P9-BYS-576

12-1-77

Dear Mom,
Send us a
post card after your
voyage down the Seine
and up the Potomac, (have
Art send us one too).

Wishing you the happiest
birthday and merry, merry more.

With all our love and wishes,

Rick and Kathie

DOWN THE SEINE AND
UP THE POTOMAC
WITH ART BUCHWALD

Also by Art Buchwald

WASHINGTON IS LEAKING
IRVING'S DELIGHT
"I AM NOT A CROOK"
THE BOLLO CAPER
I NEVER DANCED AT THE WHITE HOUSE
GETTING HIGH IN GOVERNMENT CIRCLES
HAVE I EVER LIED TO YOU?
SON OF THE GREAT SOCIETY
AND THEN I TOLD THE PRESIDENT
I CHOSE CAPITOL PUNISHMENT
IS IT SAFE TO DRINK THE WATER?
HOW MUCH IS THAT IN DOLLARS?
DON'T FORGET TO WRITE
MORE CAVIAR
BRAVE COWARD
ART BUCHWALD'S PARIS
A GIFT FROM THE BOYS (NOVEL)
PARIS AFTER DARK (GUIDE)
ART BUCHWALD'S SECRET LIST TO PARIS (GUIDE)
THE ESTABLISHMENT IS ALIVE & WELL
IN WASHINGTON
COUNTING SHEEP

DOWN THE SEINE AND UP THE POTOMAC WITH ART BUCHWALD

G. P. PUTNAM'S SON'S · NEW YORK

Copyright © by Art Buchwald, 1956, 1957, 1958, 1959, 1960, 1961, 1962, 1963, 1964, 1965, 1966, 1967, 1968, 1969, 1970, 1971, 1972, 1973, 1974, 1975, 1976, 1977.

All rights reserved. This book, or parts thereof, must not be reproduced in any form without permission. Published simultaneously in Canada by Longmans Canada Limited, Toronto.

SBN: 399-12019-X

Library of Congress Cataloging in Publication Data

Buchwald, Art.
Down the Seine and up the Potomac with Art Buchwald.

I. Title.
PS3503.U1828D65   818'.5'07   77-24466

PRINTED IN THE UNITED STATES OF AMERICA

CONTENTS

PART IV

PART V

PART VI

PART VII

PART VIII

PART IX

PART X

PART XI

PART XII

PART XIII

PART XIV

PART XV

I would like to dedicate this book to the American taxpayer who made it possible for me to go to Paris on the GI Bill of Rights in 1948, which made it possible for me to be hired by Geoffrey Parsons, Jr. of the European Edition of the Herald Tribune, which made it possible for me to be syndicated by Helen Reid, publisher of the New York Herald Tribune, which made it possible for me to get into a fight with James Hagerty in 1959, which made it possible for me to become famous overnight, which made it possible for Jock Whitney, who bought the Herald Tribune to send me to Washington in 1962, which made it possible for me to write about five Presidents, which made it possible to put out 16 books, most of them edited by Bill Targ who talked me into putting this collection of 25 years together, which made it possible for me to keep my wife, Ann Buchwald, in the style to which she is accustomed.

I would also like to dedicate this book to the American newspaper reader, whose support and loyalty never wavered even after I had failed to make Nixon's enemy list.

DOWN THE SEINE AND
UP THE POTOMAC
WITH ART BUCHWALD

"I DID WHAT I COULD"

I was sitting in the Coliseum in Los Angeles, watching the USC-Notre Dame football game in 1946 when my name was paged over the loud-speaker. I went to the nearest phone and a voice said, "Mr. Buchwald, the President of the United States wants to talk to you."

Harry Truman came onto the phone. "Can you come to Washington right away?"

"For crying out loud, Harry," I said. "You know I'm going to USC on the GI Bill of Rights, and I've got an English test I have to study for this weekend."

"This is very important," he said, lowering his voice. "I've sent my plane for you. It should be at the airport in an hour."

I went back to my boardinghouse, threw some clothes into a bag and 12 hours later I found myself sitting in the Oval Office at the White House.

Harry seemed very agitated. "Our relations with the Russians are disintegrating and Europe is in terrible straits."

"I realize that," I said. "An iron curtain has fallen over Europe."

"Churchill voiced those very words in Fulton, Missouri," the President said.

"I know," I told him. "I wrote his speech."

"Well, what the hell do we do?"

"We have to come up with an economic plan that will help the Western European countries get on their feet," I told him. "We must finance their industry and rebuild their cities. It may run into billions, but we will save Italy, France, West Germany, Britain and all the other countries from going Communist."

Truman hit his fist into his hand. "Why didn't I think of that?" he exclaimed. "Of course—an economic-recovery plan to save Europe. It will dramatize to the Soviets that we will not let those countries go down the drain. I'll call it the Buchwald Plan."

I smiled. "Harry, I don't want credit for it. General George Marshall has served his country well. Why don't you let him announce it at Harvard and they'll call it the Marshall Plan?"

Harry looked at me. "You constantly amaze me," he said. "You never want to take credit for anything."

"I always work better out of the limelight," I said.

"Well, I don't care what we call it, I want you to go to Paris and run it for me," Harry told me.

"I've still got to find a cure for polio at USC," I replied. "I'm not ready to go over until 1948. Why don't you get Averell Harriman to run the Marshall Plan for you? When I get over there, I'll give him a hand."

"All right," Truman said. "But if I win the election in 1948, I want you to be my eyes and ears in Europe."

"You'll win, Harry," I assured him.

"You and I are the only ones who think so," he said.

I patted him on the shoulder. "You and I *and* the American people."

I flew back to Los Angeles, found the cure for polio, which I called the Salk Vaccine, and took a ship to Europe.

Together, Harriman and I set up the Marshall Plan, and then, after I managed to get it running well, I landed a job with the European edition of the New York Herald Tribune.

It was a cover, naturally, but it gave me access to all the heads of state and a chance to move around without arousing suspicion.

I gave the impression I was a ladies' man and a bon vivant.

I mingled with the international set, cruised with Onassis and Niarchos, went to parties given by Elsa Maxwell and Aly Khan, and still managed to report back to Truman on what was happening in Europe. I tipped him off that the Soviets had managed to make their own atomic bomb. I had gotten the information from the wife of a

Polish ambassador after a torrid weekend we spent together in St. Tropez.

On the basis of that information, Truman decided to go ahead and build the hydrogen bomb.

I also suggested that the President set up the North Atlantic Treaty Organization to unite all the armed forces in the West against Communism. He wanted me to command NATO, but I demurred. "I'd rather do what I'm doing," I told him. "Why don't you get Dwight Eisenhower to head it?"

"But you're my first choice," he said.

"Ike is as good as I am at working with our allies," I told him. "I can help you more if I stay where I am."

So Truman appointed Eisenhower to head up NATO, and as I knew he would, Ike did a superb job.

The Korean war started and while I stayed out of it, it distracted Truman's attention from Europe. He called me only once during that period. "MacArthur," he said, "is violating my orders. What should I do?"

"You're the Commander-in-Chief," I told him. "Fire the son-of-a-bitch."

"You know what I'm going to do?" Truman answered gleefully, "I'm going to fire the son-of-a-bitch."

I offered to go to Korea for Truman but he wanted me to stay in Europe.

"Keep your eye on that bastard Stalin," he told me.

In 1952 Ike had gone back to the U.S. to run on the Republican ticket against Adlai Stevenson. I admired both men so I remained neutral. Stevenson never forgave me for this as he believed that if I had campaigned for him he would have won.

In 1953 Elizabeth was crowned Queen of Great Britain. In gratitude for not coming out publicly for Stevenson, Ike asked me to represent the United States at the Coronation. Once again I had to say no to a President. If I did it, people would begin to suspect that I was more than a columnist for the European Edition of the New York Herald Tribune; then my relations with France, Italy and West Germany would be jeopardized.

The most I would do, I told Ike, was design Queen Elizabeth's dress for the Coronation.

I would probably have returned to the United States, but Stalin died and there was a bloody struggle for leadership in the Kremlin.

The wife of a Soviet military aide told me one night while we were in bed at the Hotel George V that Beria was going to make a bid for power. I passed this information on to John Foster Dulles. Foster passed it on to Malenkov who, after arresting Beria, became the new Soviet Premier. Ike asked me to stay in Europe until the Soviet situation settled down.

I continued writing the column, and enjoyed the good life. Liz Taylor, Sophia Loren and Gina Lollobrigida kept showing up at my Paris apartment at all hours of the night, and sometimes I let them in and sometimes I didn't.

I'd like to mention an interesting sidelight that took place around 1955. I was visiting Monaco and had dinner with Prince Rainier who ran the Principalite. As we sat out in the Palace Courtyard sipping brandy one night, he told me, "You know I'm tired of fooling around, I'd like to get married and settle down."

"That's not unreasonable," I assured him.

"The only trouble is that there is just one girl I would like to marry."

"Who is it?" I asked.

"Don't laugh at me," he said. "It's Grace Kelly, the actress."

"That's no problem. I'll introduce you."

"Do you know Grace Kelly?" he asked me.

I chuckled. "My father used to row with her father on the same crew."

I called Grace and had her come to Monte Carlo. The two of them fell in love immediately. Rainier wanted me to be best man, but I declined. "I'll just come to the wedding and stand in the back."

I'm happy to say the marriage worked out splendidly and to this day I consider it one of my most successful achievements in Europe.

They were wonderful years and Eisenhower made very few demands on me. The only time I saw him worried was when he came to Paris to meet Khruschev. The Soviets had just shot down one of our U-2's and Eisenhower asked me what, if anything, he should do about it.

"Admit it!" I counselled him. "Say you ordered the U-2 to overfly the Soviet Union."

"Won't that wreck the conference?" he asked.

"Probably," I said. "But you'll be a bigger man in the eyes of the world."

Ike did as I advised and Khruschev left Paris in a huff.

The Rothschilds invited me to their Chateaux for the weekends, and I used to visit with Charles De Gaulle and discuss his return to power.

On June 2nd, 1958 I saw the fruits of all my labor in France pay off when Charles De Gaulle returned to power as Premier. How I worked this out will have to wait for another book. The fact that De Gaulle never mentioned my role in his memoirs was proof of how secret the operation had been.

De Gaulle disappointed me later in his relations with the United States, but at the time he was the only man—in my estimation—who could save France. The wife of one of his cabinet ministers told me so while we were taking a shower together. "Charles wants you to know that you will always have his eternal gratitude."

In 1960 John F. Kennedy was elected President of the United States, defeating Richard Nixon whom I never did get along with.

I flew home secretly after the Inauguration.

"What do you think I ought to do?" the President asked me.

"The Americans have to land a man on the moon. The Soviets are ahead of us in space, and we have to do something dramatic to show them that we're number one."

"But can we do it?" Kennedy asked me.

I went to the blackboard, took a piece of chalk, and wrote down a mathematical formula.

Kennedy studied it for a few moments and then said, "By God, you're right. We can do it!" He immediately proposed a crash program and the Soviets have been behind in the space race ever since.

A movie actress told me that night as she was buttoning my shirt, "Jack was very grateful for your advice."

Kennedy wanted me to stay and be his Attorney General but my heart was still in Paris, and I told him I had to go back. It was only after the Bay of Pigs fiasco that I decided I was needed in Washington. This meant giving up the good life in Europe, as well as the column, but I knew it would come to an end sooner or later.

I arrived just in time for the Cuban Missile Crisis.

Kennedy called me at home during the height of it. "We have two messages from Khruschev. One is tough—the other is conciliatory. What should we do?"

"Read them to me," I said.

He read them. After he was finished I told him, "Pretend you never got the tough one and reply to the conciliatory one."

"But. . . ." he said.

"Listen," I said, "we're eyeball to eyeball and I think they'll blink."

Later on an airline stewardess told me, as she washed my back, "Jack says you saved the world from being destroyed."

To keep from being bored I wrote a column for the Washington Post and 500 newspapers. Brilliant and incisive, it appealed to both the intellectual as well as the man in the street. It was "must" reading in the capitals of the world, and very few leaders made a move before they had read what I had to say. Walter Lippmann and I were friendly competitors and, while we sometimes disagreed with each other on the major issues of the day, we had a mutual admiration for each other rarely seen amongst Washington pundits.

When President Johnson moved into the White House he asked me to come down to the ranch for breakfast. "I want to put my own imprint on the Presidency," he said. "I want to help the poor and the blacks and the disenfranchised. But I need a name for my program—something that will grab the imagination of the American people."

I put some butter on my toast. "Lyndon, why don't you call your program 'The Great Society'?"

Lyndon stopped eating his scrambled eggs. 'The Great Society.' I like the ring to it."

Jack Valenti was pouring coffee for us. "Jack," the President said, "how do you like the name 'The Great Society'?"

Valenti said, "Mr. President, I'll sleep better at night if that's what you call your program."

Johnson later sent me a Hereford cow in gratitude for naming his domestic program.

But there were dark clouds on the horizon. The people around him were dragging him into the Viet Nam war, step by step. I tried to warn Johnson that the war would destroy everything he wanted for the American people but he told me, "I want to nail a coonskin to the wall."

One night when we were sharing a sleeping bag, a White House secretary whispered, "Lyndon's mad at you because you won't support his policy in Southeast Asia."

"Tell him," I said, as I kissed her ear, "that it could cost him the election in 1968."

She pressed closer to me. "He says that if you go along with his bombing plans he might appoint you to the next opening on the Supreme Court."

"I wouldn't mind serving on the Court," I replied. "But the price is too high. We can't win that war and the sooner he knows it the better off we'll all be."

I was right, of course, and Johnson decided not to run in 1968.

Much to my horror Nixon defeated Hubert Humphrey in the election. As I said I never trusted Nixon and while he made several attempts to get me to come to Key Biscayne and San Clemente, I felt we had little to say to each other.

My only contact with the Nixon Administration was through Henry

Kissinger. I liked Henry and I was always available to him when he sought my advice.

I don't remember if it was at my house or his, when I broached the question to him of normalizing relations with Red China.

In any case Henry grasped the value of it but he was stumped as to how to do it.

"Why don't we send a ping-pong team to China?" I suggested. "It would be a small gesture, but I think it would break the ice."

Henry went to Nixon with the plan, not mentioning it was mine. He knew that Nixon would never accept an idea if it came from me. The rest is history. After ping-pong came Henry, and after Henry came Nixon, and by recognizing the existence of China the U.S. was able to play the Soviet Union against Mao.

While I also suggested the policy of "detente" with the Soviet Union, I wasn't happy with the way Henry was winding down the war. I told him as much and our relations cooled after that. I knew he had my phone tapped, but it didn't bother me because a telephone operator, whom I used to meet for après-ski at the Marriott Motel, told me everything Henry had heard.

Watergate came as no surprise to me. I knew Nixon had a bunch of plumbers working for him in the White House. But I must admit that even I was surprised at the lengths everyone in the White House went to to cover up a third-rate burglary.

The problem was that the story was hard to break. Two young reporters from the Washington Post—Bob Woodward and Carl Bernstein—were working night and day on it. I used to meet with Woodward in a garage at three o'clock in the morning and tell him what I had found out about the case. I don't know if I was any help or not. Woodward wanted to give me credit for my role in his getting the Pulitzer Prize, but I preferred to remain anonymous. "Just call me 'Deep Throat', I told him. That will be credit enough."

One day when I was at a wild congressional orgy up on Capitol Hill, a girl who couldn't type told me that her boss, an important Congressman on the Watergate Committee, had found out that Nixon had taped all his conversations in the White House. This was the "smoking gun" I had been looking for. I called Archibald Cox, the special prosecutor, and told him about it. He told Elliot Richardson, who was then Attorney General, and Bill Ruckelshaus, the Deputy Attorney General.

Nixon found out about the call, and after stonewalling three months ordered what I named the "Saturday Night Massacre."

I know it would just be a matter of time before Nixon would have to resign.

My next two years were uneventful. Gerry Ford was a nice guy but he stumbled a lot. I was angry about the pardon he had given Nixon, but I kept these feelings to myself.

It came as no surprise to me when he was defeated by Jimmy Carter, whom I had served with on a nuclear submarine. Jimmy and I used to lust after the same women in our hearts, and I imagine I'll be seeing a lot of him during the next four years.

I can't say the last 25 years haven't been fun because they have. Who knows what I'd be doing now if I hadn't gotten that telephone call from Harry Truman back in 1946. Someday I'll probably put it all down in a book. In the meantime, to protect the innocent, this one will have to do.

A.B.

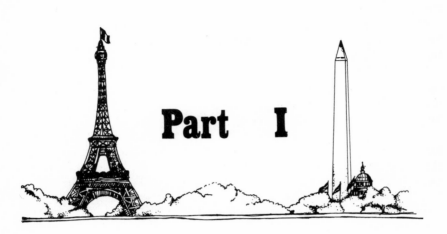

Part I

The Six-Minute Louvre

Any sportsman will tell you that the only three things to see in the Louvre are the "Winged Victory of Samothrace," the "Venus de Milo" and the "Mona Lisa." The rest of the sculpture and paintings are just so much window dressing for the Big Three, and one hates to waste time in the Louvre when there is so much else to see in Paris.

Ever since the Louvre acquired these works of art, amateurs from all over the world have been trying to cut down the time it takes to see them. Before the war the world record was held by three Scandinavians, who had managed to make the course in seven minutes thirty-three seconds. This record stood until 1935, when a Britisher, Mergenthaller Waisleywillow, paced by his Welsh wife, did it in seven minutes flat. Waisleywillow in his first attempt made it in six minutes and forty-nine seconds, but was disqualified when he forgot to make a complete circle of the "Venus de Milo."

The record stood until 1938, when a Stockholm man, known as the Swedish Cannonball, introduced sneakers and made it in six minutes and twenty-five seconds.

That record stood during the war years, and it wasn't until 1947 that an attempt was made to beat the Cannonball. This time, because of the

travel restrictions in Europe, the Americans had the course to themselves. The first one to take the Blue Riband to America was Tex Hous-
ton, from Oklahoma, who shaved two seconds off the record. In 1949 a
track star from Miami University (Ohio) made it in six minutes and
fourteen seconds. In 1951, the Australians took the title away from the
Americans with a six-minute-twelve-second Louvre.

By this time everyone was talking about a six-minute Louvre. Scientists said that under perfect conditions, with a smooth floor, excellent
lighting and no wind, it could be done. But for four years no one was
able to beat the Australian.

Then one Sunday I was tipped off that an American tourist was going to try for the record. His name was Peter Stone and he had made
several previous attempts that had failed. Mr. Stone has been cited in
many magazines and newspapers for a famous remark. After studying
the "Winged Victory" for an hour, he said, "It will never fly."

He also was once asked to leave the Louvre when he said in a loud
voice in front of a group of tourists who were looking at the "Mona
Lisa": "I know the fellow who has the original."

Stone had brought his trainer along with him. He was wearing special indoor track shoes, and he had emptied his pockets of anything
that would weigh him down. In choosing Sunday morning for the test
he had banked on several things. One was that no tickets are required
to get in and he would not lose precious seconds at the ticket booth.

Another was that the Louvre is pretty empty on Sunday mornings
and most of the halls would be clear. In order to comply with all the
rules, Stone had to get out of a taxi and tell the driver to wait. Then he
had to rush into the museum, make the course, and get back in the
taxi. The taxi had to be four feet away from the curb before he was
officially clocked. Timekeepers from the American Express, Thomas
Cook & Son and the French Bureau de Tourisme were on hand.

Stone received last-minute instructions from his trainer.

"Whatever you do, keep away from the 'Rape of the Sabines' or
you're a goner."

Stone wiped his track shoes in the box of resin that the Louvre keeps
at the door for tourists and then got into the taxi. A gun went off and
he jumped out of the taxi and rushed into the museum. The rule of the
course is you must walk; you cannot run. Keeping his eyes straight
ahead, he whizzed past the Salle Denon. At the foot of the Daru stair-
case, with just a glance at "Winged Victory," he turned left and rushed
down two small flights of stairs past the rotunda straight to the "Venus
de Milo." He circled the statue completely and headed back toward the
"Winged Victory," shortcutting through the Roman and Greek an-

tiquity rooms. His time was a fantastic one minute and fifty-eight seconds to the "Venus."

Stone took the stairs two at a time, stopped for two seconds in front of the "Winged Victory." He had a choice of two routes: the Salle Daru, where Napoleon I was being crowned, or the Salle Sept Metres, where the Italian school was hung. He chose the Salle Daru, paused only for a second at the Napoleon painting and then rushed into the Grande Galerie, where "Mona Lisa" was waiting. In thirty seconds he was at the painting. The rules state that a contestant must make some innocuous tourist remark at the painting.

Stone said, "I don't see what's so great about it," and then wheeled, this time taking the Salle Sept Mètres. He rushed down the stairs, not even bothering this time to look at the "Winged Victory," hightailed it through the Salle Denon and was out in the street and in a taxi before you could say Leonardo da Vinci. As the taxi pulled away a gun was set off and Stone's time was recorded at five minutes fifty-six seconds, a new world tourist record. The Blue Riband was brought back to America.

Turning down offers from magazines and travel agencies which wanted to use him for testimonial advertisements, Stone modestly gave much of the credit to his trainer.

"The next record I'm going after is St. Peter's in Rome," he said in an exclusive interview. "And then, who knows—perhaps I'll try the Tower of London. They say you can't do it in less than four minutes. Well, let's just see."

The champ threw his arms around his mother and the photographers started taking pictures.

The Good and the Bad

I took my son to the movies the other day. The picture was called *The Battle of the Coral Sea,* and in comparison with other war pictures it was pretty bad. It had something to do with a crew of American submariners who are captured by the Japanese and are put in a prison camp. The man in charge of the prison camp is a very civilized man, by prison camp standards, and he resists torturing his charges even though he knows they know naval secrets that could change the course of the war. But the people under the commander are typical brutal prison guards.

There is no sense going on with the plot except to say it was no *Bridge on the River Kwai.*

When we got out of the theater we went to a sidewalk café to have a drink. My son was pretty quiet after the film and it had left a deep impression on him.

At the table he said to me: "The Japanese were very bad people to do those things to the Americans, weren't they?"

"Yes," I said, "but they're not bad people now."

"Why?" he wanted to know.

"Because they don't do things like that any more."

He thought about this a minute and then said: "Why did they do all those bad things then?"

"Probably they didn't know they were doing bad things. They probably thought they were doing good things."

"Why didn't someone tell them?" he wanted to know.

"We tried," I said, "but they wouldn't listen."

"Remember that war picture we saw some weeks ago? The one about the Germans and how they beat the poor people and the children in the prison camp?"

"Yes," I said.

"The Germans are bad people, aren't they?"

"No," I said. "They *were* bad people, but now they're good people."

"Are they different people?" he wanted to know.

"No, they're the same people. At least many are the same people. You see, once you fight a war you can't stay mad at the people after the war is over. You have to forget what the bad people did during the war, because if you don't there could be another war."

"But in the movies they're still bad people," he said.

"Yes. That's to remind us they were bad people, but we're supposed to forget it."

He looked at me blankly.

"Did you kill any Russians during the war?" he wanted to know a few minutes later.

"No. Because during the war they were good people and they fought the Germans just like the British and the Americans did."

"But if they were good people during the war and killed the bad people, why are they bad people now?"

"They're not bad now. Most of the Russians are good people. But we don't agree with what their leaders say and want to do. And they don't agree with us. That's why we're having trouble in Germany."

"With the bad Germans?"

"No, with the good Germans. The bad Germans want to kick the good Germans out of Berlin."

"Then there are still bad Germans?"

"Yes. But there are also good Germans. You see, after the war the country was divided and the Russians occupied half of it and we occupied the other half."

"Why didn't the Russians kill the bad Germans if they were bad?"

"Well, the Russians don't think their Germans are bad. They think their Germans are good. They think our Germans are bad. We think their Germans, at least their German leaders, are bad, and our Germans are good. You understand?"

He said: "No."

"Well, it doesn't make any difference if you understand it or not," I said angrily. "Everyone else does. I never saw a kid who asked so many silly questions."

How to Sit at a Café

The most popular outdoor sport in France is sitting at a sidewalk café. This year, as in previous years, millions of Frenchmen and tourists will pass thousands of hours in tens of thousands of cafés throughout this great aperitif-loving country. Unfortunately, most tourists are amateurs and have never had the correct instruction or the right approach to café-sitting. As a public service, I interviewed one of the great café-sitting champions of the world, Monsieur Samm Assoir, who has logged over 16,700 hours in Paris cafés, and claims to have seen more non-flying saucers in his lifetime than any other Frenchman.

M. Assoir was reluctant at first to give out any information on his profession, café-sitters being a very closed-mouthed group of people, but he finally opened up after the seventh Pernod was served at his favourite table at the Café Select on the Champs-Élysées.

"The most important thing to know about café-sitting," he said, "is how to select the right table. The first rule of café sidewalk society is never to sit in the first row of tables and chairs facing the sidewalk. People in the first row are fair game for cigarette beggars, rug salesmen, and sniffing dogs.

"Of course, there are people who enjoy sitting in the first row because toy venders usually put their toys on the first-row tables, but this does not compensate for all the inconveniences. This is especially true of the Champs-Élysées, where automobiles drive on the sidewalk. You have never heard of a person sitting in the second row of a café being killed by a car, have you?"

I never had.

"That proves my point," said the expert. "Now, the second row is the ideal one for café-sitting. You still have a clear view of the sidewalk, you can still get up fast if you want to see somebody, and you get a much broader picture of the sidewalk scene. If you can't get in the second row, try the third. If you sit any further back than the third row, you might as well sit inside the café.

"Once you are properly seated the first thing to do is order a drink. Café waiters are very difficult men to deal with. In my forty years of café-sitting, I have never met one who looked as if he enjoyed his work. If your waiter is particularly surly and you want to get even with him, order a *citron pressé*. He is obligated to squeeze the lemons in front of you. *Café*, tea, ice cream, *aperitifs* and *digestifs* can all be ordered at sidewalk cafés, but there is an unwritten law that you never order more than one thing in any hour. The ideal, of course, is to nurse the same drink the whole day. This can be done by continually adding ice and soda water at two-hour intervals. No matter how unhappy the patron or the waiter becomes you have every right to sit there, so don't let them frighten you away.

"There are several interesting games one can play while sitting at a sidewalk café. The most popular is one called French roulette. You need two men to play the game. The man sitting on the right watches all the women coming up the sidewalk from the left and the man sitting on the left watches all the women walking by from the right.

"Each girl passing by is scrutinized very closely. If you would like to date her, you get three points; if you would like your brother to date her, you get two points; if you'd let a friend date her, you get one point. You can also make up minus points if you wish. Both sides have to agree on how many points each contestant deserves, and in case of arguments, which can get fierce, the *maître d'hôtel* should have the final word on the matter.

"In the case of a man and woman sitting at the same café table, a much milder and less rewarding sport is guessing nationalities. There is no scoring in this game, as it's impossible to check the results, but it could become interesting, especially if a man pretends he is guessing a woman's nationality when he is actually scoring her for French roulette.

"There is nothing wrong with a woman sitting at a café alone. As a matter of fact, some of the best professional sidewalk-café sitters have been women. But they must be prepared to expect the glances and approaches of the opposite sex at all times. It is safer for two girls, and you can be sure nothing will happen if there are three. So if there are more than two girls in a party, they should always split up."

"And that's all there is to sidewalk-café sitting?" I asked M. Assoir.

"For the amateur, yes. Once he has learned the elementary steps in café-sitting the rest will come easy."

How to Crash the International Set

Ever since I mentioned that I was a member of the International Set, I have received queries as to how the ordinary citizen can become a member. It is not as hard as a person might think. Anyone who has a string of polo ponies, a yacht, or an old can of caviar hanging around the house is eligible to join.

To be a member of the International Set is one of the most rewarding experiences I can think of and, in a world fraught with strife and striven with fraught, it is still nice to know there is a group of people in Europe who just don't care what is going on.

The International Set is made up of about 500 people, give or take a countess or two. We have no headquarters because we're usually always on the move. In May and June we prefer to live in Paris, making side trips to Ascot and London when the horse racing warrants it. June is one of the gayest months of the year for all of us. There are parties every night—and what parties! Orchestras are flown in from South America, lobsters from Estoril, maharajas from India and Greek shipowners from Panama.

There are private balls in people's homes, dinner parties at Maxim's, the Café de Paris and Pré-Catelan, lunches at the Ritz and Fouquet's, and dancing at the Elephant Blanc, Carroll's and Jimmy's. It's no wonder people envy us and call us names.

There are no written rules concerning membership in our set. The basis for our friendship is built on mutual understanding. If you own a boat, a stable of horses, and you are a direct descendant of Louis XIV, it's understood that you are going to be invited to our parties. If you're beautiful and rich, or ugly and rich, your chances of making the grade are infinitely better than if you are ugly and poor. (Beautiful and poor girls do get in without much trouble, but they don't stay poor for long.)

But there are many cases where people have become a member of the set without benefit of beauty, money or titles.

Take my case, for example. When I came to Paris six years ago I arrived with 87 dollars, two suits and a letter of introduction to a perfume store where I could get a 10 per cent discount. For the first year I managed to feed myself by selling black-market gas coupons, and stealing CARE packages from sleeping hoboes under the bridges of the Seine. It wasn't a particularly hard life, but I knew I was meant for better things.

One day, when I was looking for the men's washroom at the Ritz, I blundered into a cocktail party where I found a group of the set whooping it up. When I asked where the men's washroom was they thought it was the funniest joke in the world, and when I repeated the query they thought I was the funniest person that ever lived.

All night long I kept asking where the washroom was and they kept getting more hysterical, pressing drinks on me and begging me not to go. Before the party was over, I had four invitations to dinner, two invitations to go for cruises on the Mediterranean, and one invitation to go tiger-hunting in India.

In a matter of weeks I became the rage of the International Set. All I had to do was to ask where the men's washroom at the Ritz was, and I had people rolling in the aisles. Hostesses competed for me at parties, restaurant owners pleaded with me to dine at their places on the cuff; I never had to pay for champagne in night clubs.

That was five years ago, and the joke is wearing rather thin now, but occasionally when a new duke or duchess comes to town I'm asked to repeat it at a party. I've said other things that I've thought much funnier, but they never laugh at them. They all want to hear what I said at the Ritz. To be perfectly honest, I've heard it said by some of the friends I know and love that I'm not as funny as I used to be. But somehow I've never been able to top the original joke.

Frankly, I don't care. The important thing as far as the International Set is concerned is to prove yourself just once. From then on you're accepted for what you are.

And so, for those of you who have been wondering how to become a member of this select group of people, the gay international café-society crowd that you read so much about, I hope our experience will give you encouragement. The set is always looking for amusing people, and who knows when one of you will say something as funny as I did that memorable evening five years ago at the Ritz.

"Dear Mary—Please Come Home"

One of the hazards of sending an American daughter to Paris for a visit is that she doesn't want to go home. This has happened to more daughters than you can shake a parental stick at, and Americans have lost more of their young women to the French capital than to any other city in the world.

An attractive young girl from a town in Wisconsin showed me a letter the other day from her mother which I found quite interesting, since it focused so well on the problem. I've changed the names so no one will sue me.

"Dearest Mary,

"We received your letter and were very disappointed to hear that you didn't mention anything about when you were coming home. You have been over there for two years now and both your father and I are very worried about you. As your father and I have told you many times before, Paris is not a safe place for a young girl to be, and some of the stories we've heard about it, and what we've read in the newspapers, have been frightening.

"I need not tell you how shocked everyone here in town is that you are still over there. They don't come out and say it, but they feel you must be living a sinful life, and some of my friends have told me that a few people who thought you were a nice girl, now consider you, so to speak, 'loose'.

"Just the other day during our Thursday bridge game, Alice Summers said to me: 'Helen, how can you let Mary live in Paris? The Connollys just came back and the stories they tell would make your hair stand on end.'

"I know you're not doing anything your father and I would be ashamed of, but you know how the people are here and it isn't easy for us to defend your actions.

"Besides, we understand there is a revolution over there.

"I won't say any more about it. This is something you'll have to work out in your own conscience.

"There has been quite a bit of excitement here in the last few weeks. Harvey Wetheridge, he used to own the gasoline station out by Washington Boulevard, shot his wife Sunday, and is being held on a manslaughter charge. I'm enclosing the clipping from the newspaper. She was supposed to be having an affair with Carlton Smith, I believe he's a boy you went to school with, or was it his brother? Harvey said when he got out of jail he would shoot Carlton, too, but your father thinks he made a mistake saying this, as it will only hurt him at the trial.

"Sally Simpson, Eleanor's 15-year-old sister, is pregnant, and it's quite the scandal of the town. She won't say who the father is, and her parents are just going out of their minds. Everyone thinks she should have gone away and had the baby somewhere else without anybody knowing about it, but she's a strongheaded girl and actually flaunts her pregnancy in front of everyone.

"There has been some teen-age violence at the high school. A gang of young toughs from the South Side crashed a dance at the high school and when Mr. Pemberton, he's the new principal, told them to leave, one of the boys pulled a knife out and slashed him. Then a fight started between the toughs and the high school students and they wrecked the gymnasium. Three people were taken to the hospital. (I'm also enclosing a clipping.)

"Mr. Schneider, of Sam's Drugstore, was held up the other night and robbed of $50.

"Another bit of sad news is that Pop Carroway committed suicide. He apparently embezzled money from the bank and they were checking his books. We were all amazed, since Pop was so well liked in town. He had a girl friend in Lincoln and she was responsible.

"There was a head-on automobile crash at Four Corners Saturday night, and four people (none from our town) were killed. It seems some college kids from the university were celebrating a basketball victory and were completely drunk, driving at 80 miles an hour. They hit a car from California. Your father and I had driven by Four Corners an hour before, and we feel lucky we're still alive.

"That's all the news from here for the moment. Once again, dear, please think about coming home. Your father and I worry about you every day. I've said it once and I'll say it again. Paris is no place for a young girl to be alone.

"Love,

"Mother."

Louis XIV in Venice

Probably the worst thing that ever happened to my pride as a respected member of Europe's International Set was when Don Carlos de Bestegui gave a costume party in Venice and forgot to invite me. The party was the talk of two continents and I think I was the only member of the International Set who hadn't been asked. At first, I thought it was some careless secretary's mistake; so as soon as I arrived in Venice I took out my Louis XIV costume and went over to the Labia Palace to correct the oversight. But Don Carlos himself told me that it was not an oversight and that he had never had any intention of sending me an invitation to his housewarming. I told him that the 30,000,000 readers of my paper wanted to hear about the party and he said to me: "There will be princes and princesses, dukes and duchesses, marquises and millionaires, and they're not interested in what the press has to say."

The next day I saw de Bestegui and asked him again. "Why is everyone interested in my party?" he said. "It's just a small, modest affair. A little housewarming. I can't see why they should get so excited everywhere. If you want to come, you'll have to arrive before eight-thirty and I'll put you in a room upstairs until three o'clock. Then maybe I will let you come down and talk to a few guests, but be sure and eat your dinner first."

The next day Don Carlos denied that he had promised me admittance and said that if I came he wouldn't let me in. The following day he said that it was all right for me to come at ten o'clock and twenty minutes later he denied saying that. The only decent thing left to do was crash the ball.

At seven-thirty sharp, dressed in the full costume and wig of Louis XIV, I climbed into a motorboat and set sail from the Lido for the Bestegui Labia Palace. I won't deny my knee breeches were twitching. I had a lot to worry about. If I got thrown out of the place by the Venetian aristocrats who thought me a commoner, I would probably get stoned to death by the populace who mistook me for an aristocrat.

As we motored up the Grand Canal, I waved to the watching people and screamed, *"Vive la République,"* and as we turned into the Canale di Cannaregio, where the palace was, I yelled, *"Vive le Roi."* But when we touched the dock, I found to my dismay that I was two hours too early. Nobody was in costume, and the only people around the place at that hour were working men being ordered about by the excited host. I casually sauntered in and walked up to the first wall, where I sat down inconspicuously under a Tiepolo fresco.

But I didn't sit there long. Don Carlos came storming around the corner. "Who are you?" he said angrily.

"Louis the Fourteenth," I answered weakly.

"Yes, but who are you?"

I told him my name and he yelled, "You weren't invited. Get out of my house."

"But you said it was all right to come at eight o'clock," I said.

"Out, out, get out of my house," he cried, and then rushed away to get reinforcement.

I ran upstairs and ducked into the first open room I saw, slamming the door behind me. It was pitch black in the room—and suddenly I heard the rustling of costumes. When I turned on the light I found two *Life* photographers and two *Life* researchers hiding under the bed.

All of us were in a bad spot. The room we had chosen was right next to Don Carlos's bedroom and he had to go through it to wash his hands.

We couldn't leave and we couldn't stay.

"To the window," yelled one of the researchers, and we all ran to the window and huddled on the balcony, closing the curtains behind us. Don Carlos entered five minutes later and went into his bedroom to get dressed. Every time he heard a cheer, he came to the balcony and waved to the people below, while the five of us froze tightly together. For two hours we didn't move and didn't speak, except for one of the photographers, who kept muttering, "A curse on this house. A curse on this house."

Finally, Don Carlos at ten o'clock went down to greet his guests and we staggered stiffly back into the room. From then on it was clear sailing, especially in my case, because as luck would have it, twenty guests turned up as Louis XIV.

I drank Don Carlos's wine, ate his lobster and chicken and danced with some of his beautiful guests. And as a democratic gesture, I waved to the mob in the square. By six o'clock I was tired and decided to leave. As I went out I thanked Don Carlos for a wonderful time.

"I'm glad you liked it," he said, apparently not recognizing which Louis XIV he was talking to. "It was awfully kind of you to come."

Auto Polo in Paris

One day I thought I'd go over and call on Mr. Milton Wallach, an intrepid American who was living on the Right Bank before moving to the American Hospital. If you have never heard of him, he is the man who has been trying to stir up international interest in the French game of auto polo, which is now played every day on the winding streets and majestic avenues of Paris.

"I know something of the game," he told me. "For example, I know that hitting a pedestrian counts one point for each adult, a half point for each child and two points if the victim is a tourist. What I would like to know is, can I be credited with a score if my car is in reverse gear? Last week I backed into a bus and the referee waved his baton and said I was offside."

Mr. Wallach was of the opinion that Paris cars should be marked with the ratings of the driver. It is unfair, he pointed out, to pit a ten-crash car against one which has only scraped a fender. The two best playing fields in Paris for auto polo, he thought, are the Place de la Concorde and the Etoile.

The Sunday before he had achieved his best score since he'd been in Paris. "Zooming into play around the Etoile, I scored a carom shot. This involved blocking a Renault 4 CV against a Simca Aronde and then hitting two motorcyclists in such a way as to drive them into the air feet first. I'm a modest man when it comes to auto polo, but when I heard the cheers from the sidelines I'll have to admit my head swam."

In playing the game Mr. Wallach told me that he had experimented with many different kinds of mounts, but had come to the conclusion that a Ford Country Sedan was the best. "Testing it against city play, I found it responded very well and that with power steering I tired very little after several chukkers on the boulevards. My mistake was thinking that because I had achieved success in Paris I was ready for the Route Nationale.

"While perhaps it's unfair to complain about the infractions of the rules from the relative safety of a bed at the American Hospital, I do feel that clipping should not be permitted unless both offenders approach from the same direction. Just as soon as I can obtain a new motor and body from Michigan, I expect to return to the field of play and meanwhile would appreicate anything you can do to generate interest among other visitors who may wish to form an auto-polo club in Paris. I think only eight-crash ratings should be admitted."

He believed that the insurance companies are trying to discourage the game, but he said: "I do feel it will eventually prove the answer to the tremendous over production of motor-cars."

On hearing of my interest in the game, Mr. William Schwartz, the secretary of the French Auto Polo Association, wrote several days later to me to inform me that new rules of scoring had been added in the last few years.

The new rules state that French drivers are scored according to the following:

1. Accidentally hitting a pedestrian when no previously established motive can be proven . . . one point.

2. Planning a concerted attack upon a pedestrian and seeing it through to its eventual accomplishment . . . two points.

3. Singling out a specific pedestrian from among a large crowd crossing at an intersection, attacking the single pedestrian without touching the others . . . three points.

4. Pregnant women or a woman carrying a child under three years of age . . . four points.

5. Male or female tourist snapping pictures in the middle of the Avenue de la Grande-Armée or the Etoile, if hit from behind . . . five points; or straight on . . . six points.

There is currently an amendment pending concerning school children. Many French drivers consider that the point value of six for school children is too low. They claim they are often forced to chase the children and have frequent misses due to the children's nimbleness. Several members have asked that the point value be raised to seven. A compromise may be reached by giving six points for hitting a child and an extra point if he's on a bicycle.

In scoring, the French Auto Polo Association requires the signatures of two witnesses, neither of whom is related to the driver.

But auto polo is the first game that has been played with cars in Paris. For many years the French have been playing something called auto soccer. The sport, which originated at the Place de la République and spread all the way over to the Porte de St. Cloud, requires the participants to hit a pedestrian and then try to push him into the other fellow's goal. Only the tyres may be used in pushing the pedestrian toward the goal once he has been hit. Passing is permitted from one car to the other. The goalkeepers, who are Paris policemen, are the only ones who can touch the pedestrian (the ball) with their hands.

The scoring is similar to auto polo except for the penalties. If the opposing car passes a red light, then the other team has a "free throw"—the pedestrian is placed in the *clous,* or pedestrian walk, and the car, with a two-hundred-yard advantage, is allowed to hit him without interference from the opposition.

Some auto-soccer players have tried to use motor-scooter drivers instead of pedestrians, but the results have not been as good. Although the "ball" is livelier, there is too much chance of the motor-scooterist getting caught in the spokes of the car, which slows up the game no end.

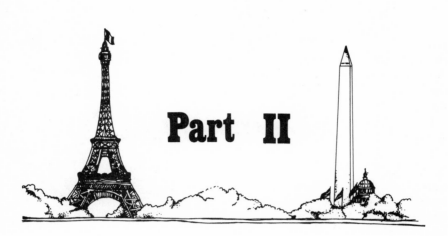

Part II

Venice à La Hemingway

Every person who comes to Venice is influenced in some way by one of the great writers who have written about the city. Hemingway has probably influenced me more than anyone, and without *Across the River and into the Trees,* I doubt if I'd even have enjoyed being there.

Take, for example, the night when I went to dinner at the Gritti Palace Hotel with my wife. It was a good dinner, an imposing dinner, a lobster dinner, and the lobster he was good. When he arrived he was dark and green and unfriendly and cost a day's wages, but when they grilled him he was red and I wouldn't have traded five suits for him.

I looked across the table at my wife. She looked good. Almost as good as the lobster. "She looks as lovely as a gondola," I thought to myself, "or Stan Musial or Joe DiMaggio. She could drive a home run into the canal if I let her." I held her hand tightly. "I love you and I'm glad you're you," I told her. "Daughter, let's go for a ride in a gondola after dinner."

"What is this daughter business?" my wife said. "And stop holding my hand so tight. I can't eat my lobster."

"My poor daughter, my little daughter, my only daughter," I said. "Who do you love?"

"If you call me daughter once more," my wife said, "I'm going to hit you with this bottle of wine. And while you're in this mood, would you mind telling me what you were doing all afternoon on the beach with Gina Lollobrigida?"

"Moon is my mother and father," I told her. "A lobster fills with the moon. When he is dark he is not worth eating, little daughter."

"I wasn't talking about the lobster," she said. "I was talking about Lollobrigida."

"Please, daughter. You must try to understand my attitude. When you have killed so many you can afford to be a little wild."

"How many have you killed?"

"One hundred and eighty sures, not counting possibles."

"And you have no remorse?"

"None."

"Well, I do, and you'd better watch your step."

"Come, daughter, come, let's not think of Lollobrigida. We will find a gondola and you will be you and I will be me and the gondolier will be him."

"I'm warning you about this daughter business."

We walked outside. Now she looked more like Mickey Mantle or a young Bobby Feller. What a pitcher she'd make, I thought.

We found a gondola which was long and good and brave and true and it was our gondola for as long as we wanted it, for that's how it is in Venice. A man can either take a gondola or leave it alone. Only tourists and lovers take gondolas in Venice, I thought. Tourists and lovers and people who can afford them. Where does that leave me?

"Why can't we take a motorboat?" my wife asked. "A gondola is awfully slow."

"Because you're my wife and we're alone and it is Venice and I want to hold you close and I want you to hold me close and anyway it's cheaper than taking a motorboat."

"The canal smells," she said.

"So does war. So do the Russians. So do lobsters and garlic and perfume. Everything smells, daughter. We've just got to get used to it. Have you ever skied in the dark?"

"Listen. I'm getting sick of this nonsense. Let's go back to the Lido and see one of the movies. You came down for the film festival."

"The pictures smell almost as much as the canal. Except for Marlon Brando and Cary Grant and Frank Sinatra and some selected short subjects, I'd rather be in a gondola with you."

"The Italian starlets seem to have attracted your attention."

"They're nothing compared to the 'Star-Spangled Banner' or baby shrimps at the Taverna or sole at the Colombo or you at first base for the New York Yankees. I looked at them as I would look at any live animals in the jungle. Let's go to Harry's for one last drink before I kiss you once and for all forever and for a day."

"I want to go back to the hotel," my wife said. "The gondola or the lobster have made me sick."

"Which one, daughter?"

"How the hell do I know?"

"All right, I'll take you home and read you Dante and tell you about war and the Krauts and the very brave boys and guys like Pete Quesada and Red Smith and the Montana National Guard. Now before you get sick, daughter, kiss me and love me straight and true."

It must have been the last "daughter," because before I knew it I was in the canal with all my clothes on. But it was good to be alive and wet and in love and in Venice. Hemingway couldn't have had a better time.

Week-end With the Mob

One day in Paris after I had become a recognized authority on the European underworld I interviewed an Italian deportee named Frank Frigenti, a convicted murderer who claimed that he had been on intimate terms with Al Capone, had knowledge of many crimes committed by deportees, and who said that he had once organized a march of deportees in Rome which never came off.

You can imagine my surprise when I received word from Naples shortly afterwards that Mr. Frigenti had told me some untruths. These letters from other deportees said some horrible things about Mr. Frigenti. For one thing, they said that Mr. Frigenti had never met Al Capone and that the only thing he knew about him was what he had read in the newspapers. For another, they said Mr. Frigenti's knowledge of crime was culled from detective magazines.

"We chased him out of Naples," one correspondent wrote, "after he came out of the hospital for twenty-six days. One of the boys gave him a kicking around because he squealed on somebody. He receives his stories from police magazines and then sells them. He is a writer like I am, and I'm no writer. His stories have made our future very detrimental; if you do not believe what I am telling you, I am willing to tell it to you in front of that punk Frank Frigenti.

"We would like to invite you down to Naples as our guest and see how us deportees are getting along; you would get astonishing stories of our conditions here. Best wishes to you from all deportees."

Well, it's hard to turn down an invitation like that, so I went down to Naples to see if all the untruths Frank Frigenti told me were untrue.

I arrived on a Saturday morning and was met by a delegation of two deportees (the Naples police frown on delegations of more than two or three deportees for any occasion). One introduced himself as Nick Di Marzo, who had done time for narcotics, counterfeiting and ship jumping. Mr. Di Marzo's last Stateside address was Lewisburg Federal Pen, where, as the prison barber, he cut the hair on the heads of such famous men as Frank Costello, Harry Gold, Alger Hiss and David Greenglass. My other escort was Enofrio Raimondo, who had a white-slavery rap in his past and was asked to leave the country for embezzling $25,000 from some liquor people.

Both men apologized for their appearance, but explained that they were short on good clothes. I told them to forget it.

"What was the last time you saw Frigenti?" Mr. Di Marzo asked.

"About two weeks ago. Why do you ask?"

"If that bum ever comes back to Naples the boys are waiting for him. How can he say we're in dope and girls? Why, we'd be rich if this were the truth."

"We have prepared an itinerary for you," said Mr. Raimondo. "We're going to show you everything you want to see. You can ask any questions you want to ask; our life is an open book."

"That bum Frank Frigenti!" Mr. Di Marzo said. "Where does he come off calling himself a big-time gangster? He's a bum."

"But he did kill his mother-in-law, didn't he?" I asked.

"Probably—but if he did, it was a crime of passion."

Mr. Raimondo told me that there were about one hundred deportees in Naples, many of whom did not belong there. Only a few, like Mike Spinelli and Lucky Luciano, had any money when they came. The rest were loaded on to ships and planes and arrived with very little in the way of spending money. When a man is deported from the United States to Italy he is greeted at the boat by the Italian police, who escort him to his place of birth.

"For most of us," said Mr. Di Marzo, "our place of birth is on the top of a mountain somewhere, with maybe two donkeys and one goat in the town. How are we going to live there?"

At his place of birth, the deportee registers and is given an identity card. Deportees must remain in the town where they were born, but most of them head for the port cities of Genoa, Naples and Palermo, where it is easier to make a living.

"The word deportee is a black mark," said Mr. Raimondo. "The Italians don't want us, the Americans don't want us. To Americans we're

Italians and to the Italians we're Americans. We advocate democracy more than anyone else, but do you call this democracy? Italy is the country that God forgot to bless."

"Lots of these guys," said Mr. Di Marzo, "can't even speak Italian. They were taken to America as kids in their mothers' arms. Most of us would rather be in prison in the United States than free men here. I got two years at Lewisburg because I asked for it. I told the judge that I would rather be there than for them to send me out of the country."

"We're always defending America to the Italians," Mr. Raimondo said. "These people say that American cars are no good, American food stinks. These people got us Americans down as bums and that gets us deportees sore. We fight them many times. They really can't be blamed. They have never seen America."

"You know something?" said Mr. Di Marzo. "I am more American than you are. I even went to school on the GI Bill of Rights, in Rome. I got an honourable discharge from the Army. What am I doing in Italy?"

Mr. Raimondo said, "Let's go see some of the boys."

I took one last look at the Bay of Naples, gulped, and followed them down through some narrow alleys to a dark bay street near the Naples port.

"The reason we come to Naples," said Mr. Raimondo, "is because it's the only place we can hustle. It's a port. There are ships coming in all the time, and merchant-marine guys befriend us. We'd go crazy if it wasn't for the port."

He explained that most of the deportees arriving from the United States were flat broke and unable to get legitimate work in Naples. The only thing they could do was wait for American ships to come into port and to offer to escort sailors and passengers around the city. As a man needed a license for this kind of work, the Italians would tip off the police, and the police would usually clamp down hard on them.

We ended up in a small, dingy restaurant near the port. There were six or seven deportees sitting around, and four or five drifted in while we were talking. I was introduced to a man called "Joe the Wop" (narcotics), "Little Joe" (narcotics), "Blackie Joe" (armed robbery), "Dominici" (robbery), "Pop" (robbery) and "Mickey" (attempted murder), and so on. Most of them told me that they had been framed and weren't doing anything more than getting caught in a crap game or playing the horses away from the tracks.

They were all interested in knowing how Frank Frigenti's health was. Mr. Frigenti had sold some stories on deportees which apparently gave a dark picture of their situation, and they resented it. They resented it so much that they asked me to tell Mr. Frigenti that if he ever cared to visit Naples again he would receive a welcome heretofore unheard of in the annals of the American underworld.

"He's a disgrace to deportees," the man named Pop said. "I'm fifty-one years old, but I can't wait to get my hands on him. He said we dealt in dope and girls. It's a big lie."

"Let's be frank," said Mr. Di Marzo. "We couldn't get into any of the rackets if we wanted to. Look at it this way: the Italian government's got the numbers racket with the national lottery. You can place a bet anywhere you want in Italy, so there is no illegal bookmaking. There are no card games and no crap games. If we try to get into contraband, the Italian contrabandists finger us and we're hauled off to jail. You can't sell junk [dope] in Naples. If we tried to heist [stick up] a bank, everybody would start yelling at once. These people in Naples don't mind their own business. And they ain't afraid of guns. You show them a gun, they'll spit in your eye. Besides, you can't make a getaway. Where could you go? It's these identification papers, they drive us nuts. Every time something happens, they start screaming at the deportees. As far as we're concerned, the United States dropped the bomb on the wrong country."

"Do these men," said Joe the Wop, "look like they could shoot anybody? They ain't even got the strength to hold a gun in their hands."

"Sure," said Pop, "we've made mistakes. But even a baby has to tumble before he walks. If they're willing to accept nine out of ten refugees—you can't tell me they ain't Communists—then why they keeping us good Americans out?"

Blackie Joe said his son was an American soldier. "If my son's good enough to be an American soldier, why should they take his father away from his family?"

"Suppose," said a man named Willie, "Italy goes to war against the United States. Then Blackie Joe's son will have to shoot his father. Is that justice?"

"Italy's the only one accepting deportees," said Mr. Raimondo. "Russia said they'd take them if the U.S. gave Russia ten grand for each man and he was clothed from head to foot. What did they do to us? We served our time and they kicked us out. It's double jeopardy, that's what it is."

"It's triple jeopardy," said somebody else.

"They got five hundred Italians working at the Navy PX and warehouses. Why don't they give us Americans a chance to work?"

We had to move on to another restaurant because the police had received word the deportees were holding a meeting.

"They hound us night and day," said Mr. Di Marzo.

At the next restaurant, which was slightly darker, Joe the Wop said, "This is the way we feel about America. They done us harm; we done them harm. I come to America in my mother's arms. My father was a pioneer. Maybe I *was* the black sheep of my family. But if I become bad, America taught me to be bad. But I'm an American through and through. If you cut my insides out, you'll only find American blood. I never made no attempt to overthrow the American government."

"We might of committed crime," said Little Joe, "but we never was Communists."

"All I did," said Joe the Wop, "was live like a New Yorker. Laws were made to break. So we broke them, and if we got caught we got jailed. But this sending us back to Italy, that's something else again."

"You know why we're in Italy?" said Pop. "It's because there's no Italian big shots in America that will do anything for us. But we love America. Every time Old Glory is flying off one of them ships in the harbour, tears come to my eyes."

Several of the men said they had attempted to jump on ships and get back to the United States as stowaways, but very few ever made it. Blackie Joe said he was going to be reunited with his family no matter what happened. Several others also expressed a determination to get back one way or another.

"That's the only thing we hold on for," said Mr. Raimondo. "That and waiting to see Frank Frigenti again."

We had to move again from the restaurant in which we were eating because my hosts were afraid the police would arrive.

"You know what we want?" said Joe the Wop, when we were able to sit down again. "We want a pension from the United States. They owe it to us. The Italians owe us nothing."

"How much would you like?" I asked him.

"We think fifty dollars a month would be fair. We have families in America who pay taxes. Why shouldn't we get a little of it? They're giving millions of dollars to Italy and why don't we get any of it?"

"Why don't they send us to Alaska?" asked Mr. Raimondo. "We could work there. We would work like hell if they sent us. We'd shoot the first guy who wouldn't work."

"Even Ike said those lousy immigration laws should be thrown into the Hudson River," said Mr. Di Marzo.

"When he got sick, we was going to send him a spray of flowers," said Pop, "to wish him godspeed and remind him about the deportees down here. But we couldn't raise the money."

"The money just wasn't there," said Blackie Joe.

The only sources of income for deportees, as far as I could tell, came from escorting sailors around Naples and taking occasional excursions into contraband cigarettes and other American commodities. Naples is one of the great contraband cities of the world. But getting in contraband requires money, and there is a strict cash policy among contrabanders which makes it hard for a deportee to operate.

"I thought you fellows were given money by the combination," I said.

"That's a big, fat lie," said Mr. Di Marzo. "The combination gave us nothing. If we wanted to, we could take care of those big guys. We could bury them if we wanted to. We got guts. I'd like to see some of the guys in the combination go through what we've been through."

"I'd like to see Mr. Luciano," I said. "How do I get in touch with him?"

"Luciano? Luciano?" said Mr. Raimondo. "The name rings a bell. Now where would I have heard it before?"

"I think there was a Luciano in Naples," said Pop. "But I don't recall him."

All the men at the table racked their brains to see if they could remember a man named Lucky Luciano.

"Seems to me," said Joe the Wop, "that a guy named Luciano used to own a candy store in my neighbourhood in the Bronx, but that's the only one I ever heard of."

I took a chance and went out to the race track, where who should I run into but Lucky himself! He was having a very unlucky time with the horses.

Mr. Luciano, who was under what is known as admonition in Naples, had to be off the streets at six o'clock at night. He could not associate with known criminals, had to stay out of bars, could not leave the city limits of Naples and had to report continually to the police.

"Are you happy?" I asked him.

"Why should I be?" he replied.

"I hear you've opened a surgical-supply house."

"Yeah. I'm selling operating tables, dentist chairs, X-ray machines and anaesthesia equipment. Here is my business card. I have all of southern Italy and Sicily as my territory. I got the franchise; the only ones who've given me real competition is the Germans."

"Do you know anything about the business?"

"No. But I'll learn. I'll have to if I want to branch out. It's a good business."

Mr. Luciano seemed to be the wealthiest of all deportees. He had a private income, lived in a five-room penthouse and even had his own business. But he found Naples as uncomfortable as the other deportees.

I asked him if he, like the others, would prefer to be in jail in the United States rather than a free man in Naples, and he replied, "Who's free in Naples?"

The Great Bat Hunt

Because of high taxation and the struggle to keep up some of the larger estates, the grand old sport of bat hunting in England is slowly dying out. There was a time when the lords and ladies of the great manors did nothing but hunt for bats. But now the trend is toward gassing them or using poison. You have to go pretty far to find people who still enjoy killing bats by hand.

It was my good fortune to meet in Sussex one of the great bat hunters of all time. His name is Lieutenant Colonel Ian Anderson, retired, formerly a battalion commander of the Home Guard, and at present a retired stockbroker, who lives in a magnificent home outside of East Grinsted called Old Surrey Hall. Old Surrey Hall was built in 1430 and is considered one of the Great Halls of England. It has a ceiling forty feet high which contains the original beams used in the building. Because of its age and its height, Old Surrey Hall also has a great number of bats, which hang from the ceiling during the daytime and fly through the rooms at night. Mr. Anderson, whose family crest boasts the legend "Sans Peur," is up every night bat hunting from midnight until three in the morning, and in less than a year he has killed six bats, two in the last week alone.

Since I expressed an interest in bat hunting, Mr. Anderson and his wife invited me to attend a bat hunt that evening at Old Surrey Hall.

It was the first time a Yank had ever been invited to attend a bat hunt at Old Surrey, and I couldn't help being just the least bit pleased.

I was at a loss as to what to wear for a bat hunt, but didn't want to show my ignorance by asking, so I showed up in a checkered peak cap, a raincoat and rubber boots. I couldn't have been more wrong.

The only correct outfit to wear for bat hunting is a hair net, a bathrobe and sneakers.

When I arrived a few minutes before midnight it was raining and thundering outside and the wind was whistling around the building. Mr. Anderson told me it was perfect bat-hunting weather.

He handed me a tennis racquet, which had been warped in more or less of a curve.

"This is your bat," he said. "You can put on this hair net and bathrobe and these sneakers in the other room."

I put on the hair net, bathrobe and sneakers, took a few practice swings with the racquet and then returned to the drawing room. There were several other people in the drawing room, including Sir Robert Haddow, the former British Consul General in Los Angeles and San Francisco; Dr. Robin Beare, a great plastic surgeon, and Felix Kelly, an English artist. The Andersons poured out whisky for everybody, which is the traditional drink before going into a great hall to swing at bats. (Or, for that matter, anything.) Each person had his own warped tennis racquet.

Once inside the great hall Mr. Anderson gave out positions. I was assigned the left wing of the balcony overlooking the great hall. Mrs. Anderson was in the center and Dr. Beare was right wing. Down below Sir Robert was standing on the couch and Mr. Kelly was hiding under a curtain. Mr. Anderson was by the open door which led into the corridor.

When everyone was in position Mr. Anderson turned on the light over his wife's grandfather's portrait. It was the only light allowed on in the room.

Suddenly the bats started flying out of the ceiling. They whushed down into the great hall at tremendous speed. At the same time we all started swinging. The object, of course, was to put a spin on the bat (that's why the racquet has to be warped).

Mrs. Anderson, who was after one particular bat (unlike the rest of us, who swung at anything), almost batted me on the head. "Watch it, Mona," her husband cautioned. "You're putting too much speed on your back-spin service."

Dr. Beare, who is a stag-beetle champion in Sussex, was using an unorthodox chop drive which the other people admired but couldn't duplicate.

Sir Robert had a forehand defense swing, and Mr. Kelly was a counter-hitter.

During the first chukker we noticed Mr. Anderson wasn't swinging at all. That confused us.

In about twenty minutes the bats became fatigued and retired to the eaves.

We all went back into the library for the second traditional drink of whiskey.

The second and third chukkers went the same as the first, with no one making a kill. But on the fourth chukker I understood why Mr. Anderson played by the open door. A bat that Mrs. Anderson was swinging at was almost hit and in its effort to escape flew out of the door of the great hall into the narrow corridor.

"Yoicks!" shouted Mr. Anderson, running down the corridor and swinging his raquet. The bat, unable to escape, made one attempt to get back into the great hall but Mr. Anderson's forehand was too fast and he killed the bat with one volley.

Everyone congratulated Mr. Anderson except Mrs. Anderson, who felt she should have gotten some of the credit. It was the only bat killed that evening, and in the true tradition of bat hunting a tankard of Bat 69 scotch whiskey was passed around. We all toasted a sporting gentleman and a man whose batting average needed no defense.

Mrs. Anderson threw a slight damp blanket on the hunt, though, when she said: "I still insist, Ian, gas would be so much easier."

Coward in the Congo

Deep down in every writer lies the horn of the hunter. To most people it may sound like gas on the stomach, but when a writer hears it, he knows Africa is calling. There was a time, many years ago, when to be a writer all you had to do was write. Today if you want to be a writer you have to shoot a big-game animal. You've got to go to the Dark Continent and prove you're a lion among men, a killer of kudu, a butcher in the bush and a fearless fellow in the forest.

While covering the European scene for the New York *Herald Tribune* in recent years I have been insulted by friends and strangers. "Hemingway has killed his leopard," they say. "Ruark has killed his lion. Pray, what have you killed?"

Several summers ago I began to feel the pressure even at home. My wife would never come out and say anything, but I could tell by the little things that all was not going well. Finally, after an unexpected outburst of tears, she told me what was bothering her. "We've been married for more than two years," she said, "and you don't have a trophy to your name. Everyone is laughing at me. They ask me what you do and when I tell them they say, 'If he's a writer, what's the name of his white hunter?'"

I tried to comfort her, but I knew I had failed her. I knew if I wanted our marriage to last I could no longer keep the killer instinct down inside me, next to my ulcer. I could no longer ignore the horn of the hunter.

I picked up the phone and called Sabena Airlines.

"Let me have two tickets to the Congo."

"Why two tickets?" my wife asked.

"You have to come with me to take pictures of my trophies. All the wives do it."

"I'm not going," she said. "I can't stand the sight of your blood. Take Joe Covello. He's a photographer and he can give you moral support. Besides, he'll make a wonderful gin-bearer."

It's funny she should have mentioned Covello. The last I had heard from him, he was in Rome photographing Italian movie stars on leopard skins. He probably knew a great deal about animals by now, and I was sure he would welcome a change. Besides, this safari would give him an opportunity to photograph animals in the flesh, instead of vice versa.

Covello seemed reluctant to leave his work, but he did admit he was running out of leopard skins, and Africa seemed like a good place to replenish his supply.

We flew directly to Stanleyville, our yellow-fever shots tingling in our arms, our eyes glassy from typhoid serum, our hands shaking from the effects of quinine pills. Even before we landed I could hear the native tom-toms beating out a message. "White hunter . . . no guts . . . white hunter . . . no guts."

In Stanleyville we took a taxi to the office of José Ingels & Son, who operate a company called Congo Safari. Ingels is no stranger to the safari business. He took John Huston out in search of wild boar, he took Katharine Hepburn out in search of wild crocodiles and he took Humphrey Bogart out in search of a drink. During the shooting of the movie *The African Queen,* he saw that Lauren Bacall had forty-five bottles of soda-water a day for her bath, and he killed hundreds of mosquitoes on producer Sam Spiegel's back. Ingels was a good man for a tough job.

I stuck out my trigger finger and we shook hands.

"Do you have any safaris for cowards?" I asked Ingels.

"Not at the moment," he replied. "I've got a group of thirty-five Americans, the oldest eighty-seven, who are going to the Albert National Park to take some movies. I could put you on that."

I was about to sign up when Cavello reminded me I had to kill an animal.

"Oh, you want to *kill* something," Ingels said, putting on his pith helmet. "Well, you've come to the right place. The Belgian Congo is full of wild game. We can offer anything you want. What about a lion?"

"Is it dangerous?"

"Heavens, no. Except of course if the creature is hiding in the bush, or if you wound him or have to follow him into the dense undergrowth. Or if the female is trying to protect her cubs, or if the lion thinks he's cornered and wants to make a fight of it, or if you attack the male and the female tries to sink her claws in you."

"What else do you have?"

"How about a nice pachyderm? Elephants are great fun, particularly if they know they're being hunted and decide to hunt the hunter. You have to get right up to an elephant to get in a good shot and naturally he'll charge if he sees you. He'll put up his flappy ears and head straight at the man with the gun. If you don't kill him on the first shot it may be your last.

"When he gets on top of you he'll grab you with his trunk and smash you against a tree or the ground. Then he'll either trample on you or gut you with his tusks. Once he thinks you're dead he'll cover you up with leaves or grass. Elephants always give their victims a proper funeral. I must warn you of one thing. It will cost you two hundred dollars for a license if you want an elephant."

"Two hundred dollars," I said thoughtfully. "That's not too bad, considering you get a burial and everything. But don't you have something a little more my size?"

Ingels measured me around the waist.

"You can try for rhino if you wish, but rhinos usually attack without provocation and there is not much to shoot at, once one is coming toward you. You'll be a big man if you shoot a rhino.

"Then there's always leopard. I'll bet you'd like to bring your wife back a nice leopard coat. Shooting leopards in the Congo is a praiseworthy business and the natives will be grateful if you do it. But leopards are not easy to find. They've been known to hide in trees and jump on you as you walk under them. They'll rip you to bits with their claws. Even if they just scratch you, the poison in their talons can kill you. But they do make wonderful coats."

Ingels ran down the list of other game. He mentioned hartebeest, waterbuck, sassabies, red and black lechwes, Varden cob, Thomas cob, impala buck, bushbuck, oribis, klipspringer, wart-hogs, Livingston eland, bongos, topis, Neuman cob and scaly anteaters.

"You are not permitted to hunt gorillas," he said. "They are protected by law."

It was the first good news I had heard all day.

Finally it was decided by Ingels and Covello that I would shoot a buffalo. The buffalo is the meanest, most thieving card-cheating, wife-stealing animal in the Congo. But Covello tried to be encouraging. "The buffalo isn't as dangerous as everyone makes him out to be. Statistics prove that in the United States more Americans are killed in automobile accidents than are killed by buffalo."

Ingels arranged to send us out with his son, a strapping twenty-five-year-old lad who would be in charge of our porters, buy our food, take care of our transportation, guns and camping equipment, and tell us true stories of other hunting safaris.

Before we left Stanleyville, Ingels and his son took me to be outfitted. They bought me regulation shorts, a bush jacket, a slouch hat, a toothbrush and a bottle of gin. There was no doubt about it, I was dressed to kill.

We loaded the car with mosquito netting and first-aid equipment and—as is the custom with anyone who is going out hunting for the first time—I was asked to pay Ingels in advance. "The executors of the estate are sometimes reluctant to pay," Ingels explained apologetically.

It is 250 miles as the crow flies from Stanleyville to Irumu. No crow would make it if he went by car. The road twists and turns through a rain-soaked Ituri forest, and the animals, which have a habit of sitting in the middle of the road are neither frightened nor impressed by an automobile horn. The law of the jungle reads that under all conditions an animal has the right of way, and in the few recorded cases where the driver and the animal have both lost their tempers, the animal has always come out on top.

As an added attraction on the safari, we stopped off at a Pygmy camp to take pictures. It cost us only twenty dollars apiece, but the Pygmies warned us if we made any postcards from the photos they wanted royalties on the sales.

In Irumu we found the white hunter. His name was Alex Pierrard and in six years he had bagged more than one hundred elephant, lion, leopard, rhino and python. His walls were jammed with trophies and you couldn't walk on the floor without slipping on an antelope or leopard skin. He had rhino horns for ash trays and elephant tusks for coat racks, and wild boar heads for door-stops. Pierrard was a white hunter to give any yellow hunter confidence.

Young Ingels explained to Pierrard that I was after buffalo, and the white hunter, who noticed that the left side of my face was twitching, looked surprised.

"I can find you all the buffalo you want," Pierre said. "But are you sure you want to do it? It's pretty risky business, particularly if you've never hunted them before."

"See here, sir," said Covello. "We know it's risky business and that's why we're out here. If you don't want to take us we'll find another white hunter."

I tried to shut Covello up, but he was very indignant. "It just so happens that my friend here is one of the best shots in Paris. Just because his face is twitching and he's cowering behind your couch is no reason for you to become insulting. My friend wants a buffalo in the worst way and he's determined to pay for it."

Pierrard apologized and said he would arrange porters and would borrow a *tipoye*—a carrying chair for rough travel—as we had a great deal of country to cover. "If it's buffalo you want," he said, "it's buffalo you're going to get."

The next morning we started out bright and early to find a camp. We hired twenty-five porters at twenty cents per head. They were in the truck with the supplies and we followed in a station wagon. Our first inkling that all would not go well on the safari came when the truck, which was being towed on a raft across a fast-moving river, sank to the muddy bottom. We saved the porters and the supplies, but it took us two days to get the truck out of the river. It was heartbreaking work, particularly when I thought about the porters costing me twenty cents a day.

We finally made camp and I was given a tent to myself and my own Gideon Bible. Modern safaris think of everything.

The best part of hunting in Africa is camping out. There—underneath an autumn moon, with a large roaring fire and the companionship of good fellows, large safari ants and malaria-ridden mosquitoes feeding on what little there is left after the scorpions get finished with you—a man is at peace with the world.

Over warm beer and pickled elephant ears, we talked the talk of men—the animals we had shot, the women we had known, the Marilyn Monroe pictures we had seen.

Pierrard cleaned and oiled the guns, Covello and Ingels practiced making tourniquets and splints in case anything went wrong, and the natives argued amongst themselves who was going to draw my bath the next morning.

It was a pleasant evening, and I thought to myself, perhaps for the last time, that it was good to be alive.

The next morning Pierrard and I went out to find my buffalo. The porters carried me for three miles in the *tipoye* and my gun-bearer walked by my side. I had intended to shoot my buffalo from the seat, but Pierrard wouldn't permit it. Besides, if the buffalo charged and the porters ran, I would be caught with my *tipoye* down.

So the white hunter, the beaters, my gun-bearer and I went into the savanna on foot. About seven o'clock we sighted a herd. We dropped down on our bellies and Pierrard indicated it was time to crawl for-

ward. I kept thrashing with my arms and legs but I wasn't going anywhere and finally Pierrard made the beaters pull me along. We got
within sixty yards and then Pierrard whispered:

"That's your boy."

He pointed to the largest bull in the herd, the meanest, cruellest
hunk of fauna in the entire green hills of Africa. He had horns the size
of two curved Eiffel Towers, and a face that would stop Big Ben. His
hump was slightly smaller than Mount Everest and each shoulder
looked like the front of the *Super Chief.* To top it off he had Native
Dancer's legs.

I tried to crawl away but Pierrard held me by the belt.

"Let's forget the whole idea," I whispered. "Live and let live, I always say."

"It's too late now. You better take him. Bust him between the neck
and the chest."

I got up on one knee and sighted. I squeezed the trigger slowly.

You think a lot of things when you're about to kill your first buffalo.
You remember a lot of people who have been close to you.

As I squeezed the trigger I thought about the boys at Toots Shor's
and how we used to sit around together with Leo Durocher, Joe Di-
Maggio, Bill O'Dwyer, Bob Considine and Tallulah Bankhead.

I thought about my good friends Leonard Lyons, Earl Wilson and Ed
Sullivan and how we used to hunt items together in much darker
places than Africa.

I thought about Sherman Billingsley. Good old Sherm. I knew I was
going to miss him, even though he used to throw me out of the Stork
Club every night. Well, that's not exactly true. He never let me in.

I thought of Elsa Maxwell and what a fine buffalo hunter she would
make if only she took it seriously. I thought of Walter Winchell and
the many Sunday nights we used to stay up together, he in his radio
studio and I in my home in Forest Hills. I fervently wished he and Len-
ny Lyons would stop feuding.

I kept squeezing the trigger.

I thought of Hedda Hopper and Louella Parsons, who had gone after
much bigger game than I had, and had Hollywood's finest collections of
shrunken heads of movie stars and producers.

I thought of Aly Khan and Rubi Rubirosa and the wonderful trophies they had collected during the years.

There was so much to think about and I kept squeezing and squeezing.

All of a sudden, just before I got to Jane Russell, the gun went off.

For a second I was blinded but when I looked up the buffalo was gone.

"I got him, I got him!" I shouted.

"The hell you did," said Pierrard. "You missed him by a mile."

"But I hit something. I could hear the thud."

"You hit a Thomas cob antelope which was standing two hundred yards to the right of the buffalo. Let's have a look."

We crawled up to the animal and found him dead. I had shot him true and straight and he had died brave and strong. I fainted.

The gun-bearers and porters whooped for joy.

They threw me over the antelope and carried the whole mess into camp.

Covello was waiting for us at the camp.

"Where's the buffalo?" he asked.

"I was about to shoot one," I explained, "when I saw this Thomas cob. They're very rare and Pierrard insisted I shoot it instead. What could I do? Buffalo are a dime a dozen, but have you ever seen a Thomas cob like that? He charged me and I had time for only one shot. Fortunately I got him in the chest, right smack in the heart."

Pierrard nodded his head, and gun-bearers didn't speak any English.

The porters gave me the tail of the cob as well as the horns and carried me on their shoulders to the airport in Irumu. It took only a half-day, so I was in my rights when I paid them only ten cents each.

I'm back in Europe now and I can already tell the difference. People are now saying, "Hemingway killed his leopard, Ruark killed his lion and Buchwald killed his Thomas cob."

Now that I'm a full-fledged writer I'm even thinking of writing a book. I've got a great idea for one, about an old man who goes fishing off the coast of Cuba by himself, and catches the biggest fish in the sea only to have the sharks eat it before the old man can get it back to shore. I haven't got a title for it yet, but it should make a whale of a story.

The Great Grimaldi Feud

Many people, particularly members of the British press, expressed surprise at the cool reception I received at the hands of the Monegasque royal family.

"We can understand it for ourselves," they told me, "but how can they snub somebody like you—somebody who got into the Mittersill Hunting Club?"

The answer is quite simple. I was snubbed at Monaco for one simple reason. The Buchwalds and the Grimaldis (the royal house of Monaco) have not spoken to each other since January 8, 1297.

The reason for the feud is lost somewhere in the cobwebs of history, but it was a time when one of my ancestors, then working for the Viking News Service, covered a battle that Rainier Grimaldi fought against the Flemish Navy. Rainier I, then an admiral, decreed that only members of the Associated, United and International Press associations could accompany him into battle, but my ancestor, disguised as a Genoese sailor, hid on board the flagship and scooped the other three news agencies by four years.

In 1523, when Lucien Grimaldi, son of Lambert, and successor to his brother Jean II, was assassinated by his nephew, Barthelemy Doria, the palace tried to hush the news up. But an alert ancestor of mine, then working for the *Volga Free Press,* broke the story and prevented Barthelemy from sitting on the throne.

And so it's gone down through history. There was talk that Charlotte de Grammont, daughter of the Marshal de Grammont, who married the Duke of Valentinois on April 28, 1659, was in love with Rudolph Buchwald, then a court reporter for the *News of the World.* But we only have Rudolph's diary as evidence, and every one in the family knows how unreliable he was.

You won't find a page in the history of Monaco where a Buchwald hasn't offended a Grimaldi or a Grimaldi hasn't offended a Buchwald. Generation after generation the families have stayed clear of each other.

Just last year, my Aunt Molly from Brooklyn was making up her guest list for my cousin Joseph's wedding to a nice girl from Flatbush.

I suggested she invite Prince Rainier, who was then in the United States.

"No Grimaldis," she said, "will be allowed at Joseph's wedding."

"But Aunt Molly," I protested, "this is the twentieth century. We've got to forget ancient family feuds. Prince Rainier's a nice fellow."

"I don't care for myself," Aunt Molly said, "but you know what a long memory your Uncle Oscar has. Besides, has Prince Rainier invited Joseph to his wedding?"

No matter how much I tried to persuade Aunt Molly, she wouldn't send the Prince an invitation to Joseph's wedding. How he found out about it I'll never know, but as soon as I received that cool reception in Monaco, I knew Aunt Molly had made a mistake. The Grimaldis still had it in for the Buchwalds.

I can understand Prince Rainier's attitude toward us, but I can't understand the Kelly family behaving the way they have. The Buchwalds have always liked the Kellys. Back when Mr. Kelly senior was turned down at Henley, my father sent a telegram to the King and said, "If Jack Kelly can't row at Henley, then I won't row either."

So what happened at Monte Carlo? Mr. and Mrs. Kelly threw a dinner for the bridal party at the Monte Carlo Casino, and do you know where I was? I was outside in the rain holding a flashlight for a photographer from a Finnish newspaper. That's the thanks my father got for sending the telegram to the King of England.

White Hunter, Red Fox

Mr. John Huston, the movie director, who lives the life of Riley in Ireland between pictures, invited me to join him at his country estate one week-end to ride the hounds and hunt the foxes with the landed gentry of County Kildare.

When I arrived Mr. Huston gave the butler my bags and took me into the library. "Now, sit down, kid, I want to talk to you."

"Yes, sir, Mr. Huston."

"Now, kid, what exactly do you know about fox hunting?"

"Well, I've been reading up on it and Oscar Wilde said that fox hunting is the pursuit of the inedible by the unspeakable."

Mr. Huston blanched. "That's just what I was afraid of. As long as you're going to be with us I think we'd better get you straight on fox hunting. Once you understand it, you'll realize what a wonderful thing fox hunting really is."

"Yes, sir."

"Fox hunting is one of the greatest and roughest sports in the world," Mr. Huston said. "It is the real test of horsemanship, sportsmanship and woodmanship. And Irish fox hunting is the best fox hunting of all."

"Why don't they just shoot the foxes and be done with it?" I asked.

"Because, kid, the only time you can shoot a fox is at night, and nine chances out of ten the farmer will only wound him and he will die a cruel, lingering death. In fox hunting, once the fox is trapped, he is entitled to a quick, clean death."

"Why don't they gas them? That would do it."

"You're missing the point. The fox serves a great purpose. The Irish people don't want to kill all the foxes. The fox is Ireland's best friend. If it weren't for the fox there would be no great breed of Irish horses, those big-boned, heavy-muscled, bold, noble creatures who are responsible for the great steeplechase races throughout the world.

"And by the same token the fox is responsible for producing the great courage in Irish people. My boy, you haven't lived until you've seen an Irish woman, sixty-five or seventy years old, sitting side-saddle on a horse, and taking one of the great Irish banks. The Irish love their fox hunting so much that every year a half-dozen oldsters fall out of their saddles and are dead before they hit the ground. They literally die with their boots on.

"And, oh, the women! The world owes a debt to the Irish women and to fox hunting. The Irish women are the mothers of Ireland's greatest export—Irishmen. I would go so far as to say that Guiness Stout and fox hunting are responsible for most of the good characteristics in Irishmen."

"What is responsible for the bad ones?" I asked.

"Irish whiskey. But don't change the subject. Not only is fox hunting a humane sport, but it gives the fox a chance to get away. A fox is caught only one out of four times. Now what could be fairer?"

"Maybe if they imported a fox blight of some sort it would kill them off in no time," I said.

"People say," said Mr. Huston, "that fox hunting is a posh sport only for toffs, but I would say it was one of the most democratic sports there is. Anyone who can ride a horse is welcome to join in a fox hunt. This isn't just true of Ireland, it's true everywhere."

I disagreed. "I had an uncle in Brooklyn who tried to join a fox hunt on Long Island, and the people set the hounds on him. Chased him all the way back to Brooklyn."

Mr. Huston was becoming annoyed. "Look, kid, once you're out in the field on a horse you'll feel differently about this. I am going to take you on a fox hunt tomorrow and you'll see for yourself exactly what I have been talking about. Now, are there any more questions?"

"Well, there is one. Why don't they set out poison? It seems that would really knock them off."

For the first time Mr. Huston looked as if he was sorry he asked me to come along.

The following morning was "a grand, soft day," which means in Ireland that it was raining like hell. Originally, I had planned to wear a cowboy suit with two .45-calibre revolvers around my waist. But when the master of the hunt saw this he made me go back and change. I was given instead a pink swallow-tailed coat, yellow vest, white tie, black boots and a tall black silk hat. They wouldn't even let me keep my revolvers.

The horse Mr. Huston had selected for me was a large, grey stallion named Lots of Lolly, a raring beast no different from any other jumping horse except that it talked a blue streak. Now there are people who say horses don't talk and it's true in most of the world. But Ireland, a country haunted by ghosts, inhabited by leprechauns and driven mad by banshees, is the exception. Horses not only talk here; you can't keep them quiet.

"You ever been fox hunting before?" Lots of Lolly asked.

"No, sir," I honestly replied.

"I thought so," he said. "You really haven't a very good seat. Well, if you're game, I guess I am. But try to behave yourself. Don't pull on my mouth, and throw that damned whip away. Just leave everything to me."

We had some time to wait before the hunt began and Lots of Lolly seemed very bored. "Say, did ya hear the one about . . ."

"Hounds, gentlemen, please," the master of the hunt said, and the whipper-ins, with the hounds neatly packed together, moved down to the first covert.

"What are they doing now?" I asked Lots of Lolly.

"Just wait. There, now the fox is going away, the hounds have the scent and they're giving tongue. Now the master is blowing 'Gone Away' on his horn and the hunt is on. Let's go."

I started off with Lots of Lolly trying to take the lead. The master of hunt's face became contorted. "If you please, sir, would you mind staying in the field?"

"Don't let him talk to you like that," Lots of Lolly said. "Are we hunting or are we not hunting? He's just a big bag of kale." I was just about to tell the master of the hunt he was a bag of kale when the first bank loomed up in front of us.

"Close your eyes," Lots of Lolly said, "let go of the reins and leave everything to me."

I closed my eyes but couldn't help peeping. When I saw what was in front of me I shrieked. Lots of Lolly became furious. "I told you to shut your eyes—or would you prefer that I shut them for you?"

I shut them and Lots of Lolly soared beautifully over the bank, landing on all fours on the other side of the ditch.

"You see?" he said. "What did I tell you? Now let's hear the music of the hounds."

We turned and headed for the woods. Lots of Lolly was running three strides ahead of the rest of the hunt. Suddenly I looked ahead and saw a bank slightly higher than Mount Everest.

Lots of Lolly shuddered. "Do you see what I see?"

"Yes, sir."

"Are you willing to take a chance?"

"Yes, sir," I said as we approached the jump.

"Well," said Lots of Lolly, "I'm not."

And with that he stopped abruptly and threw me out of the saddle, over the bank into the water-filled ditch, and then, snickering with pleasure, galloped away.

Two hours later, while I was still swimming around in the mud, Lots of Lolly came back with the brush between his teeth. "You certainly missed a wonderful hunt," he said.

"What happened?"

"Well, we found a fox at Palmerstown which went to ground near the house. We went to Forenaughts, where we had a nice thirty minutes. At Tipperhaven, the hounds drew ferness, where the fox left immediately and going for the kill he swung right-handed through Major Mainguy's bottoms leaving Arthurstown on his right. The hounds killed in the open, just short of Kilteal Finish. And because I got there first, they gave me the brush. You should have come along; you would have loved it."

"Would you give me a ride back to town?" I asked him.

"With all that filthy goop on you? I should say not. What kind of horse do you think I am, anyhow?"

I told him, and Lots of Lolly went away mad.

Bulls

The talk around the bullfighting circles of Madrid is that the bulls aren't as brave as they used to be. The explanation may lie in the fact that most bulls receive no instructions before entering the bull ring. Millions of words have been written on how to be a brave matador, a brave picador and a brave sicador (one who gets sick at a bullfight), but not one word of advice has ever been written on how to be a brave bull. Perhaps this sad state of affairs can be remedied. The following advice is for fighting bulls only.

The first thing you've got to realize is that you're a bull—you're a wild, noble, honest animal who has been bred, not for his meat, but for his courage. You are endowed with keen instincts, physical soundness, pugnacious arrogance, ferocious bravery, bull-like nobility, and when it comes to plain good looks you've got it over any other four-legged male in the world.

You've come from a long line of fighting bulls and you should be as proud of them as they hope to be of you.

For the last five years you've done nothing but eat and sleep and it's been a good life. But now the time has come to bid farewell to the ranch and the many dear friends you must leave behind. A brave bull, when leaving the breeding ranch, walks straight up the wooden ramp to the truck, never looking behind. If he falters or hesitates, his owner may think him a coward, and there is nothing more horrible for a bull than for an owner to think he's afraid.

You arrive at the bull ring tired and in need of a shower. The handlers unbox you and put you in your own corral, where you can wash and be refreshed. Because you're going to fight the next day they don't let you out in the evening.

The next morning you're up bright and early and you're excited. This is it; this is what you've been waiting five years for. Today you're going to have a chance to appear in front of twenty-five thousand people who have paid up to ten dollars a seat to see you fight. You say to yourself, "If only Dad could have lived to see me now."

You eat a light breakfast and then the fight promoters come into the corral and start pairing you off with another bull. Each matador must fight two bulls, and since there are three matadors on the programme, that means five other bulls as well as yourself are chosen. There are a couple of spare ones in case one of you loses your nerve, but it rarely happens.

You don't know how it happens but the day just flies by. Before you know it, it's five thirty. You can see through the slats in your box that the stadium is full. A band is playing and most of the people are in their shirt sleeves. They're in a gay mood, drinking wine and eating peanuts and shouting to each other. You start perspiring a little, not from fear, but from nervousness. Your blood tingles and your heart starts beating fast. You keep saying to yourself, "Is this really happening to little old me?"

Suddenly you hear trumpets and drums. The horse gate next to you opens and the matadors, banderilleros, picadors and ring servants parade into the ring to the president's box. You have a new respect for tradition.

Then you see two teams of three mules each, richly tasselled and belled, and you wonder what part they play in the bullfight. You find out sooner than you think.

The moment is near. The matadors bow to the crowd. They exchange their dress capes for fighting capes, and strut up and down in front of the beautiful women and retired bullfighters. It makes you mad to see this display of conceit and you can't wait to get your horns into the seat of their pompous pants.

A bugle sounds, the gate swings open and at last you rush into the ring. The crowd roars a cheer, the like of which you've never heard before. They're cheering you. You're so happy you want to sit down and cry. But a brave bull has to stay on his feet and you run around snorting and raging and drinking in the glory. As you run around you see a pink cape out of the corner of your eye. It's as though someone were waving a red flag in front of you and suddenly you're furious. You dig in your front hoofs and charge for the cape.

The thing that you, as a brave bull, must always keep in mind when a fight is on is that it took generations of careful breeding and scientific know-how to make you what you are today. For the next twenty minutes you have a chance to repay your owner for all the care, affection, kindness and money he has lavished on you for the past five years. No other animal except a fighting bull is given such an opportunity.

As we mentioned before, the first thing you must do when you charge out into the arena is snort and kick up your heels and charge into the fence a couple of times so the matador who is hiding behind a wooden fence can study you for any defects. He wants to know on which side you hook, how wide your horns are and if you have a tendency to chop. Don't tell him anything. And don't waste your energy on the peon. The crowd doesn't care if he gets gored or not.

Now the matador will come out. He does some experimental cape work with you and you might as well go along with it. If you don't, the audience may ask the president to send in another bull. (Besides, it gives you a good chance to study the weaknesses of the matador.) After making a few passes and getting the feel of the cape, the signal is given to let the picadors into the ring.

The real show is about to begin.

The picador, with his wide-brimmed hat, canvas pants and armoured legs, is the meanest man in the bull ring, disliked as much by the audience as he is by the bulls. He is mounted on an old blindfold horse, and since the animal is not long for this world, there is no harm in goring the poor thing and putting him out of his misery.

Once you get the horse it's only a matter of seconds before you get the picador, and the crowd will be with you all the way. A brave bull should never hesitate when charging the picador. He should charge right in, aiming for the underside of the horse. At first the pick will sting a little, but you'll be so furious by this time you won't even feel it.

Some picadors (what are we talking about, most picadors) will try to work their picks into your flesh, and this makes the crowd very mad. When you hear a roar from the fans you know the picador is not playing the game and anything you do to him will be all right with them.

The idea behind "picking" you is to weaken your neck muscles so you'll keep your head down. There's nothing wrong with this except for the way the picador does it.

After he's finished, the banderilleros come out and stick barbed sticks in you. They are supposed to correct your faults (as if you had any). After the picador you hardly feel the barbs and, since it adds colour to the bullfight, there is no reason for you to object to them.

The final act is about to take place. This is the act that separates the bulls from the calves. This is your chance to show how brave you really are. From now on it's you or the matador, and almost everyone is rooting for you.

In this stage you are more dangerous and wary than you have been before. You're on the defensive, and we hate to mention this, but you're also fighting for your life.

The matador carries a scarlet cloth called a *muleta*.

The cloth is folded and attached to a stick, which the bullfighter can use with one hand. The matador, bareheaded, walks over to the president's box and asks if he can kill you. This makes you laugh. He then dedicates you to someone in the ring, usually a beautiful lady. If you wish, you can dedicate the matador to somebody, but you usually don't have the time.

Now the matador approaches you (don't go to him; it makes him look good and you can save energy this way). You face each other. The first pass you'll probably make is the *pase natural*. It's very dangerous and beautiful when done right. Try to get as close to the bullfighter as possible without touching him. If you do it right the crowd will go mad. Now turn around and do it again. *"Olé!"* they're shouting. Do it again and again. Now take a short trot around the arena and take a bow.

The matador will adjust his *muleta* and you get back to business. He may try a chest pass, at which time you pass the matador's chest and keep going straight out. You'll probably be doing many variations of the different passes, but in order to look good you must stay as close to the bullfighter as possible. When you get bored with running back and forth you might try to gore him. The best place to gore a matador is in his chest. If you don't want him to die you might try for the groin. Toss him up in the air and then stomp on him. The crowd will go wild and you'll be the hero of the day.

If you don't gore the bullfighter, then you must face what is known in bullfighting circles as "the moment of truth." At this moment the matador stands in front of you, his sword raised, staring straight at you while you have your head down (that damn' picador). The matador suddenly runs at you and, thrusting the sword with valour and skill, he pushes it between your shoulder blades, cutting the big blood vessels of your mediastinum.

If he makes a good thrust you should drop dead on the spot.

Sometimes the matador misses and then the spectacle becomes cruel. You start coughing up blood and all the fight has been taken out of you. The crowd is very mad when this happens and they hate the matador almost as much as you do.

If you don't die right away they give you the *coup de grâce,* but you have to lie down to get it. You might as well, because if you don't, the matador will be sticking swords in you all day.

Once you're dead, those beautiful mules run out into the ring and your feet are hooked to the chains. If you've been a brave bull then you can savour your greatest hour of glory. The mules will drag you around the ring while the crowd screams its approval. It's a very moving scene.

If the matador has done well, they'll cut off your ears and give them to him. It really doesn't matter. At this stage of the game you can't hear anything anyway.

Chacun à Son Gout, or, Why We Eat Turkey for Thanksgiving

One of our most important holidays is Thanksgiving Day, known in France as *le Jour de Merci Donnant.*

Le Jour de Merci Donnant was first started by a group of Pilgrims *(Pelerins)* who fled from *l'Angleterre* before the McCarran Act to found a colony in the New World *(le Nouveau Monde)* where they could shoot Indians *(les Peaux-Rouges)* and eat turkey *(dinde)* to their heart's content.

They landed at a place called Plymouth (now a famous *voiture Americaine)* in a wooden sailing ship called the Mayflower (or *Fleur de Mai)* in 1620. But while the *Pelerins* were killing the *dindes,* the *Peaux-Rouges* were killing the *Pelerins,* and there were several hard winters ahead for both of them. The only way the *Peaux-Rouges* helped the *Pelerins* was when they taught them to grow corn *(mais).* The reason they did this was because they liked corn with their *Pelerins.*

In 1623, after another harsh year, the *Pelerins'* crops were so good that they decided to have a celebration and give thanks because more *mais* was raised by the *Pelerins* than *Pelerins* were killed by *Peaux-Rouges.*

Every year on the *Jour de Merci Donnant,* parents tell their children an amusing story about the first celebration.

It concerns a brave *capitaine* named Miles Standish (known in France as *Kilometres Deboutish)* and a young, shy *lieutenant* named Jean Alden. Both of them were in love with a flower of Plymouth called Priscilla Mullens (no translation). The *vieux capitaine* said to the *jeune lieutenant:*

"Go to the damsel Priscilla *(allez tres vite chez Priscilla),* the loveliest maiden of Plymouth *(la plus jolie demoiselle de Plymouth).* Say that a blunt old captain, a man not of words but of action *(un vieux Fanfan la Tulipe),* offers his hand and his heart, the hand and heart of a soldier. Not in these words, you know, but this, in short, is my meaning.

"I am a maker of war *(je suis un fabricant de la guerre)* and not a maker of phrases. You, bred as a scholar *(vous, qui êtes pain comme un etudiant),* can say it in elegant language, such as you read in your books of the pleadings and wooings of lovers, such as you think best adapted to win the heart of the maiden."

Although Jean was fit to be tied *(convenable à être emballé),* friendship prevailed over love and he went to his duty. But instead of using elegant language, he blurted out his mission. Priscilla was muted with amazement and sorrow *(rendue muette par l'étonnement et la tristesse).*

At length she exclaimed, interrupting the ominous silence: "If the great captain of Plymouth is so very eager to wed me, why does he not come himself and take the trouble to woo me?" *(Ou est-il, le vieux Kilometres? Pourquoi ne vient-il pas auprès de moi pour tenter sa chance?)*

Jean said that *Kilometres Deboutish* was very busy and didn't have time for those things. He staggered on, telling what a wonderful husband *Kilometres* would make. Finally Priscilla arched her eyebrows and said in a tremulous voice: "Why don't you speak for yourself, Jean?" *(Chacun à son gout.)*

And so, on the fourth Thursday in November, American families sit down at a large table brimming with tasty dishes, and for the only time during the year eat better than the French do.

No one can deny that *le Jour de Merci Donnant* is a *grande fête* and no matter how well fed American families are, they never forget to give thanks to *Kilometres Deboutish,* who made this great day possible.

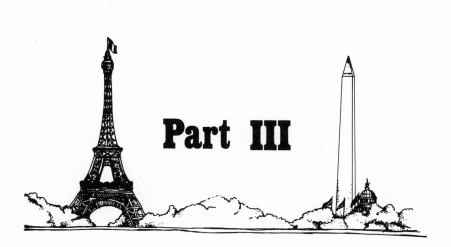

Part III

To Russia With Love

Among the many scientific questions still left unanswered during this great International Geophysical Year was: "Could an American in a chauffeur-driven car with torque flight transmission, hemispherical combustion, full-time coaxial power steering, oriflow shock absorbers, total contact braking and an automatically lighted glove compartment drive from Paris to Moscow without being arrested?"

And in connection with such a trip, would an English picnic hamper, a magnum of French champagne, a bottle of American vodka, a brie cheese, a Paris boot-cleaner and a Belgian chauffeur hold up on the Iron Curtain countryside?

In the interests of science and in the great tradition of Dr. Vivian Fuchs, who did such a splendid job in his dash across the South Pole, I volunteered to make the trip.

Of course, I had a few more difficulties than Dr. Fuchs. For one thing, Fuchs did not have to apply for a visa from the Russians and, for another, his wife apparently did not try to stop him from going.

In fairness to the Russians, it must be said that permission to go to the Soviet Union was obtained far more easily from the Russians than it was from my wife. My wife has always been noted for her capitalistic tendencies. Since she reads nothing but the bourgeois press, she was afraid I might be filling Soviet salt shakers for the next twenty years.

For a month there was much hemming and hawing over my visa application. My wife hemmed; the Russians hawed. Finally, through the good graces of a Paris travel agent named C.F. Bertoncini, and several telegrams and telephone calls to Moscow, the visa was granted.

"If the Russians say *da*," I told my wife, "you can't very well say *nyet*."

She said *nyet* and a lot more, but her aggressive antitourist policies were finally suppressed when I promised, if she would let me go, I wouldn't write any more about the counter-revolutionary hooliganism of our three children.

For a travelling companion, I chose a screen-writer named Peter Stone. Mr. Stone's qualifications for such a trip were excellent. He holds the record for getting through the Louvre Museum in less than six minutes. He was the first man to study the Winged Victory and declare: "It will never fly." Besides, he was a patsy at gin rummy and I saw no harm in making a few bucks while we were on the road.

Since I was going as an American Imperialist, the perfect car to travel in was a Chrysler Imperial. The Chrysler people were delighted to give me one of their latest models. They hadn't been able to test their cars on Russian roads and they were interested in finding out if their latest transistorized electro-touch tuner radio (with rear-seat speaker, power antenna and foot control) would be able to pick up the Voice of America.

They provided me with a chauffeur, Mr. John Van den Beroff, a Belgian who spoke Russian and was also a qualified mechanic.

Insurance was another problem. Most Western insurance companies were reluctant to insure the car, as they felt that in case of an accident there would be some difficulty in winning a lawsuit with an all-Russian jury. But finally Lloyd's of London said they would take the risk, and, if necessary, the roubles in the event the Imperial did not make it back.

Although the Russians gave me a visa for 21 days, the Czechs and Poles would give me only 48-hour transit visas.

I pointed out to the Czech and Polish Consuls in Paris that it sometimes takes 48 hours just to drive from the Arc de Triomphe to the Place de la Concorde. I said I wasn't sure I should be able to get through their countries in the allotted time. But they were both adamant. I had to get through in 48 hours . . . or else! I didn't have the heart to tell Lloyd's of London the news.

And so, on March 30, the three of us, loaded down with food, vodka, jerrycans, spare parts and long underwear, piled into the Imperial to journey eastward, to preach the gospel of enlightened capitalism to the Marxist and Leninist natives behind the snowbound curtain.

Before going, my wife insisted I devise a code word in case I got into trouble. We both discussed it all night and finally reached a decision. In case I got into trouble I could cable one word. It was: "Help!"

* * *

A westerner driving from Paris to Russia has the choice of two routes. He can go through Berlin, East Germany, Poznan (in Poland), Warsaw and on to the Russian border town of Brest. Or he can drive through West Germany, Vienna, Austria, Brno in Czechoslovakia, Cracow (in Poland), Warsaw and then to Brest. After weighing the advantages of both routes, I chose the second one, mainly because it would give me an opportunity to pass by Demel's, in Vienna, the greatest pastry shop in the world. In addition to the 48-hour visas for Czechoslovakia and Poland, I also applied before leaving Paris for a 48-hour visa for Demel's. It was finally granted and they stamped a *Sacher Torte* in my passport.

Vienna was our last contact with the free world as we know it. We packed in as much boiled beef, *Wiener Schnitzel, Schlag, Palatschinken* and *Leberknödel* as our fuel tanks would hold, kissed Yul Brynner (who was making a film there) on the head, and shook hands with all the employees at the Imperial Hotel. They seemed so happy, not because we were going to Russia, but because they weren't.

The Chrysler Imperial had been checked, oiled, washed and its tyres filled, for the last time, with "free Western" air, and it had its last drink of 90-octane gasoline. For the next three weeks, it would be running on 74-octane. It shuddered every time we mentioned it.

The Austrians couldn't understand why anyone with a new American car would want to go east, and every time we stopped to ask the direction to the Czech border they kept pointing the way back to Vienna.

On April 3, 1958, at 1:30 p.m., we reached the Austrian-Czech border. The Austrian border-guard gave us one last chance to change our minds, but, when we insisted we really did want to go to Russia, he stamped our passports, lifted the barrier and said the Czech border was straight ahead.

"You can't miss it. It's the first watchtower, behind the second machine-gun, between two large mine-fields on the left."

We waved goodbye and crossed no-man's-land. A Czech guard in the watchtower came scrambling down the ladder and rushed up to me with a machine-gun. He also thought we had made a mistake and kept pointing back to the Austrian border. We kept pointing the other way, and finally he shrugged his shoulders and told us to go on. We came to another barrier, another watchtower, some more barbed wire and finally the customs shed. We were in Mikulov. The customs inspectors came out and stared at the car. They insisted the first thing to do was open the hood. Not because we were suspected of smuggling anything, but they were just curious to see the motor. We found the same thing happening all along the way. Police and customs officials always made us open the hood to check the motor of the Imperial.

The Mikulov customs were amazed at the amount of foodstuffs and liquor we were carrying in the trunk. Peter Stone insisted they were CARE packages for Marshal Zhukov, the "retired" Russian officer, and the officials did not charge us any duty.

An hour later we were on our way to Brno, the capital of Moravia. Brno is a vry nce cty, but we ddn't get a chnce to spnd mch tme thre. Crwds gthered arnd the Mperial and I cllected lots of fngerprnts whch I snt on to the FBI. Thre are mny twns in Czechoslovakia wthout vwels, but Brno is the lrgest one of thm all. We gssed up and wre advsed to stp at Olomouc for the nght. It was hrd to lve snce we wre surrounded by hndreds of Brno ctizens.

But we were glad to get on the road where we could use vowels again.

Olomouc is the second largest city in Moravia. It has a population of 70,000 people. When we drove up to the Hotel Narodni Dům, 69,678 of them gathered around the car. Unfortunately, the Narodni Dům is located on a street with trolley tracks and there were so many people around the car that all traffic and trolleys were blocked. The people wouldn't get out of the way, and police in uniform arrived and tried to disperse them. But they didn't succeed, so they sent for the secret police in civilian clothes. The chief, in a black leather jacket, told us to move the car to a garage. I told John, my chauffeur, to find a garage, and he drove away from the hotel.

In the meantime the crowd surrounded Peter and me and the baggage. A few people spoke English and translated for the others. The people of Olomouc had hundreds of questions they wanted to ask about the United States. Some had relatives there and wanted to know if I knew them. Others wanted to know what we were going to do about the Ku Klux Klan "in the Rocky Mountains." They apparently had the Rocky Mountains and Little Rock confused.

One student had another problem on his mind. "Why is it that Tokyo is bigger than New York?"

I denied it, but he had the statistics in his pocket. He showed them to the crowd and they agreed it was so.

I had no figures of my own, so I admitted that it was possible it was true.

The student asked: "Well, what are you going to do about it?"

Peter said we couldn't do anything about it until we got back from Russia.

In the meantime John and the Imperial had returned. No garage in town would take the car because there was no room. The street was again blocked, the trolleys were stacked up and the secret police were blowing a gasket.

Finally, an inspector for the tramways, who was never going to make his norm for the day, because of the jam-up, took John to a garage. He ordered the garage manager to move out an Olomouc truck that had been parked there every night for five years and put the Chrysler in its place.

We broke away from the crowd and checked in at the hotel. Later on, after dinner at the hotel, we went to a night-club. We had been there only two minutes when the doorman came to our table and said there was a telephone call for me.

We went to the lobby, but, instead of a telephone call, there were two policemen waiting to speak to us. They weren't selling tickets to a welfare ball.

The Czech police have a reputation for being very touch and I became slightly unnerved. The doorman, a former French Foreign Legionnaire, did the translating.

"Did I own the Chrysler Imperial that was parked out in front of the Hotel Narodni Dúm that afternoon which blocked all the traffic and trolleys in Olomouc?"

I confessed I did.

"Did I know that I had violated Olomouc traffic regulations by parking a car of that size next to the trolley tracks?"

I confessed I didn't.

"Is that all I had to say for myself?"

"It wasn't my fault," I pleaded. "The imperialist automobile capitalists in Detroit were to blame. Everyone said they should be making smaller cars, but they apparently ignored the warnings. Now, because of their lack of foresight, I found myself blocking trolleycars in Olomouc." I asked them if they wanted me to sign a confession.

"No," they said. "We want to give you a traffic ticket."

I pointed out that it wasn't the car, but the people of Olomouc *looking* at the car that blocked the traffic.

Peter whispered to me, "Let them give us the ticket. We'll pay it with a bad Czech."

The police said that if we promised to leave the next morning they would forget the entire incident.

We promised, and the next morning we kept our word, but sadly we blocked traffic again in front of the Narodni Dum while we were loading baggage. The crowds in the morning were just as large as those on the previous night.

The officials were so afraid we wouldn't get out of Olomouc that they gave us a uniformed escort to the city line. The policeman was very friendly and explained there were no hard feelings. To show there were none on our part, we let him work our electrically controlled automatic windows twice and we all parted friends.

We were the only car at the Czech-Polish border at Tesin, so we received the Czech customs guard's undivided attention. Unfortunately, I took a picture of the customs house and this turned out to be an even more serious offense than parking a car next to the trolley tracks. The chief called me into his office and in strong Czech language told me no one was allowed to take pictures at the border.

He demanded my film, and, in the mood he was in, there didn't seem any reason why he shouldn't have it. I gave him the roll and he let me go.

On the Polish side of the border the officials were friendlier. Once again I explained that the foodstuffs and liquor we were carrying were gifts to Russian officials, and there was no problem on duty. A half-hour later, after filling out forms for foreign currency, we were on the way to Cracow.

The consular officials who gave us 48-hour transit visas for Poland were very optimistic people, considering the condition of the Tesin-Cracow road. It took us three hours to make the 89 kilometres, though 30 minutes of this was used up because we killed a goat.

Before anyone gets angry, let me explain that it was not our intention to kill the goat. In order to understand what happened you must know a little about Polish highways. There is very little motorized traffic on Polish roads. There are plenty of horse-drawn wagons, a few cows, occasional geese, dogs and no one knows how many people on foot.

Trying to manoeuvre a large car among all these hazards is a very difficult and dangerous thing. The odds are that you're bound to hit something. On the outskirts of a little town 50 kilometres from Cracow, it was our turn. A goat decided to cross the road at the exact moment that we drove by.

John, the chauffeur, didn't see it until it was too late, and so, as it must to all goats, etc., etc.

There is no set price for killing a goat in Poland. When we walked back to the scene of the accident a small crowd had already gathered, with the owner in the centre. In German I told them that any fair price the crowd set on the goat I would pay. They discussed it among themselves and concluded 200 zlotys ($8.00) was acceptable. The owner was in agreement and I paid on the spot.

John was very upset, and we tried to cheer him up by pointing out it was much cheaper than killing a horse. But he felt so bad he kept the windows at half-mast all the way to Warsaw.

We didn't kill anything else (except several bottles of vodka) for the rest of the time we were in Poland. Friends who had travelled the same road couldn't believe our entire bag for the trip was just one goat. "With that car," they said, "you should have gotten at least two cows." It was the first time the Imperial let us down.

* * *

It's very hard for someone to be in Poland for 48 hours and be an expert on the country. Therefore we stayed an extra 24 hours and would like to retitle the heading of this chapter "Inside Poland."

Most of my information came from foreign correspondents late at night between toasts of the local fire water (see below), and I didn't have a chance to check all the facts. Also the information wasn't given in order. But my own observations weren't any clearer.

I was surprised to see in the Warsaw food stores such American delicacies as Maxwell House Instant coffee, Nescafé, Stokely's orange, pineapple and grapefuit juices on the same shelves with Chinese mandarins, tea and jam and Bulgarian canned stuffed cabbage. I also discovered many brands of Chinese cigarettes on sale: One of the correspondents told me: "They don't give you cancer—they give you Asian flu."

There were long queues in all the food stores and things were very expensive. The national drink in Poland is called *Spiritus Rektifikowanis* and is 96 per cent alcohol. It can be diluted with anything, mostly Stokely's fruit juices. The normal dilution is two cups of *Spiritus Rektifikowanis* with two teaspoons of fruit juice.

Coca-Cola is more popular in Poland than caviar. The reason is that Coca-Cola is American and caviar Russian. The Poles make their own Cola, I was told, but, according to a girl friend of one of the correspondents, it tastes like "grey soup."

Eggs are an obsession in Poland. They are so popular, I was told, that it's difficult to get a haircut without an egg on top. Lemons are also very much in demand. Herring is the national dish.

There is a great deal of trade going on among all the satellite countries, but, rather than helping relations between the countries, it sometimes makes them worse.

When anything is good, a satellite country exports it. If it's bad, it's used for home consumption.

The case of the Bulgarian tomato-juice is a good example in point. Recently the Bulgarians exported excellent tomato-juice to Poland. The Poles were delighted with the tomato-juice. During the same period, though, the Bulgarians were drinking very bad tomato-juice. The trouble started when the Bulgarians came to Poland and the Poles congratulated them on the excellent quality of their tomato-juice. The Bulgarians thought the Poles were making fun of them, as all Bulgarians believed that if there was one thing they didn't make well it was tomato-juice. If the Bulgarians hate anything, it's the Poles making fun of them. So ever since the tomato-juice arrived in Poland, relations between the two countries have been strained.

The Poles, on the other hand, are suspicious of anything they make themselves. Polish soap is excellent, but the Poles can't believe it. If it was good, they figure it would not be on sale so they go on buying inferior foreign soap at higher prices.

"Books and magazines in Poland are very cheap," a correspondent told me, "in compensation for the toilet paper being very expensive."

Horse-racing is very popular in Poland, with or without the horses. A friend reported he went to the track one day in Warsaw.

"It was a beautiful race-track, very modern, and I had marvellous seats. There were about two or three thousand people there, all studying their racing forms and placing bets. Usually you see a few horses at a race-track, but this day I couldn't see any. Then suddenly a bell rang, everyone stood up in the stands and, although there weren't any horses running on the tracks, in three minutes the winners were posted.

"Several people tore up their tickets in disgust and others went to get paid. Then everyone studied his programme again, people made bets, a bell rang, they all poured out to the rail, no horses came out and in three minutes the winners were once more put up."

My friend couldn't stand it any longer and demanded what was going on from one of the pari-mutuel clerks. The clerk explained. Poland has only one string of race-horses and that day they were racing at Sopiat, 400 miles away. But they still kept the Warsaw track open in deference to all the people who wanted to bet and didn't care whether they saw the horses or not.

When you see two men kissing each other on the street in Poland it doesn't necessarily mean they are related. They may be just two strangers whispering something to each other.

Briefly, the political picture in Poland at the moment is as follows.

Gomulka is stable.

Sambrowski, of the shadow government, is bothered with stomach trouble.

Mr. Ochab, the Agriculture Minister, is consolidating and can now be considered No. 2 man.

And Mr. Cyrankiewicz, the President, is extremely happy with the performance of his new Mercedes-Benz.

The zloty, pegged officially at 24 to the dollar, is selling on the black market at the rate of 120 to the dollar.

"The one time the zloty hardened," an informant told me, "was when the Russians sent up their first Sputnik. Poland was the only country in the world that thought the Russian Sputnik was a triumph for the American economy."

The great sport of football has been endangered in Poland because of a star footballer named Trampicz, who plays on the Polonia team in Bytom. Trampicz, when playing on the visitors' grounds, keeps showing his disdain for the crowd by pulling his pants down on the field. They have tried to stop him, but with no success. Once a crowd in Lodz got so angry that they started a riot. But Trampicz is so popular in Bytom that he keeps on playing. "It's been very bad for Poland," a correspondent told me, "and very bad for football. And it's also very bad for Trampicz, particularly when he plays in the wintertime."

*　*　*

We left Warsaw early Monday morning. We had overstayed our transit visas by 24 hours, but it wasn't our fault. We tried to get them extended but we were in Warsaw on Easter Sunday and everything, including the police station, was closed. The manager of the Hotel Bristol gave us a letter testifying to the fact that we had gone to the police station and that there was no one to receive us. We left $5.50 behind for the extra day which the manager of the Bristol promised he would hand over to the police on Monday.

At noon we were driving eastward towards the border town of Terespol when the most embarrassing thing that can happen to a Chrysler Imperial took place. We got stuck in the snow. The Chrysler Imperial is a low, fast car with 325 horsepower. But if you drive through Poland in April you should always carry a spare horse. When we couldn't get out of the snow we went to a peasant farmhouse and asked if someone or something could give us a tow. The woman of the house was very cold.

"You go to Russia?" she asked in German.

I said I did.

"English?"

"No, Americanski."

"Communist?"

"No," I said. "Capitalist."

For the first time she smiled. "Gut. You can have my horse."

Her husband, when he heard I was a capitalist, insisted I pay 100 zlotys ($4.00) for the horse. Since I had paid 200 zlotys for a dead Polish goat a few days before, 100 zlotys for a live Polish horse did not seem an unreasonable price.

The horse was hitched up to the Imperial and, while the villagers stood by, it pulled the Imperial out of the snow without any strain. The peasants were delighted. It proved to them once and for all that a horse was worth an $8,000 (800,000 zloty) car, at least on the snowy roads of Poland.

We arrived in Terespol at noon. We were told by the Polish border officials that we were the first American car through this year. A Volkswagen with three students had gone through the day before and a Mercedes-Benz with a couple had gone through a few days before that. There was some question about our overstaying our visas, but we produced the letter from the hotel manager in Warsaw, and told the captain in charge of the border post we couldn't stand the thought of leaving religious Poland for atheistic Russia on Easter Sunday.

This seemed to be a reasonable argument (any argument against the Russians, the Poles consider is a reasonable argument) and we were allowed to go. We crossed the bridge over the River Bug and a young Russian soldier with a machine-gun stopped us on the other side.

Peter Stone said to the guard in English, "Take us to your leader."

But the guard didn't understand. He indicated that we should wait. Forty-five minutes later, and don't let anyone tell you the bridge on the River Bug isn't cold, two cars arrived. One was filled with Intourist people and the other with military personnel. They checked our passports, and then, when everything seemed in order (they were expecting us and we had been ordered to be on the Terespol-Brest border on April 7), introduced us to our Intourist guide, whose name was Vladimir and who would be our bosom companion for the entire time we were in Russia.

After we were taken to the Brest railroad station for customs inspection (no one bothered to look into any of our bags), it was "suggested" we leave Brest after lunch to go to Minsk.

We were assured there was nothing of value to see in Brest. It was just a military border town, and Minsk held far more tourist interest.

"Couldn't I sleep in Brest and go to Minsk in the morning?"

The Intourist man assured me the beds in Brest were very hard and the beds in Minsk were very soft. It would be much more advantageous to leave for Minsk as soon as possible. As soon as lunch was over, he thought.

"I think," Peter said, "he's trying to tell us something."

In the dining-room we got to know Vladimir, our guide. Vladimir was a young (27 years old), nervous, chain-smoking member of Komsomol, the Young Communist League. His English was excellent, and he seemed happy to be travelling in a Chrysler Imperial. The last party to leave Brest was in a Volkswagen and the word from Minsk was that because of the roads the Intourist guide and the three passengers had to carry the car most of the way on their shoulders.

"I'll make a deal with you, Vladimir," I said after we all got on first-name terms. "I'll show you my notes at the end of the trip if you show me yours."

Vladimir sucked in on his cigarette.

"We're not concerned about what you're going to write," Peter assured him. "It's just that we may have gotten off a good anti-communist crack, and forgotten it."

Vladimir laughed nervously.

"Don't worry," I assured him, "if you get into any trouble because of us, we'll drive you to Siberia in our new Chrysler."

Before leaving Brest, the Russian border town, we were given a small pamphlet concerning the drive. It is 1,053 kilometres from Brest to Moscow. We were scheduled to pass through such well-known towns as Kobrin, Ivatsevichi, Stolbsty, Minsk, Boriskov, Tolochin, Jurtsevo, Orsha, Smolensk, Izdehkovo, Viazjma, Gzhatsk, Moshaisk, and then Moscow.

"How can we drive through them?" Peter asked Vladimir, the Intourist guide. "We can't even pronounce them."

We discovered we didn't have to pronounce them, since we weren't allowed to stop at any of them anyway, except for Minsk and Smolensk.

"Why aren't we allowed to stop at any of the other towns?" I asked Vladimir.

"Why would you want to stop at any other towns?" Vladimir asked, and this seemed to answer the question as far as he was concerned.

The pamphlet also had instructions for tourist drivers. The most important one was: "When necessary, the car should be stopped in time to avoid an accident."

We left Brest at five in the afternoon after being assured by everyone that the road between Brest and Minsk was fine. John, our capitalist chauffeur, was in the front seat and Peter and Vladimir were in the back with me.

The first sixty miles were fine, but then we found out why Napoleon turned back. We hit the same kind of snow he did. It had been snowing for three days and there was at least eighteen inches of snow and ice on the roads. The only transportation on the road had been large trucks that had left deep valleys in the snow. The undercarriage of the Chrysler had not been built with the Brest-Minsk road in mind, and we were scraping ice and snow with our gas tank.

There was nothing in sight for miles in either direction, and the only inhabitants of this part of the country, we understood, were large hungry Byelo-Russian wolves who waited for a car or truck to break down.

Peter was sulking and Vladimir asked him what the matter was.

"Our travel agent," Peter said, "told us people would be throwing flowers in front of the car all the way from Brest to Minsk."

Vladimir, who was getting used to us by now, said: "That's only if you take the Deluxe Tour."

Finally John, who was driving with his left wheels in the snow and his right wheels in the ruts, got caught in two truck ruts and the car settled on its undercarriage with all four wheels off the ground.

We got out of the car, but there was nothing we could do. Off in the distance I heard a mother wolf calling all the other wolves to dinner.

But in a half-hour several Russian trucks arrived, and, without exception, they all stopped to give us a hand.

They had a meeting to decide whether to push or pull. The majority voted to push and it took twelve of them to get the Chrysler off the snow and ice. It was a great demonstration of Russian-American friendship, and how the Russians and Americans, when in trouble, can work together. In this case the Russians pushed, while the Americans took photographs.

Once we got the wheels on to the right ruts again, two of the trucks followed us to see we didn't get into any more trouble.

About five miles further on down the road I saw six trucks parked off the road.

"What are the trucks doing there?" I asked Vladimir.

Peter, who was still shaken by the experience, said: "That's where the truck drivers get eaten."

The rest of the ride was a Russian nightmare, with the Chrysler slipping down into ruts, riding high on snow banks, and skidding sideways when there didn't seem much else to do. It was dark, the trucks had left us by now and we were strictly on our own. Then the final blow fell. We discovered Vladimir didn't believe in God.

"Couldn't you have waited until we got to Moscow before you told us?" Peter asked.

It may have been my imagination, but I kept seeing wolves running behind the Chrysler, snapping at the tyres. John had tuned in Radio Minsk for navigational purposes, and Vladimir, who had run out of cigarettes, was now chain-smoking his thumb.

They will be arguing for years in Brest and Minsk over how we made it under the road conditions of that night.

Vladimir insists it was because of socialist fulfilment of superior road-building equipment. John, a loyal Chrysler employee, insists it was because of the Imperial's independent front-wheel suspension with torsion bar springs, and Peter believes it was because of his ability to call on the Almighty in times of great peril.

But the real secret is that I kept throwing rouble notes out the windows for the wolves. By the time we reached the outskirts of Minsk they had enough money to buy themselves a good meal at a collective farm, and they didn't need us for dinner after all.

* * *

There is no hostility towards an American tourist travelling in Russia. On the contrary, everywhere we went we were treated with kindness and curiosity by the people we met. A new American car is probably one of the best mediums of good propaganda the United States could send to the Soviet Union. In Minsk and Smolensk, and even in cosmopolitan Moscow, our Imperial was surrounded by hundreds of friendly people with hundreds of questions about it, us and America.

In every group there was always someone who spoke English, French or German, and he did the translating for the rest of the people.

(There are 41,000 English teachers in Russia, and even in the small towns we found young children speaking English.) The questions more or less followed a pattern.

What kind of car was it?

How much horsepower, how many miles to the gallon, how much did it cost? Why didn't America sell such cars to the Russian people?

In Minsk, a well-dressed man asked me how much the Imperial cost. I translated at the official rate and told him 40,000 roubles. The best car on sale in Russia is an imitation of the English Ford called the Volga which sells for 60,000 roubles. The man whipped a fistful of roubles out of his pocket and said: "I'll buy it from you for 50,000 roubles."

The biggest thrill to the crowds, comparable to seeing Marilyn Monroe's dress blowing up above her head in New York City, was when we let them have a peek at the motor. Many of them wanted to crawl right inside, and had to be restrained by cooler heads in the group.

Once their curiosity about the car was satisfied, they wanted to know all about us. How much money did we make a month? What newspaper did I work for? And finally, could all newspaper-men in America own Imperials? I assured them that all the American newspaper-men I knew (Henry Luce, William Randolph Hearst, Roy Howard, Ogden Reid, Joseph Pulitzer 2nd), owned Imperials, Cadillacs or Lincolns. This pleased them very much.

There was a great deal of joking going on at these "Summit Conferences." A boy of about twelve was trying to get near the car in Smolensk, but his father was dragging him away. The boy kept crying he wanted the car.

Peter Stone patted him on the head and said, "Don't cry, little boy. I understand you're getting a much better education than your counterpart in the United States."

Although there is no private enterprise in the Soviet Union, there is plenty of outdoor advertising on the roads. A great deal of this is devoted to making everyone fulfil his quota, and we saw several which urged the Russians to "Beat America."

But a few were confusing.

There was one on the road between Minsk and Smolensk which said: "Fight for 10 per cent increase in dairy products."

I asked Vladimir, "How can I fight for an increase in dairy products?"

"You can't fight for the increase," he said. "You're a tourist."

"How can you fight for the increase?" I asked him.

"I can't fight for it either," he said. "Only the dairy collective farmers can fight for it."

"But they would never see the sign," I protested.

"Is that a provocative capitalist question?" he asked.

"No," I replied. "It's a provocative capitalist statement."

"I didn't put the sign up," Vladimir said. "But there is probably a reason for it." That seemed to end the subject.

It was very hard for us to get news of the world while driving through Russia. Our only source of information was Vladimir, and his only source of information was Radio Moscow.

Once when we asked Vladimir what the news was, he said: "I just heard six American destroyers sailed into a Greek harbour to influence the election."

"Six destroyers," Peter said in amazement. "It must have been a municipal election."

* * *

The road between Smolensk and Moscow was excellent and we made it in an afternoon after gassing up outside Smolensk on the highway. There were ten trucks at the gasoline station waiting to be fuelled, but because we were foreigners we had priority at the pump. This was true everywhere we went in Russia. A foreigner is in a privileged class. With his guide he can go to the head of any line, and there isn't anything in the Soviet Union that doesn't have a line except perhaps the Stalin statues.

The Russians don't seem too disturbed by this linecutting, and we heard no complaints. There are two kinds of visitors to the Soviet Union. Any number over two is considered a delegation. Any under two are "tourists without party."

The gasoline stations in Russia are few and far between. Most of the station attendants were husky women who looked as though they could change a flat tyre with one arm and grease an axle with the other. They had to pump the gasoline by hand and there was only one pump at each station.

Friends briefed us on driving in Moscow. There are no blood purges in the Soviet Union at the moment, except on Moscow streets. Under Czarist rule, pedestrians were oppressed by the privileged classes, who drove down the streets of Moscow spattering mud on the workers and peasants. But now this has all been changed. Only state-owned trucks, buses and party functionaries may spatter mud on the workers and peasants.

The ORUD (Moscow Militia) is charged with traffic direction and there are certain regulations in force that would never work in a Western country.

Back-seat driving, for example, is forbidden. Section I, Article 4 says: "All persons, without exception, who use motor transport, are forbidden to give orders to the driver that contradict regulations, and drivers are forbidden to carry out such orders." They wouldn't sell a car in the West if this law were adopted.

Another traffic regulation that would raise havoc in the West is Section IV. Article 16, which says: "It is forbidden to play, skate, ride scooters or ski on sidewalks, bridges, or the side of the road."

Also, you are not allowed to hit military columns with your automobile and it's absolutely forbidden to shoot landowners or Trotskyites from a moving streetcar.

Moscow looked great to us after Minsk and Smolensk. We were put up at the Hotel Metropole, a veritable palace which sleeps 350 people and employs 700. Three hundred and fifty of the 700 watch the guests and the other 350 watch the employees. This leaves very few people to do the actual work.

Getting a meal is a very difficult feat in the Soviet Union, particularly in Moscow. All the tailors left Russia in 1905, all the cooks left in 1917, and all the waiters left after they took our order.

Under the socialist system, tipping was previously forbidden by the Communist party. Tipping was considered by Communists a degrading anti-Marxist conspiracy to cheat the workers of their just desserts. The anti-tipping ruling had many advantages. It saved the guest money, there was no discrimination over tables, and there was no personality cult amongst the headwaiters. There was only one disadvantage. You couldn't get any food.

At first I thought the bad service was due to the fact that the waiters were lazy. But on further investigation I discovered all Soviet restaurants have a state-controlled system. The waiter not only hands in the order, but he must pay for it before he gets it. So if a waiter has a bad day at the track, or if he had to give his wife house-money, none of his tables will get any food that day.

Once the order is placed and paid for, a meeting of the Central Kitchen Committee is called, at which time suggestions on how the dish is to be prepared are made by everyone, from chef down to dishwasher. Then a vote is taken and, if everyone approves, an order is made to a collective farm for the ingredients. But the collective farm cannot send the food to Moscow until the tractor station gives its approval. This all takes time and is known as "the withering away of the restaurant customer."

In recent years Russians as well as foreigners have been trying to beat the socialist system by handing out tokens in restaurants. This has produced amazing results, and production of hot cooked dishes of beef stroganof, shashlick and chicken Kiev has increased by 43 per cent.

One shocked waiter at the Hotel National was so encouraged by tips he received from Truman Capote that he tripled his borscht quota in three weeks and was given the Order of the Red Plate Special, the highest decoration a waiter in the Soviet Union can receive.

Although the giving of gratuities in restaurants is heresy in the Leninist doctrine, the Communist party hasn't done anything serious to squelch it. The reason is that it has solved one of the greatest scientific mysteries in the country . . . the waiter's re-entry problem. Up until people started giving out rouble notes, people knew how to send a waiter out, but no one knew how to get him back again. As with any missile, the secret was all in the tip.

* * *

The first question everyone asks you on your return from the Soviet Union is: "Were you followed?" Every Western tourist likes to think he was. There is really no fun going to a police state if you're not followed by someone. In the Hotel Metropole in Moscow I had the feeling I was always being watched, but it was always by other tourists who thought I was *watching them.* It's kind of discouraging, when you think someone is on your tail, to discover it's a student from the University of Southern California who is competing in a music festival.

But no one knows when he's being followed or if there is a hidden microphone in the hotel room. Once I decided to test it to see whether there was a hidden mike in the room. I shouted at the top of my lungs: "Why doesn't this blankety-blank hotel have any hot water?"

The next day, sure enough, there was hot water in the room. It might have just been a coincidence, but I prefer to think the tape recording of my questions got to the right person.

Peter Stone used to cause trouble in Moscow restaurants, when, after a few vodkas, he would yell: "My KGB man can lick any KGB man in the house."

My friends in Moscow told me that if you were considered important enough they might plant an *agent provocateur* on you, in many cases a beautiful woman. This naturally got me very excited, and I hinted to my Intourist guide that if the right person approached me, I might pass on the secret of the main control switch for the Memphis Holiday Inn. A few nights later I received a telephone call from a woman who purred in French, "I have to see you."

"Do you have an *agent provocateur* for my friend?" I asked excitedly.

"I must see you alone."

We made a rendez-vous to meet in the lobby of the Peking Hotel, and I took along the torn half of an Imperial instruction book to show her I meant business.

But she never showed up. I went back to the Metropole and at two in the morning she called again. "Where were you?" she asked.

"I was there, where were you?" I said.

"You weren't there. But I'm at the apartment now and I'm very lonely."

"What's the address?"

"You know where it is," she sighed, and hung up.

Two days later she called again. "I want to see you."

"I know," I said. "I want to see you too."

"Meet me in front of the GUM department store," she said.

"How will I know you?"

"I'll know you."

I waited in front of the GUM department store until midnight, but she never came.

The next day she called again. "Where were you?"

Finally it dawned on me that perhaps she was looking for someone else. I asked her who she thought she was talking to.

"Aren't you the Syrian boy in Room 577?"

"I'm in 577 but I'm not Syrian."

"Then he left without saying goodbye!"

"It looks that way, sister, but couldn't I be of . . ."

She hung up. It was probably just as well. It's bad form to fool around with somebody else's *agent provocateur*. The Security people don't like it, and somebody's bound to find out about it sooner or later.

An American passport is treated with a great deal of respect in Russia, as Peter and I discovered one afternoon when we decided to see Krushchev at a mass meeting given for him at the Lenin Sports Palace. We asked our Intourist guide if he would take us and he said it was impossible for us to go. The rally was only for Communist dignitaries. We asked all the American correspondents in Moscow if they could get us in, but they said it was impossible. Security was so strict we wouldn't be able to get within three traffic lights of the stadium.

But we had nothing else to do, so we got into the Imperial and told John to drive us to the palace. There were militiamen along all the roads, but when they saw the Chrysler, which I had instructed John to drive at high speed in the lane reserved for Soviet Zims, they all waved us on. We screeched up at the palace and, as John opened the door, all the militiamen on duty outside the stadium saluted, we returned the salute, and, to make it more authentic, Peter gave John a dressing down in front of everyone. We walked through the gates without difficulty. But inside, where the KGB were checking invitations, we didn't have the car. Instead I whipped out my American passport and smiled. The KGB man kept looking for an invitation, but couldn't find one in the passport. He called other KGB men, and they also seemed confused. Finally a secret policeman who spoke English looked at the passport.

"Where is your invitation?" he asked.

"I don't have one."

"Who told you you could come?"

"The American correspondents said it was all right."

"Okay," he said, returning the passport, and he ordered one of the men to give us two of the best seats in the house.

We were disappointed when Krushchev said some uncomplimentary things about the United States at the rally, but we couldn't very well complain, since we weren't formally invited.

It did show, though, that an American passport means more in Russia than it does in Western Europe. I remember very well producing my passport when I tried to get into the Royal Enclosure at Ascot a few years ago, and how the security people there took one look at it and ushered me off the track.

The only good story I heard the entire time I was in the Soviet Union was told to me by a little Jewish man in answer to a question as to how he liked living in Russia.

"They tell the story of Abramovitch," he said, "who was told to report to the KGB.

"The KGB man said to Abramovitch: 'Do you have any relatives abroad?'

"Abramovitch said he didn't.

"'Don't lie to us, Abramovitch,' the KGB man shouted. 'Do you have any relatives abroad?'

"Abramovitch said: 'I swear I have no relatives abroad.'

"The KGB man took a folder off his desk. 'Do you know Jacob Abramovitch, of Tel Aviv?'

"'Yes.' replied Abramovitch. 'He's my cousin.'

"'Hah,' the KGB man said. 'I thought you didn't have any relatives abroad.'

"Abramovitch replied sadly: 'I don't have any relatives abroad. He has relatives abroad.'"

Before I knew it, it was time to leave Russia. I decided to fly out and let John drive the Chrysler Imperial back. There were many tearful goodbyes at the airport. Vladimir was crying because he knew that, after my articles, the Intourist people would not give him anything to ride in but Volkswagens driven by women (punishment is severe in the Intourist system). John was crying because he had to drive back alone. Peter Stone was crying because he had to pay overweight on his baggage. And I was crying because I was leaving a country (Russia) with such a strong government, to go to one (France) that had no government at all.

A Week-End in the Country

One of the most sacred traditions in the British Isles, an American discovers, is the "Country Week-End." Many of my British friends have told me point blank that England wouldn't be worth living in if it wasn't for the *News of the World* and the "Country Week-End."

Since it's so sacred, you can imagine my surprise and pleasure when I was invited down to a real country week-end party in Sussex. My hostess was Mrs. Fleur Montague-Meyer (the former Fleur Cowles) whose husband, Mr. Tom Montague-Meyer, is a wealthy lumber-man, a distinguished sportsman and a gentleman farmer.

One does not accept a country week-end invitation in Sussex lightly. There are certain responsibilities that go with it, not the least being to see that one is properly clothed for all occasions. Not wanting to embarrass my hostess, and uncertain as to what one wears on a week-end, I hied myself off to Simpson's fashion expert for week-ends, who was dressed in morning coat, striped trousers and grey waistcoat.

He took out a striped pad and a grey pencil and said:

"What kind of people are you going to?"

"What kind of people?" I said proudly. "None other than Mr. and Mrs. Tom Montague-Meyer."

The expert tapped his pencil against the pad. "Oh," he said, "I see."

Then he started writing. "The first thing you'll need is a mack."

"I'll need a truck?"

"No, no," he said patiently. "A mack, a raincoat."

"Oh."

"Then, a double-breasted blazer."

"Double-breasted blazer? Won't a single-breasted blazer do?"

The expert looked at me sternly.

"Double-breasted, and no nonsense.

"Then, sports shirts, a neck scarf, a pair of grey flannels, one pair of calvalry twill trousers and a sports jacket. Also, I would advise a fine hopsack, lightweight, single-breasted dinner jacket."

"Not double-breasted?"

His eyes narrowed. "Single-breasted."

"Right-o," I said, trying to get off the hook.

"Black suede shoes for dinner wear," he continued writing.

"No patent leather?"

He stopped writing. "No patent leather."

"I got a pair of velvet slippers with my monogram on them," I said hopefully.

"Not in our country you don't," he flushed.

"I was only trying to save a few quid," I apologized.

"Let's get on with it," he said.

"You'll need a contemporary check sports shirt and two cotton wind-cheaters. Saddle or canary are rather attractive. Now, are you going to church on Sunday morning?"

"Of course I am. What do you think I am, a heathen?"

"Well, then, you had best take a formal suit."

"Can't I wear a blue blazer?"

He looked up, shocked. "I say."

When he recovered from the question, he continued: "Now you have an option on headwear. You may either wear a plain or checked cap or trilby hat."

It was a hard choice for me to make and I was sorry he was so indefinite.

"After that, if your hosts have a swimming-pool, you'll need a bathing-costume."

"What about linen shorts?" I asked.

"Where are you going?"

"Sussex."

He shook his head sadly. "No linen shorts."

He wrote on. "Naturally you'll need neck wear, bright Argyles and Chukkaboots."

"I beg your pardon."

"Chukkaboots. They're shoes."

"What a fool I was for not guessing," I cried.

"That should do it," he said, checking the list.

"How much will it cost me?" I asked out of nervous curiosity.

He took a pencil and pad and started adding. "89 pounds 6 shillings," he said.

"And there is no way of cutting down on the list?"

He went over it again carefully.

"Can't see how I can do it. I've only given you the bare necessities for a country week-end. I've kept it down to three days."

He turned me over to a clerk who had me in a pair of Chukkaboots before I could say "Lord Altrincham."

There was only one slight hitch. After I paid for the clothes, I didn't have any money left for my train fare. Early Saturday morning, I was still on the road trying to get a hitch to Sussex. You'd think people would give a ride to somebody in a trilby hat, a double-breasted blue blazer, cavalry twill pants and black suede shoes, but they just kept passing me by.

When I told my English friends I was going to Mr. and Mrs. Tom Montague-Meyers' estate in Sussex for a country week-end, they were almost as excited as I was. But knowing how easy it is for an American to make a gaffe on such a sacred occasion as an English week-end, everyone thrust advice on me.

"Whatever you do," one said, "don't talk politics. The British hate to talk about politics on a week-end."

"I shouldn't mention the Sultan of Oman and Muscat?" I asked.

He shook his head.

"Not even the Imam of Oman and Muscat?"

"Especially not the Imam of Oman."

"Well, what else is there to talk about?"

"Shooting, hunting, riding, horses, beagles, grouse, cricket, and, as long as you're going to Sussex, you might read up on stoolball."

"Stoolball. What is it?"

"No one really knows except it's only played in Sussex, by women I believe."

As I left, one final bit of advice was thrust on me.

"If you're not sure on any point, always ask the butler. He knows the right thing to do."

I arrived there by noon on Saturday. Other guests were already down for the week-end, but no one had yet put on his cavalry twill trousers.

The butler, a distinguished gent, showed me to my room.

"I say," I said confidentially, slipping him my last ten shillings, "what's the form around here for lunch?"

He looked at me blankly.

"Look, old boy, be a sport and tell me what to wear to lunch."

He shrugged his shoulders and said: "Me Italian. I no speaka da Inglish."

I had to go it alone. I decided on charcoal grey flannels, a checkered sportscoat, a two-way shirt with a neckerchief, chukkaboots, red argyles and handkerchief to match.

When I came down for lunch, everyone else was in T-shirts and swimming shorts.

The English guests looked at me suspiciously. One chap, a Beaverbrook employee, said: "When are the American oil interests going to get out of the Middle East?"

Remembering my friend's advice about the British not wanting to discuss politics, I said: "Why is it that in stoolball the wickets are only sixteen years apart and yet the bowler delivers underhand from a distance of ten yards?"

Later on, the same Beaverbrook man said: "I understand the penal system in America is the worst of any place in the world."

I rushed upstairs and changed into a blue blazer before I said anything I'd be sorry for.

Saturday afternoon in the country is usually spent hacking, grousing, cricketing or, in the case of Sussex, stoolballing. Then everyone comes in for tea, after which a game of bridge or billiards is arranged between the gloaming and the sounding of the dressing-gong. Then everyone goes upstairs to arrange his toilette.

Saturday evening, on a hunch, I got into my light hopsack single-breasted dinner jacket and black suede dinner shoes. Everyone else was in sports jackets and grey flannels except for the Beaverbrook man, who was wearing a sweater and a scowl.

"Do Americans always dress in such silly costumes?" he asked.

Bitter tears came to my eyes. "I'm only trying to do the right thing," I cried. "I've never been on an English week-end before."

Mrs. Montague-Meyer held my head as I sobbed uncontrollably.

The other guests ate their oatmeal bannocks in silence.

Sunday morning I came down in my formal suit, to discover everyone back in T-shirts and shorts again, except for the Beaverbrook man, who was still in his bathrobe and reading *The Sunday Express*. He looked up and laughed.

I couldn't control myself any longer, so I shouted "The Sultan of Oman!"

He dropped his paper in horror: "I say, that's a bit thick."

"Well, you asked for it, Milton," said Mrs. Montague-Meyer. "You can push an American just so far."

Now it was my turn to laugh, "And while I'm at it, the Imam of Oman and Muscat!"

It was too much for him and he rushed out of the room.

The rest of the day I spent in a windcheater and cavalry twill trousers. Nobody dared say a word to me.

The Mona Lisa Crouch

Whenever I have a fight with my wife or get depressed about the price of apartments in Paris, I hie myself off to the Louvre to look at the "Mona Lisa." I have been there many times lately and have had the opportunity to get more familiar not only with the famous painting, but also with the people who come from all over the world to look at it.

"La Joconde," as it is known to the French, hangs in the Grande Galerie on the first floor of the museum. It is covered with a pane of glass, presumably to keep tourists from cutting their initials into it. A guard stands by it all day long to see that people don't set off the burglar alarm that is attached to the back of the canvas.

The painting is no longer considered a work of art, but more an idol to be viewed by tourists with awe and reverence.

People do not approach it as if it were a painting. Instead they go forward in what has become known as the "Mona Lisa Crouch." It could best be described as semi-crouch. The tourist bends forward and makes a slow advance on the canvas. Then, keeping his eyes on the picture, he makes a semi-circle to see if the eyes are following him, as most guidebooks claim. He finally returns to the painting, straightens up, and keeps staring at it, waiting for something to happen.

There is a small minority of tourists (the ones who don't want to go where the tourists go) who pretend they are not interested in the "Mona Lisa." These tourists pretend they have come to study the Titian on the left and the Corregio on the right while sneaking glances of the "Mona Lisa" on the sly.

Many tourists have their pictures taken next to the "Mona Lisa" and one of the more common comments heard in front of the painting is, "What opening shall I give it?"

If two or more tourists view it, the remarks are quite interesting.

The other day I recorded some of them.

A guide came up with an American man and his wife.

The guide: "You really must get the extraordinary expression. You see . . . she doesn't smile much, does she?"

American man: "Unnnhhh."

Guide: "Notice how her eyes follow you . . . don't they?"

American man: "Unnnhhh. Very good art."

They moved to the side and the guide said, "Here again she is looking at you. That is why she is so human . . . you get a funny feeling when you look at her . . . she seems to understand what we are saying. I feel uncomfortable after talking in front of her. I'm sure she understands what we are thinking."

American woman: "Who is she?"

Guide: "She is supposed to be somebody's wife . . . but she is really a portrait of Woman . . . just women in general, as Leonardo thought of them."

American woman: "I'd love to know who she really was."

A German couple came up. "It's the mouth, nein?"

"Ja," replied the other. "It's the mouth."

An English couple walked past. The woman stopped and the man said, "Oh, come on. We've already seen it."

Three Americans approached.

"Is this it?"

"I don't think so." (Looks at metal tag under painting.) "Yes, this is it."

"It's the original, isn't it?"

"I think so. Let's ask the guard."

One of them went over to speak to the guard.

"*Est-que ça l'original de Mona Lisa n'est-ce-pas?*"

"*Oui,*" the guard replied. "*C'est l'original.*"

The American returned to the other two: "Yup, this is it."

"I expect it's the most expensive picture in the world."

"Yeh, but they wouldn't sell it."

"Come on, let's go see the Venus de Milo." Two Italian men came up. "They say it's a man."

"They lie. Look at the bosom."

Several people came up by themselves and said nothing.

Then an American with a camera and his wife stopped.

"Well, here it is," said the wife. "What do you think?"

"The light's no good for colour film. What's next?"

I left on this note. But I couldn't help thinking as I walked out into the Tuileries that the guide who told the American couple that the "Mona Lisa" knows what the people are saying is wrong. If she did, she certainly wouldn't be smiling anymore.

The Order of the Three-Star Liver

Recently, I have had what is commonly described as a liver ailment. I am quite sure there is no more than one American (including my wife) who cares whether I have liver trouble or not, but I discovered during that time that 40,000 Frenchmen care. There is nothing in this world that will stir up as much sympathy among the French as to hear someone has a liver malady. It is a badge of honour and a disease one does not have to be ashamed of. A bad liver is to a Frenchman what a nervous breakdown is to an American. Everyone has had one and everyone wants to talk about it.

It all started off with flu and a temperature of 103. Neither the cook nor the cleaning woman nor the concierge was impressed. The cook was annoyed because I was taking my meals in my room. As the flu subsided, word leaked out to the kitchen that I had liver trouble. Immediately the cook's attitude changed. This was an illness she could cope with. She insisted the best cure for liver trouble was lemon juice . . . and this while I was getting yellower all the time.

The cleaning woman, who had heard the news from the cook, sneaked into my bedroom when my wife was out. "Monsieur, you must not eat any beans."

I stopped writing my will. "Not even string beans?"

"Beans," she said, "are the worst thing for the liver."

The concierge, who was up within an hour after the diagnosis, barged into my room. "My poor husband—I remember when he had liver trouble. It was just after the first war. His face was yellow—almost as yellow as yours. The doctor put him on a regime. No fried food, no fats, and, alas, no wine. He didn't mind giving up the fried foods, but giving up the wine was too much. He stopped drinking wine and died of heartbreak."

The diaper man, the grocery man and the electrician were all informed of my illness. Each found some excuse to come into my room and discuss it with me.

"Rest," said the grocery man, waking me out of a deep sleep, "is the only thing that will cure liver trouble. You must sleep on the left side of your body so you do not do any damage to the gland."

The electrician was called in for consultation. His cure was just the opposite. "Exercise is the most important thing to make the liver function properly. You must breathe deeply by an open window twenty times a day. The liver needs oxygen."

The diaper man was the most pessimistic of the trio. "Once you have liver trouble, you'll never be the same again."

The telephone operator at the office called me at home when she heard the news. "This month's *Reader's Digest,*" she said, "says you must be careful the liver gets all the right vitamins. Vitamin C and Vitamins B and B12, a powerful fat mover, are being given to patients in large doses. It also says, 'Preventive nutrition is a cheap price to pay for a strong liver—our best chance for top vitality.'"

My wife, on returning from a mission, always had a new cure to report. The girl who sells magazines at the Hôtel George V said liver extract was the best thing, and my wife's dressmaker said the only cure for liver trouble was large doses of shots administered where one usually sits.

Out of curiosity, I asked my wife: "Has anybody thought to call the doctor?"

It had slipped everybody's mind.

The doctor came and suggested I go to the American Hospital for a few days. My wife took me out in a taxi. The taxi driver, in true fashion, was clipping along at 60 miles an hour.

"My wife is pregnant," I told him, thinking I could slow him down. It made no impression at all.

"My husband has liver trouble," my wife said desperately.

The driver immediately slowed down and drove in second for the rest of the way.

A funny thing has happened since my liver trouble. The cook, the cleaning woman, the diaper man, the grocery man, the electrician and the concierge have suddenly become my friends. It's as if I've finally become a member of a club—the Order of the Three-Star Liver. I've discovered that once you've had the ailment you're accepted by the French as being one of them.

If the United States wants to help create better Franco-American relations, I suggest the best way of doing it is to send over diplomats with liver trouble. They'll be surprised at the wonderful reception they receive.

The Time-Killer

According to Nunnally Johnson, the Hollywood director and writer, the hardest thing for a male tourist in Europe to do is to kill time.

"There is absolutely nothing for a guy to do in Paris," said Mr. Johnson, "if he is not interested in sightseeing or going shopping with his wife."

Mr. Johnson claims to be an expert on killing time in Paris and thought he might be able to advise other husbands who are bent on doing the same thing.

"The first thing to do," said Mr. Johnson, "is to clear your day. Don't make any appointments that might interfere with your time-killing.

"It will take about one hour to get your wife off on her shopping excursion. You can kill some time with her explaining the franc equivalents and discussing where you'll meet her for lunch. It isn't the best way of killing time, but it has to be done. Once she is out of the way you can become serious.

"One of the best ways I've found of killing time in Paris is to look for someone you know who is in the city, when you're not sure of where he is staying. I go from hotel to hotel asking for him. I always look for someone I'm not very interested in finding, so if I happen to find where he is staying, then I can start looking for someone else.

"Some days when I can't think of anyone to look for, I look at the list of arrivals at the American Express which are printed in the *Herald Tribune.* The other day I saw: 'I. Rappaport, of Detroit.' I once knew an Irving Rappaport in Atlanta, Georgia, but he could have very well moved to Detroit. Although I spoke to him only once at my brother's wedding, I distinctly remember his saying he didn't like Atlanta and was thinking of moving.

"So I called the American Express, which took an hour in itself, and asked them if the I. Rappaport of Detroit reported in the papers could be Irving Rappaport who used to live in Atlanta. The girl said she didn't know, so I said I would come down and look at the book myself. She said this was all right with her.

"Well, it took me an hour by taxi to get there, and then it took me a half-hour deciding whether to buy *Time* magazine or *Newsweek,* which were on sale in front of the building. Then I went in and asked to see the register. I started looking through it slowly, reading a lot of other names, and finally, after half an hour, I came to Rappaport's name. But it was Ida Rappaport, and I distinctly remember Irving's wife was named Sarah. All told, it killed three hours, which I was very grateful for.

"Another way of killing time is to go to different places and check to see if there is any mail for you. You can go to American Express, Thomas Cook, Morgan's Bank, TWA and the American or British Embassy, all mail drops for tourists. If you make the rounds on foot it can kill two and a half hours easily.

"If you have a couple of hours to go, you can always step into a plane or ship reservation office and inquire about a trip you have no intention of taking. To do it properly you must inquire about schedules and make the reservation clerk constantly check his time-table. If you haven't killed enough time you might ask about making a connection with another airline or a train.

"One of the most successful methods of killing time is to pay your respects to the Paris branch office of your company. You call up the manager and tell him you're in town for a few days and would like to stop by and say hello. In my case I go to 20th Century-Fox. Sometimes there are other people waiting to pay their respects, but I'm not in a hurry. The fact that you have to wait serves a purpose in itself. Once you're in the manager's office you can ask any questions you want to about the operation, and since you're from the home office and he doesn't know how you stand with his boss, the manager has to answer them. I once killed two and a half hours by simply asking the 20th Century-Fox man: 'How do you dub pictures into French?'

"Another time I killed four hours by asking: 'Why does France keep changing its Premiers?'"

When Mr. Johnson has run out of ideas he sits in his room and sulks about his wife's shopping. This can kill some time, but it isn't healthy time-killing, because if he thinks about it too long he gets mad.

I spent about two hours with him and he was very grateful to me. He said as soon as I left he was going to call up a French producer and discuss a co-production with him. "I have no intention of making it," he said, "but I know if we start discussing money, I'll get through the afternoon. If not I think I'll look up Ida Rappaport. It's very possible she could be Irving's sister."

Only a Passing Interest

There is a rumour around that I own a Chinese restaurant. This isn't exactly true, and I'd like to set the record straight. There is nothing wrong with owning a Chinese restaurant in Paris (you can own a lot worse things than that), but it would be unfair to the dedicated people who have spent so much time and energy in this enterprise to say that I am more than an interested party in this affair.

To squelch the rumour, I have to go back five years when I hired a Chinese cook and valet named Tsien (pronounced Chun). Tsien was the greatest cook and manservant in Paris. Besides doing all the marketing he cooked the most exquisite Oriental dishes, he did my shirts to perfection and he never complained about the long hours or the hard work.

Friends used to come to our house and rave about the dinners. My wife was a very happy woman. She couldn't wait to entertain our vast store of acquaintances. We had what marriage counsellors would call a "happy home."

Occasionally a friend would say in front of Tsien: "You should put this fellow in the restaurant business." I looked at my wife and chuckled, first because I knew Tsien didn't understand a word of English, and secondly I knew it would be impossible for Tsien to open a restaurant on what I was paying him.

But one day about a year and a half ago, when my wife was away on a trip, Tsien announced he was going to quit. He said he was unhappy being just a cook and valet and wanted more out of life. I tried to impress on him that he should be satisfied to be a good cook and a good valet, for if a man was good at what he was doing he was at peace with himself.

"What do you want to do?" I asked him.

"All your friends say I should be in the restaurant business," he said.

I told Tsien my friends were only joking and they would be very hurt if he ever left us. But Tsien couldn't be disuaded.

"I want to leave at the end of the month," he said.

Fearing what would happen if Tsien wasn't there when my wife returned, I said: "I'll make a deal with you. If you ever find a location for a restaurant that you like, I'll speak to my friends and maybe they will contribute something to the opening. Now let's forget this foolish talk and discuss whether we shall have sweet and sour pork or Peking duck tonight."

One week later Tsien found the location. It was on the rue Francois Ier, off the Avenue George V. He asked me to ante up some francs so he could take an option on the lease. An Oriental promise made is an Oriental promise kept, and I spent the next few weeks raising some capital among the "friends" who insisted Tsien should be in the restaurant business.

I put the arm on John Huston, Darryl Zanuck, Anatole Litvak, Faye Emerson, Irwin Shaw and Joan Crawford. I emptied my own cookie jar, where I was saving for my son's education. Tsien said it would be a matter of a few months before the restaurant opened.

My wife came home from her trip and asked where Tsien was. I said he was around the corner opening a Chinese restaurant. She threw the empty cookie jar at me.

One year later Tsien was still opening his restaurant. Backers were demanding dividends and I was demanding backers. I spent every afternoon with Charles Torem, my lawyer. Tsien by this time had hired his own lawyer. Then Huston, Zanuck, Litvak, Emerson, Shaw and Joan Crawford sent over their lawyers. These lawyers met with contractors' lawyers who met with French government lawyers. Yet not one bowl of fried rice had been cooked.

The only thing we could all agree on was to call the restaurant China

Bistro. But when the awning we had ordered came back from the manufacturer it was marked Chinatown so we had to change the name to correspond with the awning.

As the months went by I spent more and more time at the restaurant and less and less at my office. Finally Chinatown opened. My wife cried during the entire opening. Not only had I given away our cook, but our son's education was going up in steaming bowls of soybeans.

Although I have only a minor interest in the restaurant, I have suffered indignities that no columnist should be made to endure. Just the other night Mike Todd took over the entire restaurant for a party after the première of his picture. Tsien was short of help and I had to fill in as a waiter. Not only did I have to wait on the two United Artists press agents who were trying to get me to write something about their picture, but I was accused in front of all the guests by Todd of filling the Evian bottles with tap water. He also accused me of leaving the neon sign on outside so strangers would walk in and he would be charged for them.

The next day I had to go around to the hotel at six o'clock in the morning in case the producer was planning to check out early, and had to wait until noon to get paid.

Outside of the fact that I'm being sued by our backers and I work there occasionally as a waiter, and I do the marketing at Les Halles when Tsien is tired, and my wife does all the shirts of all the waiters, I just have a passing interest in Chinatown and I don't know where the rumour about me owning a Chinese restaurant started.

Calling Your Loved Ones

The telephone companies have been urging fathers to telephone home to their loved ones when they are away from home, and I'm beginning to understand why. If everyone has the same experience I had calling from Sicily, the telephone company stands to make a fortune.

It took me two days to get my loved ones on the phone. Every time I placed the call, I was informed the lines were down, Rome wouldn't let the call go through, there was fog over Mount Etna or the Mafia had cut all the lines.

And every time I told them to forget it, they informed me there was a surcharge for cancelling the call.

"But I never received the call. How can you charge me for a call I never got?"

"But it was your intention to telephone and this is all we need. It is not us, Signor. It is the Italian Telephone Company. Don't cancel and then we won't charge you."

"But I can't get Paris on the phone."

"We know that, Signor. But as long as you can't get Paris they cannot charge you. If you tell them you don't want Paris, then they can charge you. This I'm sure you understand."

In order to save money I let the call stay in, and finally it came through. There was great excitement in the hotel, because, although many people in Sicily have in the last few years put in calls to Paris, only two or three have ever gotten through.

As I picked up the phone, all activity in the lobby stopped.

The waiters came out of the dining-room and the chamber-maids came down from upstairs. They all stood around with pleased smiles on their faces. Everyone felt they had played their part in getting the call through.

I had placed the call on the maid's day off, and, in order to save money, did not bother to make it person-to-person. Since the call came in the next day, the maid was there and she answered the phone.

"This is Mr. Buchwald," I said.

"No," she said. "Mr. Buchwald isn't here."

"But this is Mr. Buchwald speaking."

"He's on a trip."

"Where did he go?" I asked out of curiosity.

"Just a minute," she said.

It took her two minutes. "He's in Sicily."

"Oh," I said. "That's too bad. Then can I speak to Mrs. Buchwald?"

"Who's calling?"

"Mr. Buchwald."

"He's in Sicily. He won't be back for a week."

"Just tell Mrs. Buchwald it's a friend."

"*Ne quittez-pas.*"

There was a pause on the phone. The Italian operator came on. "Are you finished?" she said.

"No," I said.

Thirty seconds later the French operator said: "No, he hasn't."

Finally my wife got on the phone. "Hello."

I introduced myself.

"How wonderful of you to call," she said. "Just a minute, Jo-jo [our three-and-a-half-year-old] wants to say hello."

There was dead silence. Then I could hear my wife say, "Jo-jo, say hello to Da-da."

Dead silence.

The Italian operator came on. "Are you finished?"

"No, we're not."

My wife came on. "It's funny, he's been talking about you all week. Wait a minute, now he wants to say something."

Dead silence.

"Say something, Jo-jo. It's Daddy," I could hear her saying.

The French operator came on. "Are you finished?"

Before I could reply, my wife came back on. "I don't understand it. He said he wanted to talk to you. Wait a minute, Connie [our two-year-old] wants to speak to you."

Dead silence.

Then I could hear Jo-jo screaming for the phone.

I heard my wife say, "You both can talk to Da-da. Jo-jo first."

Dead silence.

"All right, let Connie talk then," my wife said.

Dead silence.

"They're both shy," my wife explained to me. I could hear screaming in the background. Apparently they were both fighting to get at the phone.

Dead silence.

"I can't talk to you now," my wife said, "because they're fighting. Can you call me later?"

I said no, I'd write her a letter.

"Say goodbye to Da-da," my wife said.

Dead silence.

"Goodbye," I said and hung up.

The people in the lobby seemed a little confused by the conversation, but I didn't try to explain. I went over to the concierge.

"How much did that call cost?" I asked.

The concierge called the hotel operator. He said to me, "She wants to know if you're finished."

I said I was. "But how much is it?"

"She doesn't know," the concierge replied. "We've only been charging people for cancelling their calls. She's been here for just four years and this is the first time anyone has called Paris and got their party on the line. She's quite upset. Perhaps we'll know more about it tomorrow."

When I finally got the telephone bill I realized I would have to cut my trip short by two days to make my expenses. But it was worth it. It isn't every day a father gets to talk with his loved ones by long distance from Sicily.

The Facts of Life No. 1

Many people who have lived abroad have heard atrocity stories about servants in the United States and therefore decide to take their foreign help home with them. On the surface it seems like a good idea, but it doesn't always work out the way they hoped it would.

Last year some friends of mine who lived in Paris, let's call them Jones, because that is what their name was, decided to take their cook, Yvette, back with them. Yvette was in the *cordon bleu* class, and when she wasn't in the kitchen cooking up a soufflé for Mr. Jones, she was cleaning the house, doing laundry or pressing clothes. Yvette worked from seven in the morning until ten in the evening, six days a week, and received $60 a month. She was a happy, well-adjusted French servant.

In order to get a visa for Yvette, the Joneses had to list their assets, supply documentation that they were reliable citizens and swear that no matter what happened in the United States their servant would not become a public charge. The Joneses spent six months getting all the papers in order, and finally Yvette received her visa. It was a happy day for everyone.

When she first arrived in New York, Yvette was thrilled with everything. She couldn't get over the skyscrapers, the department stores, the super-markets. For the first month Mrs. Jones did all the marketing since Yvette's English was limited. But Yvette was happy to stay in the East Side apartment cooking, cleaning, laundering and pressing. She had been raised to $65 a month, which made her deliriously happy.

The Joneses were one of the few families in New York who could dine at 8.30 or 9 o'clock in the evening. Yvette would stay until midnight if she had to, and she had no trouble turning out the same wonderful meals with American comestibles.

The Joneses were very careful never to introduce Yvette to any of their friends in fear that one of them would try to hire her away. They always changed the subject when someone complimented them on their dinner and listened with great sympathy when others complained about their help.

Then one day, about two months after Yvette had landed in New York, she went out shopping alone. As she came home and entered the service entrance a woman in a mink coat with a French poodle nodded, brushed by her and got into an Oldsmobile and drove away.

Yvette thought it strange that a mistress should use the service entrance and she thought she would never understand the ways of Americans.

A few days later she met the same woman in the elevator and they started talking.

"You're the French maid that works for the Joneses ain't you?" the lady in the mink coat asked.

"Yes, Ma'm," Yvette replied.

"Don't Ma'm me, honey," the woman said. "I'm the Grants' maid. I work on the tenth floor. How do they treat you?"

"Oh wonderful," Yvette said.

The maid on the tenth floor, whose name was Connie, offered to drive Yvette to the market.

"Do your people allow you to drive their car to the market?" Yvette asked in a surprised voice.

"Their car," Connie laughed. "Honey, this is my car. The Grants have a Ford."

In a few weeks Connie and Yvette became fast friends.

"How much do they pay you?" Connie asked.

"Sixty-five dollars," Yvette replied.

"A week?"

"A month."

Connie almost hit a boy on a bicycle with her Oldsmobile. She parked the car and said: "Honey, I better tell you the facts of life."

Connie told Yvette the facts of life. She also introduced her to other servants who told her the facts of life. In a few months' time things began changing around the Joneses' household.

Yvette asked if she could serve dinner around eight instead of 8.30. Then she suggested 7.30—and finally seven o'clock. The Joneses decided to humour her and agreed. In a short while Mrs. Jones noticed that Yvette spent more time shopping than she did cleaning. She also started appearing in new clothes. Mrs. Jones knew she couldn't afford them and asked her where she had gotten them.

"Oh, you don't need money, Ma'm," Yvette explained, as if she were talking to a child. "You just go in and sign some papers and give them a dollar and you can buy anything you want. It's called credit."

In a month Yvette came to the Joneses and told them she had established so much credit that she would need a raise. The Joneses suggested $70 a month, but Yvette said she would need at least $100 a month to meet her commitments.

A few months later the Joneses were eating at six o'clock every evening, except on Saturdays and Sundays, which Yvette had demanded as her days off. They had increased her salary to $150 a month and Mrs. Jones was doing the laundry.

The final blow came when Yvette announced she was going to buy an Oldsmobile on credit. Mrs. Jones said this was too much.

"But," protested Yvette, "I'm going to get a French poodle and I need a car to take him to the country on weekends."

Mr. Jones pulled his trump card: "Yvette, if you keep acting this way I'm going to be forced to fire you and you will become a public charge."

"I don't care. If that's the way you feel, I quit."

Yvette has since become one of the most highly paid public charges in New York City. She is cooking (no cleaning) for a family on Park Avenue for $350 a month, plus garage fees for her car, and, besides the week-end, she gets off every Thursday to have her French poodle clipped.

The Joneses have a woman who comes in three times a week to clean. She costs them exactly $65 a month.

No Finger in the Dike

Travelling can be a very disillusioning affair. Take my trip to Holland as an example.

"Is it the first time your trip to Holland?" kind Dutch friends have asked.

I admit it is the first time my trip.

"It is a very nice country," they reply, "but please do not believe all the stories you hear about Holland. It is stories just for tourists."

"You mean the story of Hans Brinker and the silver skates is not true?"

They shake their heads. "Lies, all lies."

"What about the kid who stuck his finger in the dike? Surely that's a true story."

"Lies, all lies. Just for American Express and Thomas Cook. The Dutch people know of no such boy. Besides, everyone knows if he stuck his finger in the dike, it would have caused a much bigger flood than if he'd let the water run off."

"And the wooden shoes?"

"Who wears wooden shoes?"

"Windmills?"

"A few, but only on the main tourist roads. Electric pumps we have. They work much better."

"What can a man write about in Holland?"

"You can write about the fog, which is as thick as pea soup and about the pea soup which is as thick as fog. Then there are always the canals in Amsterdam."

"What's so different about the canals in Amsterdam?"

"They're constructed in such a way that you can drive your car right into them.

"Cars go into the canal on the average of one out of every three days. Most of them sink immediately to the bottom, and then it's hard for the people to get out and call their insurance companies."

"How do you get out?"

"There are two schools of thought. One school says you should sit in your car quietly under water at the bottom of the canal until the water seeps in through the cracks and the water pressure outside and inside becomes the same. Then you just open the door and float to the surface. But for nervous people this is not so easy to do, so the nervous school advocates rolling down the windows and letting the water pour in and then escaping out of the window when the water pressure gets equalized, not floating, but kicking, to the top."

"But why don't they have barriers along the canals to prevent the cars from going in?"

"Oh, they tried that. But it worked, so they tore them down. The Amsterdamers claimed it took the sport out of driving."

"Do people fall into Amsterdam canals?"

"They can if they want to, but there is too much danger of being hit by automobiles that fall into the canal, so they prefer to take their chances on dry land."

"Is that all there is to Holland?"

"You can speak about the bicycles if you want to. That is not a lie. Holland has ten and one-half million people and five and one-half million bicycles. The bicycle is to the Dutchman what the sidewalk café is to the Frenchman, the bullfight is to the Spaniard, the sauna is to the Finn. It is a way of life. Without the bicycle we should just be another country below sea level. The reason the Dutch are constantly reclaiming the land from the sea is that they need more room for their bicycles. Queen Juliana rides a bicycle, the army moves on bikes, the workers, the students, and lovers even woo each other on bikes."

"Lovers on bikes?"

"Yes. It's a very moving experience."

"It sounds like a vicious cycle to me."

"Don't make fun of us. You don't know what it is to live in the Netherlands until you've tried to pass a fat Dutch woman who is riding down the middle of the road on her Solex. It's a sight you'll never forget."

"And besides canals and bicycles?"

"The rest is for the tourists. You can go see the rest of the country, but you'll only make a fool of yourself. If you do go, don't believe anything you see. It really isn't Holland at all."

A Strange Amusing People

Tucked away in the Engadine Valley, shut in by snow-capped mountains and unspoiled by civilization, is a small town called St. Moritz. Here for over 100 years the nomadic tribes of Europe have come for the winter to find grazing lands for their herds of Rolls-Royces, Cadillacs and Mercedes-Benzes. These nomadic tribes are shy people by nature and avoid being interviewed by anthropologists and newspapermen. I am probably one of the few anthropologists ever to get into their confidence and I believe this is the first full report ever issued on this strange, yet amusing race of people.

The St. Moritzers, as we shall call them (the scientific name is E Pluribus Unum), have some very quaint customs. They live in dwellings called "hotel suites," sometimes as many as two in a room, and eat in community halls called "grill rooms" and "night-clubs."

The St. Moritzers are not cannibalistic by nature (though there have been cases known of one of them biting another's head off) and their main food staple is grey raw fish eggs, which they call "caviar," and which they eat on slices of toast washed down with a bubbly drink made from grapes.

Instead of barter, the St. Moritzers use a currency called "money." Some of them save up this money all year long, then bale it and bring it with them. Each bale of money can be traded for one glass of grapes.

If it is discovered one of the St. Moritzers does not have any money he is taken by two or three of the elders in the village to the highest peak surrounding the Engadine Valley and pushed off.

Although this may sound primitive and cruel to the outsider, every St. Moritzer knows the risks he takes when he comes here, and if he is caught without money he usually accepts his fate quietly.

The women of St. Moritz are probably the most interesting. They are tall, well shaped and wear silk robes which they call Diors, Balmains, Desses and Givenchys. They do not have to cook, sew or clean (they have slaves known as "the Swiss people" for these things), and their sole purpose is to make their menfolk happy.

The mores of the St. Moritzers are such that each man may have one wife and one mistress but, unlike some Middle Eastern countries, the women are not allowed to live in the same dwelling. When a man takes to himself a wife or a mistress he gives her a shiny stone called a "diamond." Some of the tribeswomen wear these stones around their necks, and others on their fingers, or on their bosoms, and still others hanging from their ears. The more stones they have, the higher their standing in the community. Other stones that the native women collect are called emeralds, sapphires and rubies. (I tried to trade some packs of chewing gum for some of these stones, which I wanted to take back as samples, but apparently they have some religious significance because all the women refused.)

When a woman no longer wants to stay with her husband she gets what is called a "divorce." The husband must then pay the wife large sums of money (sometimes as much as 2,000 bales), either monthly or all at once.

This is called "Ali Moanie," named after the famous prophet of the tribe.

For recreation (that's about all the St. Moritzers are good for in the winter) they tie long sticks on their feet, and, by holding two poles in their hands, they slide down snow slopes standing up. The object of the custom seems to be to see how fast they can go before they break a leg. When a native reaches the bottom of the slope in one piece, he turns around and goes right up again to do it once more. This has led many anthropologists to conclude that the St. Moritzers, by and large, are not an intelligent race, but rather creatures of habit.

This being true or not, I was still impressed by their friendliness, love of life, appreciation of material things, courage in the face of hardship (sometimes they don't catch a smoked salmon for days), and ability to remain unchanged in a changing world. I hope the St. Moritzers will always remain the unspoiled, simple people they are today and that no well-meaning missionaries will invade the Engadine Valley to change their way of life.

Salesmanship in Europe

During the past years I have made a scientific study of the attitude of European sales people towards a foreign customer. They vary in each country according to temperament, and while it isn't fair to generalize, that's exactly what I'm going to do.

In Italy, when a customer walks into a store he is greeted like a long-lost brother.

"Welcome, signor; welcome, signor. Please come into the shop where it is nice and cool. You do not have to buy anything. You can just look."

"I would like a poplin shirt. Do you have any?"

"Do we have any? That's all we have is poplin shirts. We specialize in poplin shirts. Mama, give me the best quality poplin shirts for these nice people."

While Mama is dragging out the shirts the man says: "Are you from America?"

You say you are.

"I have relatives in Chicago. You know them. The Qualliteris. Look, here is their picture. My cousin has seven children. Please to look. That is Rosita, Antonio, Carlotta, Alfredo, Guiseppe, Charles and Thomaso. Rosita is seven, Antonio is, etc., etc."

The shirts finally come. The man says: "Beautiful Egyptian cotton. Notice the pearl-like quality of the buttons, how the tail of the shirt is rounded gently, the pleated pocket and the firm rich feel of the collar. Please to touch it yourself. Where, where in the world can you find a shirt like this? Take a dozen. In America you will thank me for selling you these shirts."

You are touched by his kindness. You buy a dozen. His wife gives your wife a bouquet of flowers. They both escort you to the door. You shake hands with them, they shake hands with you, they ask you to come back soon. They tell you not to miss a visit to St. Peter's, and they give you the names of a trattoria in Rome and friends in Florence. There are tears in their eyes as you walk away. Everybody is happy.

In London you walk into a store and you are greeted by a man in a tail coat who bows and asks if he can be of help. You ask for the shirt counter. He clicks his fingers and calls for a salesman, who rushes up and stands at attention as the man in the tail coat snaps out: "Shirts for this gentleman."

The salesman says: "Right this way please," and takes you to the counter. "What size and what colour?" he asks.

You tell him you want a poplin and a button-down collar if possible.

He looks down embarrassed, as if you had just asked him how much salary he makes.

"Is there anything wrong with a button-down shirt?"

"To be frank, Sir, in England we don't think too much of the button-down collar. Of course, you Americans like that sort of thing, but we consider it rather iffy, if you know what I mean. It's just not the sort of thing you would wear except to a very bad cricket match. Of course, if you want a button-down shirt, I'd be very happy . . ."

"Heavens, no," you say. "What is the proper shirt to wear?"

"Ah, the proper thing," he smiles. "This is the style now. You'll notice the Duke of Norfolk wears only this type of shirt. It is worn by gentlemen of distinction of every profession. I'm sure a distinguished person like yourself would wear only the latest attire."

He shames you into buying a dozen.

But in France everything is different. You walk into a shop which is quite empty, with six or seven sales people standing around.

You wait fifteen minutes and finally someone comes up to you and, speaking in the tone that a Poujadist would use on a tax collector, he says: "What do you want?"

You tell him you want a shirt.

"What size?" he says sneeringly.

"Size 17."

"Ha!" he shouts. "We don't have your size. Do you think we can carry everyone's size? How much place do you think we have here? The largest size we have is 16½."

You tell him you'd like to see it.

A look of disappointment comes over his face.

"What colour?" he says.

"White."

"Ha!" he shouts. "We don't have white. We only have them in colours. Do you think we can stock both white and coloured shirts?"

Another salesman comes over and asks, in French, what is the trouble. The fellow salesman tells him in French: "This idiot wants a white shirt. First he asked for a size 17 and now he wants it in a 16½. What kind of a store does he think we run?"

"These Americans are all crazy."

You say you'll take a coloured one. The salesman is furious. He shoves the box of shirts in front of you and says: "Please don't touch them or you'll have to pay for them."

You select one and he throws it into a bag. "Four thousand francs," he says.

You give him a five-thousand franc note.

"Don't you have change? Do you think we can make change for everyone who comes into the store?"

Everyone looks at you as if you had just slapped the man in the face.

You say you have no change, and there is a conference of the salesman, the manager and the cashier. They keep looking at you and whispering to each other and finally the cashier, who writes the entire transaction in a large ledger, produces the 1,000 franc note.

The salesman slaps the purchase into your hand and throws the change down on the counter. As you walk out of the door you hear him saying to the other people: *C'est incroyable. Incroyable.*

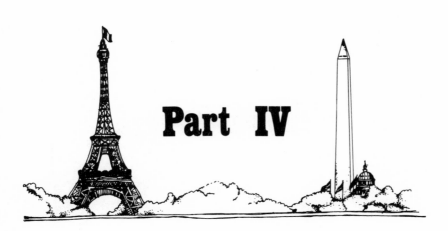

Part IV

The Seven-Year Itch

Last year my wife and I celebrated our seventh wedding anniversary. I'm not bragging. As a matter of fact it was a very disturbing thing. When I looked around I discovered that so many of my friends who were married around the same time were either separated or divorced. There were so few who were still happily married that I decided there was something wrong with us.

"We're sick," I said to my wife. "What's happened to us?"

She agreed. "We're abnormal. Everyone is talking. Most of the girls I went to school with have been married at least twice."

"For the last seven years we've been drifting together," I said. "I think we need some outside help."

"I was going to say the same thing," she said. "I'm willing to seek it out if you are."

"I'm willing if you are," I said.

It was good to clear the air and we immediately made an appointment with a divorce counselor.

A divorce counselor operates like a marriage counselor, except, instead of trying to get people together, he tries to break them apart.

Most people go to a divorce counselor only as a last resort—when it looks like the marriage is going to last forever.

We arrived at his office together. This was our first mistake. The receptionist asked us to enter separately.

The reception room was simply furnished, with chairs and a low table with magazines featuring stories such as "Wedding Bells Drove Me Mad," "My Secretary Made a Better Wife Than My Wife Made a Secretary," and "How I Invested My Alimony and Made a Million Dollars."

On one wall were pictures of men, and on the opposite wall were pictures of women, whose marriages the divorce counselor had managed to break up.

The counselor came out and nodded to us to come in.

We sat down, and the first thing he said was, "I'd appreciate it if you didn't hold hands in this office."

We both put our hands on our laps.

"Now tell me your story from beginning to end, and don't leave out any details. The smallest thing that may seem unimportant to you could shed a great deal of light on the case for me."

We told him everything: how we had met, about our home, how, although we had occasional fights, we always made up.

He kept tapping his pencil against his ear.

"Do you have any arguments about money?" he asked.

"No," I said, "I give it to her and she spends it."

He frowned.

"Now, when you have a fight, does she ever threaten to go home to her mother?"

My wife replied, "My mother lives in Pennsylvania. It's too far to go home, and besides, the children are in school and I hate to have them miss a term."

"Do you ever send your wife flowers?"

"All the time," I replied. "I go down to Les Halles and get them wholesale."

"Does he notice when you go to the hairdresser or when you buy a new dress or hat?"

My wife said, "Oh, yes. I can't buy anything new without him commenting on it."

"What does he say?"

"He wants to know how much it costs."

"And then when you tell him does he get mad?" the counselor asked hopefully.

"No, he just shrugs his shoulders and walks into another room."

The counselor broke his pencil in half. "Do you have things in common to talk about?"

I said, "Lots of things."

"Like what?"

"All our friends breaking up."

"What about your girl friends?" he said to my wife. "Do they ever call you up and tell you they saw your husband having lunch with a beautiful girl?"

"Oh, yes," my wife said. "But that's his job. If he didn't talk to beautiful women at lunch, I wouldn't be able to buy any new clothes."

The counselor threw the broken pencil across the room. "This is the most hopeless case I've ever tackled. Why don't both of you grow down? Everything you've told me makes no sense at all. You have too much in common. You should have gotten married when you were both younger and didn't know what you were doing. If it had only been a war marriage, I think I could have helped."

"You mean it's too late?"

"It's never too late to get a divorce," he said, "but you have to want it. My advice to both of you is as follows: Go home and try to get on each other's nerves. You must be a jealous wife," he said to my wife, "and you have to show a little more immaturity," he said to me. "Keep track of each other's faults. Blow up little things until they seem like big problems. Move into smaller quarters; infringe on each other's thoughts." He lectured us sternly. "Remember this—love and happiness aren't everything."

I thanked him profusely as he escorted us to the door. But when I opened the door for my wife he blew up.

"For heaven's sake," he screamed, "you're not even out of my office and you're already opening doors for her. How are you ever going to break up if you keep doing stupid things like that?"

How to Get Your Heater Fixed

Last winter the hot-water heater in our house broke. Now only people who have lived in France can understand what this means. My wife, one of the coolest cucumbers that ever grew in western Pennsylvania, loses all control of herself when something like this happens, and it is only my comforting presence which prevents her from packing her bags and taking the next jet to America.

When the event occurred on Saturday morning, I saw no reason to panic. It was an electric hot-water heater, and since we were getting cold water, it was obviously a job for an electrician. I called the electrician and told him the electric hot-water heater was on the blink.

He listened sympathetically and then said that since it was a water heater, it was a job for the plumber. I called the plumber, and when I said it was an *electric* hot-water heater, he advised me to call the electrician. I told him I had called him and had been advised to call the plumber. He replied that the electrician was just passing the buck and there was no sense in his coming, as it was out of his jurisdiction. Even if it was in his jurisdiction, which he once again assured me it wasn't, he told me he would not be able to come until March 1962.

I called another electrician, but this time I didn't tell him what was broken. He said he could come sometime in February. I told him it was a matter of life and death and there was a chance of the whole house burning up if he didn't send someone right away. The electrician said he couldn't come, but would send one of his workers. If it was really true that it was a matter of life and death, he himself would come at the end of January.

I spent the rest of the day hiding my wife's valises so she wouldn't leave. Around six in the evening the electrician's helper appeared.

He was a short man, dressed in greasy khaki shirt and pants, and seemed annoyed at having to make a call so late on Saturday evening.

Before bringing up the problem I offered him a glass of wine, which he accepted gratefully. We talked about the Fifth Republic, soccer results, cycling, and the third race at the Auteuil race track. My wife, who was twisting her handkerchief nervously, couldn't stand the suspense.

"Tell him," she cried.

This broke the friendly atmosphere and the man remembered he was on a job and became surly again. There was nothing to do but take him into the room with the heater.

He took one look at the heater and said, "Call the plumber."

"He told me to call you. Just look at it. I don't expect you to fix it. I just thought you would be interested in seeing a broken hot-water heater."

The man studied it carefully. "Your counter is broken. It's a hundred years old. So is the boiler. The situation is impossible. You would have to tear out every wire in the house and even then it is doubtful that anything could be done. Impossible! Impossible! There is nothing to be done."

"You are so right," I said. "I was foolish to call you. We're idiots to have thought anything can be done. It's hopeless, absolutely hopeless and I should have known it all the time. You have never been more right."

"But," the man protested, "it has to be fixed."

"No man could fix that boiler," I said. "It's no good."

"I could fix it," he said indignantly. "I can fix anything."

"I beg to differ with you in your own country," I said, "but you couldn't fix *that* boiler, not in a million years."

"There has never been an electric boiler that I could not fix," he shouted. "I have fixed boilers twice as bad as this one."

"Monsieur, I am not one to challenge the word of a man I do not know, but in this case I am afraid you overestimate your talents."

The little man was enraged. "I will come tomorrow and I will show you if I can fix that heater or not."

"Tomorrow is Sunday."

"It doesn't matter. I will be here and you will see who knows about electric heaters."

"No," I said. "You would just be wasting your time."

My wife, who had caught on to the game, said: "Let him try, if he thinks he can fix it."

I reluctantly agreed to let him come on Sunday, and in a half-hour he had the heater working in perfect order. I gave him a glass of wine and apologized for doubting his word.

Flushed with victory, he said it wasn't our fault. After all, in America, he said, when an electric heater breaks we throw it away, but in France one has to know how to fix them.

He left a happy man, and I felt rather pleased with everything. It's rare that an American can bring so much happiness into the life of a French worker.

It's Better to Give?

The giving and receiving of presents, as dramatized by the last pocket-breaking Christmas, usually works a great hardship on the master of the household. I don't know about other people's homes, but it certainly has gotten out of hand in mine. I am not only exchanging gifts with relatives and childhood friends, but with people I don't even know. I have no idea how I ever got myself in this bind, but I am sure it could happen to anyone.

To give you an example of what has happened I cite the following incident:

About seven years ago we met a couple on the boat, whom I'll call

Mr. and Mrs. Irving Hoffman. When it came holiday time my wife sent them a Christmas card, which also wished them the best wishes for the New Year.

They in turn sent us a souvenir letter opener from St. Moritz, which, on the surface, seemed to be a friendly gesture.

But when the next Christmas came around, my wife, who keeps the accounts in our house, said, "We have to get the Hoffmans a gift. They sent us a letter opener last year."

I protested that it wasn't necessary and that another Christmas card, perhaps with more elaborate printing, would suffice. But she was adamant. And so she went out and bought a paperweight, which she promptly dispatched with the season's greetings.

The day before Christmas a special delivery package arrived which contained four bottles of Scotch. It was too late to retaliate and my wife's Christmas was spoiled, thinking what the Hoffmans were thinking about us for sending them a lousy paperweight.

The next Christmas I went out and bought them a record album of Beethoven's nine symphonies, which set me back fifty dollars but gave my wife her pride back.

The Hoffmans, who must have had some inkling of what I was up to, sent us a television set. Another Christmas was spoiled.

Fortunately we didn't have to wait for Christmas to get even. We were invited to the wedding of one of the Hoffman daughters and we sent as a gift a silver service from Cartier's.

We were feeling pretty good for a few months, but when my anniversary came around in October I received the complete works of the Encyclopedia Americana in leather bindings.

These people were playing for real.

The next Christmas I bought them a small Van Gogh etching for one thousand dollars and gloated, but not for long. They sent us a set of Louis XIV chairs.

I was all for calling a truce, but my wife insisted I had to go on, even if it meant cutting down on gifts for the children.

"His birthday is in February," she said, "and yours doesn't come up until October. We'll have six months of peace."

I bought him a Vespa scooter for his birthday and delivered it myself just to see him eat his heart out.

It was a blow below the belt, but he recovered fast. Somehow he wheedled out of my wife that my son would be four years old in April.

When April came Hoffman sent ten shares of American Tel and Tel stock as a gift for the boy.

The gift exchanging went back and forth for the next few years without let-up. Feelings were so bitter that we didn't even talk to each other and did all our gift-giving by mail.

This Christmas I decided to fix Hoffman once and for all. I was going to give him a Thunderbird.

But while I was down at the dealer's looking them over, I got a call from my wife.

"Hold off," she cried excitedly. "All we got from the Hoffmans this year was a Christmas card."

"It's just a diversion," I said. "He's going to spring something on us Christmas Eve."

"I don't think so. It was a very cheap card and it had no return address."

"You really think they've given up?" I asked.

"I'm sure of it," my wife said.

"Why, that no good yellowbelly," I chortled. "He lost his nerve. I've got a good mind to send him the Thunderbird anyway."

"Oh, please don't," my wife begged. "He's probably suffering enough as it is, and it is Christmas."

"Okay," I said. "I'll let him off this time, but he better not start up with us again."

Pay the Two Francs

Like I said, we had this party with chopped chicken liver, turkey, ham, and various salads. But since we were giving the party with another couple, the Bernheims, we had to share with them the left-over food and also return a large, silver tray which we borrowed for the party.

So we called a taxi and carried all the food downstairs to go to the Bernheims. Every once in a while you get a taxi driver in Paris who talks to other chauffeurs. In his opinion, every driver on the road is an idiot, and also yellow. To prove it, our driver challenged every car on the Champs Élysées. All of them did prove yellow except one, another taxi driver. They both put on their brakes at the same time, avoiding a smashup, but the tray with the chopped chicken liver, ham, turkey, and salad went flying on to the floor of the taxi.

This was too much for my nerves, and I told the driver to stop the cab and let us off at the Hotel California, on the Rue de Berri. Insulted because we didn't trust his driving, he blamed us for not holding on to the tray when he had to stop to avoid an accident. He said we didn't know how to ride in a taxi. I said he didn't know how to drive one.

At the California I told my wife to get out of the cab. Then I bent down in the cab to pick up the food and the tray.

The driver said, "Pay me now."

I replied, "After I take the food out of the taxi."

He said, "I want my money right now."

I said, "You'll get it after I take the food out of the cab."

"Then we're going to the police," he said. And with the door open he put the cab into gear, and away we went, leaving my wife standing on the sidewalk.

"Nobody refuses to pay me," he said, as he drove madly in search of a police station. Unfortunately he didn't know where one was, and we kept driving around in circles. Finally he arrived not at a police station, but a police barracks where they round up Algerian terrorists.

Four policemen with submachine guns greeted us at the entrance.

It didn't seem like the place for two people who were having an argument about a taxi to get it settled, and it turned out I was right. A police captain came charging out of the barracks, furious that he was bothered. He started bawling out the taxi driver for coming there.

I was enjoying the show when he turned on me and bawled me out for not paying the taxi driver. He demanded my identification papers and told one of the policemen to take me and the driver to a commissariat—a regular police station.

The nearest one was located in the basement of the Grand Palais, where the Paris Automobile Show is held. When we arrived the police lieutenant demanded to know what was wrong.

"Well, we had this chopped chicken liver," I said.

"You had what?" he asked in amazement.

"Chopped chicken liver in the taxi."

Everyone in the station looked up from their work.

"And we had turkey and ham and salad, and he's a lousy driver," I said.

"He won't pay me," the taxi driver said. "He had all the food on the seat, and he didn't hold on to it. Is this my fault?"

The lieutenant scratched his head. "Ça, c'est extraordinaire."

"I wanted to pay him, but I wanted to get the chicken liver out of the taxi first," I said.

"It is not true," the taxi driver said. "His wife knows it's not true."

"Where is his wife?"

"He left her standing in front of the Hotel California," I screamed.

"Calm down," the lieutenant said. "Nothing can happen to her in front of the Hotel California. Where is the chicken liver now?"

"In the bottom of the taxicab where he put it," I said accusingly.

"No," the taxi driver said, "where he let it fall."

Everyone in the police station was breaking up with laughter, and I could see I was losing the battle.

"Do you want to pay him, or not?" the lieutenant asked.

"I'll pay him after I take the food out of the taxi."

"All right," the lieutenant said. "Take the food out of the taxi and pay him."

I went back outside, and while a dozen gendarmes looked on with interest, I put the food back on the silver tray. I heard one say to another "C'est extraordinaire. Foie de volaille haché. C'est plûtot cannibale." ("Chopped chicken liver. It's extraordinary—almost cannibal.")

I paid the taxi driver, refusing to give him a tip, and he drove off, screaming.

I didn't have the nerve to ask the lieutenant to call me another taxi, so I picked up the silver tray and, with the laughter of the police still in my ears, I walked up the Champs Élysées for five blocks.

It will be the last time we give a party with somebody else.

The Storyteller

Have you ever noticed how helpful wives are when a husband is trying to tell a story? I've noticed it—many times. Just recently I was out with some friends, and one of the wives said, "Dear, tell them what happened to us in Monaco last summer."

"Aw, they don't want to hear about *that*."

"Yes, we do," we all chimed in.

"Go ahead, tell them," the wife said.

"Well, all right," the husband said. "We were driving up from Rome."

"Actually it was Florence," the wife said.

"That's right, Florence," the husband agreed. "We were in Rome before we went to Florence. I was driving."

The wife said, "I don't like to drive on European roads. I think they're very dangerous."

"Yeh, and we came into Monaco."

"Tell them why we drove to Monaco."

"Because there were no rooms in Portofino," the husband said. "But anyway we got into Monaco around five o'clock at night."

"You forgot to tell them what the man at customs said," the wife said.

"It's not important to the story," the husband said.

"I think it's cute," the wife replied.

"If it's cute, tell us," we all begged.

"I don't think it was so cute," the husband said. "He asked if we had any gifts for anyone in France, and we said we didn't know anyone in France, and he said neither did he."

"It was funnier in French," the wife admitted.

"Anyway," the husband said, "the first thing we did was look for a hotel."

"You forget to tell them why we were so anxious to get to a hotel," the wife said.

"We hadn't slept the night before," the husband said. "We thought we'd sleep in Portofino."

"But there wasn't a room to be had in Portofino," the wife said.

"I already told them that," the husband said.

"Well, it's important to the story," the wife said.

"Do you want to tell the story?" the husband asked.

"No," said the wife. "You tell it so much better."

"Okay," the husband said. "So we drove around Monaco for an hour and finally got a room at the Hermitage. We checked into the hotel and went straight to our room. It was summer and still light out, so we pulled the curtains."

"We had agreed," the wife said, "not even to have dinner. All we wanted to do was sleep. Anyway, we've been to Monaco before, and after you've seen the Palace, the gambling casino, and the Onassis yacht, there isn't too much else to see. Wild horses and an invitation from Princess Grace herself wouldn't have gotten us out of that room. That's how tired we were. Go on, dear."

"I set the alarm clock for eight o'clock."

"You forgot to tell them we always carry our own alarm clock," the wife said, "so we don't have to depend on telephone operators to wake us up."

"So I did," the husband said.

"It's important to the story," the wife explained to us.

"Anyway, we went to bed immediately."

"Did you tell them the reason we wanted to get to bed early was because we wanted an early start the next morning so we could drive to St. Tropez?" the wife asked.

"No, I didn't," the husband said. "All right, so we hit the bed and went fast to sleep, both of us."

"Now comes the good part of the story," the wife said. "We were awakened out of the sleep by the alarm ringing, and we got dressed."

"Will you let me finish?" the husband said.

"Of course," the wife said. "It's your story."

"I paid the bill and got in the car and started to drive off. There seemed to be a lot of traffic that early in the morning. And then suddenly, as it got darker and I started . . ."

The wife interrupted. "You see what happened was George had set the alarm for eight, and he had forgotten it was seven when we went to sleep, so actually we only slept an hour, and we were so tired we didn't even realize it. So we paid for a room for an hour, and had to find another place to sleep in Cannes. The extraordinary thing is in France they probably don't think it's strange for people to take a hotel room for an hour. It was very funny, though it didn't seem funny at the time. Anyway, George has been dining out on the story ever since."

Little-Known Festivals in Europe

There are many folk festivals in Europe, some dating back to time immemorial. There are also music festivals, film festivals, drama festivals, dance festivals, bullfight festivals, and gastronomic festivals.

While the major ones are publicized, there are others that rarely receive the attention they deserve. It is a pity that more people don't know about them.

For example, there is the Gazpacho Festival, which is considered one of the most unique and colorful festivals on the Continent. Every year on the second Tuesday after Mother's Day the people of Gazpacho get dressed up in their colorful Tequilas, Rizzotos, and Hakims, and at dawn they start to dance through the streets of the town, stopping occasionally at the café to refresh themselves with ice-cold glasses of the strong Motherherring wine.

The procession takes a circuitous route through the narrow streets of Gazpacho, where more celebrators join in the parade while others wave gaily from decorated windows. Finally, at around ten o'clock in the morning, the procession, led by the town band, arrives in the Gazpacho Main Square, where tourists who have paid anywhere from six thousand to ten thousand fandangos are seated in specially built stands to watch the hilarity.

In the exact center of the square is a pile of cobblestones which the natives have collected all year long. The natives dance around the pile and then, at a signal from the mayor, each person picks up a cobblestone and suddenly starts throwing it at the tourists. No tourist can escape, and when all the visitors are stoned to death the festival is considered over. After the square is cleaned up the natives take off their colorful costumes and put them away for another year.

There have been some protests from neighboring towns about this fiesta, but the people of Gazpacho always reply, "We don't like tourists and this usually teaches them a lesson."

The Feuerfest in Gesundheit is also one of the most colorful in Europe. The story goes that in 1190, on the day before the crops were to be brought in, Black Frederick, the Prince of Lower Gesundheit, ordered all the crops of Upper Gesundheit to be burned so Lower Gesundheit could raise its price.

Good King Achoo of Upper Gesundheit became so enraged he ordered his people to set fire to all the crops of Lower Gesundheit, and for the next few years no citizen of either Lower or Upper Gesundheit would leave his house without a flaming torch.

From this humble beginning was started a custom which has come down from generation to generation. Every year since 1190, on the day before the harvest, the natives get dressed up in their colorful costumes and set fire to each other's lands.

In the evening there are fireworks, and street dancing, lighted by the fires which can be seen for miles around.

The bitterness has long since died between Upper and Lower Gesundheit, but neither side will break with tradition.

And although the natives lost all their crops and haven't eaten well since, Feuerfest is, for them, the high spot of the year.

The last exciting event worth mentioning, though there are hundreds more if we had the room, is the Children's Fair at Kecknivek. Every year the parents of Kecknivek dress up their children in their native custumes and bring them to the colorful fairgrounds, where they are sold.

Prices range anywhere from seventy zaphnicks for a little girl to three hundred zaphnicks for a strapping boy.

Beside finding the festival a major source of its income, Kecknivek prides itself on the fact it has never had a juvenile delinquency problem. The town is considered a model community throughout the rest of Europe.

In the evening there is street dancing and fireworks, and everyone has a good time.

The Children's Fair always takes place the first week in June so it will save the parents the expense of sending their children to camp.

A Promise Made
Is, Etc., Etc.

The Swiss mountains were getting me down and so I put in for a transfer to Monte Carlo.

"Why don't you go alone?" my wife said.

"It wouldn't be any fun alone," I said, flushing with excitement. "But then again it hardly seems fair to drag you and the children away from this paradise."

"You need the rest," she insisted. "Besides, you didn't bring a raincoat here and we did."

"Well, as long as you put it that way, I'll just make a fast trip down there to take a swim, and I'll be back before the snow melts on the Matterhorn."

"All right," she said, accepting a pair of pearl earrings as a gift. "But promise me you won't talk to any single woman."

"I won't even talk to married women," I promised. "You don't have to worry about me."

Before she could change her mind, I was on a plane to Paris and then on the Blue Train to Monaco.

The Blue Train arrives in Cannes at eight o'clock, in Nice at eight thirty, and in Monte Carlo at nine thirty. The train was full when I left Paris, but, by the time I arrived in Nice, there were only two of us left in the car. Besides myself there was an attractive woman who seemed to be traveling all alone. As the train pulled out of Nice, both of us were standing in the aisle looking out the window.

She smiled at me, but I didn't smile back

"Everybody got off the train," she said.

I didn't reply.

"It's so lonely."

I turned the other way.

"Are you going to Monte Carlo?"

I nodded yes.

"So am I."

I smiled.

"Traveling can get to be so lonely. Have you ever had the feeling you want to talk to somebody in the worst way?"

"Once in a while," I said, breaking the silence, "but not very often."

"I love to talk to people, but very few people talk to me."

I didn't say anything.

"I have a wonderful story to tell someone."

I pretended I was trying to close the window.

"It's filled with sadness and loneliness," she continued. "But no one will listen to it."

I got the window closed.

"Would you believe it, you're the first stranger I've wanted to talk to in thirty years?"

I opened the window.

"I guess I've always been frightened of people."

We went into a tunnel.

When we came out she said, "You have a sympathetic face. Would you listen to my story?"

I shook my head.

The silence was embarrassing.

"Wouldn't you even listen to part of it?"

I shook my head again.

"One small anecdote?"

I shook my head again.

"That's the trouble," she sighed. "When I finally meet someone I want to talk to, he doesn't want to listen."

I wanted to explain to her the promise I made to my wife, but she wouldn't have understood. Instead I said, "I want to be alone," and went back into my own compartment to read the newspaper.

When I arrived in Monte Carlo there was only one porter and I had to share him with the lady. As I got to the gate, I saw a friend of mine, George Schlee, run up to the woman and kiss her.

Then he shook hands with me, and said, "I see you've met Greta."

"Greta who?" I said, turning to the woman.

"Greta Garbo."

I threw myself in front of the next train going back to Paris.

It Puckers Your Mouth

"There are not in this world any lords of higher lineage than the great wines of Médoc, which form the first nobility of the vintages of France, whether they be Margaux, Saint-Julien, Saint-Estéphe, Paulliac, or Moulis. They rival each other in their incomparable elegance and in their rich, ruby-red color."

That is what they would have told you if you had gone to Bordeaux for the harvesting of the 1959 grapes. As a guest of Alexis Lichine, proprietor of the Château Prieuré-Lichine and Lascombes, I spent a few days in the Médoc, watching one of the great vintages being brought in. The sight was one to make the heart beat faster. The dry French summer and fall, which had played havoc with vegetables and dairy products, had been a boon to the grapes. Not only was it a great year in quality, but in quantity as well.

In one of those inexplicable French economic explanations we were told that the price of wine would not go down because it had been a successful year. The previous years, 1956, 1957, 1958, were bitter and cold years for the wine growers, and very little wine was made. The short-age sent the price up. This is reasonable. But last year, with wine in quantity, the price still went up.

I made the mistake of asking one of the growers why.

"Because," he said, as if talking to a child, "it is a great year and ev-erybody wants it."

So much for the economics of wine.

M. Lichine promised to take me on a tour of the Médoc and we start-ed, quite naturally, with his own Château Lascombes. He told me that in the course of the tour I would be asked to taste some wines and he didn't want me to disgrace him.

I practiced by tasting some wine from one of his vats. It tasted good, and I swallowed it.

"No, no, no," he said. "Don't swallow it. Swish it around in your mouth."

"Clockwise or counterclockwise?"

"Clockwise. Counterclockwise is for Burgundy. And then spit it on the floor."

I practiced a few times until I got it right.

"Now say something," he said.

"It sure puckers the inside of your mouth."

"No, that's not what you're supposed to say," M. Lichine cried. "You're supposed to say something beautiful like, 'How full and gener-ous. It will fulfill its promise.'"

"Okay, but it still puckers the inside of your mouth."

Our first stop was Château Margaux, one of the four greatest wine châteaux in France. We visited the chai, the long shed where the grapes are put in vats and barrels. The master of the chai asked me if I wanted to taste some. I nodded, and he gave me a glass.

I swished it around and spat it out. Lichine looked pleased at his pu-pil. "It has a texture all its own," I said. "It tastes like cotton."

Lichine kicked me in the leg. "What he means," he said to the mas-ter, "is that it tastes like velvet."

After we were shown around the Château (I discovered that no one in Bordeaux presses wine in their bare feet any more) Lichine took me to the Châteaux Latour, another of the four greatest vineyards in France.

I tasted the Latour wine and said, "A great wine. It has such a rich, soft flavor."

Lichine smiled.

"Could I have some water?" I asked of the owner, Count Hubert de Beaumont.

Lichine's face dropped.

"Water?" The count looked puzzled. "Do you want to wash your hands?"

Before I could say I wanted to drink the water, Lichine dragged me away.

"Never, never, never ask for water in Bordeaux," he admonished me.

"But I tell you my mouth is all puckered up. My cheeks are stuck to my teeth."

Lichine would have none of it. The last château we visited belonged to Philippe de Rothschild, owner of the Mouton-Rothschild vineyards. M. Rothschild, a gracious host, showed us through his caves and invited us to have a glass of champagne with him in his house, one of the most beautiful in France.

We went upstairs and a servant served us each a bubbling glass. Lichine toasted his host and we each sipped some. Then as Lichine looked on in horror, I swished it around in my mouth.

He screamed, "No!"

But it was too late. I spat it on the floor.

The Frenchman and His Car

Not long ago a man was arrested in the Bois de Boulogne, Paris' largest park, for *misbehaving* with a woman (not his wife) in a tiny Renault automobile. The man pleaded not guilty on the grounds that it was physically impossible to misbehave in a Renault 4CV. The judge who had never tried it, turned the question over to several experts who came back in a few weeks with the following verdict: It was difficult to misbehave in a Renault 4CV, but not impossible. The man was found guilty.

The reason the trial attracted so much attention in France was not that it concerned *misbehavior*, since the French don't even recognize such a thing, nor that the woman in question was another man's wife, but that an automobile was involved. The average Frenchman loves his automobile, and the only reason he wouldn't misbehave in it is he is afraid to damage his car.

There is probably nothing as dear to a Frenchman as his automobile. He may take his wife for granted, but his car is something he lavishes love and affection on and keeps on a pedestal when he isn't trying to get through traffic.

If you so much as bump his bumper, the Frenchman will jump out of his car, raging mad, and scream for a half-hour about the crime you have committed against his prized possession. But if you knock over his wife in a department store, he will shrug his shoulders and may even apologize for his wife's getting in your way.

It is safe to say that if a Frenchman has the choice between a car and a woman, he will in almost all cases take the car. For one thing a Frenchman has only one car, but he usually has access to many women.

Unlike Americans, the French do not consider their automobiles status symbols. The French divide themselves between those who have cars and those who don't. The man who drives a small Simca, a Peugeot, or Renault has no inferiority complex toward someone who drives a large Citroen, Versailles, or Mercedes-Benz. As a matter fact, if anything, the driver of the smaller car is more aggressive about it and, like small people, feels protected because of size.

This doesn't always work. Once I was standing at the Place de la Concorde when a four-door Buick bumped a Simca Aronde. The driver of the Simca got out of his car red-faced and started to scream at the Buick owner, also a Frenchman.

"You are an imbecile and an idiot," the Simca owner screamed. "Look what you have done to my bumper. You scratched it. You should be thrown into prison and your horrible car with you."

The Buick owner stood by passively as the Simca owner went on and on shouting epithets and threats. I thought the Buick owner was going to hit the other man. But instead he got back into the Buick, backed it up about ten feet, stepped on the gas, and smashed into the back of the Simca crushing it like an accordion.

Then the Buick owner got out of his car and said to the Simca man who was speechless, "There, now you have something to scream about."

It is hard to describe the passion a Frenchman has for his car. For one thing, it is rare that an eighteen- or nineteen-year-old French boy owns an automobile. For another, his father would never let him use the family car. So most Frenchmen must wait a long time before they possess a motor vehicle, much longer than they have to wait to possess a French girl. Therefore, while most of them have experienced a woman at an early age, few of them have experienced the pleasure of sitting behind the wheel of a car. Since a Frenchman has to work harder and longer for an automobile, it is only natural he would love it more.

Once the Frenchman has his car he treats it like a jealous lover. He feels, and rightly so, his car is the only one on the road, and he becomes frantic if anyone else comes near it. Although a Frenchman is considered an expert when it comes to making love, all Frenchmen are amateurs when it comes to driving a car. There is only one rule that they obey—that is, the car coming from the right has the right of the way. After that it's every man for himself.

In August 1954 the Paris Prefect (Chief of Police) decided to stop all horn-honking in Paris. This came as a blow to the French driver—for many drivers the horn on a car was the most attractive part of the body, and there was nothing that gave a Frenchman more pleasure than pressing down on it at every corner.

Strangely enough, the Chief of Police's edict worked, and ever since then there has been no horn-blowing in Paris. Now there is only shouting and arms flailing away on the sides of automobile doors.

If the French driver gives short shrift to other cars, he has no shrift for pedestrians. The late Fred Allen was once wondering why there are so many churches in Paris. Then he discovered that it was because it gave someone an opportunity to stop in and pray before crossing a street.

It is very hard for a foreigner who is unfamiliar with French drivers to catch on to driving in Paris.

A few simple things to keep in mind might help them.

1. If someone extends his hand, that means the window is open.

2. If someone stops at a red light, it means his foot has slipped off the accelerator.

3. If the left rear blinker light is lit, it means the car will either turn left, right, or come at you in reverse.

4 If the right rear blinker light is lit, it means the car ahead will either stop or has a short circuit.

5. If you hear curses coming from another car, it means that you have done something that irkes the other driver because he didn't think of it first.

6. Sounding the horn means the car has just struck a pedestrian and the driver would like someone to be a witness.

7. A policeman with one hand up means he has just witnessed a very gory accident and doesn't have the nerve to look at it. He is shielding his eyes with the other hand.

8. When a driver waves his hand up and down it means the girl with him is not his wife, and he would appreciate all courtesies.

The Health Nuts

"Hollywood is on a new kick," said Larry Gelbart, a TV writer who was filling me in on the latest American fads. "First it was psychiatry, then it was dieting, and now the health nuts have taken over. Many of those motion-picture stars and comedians, having done everything to their heads and the outside of their bodies, are now turning inward to help themselves. As part of the campaign for self-improvement, they have become organic food specialists. Instead of food, they're eating dandelion hearts, roots of moss, and eucalyptus bark. It's very dangerous to be invited to someone's house for a meal. For one thing, you can't walk on their lawn because that may be your dinner. For another, it isn't enough that your friends are health nuts; they spend the whole evening trying to convert everyone else.

"I was invited to the house of a Hollywood couple a month ago. They had a little girl, aged five. Unfortunately I had a cold and I was sniffling.

"The father turned to the little girl and said, 'You see what happened to Uncle Larry because he ate lamb chops.'

"It's hard to get a drink in a health nut's house. They either offer you a glass of honey or a handful of sunflower seeds. I was trying to think of some reason why I couldn't stay for dinner, but it was too late. The butler announced dinner was served. Dinner? It consisted of boiled peanut water, wheat-germ pancakes, soya beans cooked in their own soy, carrot salad, and cider vinegar. But this wasn't all. After we ate the food the butler came in with a silver tray filled with jars of pills.

" 'What are these for?' I asked foolishly.

" 'They're the supplements,' the hostess explained.

" 'The supplements for what?'

"They thought I was crazy. 'For the things we didn't eat,' she said. 'The brown bottle is a bread supplement; the green bottle is the salt supplement; the red bottle is the protein supplement; the black bottle is the starch supplement; the red-white-and-blue bottle is the vitamin supplement; and the tall bottle with the clear liquid is the energy tonic.'

"I said I was full and I just couldn't eat any more, but the hostess seemed very upset. She said the druggist had been preparing the meal all day, and he would be very hurt if I didn't eat everything.

"After dinner we went into the living room to hear the little girl play the piano. She played very well, and her father said, 'That was very good, dear. You can now have a piece of candy.' And, so help me, he went to a bin, and handed her a raw potato.

"After this experience, I started to look into the health craze in Hollywood. It seems now if you have a small party, you hire the family doctor. But if it's more than twenty people it's catered by the Mayo Clinic.

"The reason this thing is spreading so fast is that there are usually about thirty people dependent on one star for their living. So in order to keep their jobs they have to go on health kicks too. The same men who used to sit around Schwabs Drug Store eating cheesecake and laughing at their boss's jokes are now eating weed sandwiches at the Cavendish Health Bar—and they're not laughing quite as loud.

"One of the big things for the health nuts is tiger's milk. I made the mistake one night of asking a comedian who drinks it four times a day, 'How do you milk a tiger?' I suggested, perhaps you have to sit on a short stool with a long gun, and do it very gently. But he didn't think it was very funny and I didn't get the job.

"The health addicts don't laugh much, and I can understand why. They figure they'll be around for a hundred and fifty years, and you've got, at the most (if you keep eating steak and apple pie), four years. So they feel, How can they laugh at another man who is just about to die?

"The only thing worse than going to a health addict's house for dinner is his coming to yours. He arrives with his little plastic bag of super-nutritional cereal, tiger's milk, and tea herbs, and says to your wife, 'Just give me a bottle of hot water.' Then, while the rest of the guests sit transfixed, their turkey getting cold, he starts mixing it all into a soup plate, tastes it, smacks his lips and says, 'I just signed a contract to do a film for M-G-M in A.D. 2960.'

"It's kind of tough on the kids. They don't really understand about health foods, and I know one kid who used to hide advertisements for cake mixes under his mattresses. His mother caught him and had his father give the kid a licking for keeping dirty pictures."

Let's See Who Salutes

Have you ever wondered what would have happened if the people who are in charge of television today were passing on the draft of the Declaration of Independence?

The scene is Philadelphia at WJULY TV. Several men are sitting around holding copies of the Declaration.

Thomas Jefferson comes in nervously.

"Tommy," says the producer, "it's just great. I would say it was a masterpiece."

"We love it, Tommy boy," the advertising agency man says. "It sings. Lots of drama, and it holds your interest. There are a few things that have to be changed, but otherwise it stays intact."

"What's wrong with it?" Mr. Jefferson asks.

There's a pause. Everyone looks at the man from the network.

"Well, frankly, Tommy, it smacks of being a little anti-British. I mean, we've got quite a few British listeners and something like this might bring in a lot of mail."

"Now don't get sore, Tommy boy," the agency man says. "You're the best declaration of independence writer in the business. That's why we hired you. But our sponsor the Boston Tea Company is interested in selling tea, not independence. Mr. Cornwallis, the sponsor's represent- ative, is here, and I think he has a few thoughts on the matter. Go ahead, Corney. Let's hear what you think."

Mr. Cornwallis stands up. "Mr. Jefferson, all of us in this room want this to be a whale of a document. I think we'll agree on that."

Everyone in the room nods his head.

"At the same time we feel—I think I can speak for everybody—that we don't want to go over the heads of the mass of people who we hope will buy our product. You use words like despotism, annihilation, mi- gration, and tenure. Those are all egghead words and don't mean a damn thing to the public. Now I like your stuff about 'Life, Liberty, and the pursuit of Happiness.' They all tie in great with tea, particu- larly pursuit of happiness, but it's the feeling of all of us that you're re- ally getting into controversial water when you start attacking the King of Britain."

Mr. Jefferson says, "But every word of it is true. I've got documen- tary proof."

"Let me take a crack at it, Corney," the agency man says. "Look, Tommy boy, it isn't a question of whether it's true or not. All of us here know what a louse George can be. But I don't think the people want to be reminded of it all the time. They have enough worries. They want escape. This thing has to be upbeat. If you remind people of all those taxes George has laid on us, they're not going to go out and buy tea. They're not going to go out and buy anything."

"Frankly," says the network man, "I have some strong objections on different grounds. I know you didn't mean it this way, but the script strikes me as pretty left-wing. I may have read the last paragraph wrong, but it seems to me that you're calling for the overthrow of the present government by force. The network could never allow anything like that."

"I'm sure Tommy didn't mean anything like that," the producer says. "Tommy's just a strong writer. Maybe he got a little carried away with himself. Suppose Tommy took out all references to the British and the

King. Suppose we said in a special preamble this Declaration of Independence had nothing to do with persons living or dead, and the whole thing is fictitious. Wouldn't that solve it?"

Mr. Jefferson says, "Gentlemen, I was told to write a Declaration of Independence. I discussed it with many people before I did the actual writing. I've worked hard on this declaration—harder than I've worked on anything in my life. You either take it or leave it as it is."

"We're sorry you feel that way about it, Tommy," the agency man says. "We owe a responsibility to the country, but we owe a bigger responsibility to the sponsor. He's paying for it. We're not in the business of offending people, British people or any other kind of people. The truth is, the British are the biggest tea drinkers of anyone in the colonies. We're not going to antagonize them with a document like this. Isn't that so, Mr. Cornwallis?"

"Check—unless Mr. Jefferson changes it the way we want him to."

Mr. Jefferson grabs the Declaration and says, "Not for all the tea in China," and exits.

The producer shakes his head. "I don't know, fellows. Maybe we've made a mistake. We could at least have run it up a flagpole to see who saluted."

"As far as I'm concerned," Mr. Cornwallis said, "the subject is closed. Let's talk about an hour Western on the French and Indian War."

Economy Drives We Have Known

Companies throughout the world are either in the midst of expanding or in the process of economizing. It depends on what the last financial report looked like. The motion picture companies for the most part are economizing. One major studio has closed down all its European supervisory offices in a wave of economy the likes of which hasn't been seen since the last economy wave.

Since most people are innocent victims of economy drives, I have, as a public service, contacted Mr. Robert Goldbogen, who specializes in studying economy drives and their effect on the economy.

"Mr. Goldbogen, what does an economy drive really mean?"

"It means," Mr. Goldbogen said, "that the president of the company has had to report to the stockholders that the profits are lower than anticipated; there is in fact a loss and he is immediately instigating the necessary measures to turn the tide. As a start, he announces an economy drive will be put in effect. If he's still president after the report he has to follow through on his promise."

"What does he do first?"

"He fires two men, one in the mail room and the elevator boy."

"But who runs the elevator?"

"At a cost of only twenty-five thousand dollars, a self-service elevator is installed."

"That's all?"

"No, it really isn't as economical to fire the mail room boy as one might think. Someone has to deliver important packages and letters by hand, so a higher-priced employee is sent instead. This employee, not familiar with the city, takes twice as long to do the job as the mail room boy did.

"When the president discovers the firing of the mail room boy and the elevator boy has not solved his problem, he makes further economies."

"How does he do this?"

"Every large company has certain people that they employ just to blame things on. They have to be on the job when things go wrong. Each vice-president might have one chief blame-taker and three assistants. The chief blame-taker distributes the blame among the others. Since there are enough people to spread the blame about, no one gets in trouble. But then the president sends down word to the heads of the departments that they have to cut their staffs and instead of four people, they can only have one."

"The department head naturally keeps the chief blame-taker?"

"Not necessarily. The department head keeps the one who takes the blame the best. The chief blame-taker may be good at dispensing blame, but weak on taking it himself."

"Then the economy problem is settled?"

"On the contrary, this is the most dangerous type of economy there is. Since the head of the department keeps blaming one person for everything that goes wrong, eventually the president asks why the head of the department doesn't fire him? We know the answer. If the head of the department fires him, then he will have to take the blame himself.

"When he takes the blame, he will be fired as well, and pretty soon the president will have to take the blame. Then the stockholders will force *his* resignation. When you start firing people who absorb blame, you're really in a fix."

"What can one do to make sure one is not a victim of an economy cut?"

"Take the bull by the horns, as we say on the back lot in Pamplona. When you smell an economy cut you must immediately go in to see the boss and ask him to let you go.

"Tell him you're expendable, and you feel the company is not getting its money's worth. The boss will immediately smell a rat and decide you're trying to go over to the opposition and you will be kept on the pay roll until hell freezes over.

"Another method of staying on is that as soon as an economy wave is announced the person must demand a raise and a vacation. The boss will figure anyone who would do such a thing at a time like this must be worth a great deal to the firm, and you'll survive the cuts and possibly even get the raise.

"There are other methods. I know one man who owned two cars. One he drove and the other he kept parked in the company parking lot next to the spot reserved for the president's car. No matter what time the president came out, day or night, the man's car was there, and the president assumed he was inside working for Dear Old Inc. Incorporated. It made quite an impression on the president, so much so that when the president had the choice of firing the man or himself, he immediately resigned and the man who owned the car is now president of the company."

The National Italian Sport

The site for this year's summer Olympics is Rome. The Italians are great sports lovers, and the national sport of Italy is Far Rumore (translation—"to make noise"). The sport originated some time in the Middle Ages in Sicily when it was discovered that visitors to the island were sleeping instead of buying souvenirs in the shops.

This infuriated the Sicilian merchants so much that they hired men and women to stand under the windows of tourists and shout at each other.

Later on they hired pig beaters and donkey-cart owners to drive around the main streets at three and four in the morning. The screaming of the pigs and the rattling of the carts drove the visitors out into the streets, where they had nothing else to do but shop. The Sicilian merchants prospered, and the idea soon caught on on the mainland.

Today there isn't a town in Italy that doesn't have several first-class Far Rumore teams. While refinements have been added, the objective of the sport is still the same—to keep tourists from sleeping.

In some cities, motor scooters and Ferraris have replaced the pigs and donkey carts, and the automobile horn is as important to the Far Rumore player as the cape is to the matador.

Roger Price, who was recently in Naples, reports he was there for the regional tryouts, which were held in front of his window at the Hotel Excelsior. The people around Naples, he said, shun modern methods and prefer to holler.

"The champion hollerer of Naples had died since the previous tryouts," Mr. Price told me, "and so they held a minute of noise for him.

"Then they got on with the games. The tryouts are always held between midnight and eight in the morning. There are different categories. But the results are always the same. The one who wakes up the most tourists, wins.

"There are the singles matches, when each participant must holler alone. Then there are the mixed doubles, when husbands and wives compete against each other. Finally there are the team matches, in which teams composed of men who have consumed a bottle of wine apiece start shouting at each other.

"The teams are cheered on by spectators, and there is always a great deal of arguing after the matches about who made the most noise, the teams or the spectators."

In Rome the mixed doubles are held between teams of sports cars and motor scooters on the Via Veneto. The mufflers are taken off the vehicles exactly at midnight, and the contest goes on until dawn. It isn't necessary for the vehicle to move; as long as their motors are running they are in the game.

As you go farther north, Far Rumore takes on a different flavor. In Florence William Dana, an American tourist, reports, Far Rumore is played with garbage pails, and the teams are made up of the building superintendents on one hand and the garbage collectors on the other. For years, the building superintendents won the contest, but recently the garbage collectors have been winning, thanks to a new coach named Giuseppe Casaldiavolo. The coach invented the famed "Casaldiavolo pass," in which the garbage pail is slammed against the side of the truck before the garbage is emptied. Since then the tourists have given the nod to the collectors, and the superintendents are looking around for a new coach.

In Venice Far Rumore is played between the gondoliers and the motorboats. The gondoliers used to sing to keep tourists awake, but in recent times, every time they started, the motorboat owners revved up their engines and drowned them out.

This so infuriated the gondoliers that they brought in a team of hollerers from Naples, and now, instead of singing, the gondoliers holler oaths at the motorboats. Since then the matches have been even.

Even in the smaller towns Far Rumore is played. Mr. Price reports he was in a small town near Genoa, where, instead of hollering or racing their motors, the peasants played by banging a stick against his car.

The world record for a tourist sleeping in Italy is three hours and forty-seven minutes. It's held by a ninety-year-old Frenchman named Alain Bernheim, who lost his hearing aid an hour before he went to sleep, and the motor scooter assigned to his window ran out of gas.

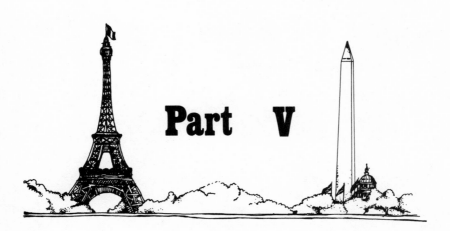

Part   V

Anyone for Hamburger?

I almost had dinner with the Vice-President of the United States, Lyndon Johnson, and it was almost one of the greatest evenings I ever spent in Paris.

This is what happened. The Vice-President and his wife had arrived to spend one day and night in Paris and asked a very good friend of theirs, who also happens to be a very good friend of mine, if he would select a restaurant to give the dinner. My friend called me up and said: "How would you like to have dinner with the Vice-President of the United States and his wife?"

I said it would be nice.

"Well, I haven't cleared it with them yet, but I'm sure it will be all right. What restaurant should we dine at?"

"Why don't you reserve at Novy's? It's got White Russian music and a nice atmosphere."

"Good idea," he said.

"Where shall we meet?" I asked excitedly.

"At the ambassador's."

"What ambassador?" I asked.

"Haven't you been invited to the cocktail party the Gavins are giving for the Vice-President?"

"No," I said.

"Well, I'll call the embassy and tell them you're going to have dinner with the Vice-President and I'm sure they'll invite you."

[141]

"Gee, that's swell," I said.

I couldn't wait to telephone my wife and tell her. But she wasn't home and I told our cook, Danielle, to tell my wife as soon as she came in that we were having dinner with the Vice-President of the United States. A few minutes later the American Embassy called and said they would be very happy to have me come to a cocktail party the ambassador was giving for the Vice-President.

I said I'd be very happy to go.

Then I went out to lunch and told everyone I met I couldn't have dinner with them because I was dining with the Lyndon Johnsons.

In the meantime my wife had come home and when Danielle told my wife about our dinner plans, she dashed out of the house and rushed off to Alexandre's, the famous Paris coiffeur, to get her hair done.

Alexandre's is a very fashionable place and you can't get in without an appointment. But when my wife explained she was going to have dinner with the Vice-President of the United States, they threw a duchess out the window and gave my wife her chair.

Meanwhile, back at the office, I was reading up on protocol and the great Vice-Presidents of our country when the phone rang, and it was my friend, who was so embarrassed he could hardly talk. It seems the Johnsons had insisted on a small dinner party made up of just their friends, and he said he couldn't invite me.

"That's okay," I said, trying to keep my tears away from the mouthpiece. "Let's do it some other time."

"I'm terribly sorry," he said. "I should have asked them before I asked you."

"Really, it's nothing," I blubbered. "I'll be happy to stay in and read a good book."

"But aren't you coming to the cocktail party?" he asked.

"We can't," I said. "The reason we were invited to the cocktail party was because we were going to dinner with the Vice-President. We'd feel like impostors if we showed up for drinks and weren't going on."

"I guess you're right," he said and hung up.

Five minutes later my wife called up, deliriously happy. "Hi," she said, "this is quite a day. One minute we're going to eat hamburgers at home for dinner, and the next we're going out with the Vice-President of the United States."

"Wait a minute, social climber!" I shouted. Then I explained quietly what had happened.

"But what will I tell them the next time I go to Alexandre's?" she cried.

"You can fake it. They'll never know."

"What about Danielle? She's told everyone in the neighborhood. What can I tell her?"

"Tell her . . . tell her . . . not to throw the hamburgers away."

The Mothers-in-Law

My mother-in-law is back in Paris making an on-the-spot investigation for the United Nations of conditions at my house, where several factions have been fighting for supremacy since my three children came back from their Swiss vacation.

Inadvertently my mother-in-law made me lose a lifelong friend, Alain Bernheim, and I have only myself to blame.

This is what happened.

Anatole Litvak, the director, was about to make a film in Paris called *Goodbye Again* with Ingrid Bergman, Yves Montand, and Tony Perkins, and to launch his film he held a press cocktail party at the Hotel George V.

My mother-in-law is a big fan of Miss Bergman's and so I took her to the party. Miss Bergman was very gracious and my mother-in-law was thrilled. She also met Sam Taylor, who wrote the script for *Goodbye Again* and he invited us both to dinner at the Plaza Athénée after the press party. As luck would have it, his date was Miss Bergman.

Well, you can imagine how thrilled my mother-in-law was—not only to meet Miss Bergman, but to have dinner with her.

To make matters even better, James Stewart, who was staying at the Plaza, stopped by to say hello to Miss Bergman and so my mother-in-law met him too. Celebrity-wise speaking, it was a memorable evening in my mother-in-law's life and I went to bed happy in the knowledge that Warren, Pennsylvania, would soon have a firsthand report on Ingrid Bergman, James Stewart, Tony Perkins, and Yves Montand.

But unfortunately the next day my mother-in-law had a luncheon date with Mr. Bernheim's mother-in-law, Mrs. Lillian Kessler, of Los Angeles. Somehow, I'll never know how, my mother-in-law mentioned to Mr. Bernheim's mother-in-law where she had been on the previous evening and also whom she had met.

As I understand it, my mother-in-law laid it on pretty thick and no matter how Mrs. Kessler kept trying to change the subject, my mother-in-law kept coming back to "Ingrid," "Jimmy," "Tony," and "Yves."

That evening Mrs. Kessler confronted her son-in-law, who used to be my best friend, at the dinner table, and said: "Marie McGarry's son-in-law took *her* to dinner with Ingrid Bergman."

Mr. Bernheim flushed.

"He also introduced her to James Stewart, Tony Perkins, Yves Montand, and some Taylor, probably Elizabeth. It's funny that you don't introduce me to anybody except some of your wild French friends."

Mr. Bernheim protested: "I introduced you to Paulette Goddard in Ascona."

Mrs. Kessler said: "She's not Ingrid Bergman."

Mr. Bernheim said: "I knew Bergman before Mrs. McGarry's son-in-law knew her."

Mrs. Kessler said: "The difference is he introduced her to Mrs. McGarry, but you would never think of introducing me to her."

"It's not true," Mr. Bernheim protested. "The next time I see Miss Bergman I'll introduce her."

"Yes," said Mrs. Kessler. "But will she go to dinner with me, like she did with Mrs. McGarry?"

"I can't promise that," Mr. Bernheim said.

"I thought so," Mrs. Kessler said. "There are some sons-in-law that care more about their mothers-in-law than other sons-in-law."

Mr. Bernheim was starting to feel pretty bad, but Mrs. Kessler wouldn't let up on him.

She said icily, "Do you know Jimmy?"

"Jimmy who?" Mrs Bernheim asked.

"I thought so," said Mrs. Kessler. "You start and stop with Paulette Goddard."

At this point Mr. Bernheim couldn't take it any more and he went to the phone. On the basis of what my mother-in-law had told me, I was expecting his call.

"What the hell are you doing to me?" he screamed.

"I'm sorry," I said. "How did I know my mother-in-law would talk?"

"After all I've done for you," he sobbed, "this is how you repay me."

"Look," I suggested, "why don't you take her to dinner with Paulette Goddard?"

Mr. Bernheim hung up on me. I never knew him to be such a sore loser.

Four Sleepless Nights

I can hardly wait for the year 1980 when I gather all my grandchildren around me and say: "Did I ever tell you about the night when the paratroopers almost landed on your grandfather?"

Yes, it was a wild, sleepless four nights for those of us who live in the

City of Light, and now that the threat of civil war is over I'm prepared to sell the diary I kept during the troubles.

Saturday, April 22— Received word of paratroopers taking over Algiers. Called wife to lay in supply of sugar just in case. Tourists called up and asked whether they should stay or leave. I urged them to leave. Easiest way I ever had of getting rid of visiting firemen.

Sunday, April 23— Went to movies with son and we discussed paratroopers landing in our neighborhood next to the Parc Monceau. My son assured me paras could never land in Parc Monceau, as it is absolutely forbidden for anyone to land on grass, and besides the gardiens of the parc were not only armed with pistols but also with whistles. He was most reassuring until Premier Debré went on air late Sunday night to inform the French population that paratroopers might be landing on Paris and to urge everyone to be ready for them.

Premier Debré told Paris populace that as soon as they heard the air-raid siren they should go by car or by foot to meet the misled paratroopers (many from the French Foreign Legion) and tell them of the mistake they were making.

Called up a friend and asked him if he had any intention of meeting the Foreign Legionnaires and talking to them.

"What's the use?" he said. "I don't speak German."

Monday, April 24— My wife's dressmakers started calling in to pledge their fidelity to her in the crisis, assured her they were backing her to the limit, and asked her was there any chance of her paying up in case they had to leave France in a hurry.

Went down to Crillon Bar in hopes of picking up inside information from embassy sources. Met one of top men, but before I could ask him anything, he asked me: "What do you think will happen tonight?" Not much help there.

Only good news of day was no one was trying to break any windows at the American Embassy, the first time in years American window-panes were safe.

Received call at four in afternoon from visiting firemen who said a taxi driver in front of their hotel offered to drive them to Switzerland immediately for $500. Did I think this was excessive? Looked up taxi tariffs for army coups d'état and found price was in line. Urged them to go.

Monday night went down to Grand Palais, where French had asked for volunteers for a people's army to defend France. Frenchmen from all walks of life, many of them prosperous middle-aged businessmen, showed up and fought to get into uniform.

Met one business acquaintance who said it was very inspiring and he had met many buddies he hadn't seen since World War II.

"What did you talk about?" I asked.

He shrugged his shoulders. "Business."

Tuesday, April 25— Parc Monceau still safe, according to my son. But everything else uncertain.

Everyone still scared silly. Can hardly eat sugar.

But then afternoon paper *France-soir* came out on stand with following headlines: "The American Secret Service Believes the Rebels May Possibly Attack the Mainland in Five Days." The story came from the *France-soir* correspondent in Washington, quoting CIA sources.

On the basis of previous CIA estimates, we all knew for certain the army rebels were finished. France had been saved!

Old Buses Never Die

If the taxis of the Marne saved France in World War I, the autobuses of Paris saved France in 1961. The army insurrection of April 22 is still being hashed over in Paris and in all the excitement no one has given credit to the role played by the retired buses of Paris, which were called up at an hour's notice on Sunday night to repel the paratroopers.

In France's greatest moment of danger, Premier Debré mobilized the French buses to drive out the would-be invaders.

It is to their credit that although many of them broke down and shuddered, when the call came not one bus refused to go out into the streets, even though many of them knew they would never come back.

An eyewitness who was at the retired-bus depot near the Porte de St. Cloud told me he happened to be there on Sunday night when the buses were called up. He said it was one of the most dramatic scenes he had ever viewed in Paris.

Many of the buses, twenty and thirty years old, were awakened from a sound sleep by a klaxon. They could hardly open their headlights when the inspector general of the bus-transportation system strode into the chilly barn that had been turned into an old bus home.

"Mes Vieux," he said to the buses, "France is in danger, and you are being mobilized to save her."

Old 83, which used to shuttle between Porte de Champerret and Place d'Italie, coughed nervously.

Old 91 shed a drop of oil and a weary 73 leaned heavily on 95.

"I know what you're thinking. Why can't the younger buses go?" the inspector general said. "Well, the answer is we need the younger buses to carry volunteers to their posts. You buses have been selected for far more dangerous works. Some of you will be driven out to the airports and stationed on runways so the paratroop planes can't land."

Old 85, which had been painted yellow, screeched in agony.

All the other buses stared in embarrassment.

"Other buses will be stationed near the bridges of the Seine," the inspector general said. "When the siren sounds we will take the air out of your tires and you will act as a barricade against the paratroopers."

Several buses shifted from first into second.

One of the buses in the back stripped its gears in anguish.

"If the rebels have tanks, you will throw yourselves in front of them to stop them from driving on the city."

There was an uproar in the barn as the buses let out their exhausts.

"I'd like a little quiet," the inspector general shouted. "We will give you each enough gas to get to your destinations, but don't try to roll away because if you do, I'll brake every one of you."

Several of the buses started to perspire grease, and one bus got sick and threw up all its antifreeze.

"Autobus Français," the inspector general said, "this is your finest hour.

"General de Gaulle expects every vehicle to do his duty. Let it be written in the omnibuses of history that because of you the Fifth Republic was saved."

All the buses straightened up proudly and with their indicator arms saluted smartly and roared out into the night.

Everyone knows the rest of the story—the story which bears out the saying that "old buses never die; they just make barricades."

If You're a Woman—Don't Vote

The story of the Bull Moose Party is one of the great stories of American politics, and I think it should be told again.

It was started because it was discovered that although the American woman had more in the way of material comfort than ever before, she was, according to all the experts, discontented with her lot.

Although many experts had been called in and millions of dollars in research had been spent to find out why American women were unhappy (mostly by aspirin companies who wanted to keep it that way), it was only last year that a group of selfless, nonpartisan, distinguished Americans were able to get to the root of the problem.

All seven of us, happily married men, were worried about our unhappily married wives. Our wives were the best-clothed, best-fed, best-loved American women that any of us knew, and yet lurking down inside them was a "discontent syndrome." Where had we, as American men and husbands, failed?

We began by discarding all the usual reasons an American wife gives her husband for her unhappiness, such as "You never talk to me at night," "You never want to do *anything*," and "All I seem to be running around here is a hotel." Then we threw out such red herrings as "lack of fulfillment," "drudgery in the home," and "undependable diaper service."

After several weeks of elimination, we finally hit on the American woman's main problem. She has the right to vote!

In the pre-Nineteenth-Amendment era, the American woman was placid, sheltered, and sure of her role in American society. She left all the political decisions to her husband and he in turn left all the family decisions to her. Today a woman has to make both the family and the political decisions and it's too much for her.

It was so obvious to us that American women were incapable of voting and also fulfilling their functions as wives, that we wondered why no one had thought of it before.

There was only one thing to do. We had to work for the repeal of the Nineteenth Amendment.

We knew we could count on the support of every man in the United States, but because women had gotten into the habit of voting, we foresaw a certain amount of resistance from some fanatic females who couldn't realize we were really trying to help them.

It was determined that an official organization had to be formed and funds raised to get the campaign under way.

After much discussion we decided to call the organization "The Bull Moose Party" in memory of those wonderful days when women thought a voting booth was a place to change their bathing suits.

Mr. Robert Jones, an advertising art director and one of the great experimental printers in the United States, was ordered to start printing posters to be distributed all over the country.

His first one is considered a masterpiece in political circles.
It said:

THESE ARE THE FACTS!

WOMEN CAN'T COOK
(96.4% of all professional chefs are men)

WOMEN CAN'T SEW
(89.3% of all couturieres are men)

WOMEN CAN'T EVEN HAVE BABIES
WITHOUT HELP
(92.7% of all babies are delivered by men)

If they can't do the things
they're supposed to do
WHY SHOULD THEY HAVE THE VOTE?

THE BULL MOOSE PARTY
dedicated in perpetuity
to the repeal of the 19th Amendment

The Bull Moose Is Man's Best Friend

Other posters pointing out "Votes Are Like Mustaches—FOR MEN ONLY" also had their effect.

But while the reaction to these posters, particularly in YMCAs, was terrific, it was felt by some members that an appeal to reason should at least be tried on the American women.

Jones went back to his printing press and came up with this one, which is considered one of the most reasonable posters in American politics.

> To the Ladies (God Bless 'Em) . . . This is your fight too. A fight for glamour, a fight for romance. A *fight for you* . . . The Bull Moose Party thinks you're wonderful. Too wonderful to stand in line on Election Day. Too wonderful—yes, and too lovely—to vote . . . The 19th Amendment made a voter out of you. The Bull Moose Party will make a woman out of you. (And remember—a woman can make a man vote *her way*.) STOP THE ROT!

We asked the League of Women Voters to distribute this poster for us, but they refused, and several of our members were arrested trying to stick them up in women's locker rooms in country clubs.

But the impact of the message hit home and while it is too early to know the outcome, the Bull Moose Party feels that the coming elections will show the results of its work.

You are probably saying right now: "What can I, as a woman, do to help?"

The answer to this highly sensible question is: Stay away from the polls in November. Go to the hairdresser on Election Day and look beautiful when your husband comes home from casting his ballot. Show him you love him by trusting his judgment. After all, if he doesn't know who the President of the United States should be—who does?

The Social Climber

Well, it was bound to happen sooner or later: I was invited to the de Gaulles' the other night for a reception in honor of President John F. Kennedy and his lovely wife, Jacqueline. The invitation called for white tie and decorations, which is usually embarrassing for most Americans because they always have to rent both. But as far as I was concerned, no price was too great to pay for a reception of this magnitude and I was as excited as a French general at his first court-martial.

Since my wife wasn't going (I've made it socially, but somehow she never has), she helped me get dressed and told me what to say when I met General de Gaulle and President Kennedy. What you apparently say is: "Mes respects, Monsieur le Président" to General de Gaulle, and "Good evening, Mr. President" to President Kennedy. It seemed easy enough and I kept saying it over and over again in the taxi so I wouldn't forget.

It was raining like the devil and although I started off at 9:30 I was five blocks from the Champs Élysées in a long line of cars filled with people in white ties and decorations at 10:15, the hour the reception was supposed to start.

It looked so hopeless I decided to hop out of the cab and make a run for it. So did everyone else, and I found myself in a 1,000-meter steeplechase being paced by a woman in a long evening gown and a fur cape who had jumped out of the chauffeured car in front of me.

Fortunately her husband was carrying ten extra pounds of decorations and he floundered in the mud at the last hurdle, so I beat both of them to the door.

A member of the Palace Guard took my invitation and I was directed to the hat-check line, which was also five blocks long, though at least it was out of the rain. But I didn't mind waiting because it gave me a chance to rehearse my lines. "Mes respects, Monsieur le Président," "Good evening, Mr. President."

After I checked my coat I was told to go into a waiting room where I was joined by the cream of French society, including the Cyrus Sulz-

bergers, the Joseph Alsops, the Marquis Childses, the David Schoen-
bruns, and the Garde Républicaine.

Beautiful women who had been sitting at hairdressers' for weeks,
and had paid hundreds of dollars for their gowns, were crushed against
perspiring husbands in starched collars and soaked shoes squishy from
the rain. All of us were bunched together like French asparagus, staring at each other's necks, waiting to move forward in what appeared to
be the direction of the receiving line.

But the line hardly seemed to be moving. The men were fretting and
the women were frothing.

By 11:30 I had advanced from the first waiting room into the second.
Somewhere ahead I could hear faint sounds of music. It sounded like
someone was having a reception, though you could not prove it by me.

Suddenly, at 11:40, the line broke and everyone rushed forward at
once. The reason was that both General de Gaulle and President Kennedy decided to forget about the receiving line and go to bed.

By the time I got in the main hall where the orchestra had been playing, the liquor was cut off and the reception was declared officially
over.

I had no choice but to turn around. The same group pushed slowly
back toward the cloakroom to get their coats. An hour later I was back
out in the street, the rain mixed with my tears, my shoes squishing as I
kept mumbling to myself: "Mes respects, Monsieur le Président," and
"Good evening, Mr. President," over and over again.

The Missile Explained

In the now famous Air Force manual, withdrawn temporarily but
not forgotten, one of the paragraphs aimed at Air Force Reservists
said: "The idea that Americans have a right to know what is going on
is foolish."

We poor, ignorant civilians can't be blamed, then, if we have to resort to conjecture about what is going on with such things as our missile program, which is no longer known as a missile program but a missile gap.

I was as confused about our missiles as anyone else until I had lunch
the other day with an industrialist who explained it to me. He asked
that his name not be mentioned, and since the Air Force won't tell me
their secrets, I won't tell them mine.

"The trouble with most Americans," he said, "is that they think
ideas for a new missile come from the top. On the contrary, most ideas

for missiles are thought up by some $10,000-a-year civilian engineer in some tiny office thousands of miles from the Pentagon.

"Let me give you an example of how a missile is born. One day a civilian engineer has to think of something new, so he writes a paper suggesting we develop an anti-anti-missile missile.

"The civilian, after developing the paper at length, turns it over to a second lieutenant, just out of ROTC, who, knowing less than anyone, immediately signs it and passes it on. The captain over him adds his signature, because he also doesn't understand it and doesn't have enough reasons for rejecting it. The paper continues on up through the channels with more and more signatures, each office signing it on the assumption the guys down below know what they're doing. This is what is known in government circles as 'management from the bottom up.'

"Finally it goes to the Pentagon, who assume the problem, on the basis of all the signatures, has been thoroughly studied, and they take it over to the Appropriations Committee, who appropriate the money because they don't understand it either and therefore can't say it won't work.

"Besides, all they need to get the missile started is $10,000,000, and as long as it's such a reasonable request no one wants to argue about it.

"As soon as the money is appropriated the public-relations people put out a release announcing their branch of the service will soon have an anti-anti-missile missile that, although not the final deterrent, will be the gap filler which everyone has been waiting for 'until we catch up with the Russians.'

"The program is under way now, and in no time at all the appropriations are used up. Nothing has come of the missile, but this is an advantage, not a disadvantage. The people in charge believe it is really an advanced idea, otherwise it would be working already. The reason it couldn't be done, according to the people in charge, is that there wasn't enough money. So appropriations are increased to $75,000,000 and, whereas only a few hundred men were connected with the original work, thousands are now added, on the theory that if you put enough people on a project long enough, they will get the job done. This is known as 'snowing the job with manpower.'

"The only thing that has been working so far has been the mimeograph machines in the public-relations department, and they have promised the American people an anti-anti-missile missile come hell or high water. When the $75,000,000 is used up, it's no problem to get more money for the project, because as long as you keep asking for more money in the Defense Department no one is going to ask you what you did with the other money. But as soon as you stop asking for money you're admitting the project is no good. No one has the courage to stop the project after so much money has been expended.

"Finally the time comes when you have to test-fire your missile. It doesn't go off. But even this is not a defeat as far as the service goes. After the failure, a general is on tap to explain that it's really a good thing to have failures, because they represent progress. If it worked it would not be an advanced missile but an obsolete one. Anything that works in missiles is obsolete.

"Therefore, the general explains, the Russians, although they seem ahead in the missile race, are really behind, because their missiles work better than ours. Anyone knows a really advanced missile is one on paper that can't get off the ground.

"In the meantime, the engineer who thought up the idea has corrected his original figures. But it's too late. Who is going to listen to a $10,000-a-year civilian engineer when $200,000,000 has been poured into a project?"

Lovlost Finds Its Way

Many people are still not too clear about what exactly is happening with the gold reserves in the United States. It appears from what President Kennedy has said, and what Secretary of the Treasury Douglas Dillon has tried to do, that the situation is serious.

Nothing could dramatize the plight better than what has happened in Lovlost-by-the-Sea, that tiny European country that has been a bulwark against Communism and friend of the United States since the early days of 1946.

As everyone knows, Lovlost was on the side of the Germans in World War II and was therefore entitled to immediate financial aid from the United States once the hostilities had ceased.

Since 1946 Americans have poured in $150,000,000, until today she has one of the strongest economies in Western Europe. Just before the Marshall Plan went into effect, Lovlost's currency, which is known as the "bardot," was one of the weakest in the world and it took five hundred bardots to make a dollar. Now it takes five hundred dollars to equal one bardot.

It is this strengthening of the bardot that has caused a drain on the United States gold reserves.

To make matters worse Lovlost is a vital link in the chain of Western European defenses, and it has the only carrier pigeon station in NATO.

While the bodies of the pigeons can be handled by Lovlost, only the beaks may be touched by the Americans. It is for this reason that American troops, a private and a corporal, have been stationed in Lovlost.

When President Eisenhower put out his edict that Army dependents had to come home, it raised a bitter fuss in Lovlost. The corporal, who had a wife with him, said nothing, as he was carrying on with a girl from Lovlost. But the private, who was unmarried, was furious, because he was in love with the corporal's wife.

The private protested to the Secretary of Defense, pointing out that if the corporal's wife was sent home, morale among the United States forces in Lovlost would go to hell. But while the Secretary was sympathetic, he said that no matter how noble the cause "no exceptions could be made."

The first step in America's dramatic effort to halt the flow of gold to Lovlost was made.

The next step was even more dramatic. The Army PX in Lovlost, one of the largest in Europe, with five hundred civilian employees, was forbidden to sell Scotch, Canadian whisky, or French champagne. Since the corporal drank beer, and the private made his own liquor from raisins, not too much of a saving was made there. But, as Pentagon officials explained, if the corporal was promoted to sergeant he "might" start drinking Scotch, and it was better to lock the barn door before the horse was stolen.

The third step was by far the most dramatic. The President decided to send the Assistant Secretary of State for Lovlost Affairs to plead with the Lovlost Prime Minister to pay for the costs of maintaining American troops in Lovlost.

In one of the worst slaps to American prestige the Prime Minister turned down the Assistant Secretary flat and said: "Thanks to American aid, the bardot is now the strongest currency in the world. If we helped share the military burden, the bardot would be weakened again and then we would have to ask for an increase in American dollar aid, something we don't want to do, as you yourself say the dollar is in trouble."

The only thing that came out of the Assistant Secretary's visit is that everyone in Lovlost started to panic and exchange dollars for Spanish pesetas.

But as the Assistant Secretary pointed out when he got home, "Lovlost is now aware of our situation and for that reason alone my trip was worthwhile."

Two Happy People

As someone who has made a close study of tourism (there must be a cure for it) I believe I have isolated a certain type of tourist that for some reason has become more prevalent in recent years. This is the type of tourist who hates traveling.

While I've written in the past about individual tourists who hated traveling, I have discovered a new type of tourist who needs somebody else to hate it with.

There are couples now traveling who know before they even leave the United States they're going to hate it. But no matter how bad they think it's going to be, the reality is even worse than their wildest nightmares.

I met a couple like that the other day. They had been touring Europe for a month and they were on the homestretch in Paris. When I caught up with them they couldn't decide which they hated more, Venice or Rome.

"Jane," the man said, "didn't like Rome, but I still thought it was better than Venice."

Jane said: "That's because Harry didn't have the experiences I had. I still maintain I'd rather spend four days in Venice than two in Rome."

"It was that bad, huh?"

Harry said; "Well, it wasn't as bad as Zurich."

Jane agreed: "We both hated Zurich. We didn't have any fun in Zurich at all. It was almost as bad as Copenhagen."

"You didn't like Copenhagen, huh?" I asked.

"Does *anyone* like Copenhagen?" Harry wanted to know. "Would you like to hear what happened to us in Copenhagen?"

"Not particularly," I said.

"We were terribly disappointed in Amsterdam," Jane said.

"Almost as disappointed as we were in Brussels," Harry said. "We couldn't wait till we got out of there and got to London."

"Which," said Jane, "turned out to be dreadful."

"The funny thing," said Harry, "I hated it, but I thought Jane liked it, so I said I liked it."

"And," said Jane, "I thought Harry liked it so I didn't tell him I hated it. You can imagine our surprise when we discovered we both hated it. If we had known it at the beginning we would have left right away."

"But where would you have gone?" I asked.

"Not to Monte Carlo, that's for sure," Harry said.

"I don't see what Princess Grace sees in *that place,*" Jane said.

"You can have the entire Riviera as far as we're concerned," Harry added. "Just try to get a good dry martini on the Riviera. Just try."

"I know some good places where you can get a dry martini," I said.

"You've been living abroad so long," Harry said, "you don't know what a good dry martini is."

"Well, what about Paris?" I foolishly asked.

"The worst," said Jane. "The people are so unfriendly and the prices are high, and I don't see what there is that's so special about Paris."

"Jane and I hate it," Harry said.

"You two seem to hate the same things," I said.

"Well, we know what we don't like," Jane said.

Harry said: "Europe's overrated. But we're glad we came because now we can understand why other people don't like it either."

I left the couple on the Champs Élysées. Harry was explaining to Jane why he didn't like the Arc de Triomphe, and Jane was telling Harry why she didn't like the Place de la Concorde. You couldn't find two happier people.

The Best-Dressed Man in Hong Kong

This city, which has now become the PX to the world, has a population of 3,239,548 people, of whom 3,239,546 earn their living as tailors.

The making of suits in Hong Kong is the most important industry in the country, and in the struggle for the backs of men, this British crown colony looks like Gimbels basement on a Saturday afternoon before Father's Day.

I didn't realize how important it was to have a suit made in Hong Kong until, after I took off from Rangoon, the stewardess gave me a police card to fill out. It demanded my name, my nationality, my passport number, and wanted to know if I preferred a single- or double-breasted vent in my jacket. I dutifully filled it out and gave it back.

When I landed at the Hong Kong airport I was whisked through the health authorities and sent to customs. The customs inspector asked me: "Do you have anything to declare?" I hesitated for a moment and then decided to come clean. "Yes," I said, "one shoulder is slightly higher than the other." He took his chalk and made a few marks on my sleeve. "Don't worry," he told me, "it will mean an extra fitting, but we'll be able to correct it."

On the airport bus going into town the bus driver, while stopping for a red light, showed me several bolts of cloth. I selected a Dacron-wool mixture which he himself approved of. At the hotel, while I was signing the register, I had my first fitting by the bell captain, who called off the measurements to the room clerk.

Since I had already selected the material on the airport bus, the reception clerk told me there would be no delay in getting my room. On the elevator I had my second fitting, and then while I was waiting for my baggage to be brought up, I had the final fitting.

Before I could get my suitcase open, the completed suit was delivered with sincere apologies for delays and inconveniences caused because the material had to be pre-shrunk before it could be cut.

Since then it's been one fitting after another. I don't really need so many suits, but because I bought one I've been forced to buy the others.

For example, the first evening I was in town I went into a drugstore to buy a toothbrush. While the druggist was wrapping it up he inquired where the new suit I was wearing was made. I said at the hotel, and he shook his head sadly. "They gave you a split sleeve with a slanted cuff and flap pockets."

"Is there anything I can do about it?" I asked nervously.

"Well, I'm not a doctor," he said, "but I'll see what I can do."

He took a bolt of English herringbone cloth out of one of the medicine cabinets and let me look at the magazines while he cut the pattern. In half an hour the suit was ready, and he was so proud of his work he told me: "You look so nice in my suit you can now meet a beautiful dance girl at Princess Garden."

He gave me the address and I rushed over. The Princess Garden is a famous Hong Kong restaurant and dance hall. You pay a dollar and forty cents an hour to dance with a beautiful Chinese girl or ten dollars for four hours, whichever is more.

It must have been my new suit, because as soon as I was seated a woman who looked like a combination of Suzie Wong and the Dragon Lady came over to the table and sat down.

"You beautiful American man," she said, taking my hand in hers. "We dance for a little while and then go to my place."

"Well, really," I said feverishly.

"Don't worry," she said, "I make you very happy."

An hour later we arrived at her apartment. She opened the door and took my hand and led me in. Then she turned on the lights. Seated in every corner of the room was a member of her family at a sewing machine. Her father started taking the measurements and damned if I didn't wind up with another suit.

Italians Excel in Pinching Miss Taylor

There were many ways to see the Olympic Games. One of the most interesting but also the most dangerous was to go to one of the events with Miss Elizabeth Taylor. Miss Taylor was there only as a spectator, and could no longer compete in the Olympics for the United States because she lost her amateur standing by signing to play Cleopatra against Marc Antony for a cool million dollars.

The actress stopped off in Rome with her husband, Mr. Eddie Fisher, and her doctor, Rex Kennemer. Although the Italians love sports, they love women more, and Miss Taylor received her share of admiration from the hot-blooded Romans.

Because of the heat she had only been attending the evening events, mostly water polo. It wasn't that Miss Taylor was a great water-polo enthusiast. It was just that by the time she got ready, water polo was the only sport still going on.

One night I was invited to attend the water-polo matches with her, and it was quite an event—not the water polo, but going with her.

When we arrived at the swimming stadium the crowds immediately recognized her and surged forward. Helpful hands reached out and touched her and Miss Taylor shouted to Mr. Fisher: "Someone touched my chest."

"Who?" Mr. Fisher wanted to know.

All the Italians around us held up their hands to show it wasn't them.

We moved forward slowly and suddenly Miss Taylor yelled again: "Someone is pinching me."

Mr. Fisher shouted: "Who?"

"I don't know," she shouted, "I'm being pinched in the back."

"Where?" the doctor wanted to know.

"You know where," Miss Taylor said.

"Bella, bella," the Italians shouted.

Mr. Fisher yelled to me: "You protect her in the back, I'll protect her in the front, and the doc can take the flanks."

The flanks at this point were the most vulnerable and not only the Italians but players from Spain and France had joined the sport.

The scoring I figured out later went something like this. A pinch on the lower part of Miss Taylor's flanks was worth one point. On the lower part of her back was three points, and on her chest, which in Italy is the equivalent of a touchdown, was worth six points.

Since I was covering the rear I had the job of being the goalie. Several fingers intended for Miss Taylor pinched me instead. "You're not

allowed to pinch the goalie," I cried out in pain. But officials were looking at Miss Taylor and paying no attention to me.

Slowly we made our way forward. The Italians had sent in substi-
tutes and Miss Taylor screamed again: "They're still pinching me."

"Walk sideways," I suggested.

But this didn't work either, and the Italians were scoring all over the
place.

At this point the photographers joined in and they kept stopping us
so that they could take pictures of the event—which was certainly an
Olympic pinching record.

It must have been twenty-five minutes before someone finally blew a
whistle. It turned out to be a policeman, and the game was over.

The final score, Mr. Fisher told me the next morning after making
the tally, was 334 pinches and 12 touchdowns against the Americans,
the worst beating the United States has ever taken from Italy since the
Olympic Games started.

The Italians have asked for a return match but Miss Taylor refused
so far to give them one. If she does she's going to have to find a new
goalie, because I haven't been able to sit down since.

Hagerty Was Here

Among the more distinguished members of the press who were in
Paris when President John F. Kennedy arrived last spring was Mr.
James Hagerty, the former press secretary of the former President of
the United States.

Mr. Hagerty came in connection with his new job as vice-president
in charge of public affairs of the American Broadcasting Company.

Now, a lot of my colleagues were rubbing their hands with glee at
the thought of my meeting Mr. Hagerty again, because the last time
we saw each other was in November 1958, in Paris, at which time we
had words, many of them printed in the world's newspapers.

If my colleagues expected me to resume these words when Mr. Hagerty arrived, they were disappointed. I have nothing but warm feelings
for Mr. Hagerty, and he has done more for me than any living Presidential press secretary I know.

Look at it from my standpoint. Before Mr. Hagerty decided to single
me out from the vast multitude of the press corps, and said I wrote "unadulterated rot," I was a poor, struggling syndicated columnist who
didn't know where his next newspaper was coming from. My wife
owned a cloth coat and my children had to go to public schools.

Although we had a nurse and cook, we could only afford a part-time cleaning woman. Things were very rough for us, and I was thinking of chucking the whole thing and getting a high-paying job with the CIA.

Then Mr. Hagerty, as he himself has since admitted, lost his temper, and by the strangest quirk of luck he lost it on me.

There I was, sitting in the briefing hall of the Crillon Hotel, jammed in with the cream of the White House press corps, surrounded by men who not only had so much more experience and stature, but some who had triple my syndication—and suddenly Mr. Hagerty said the magic words "unadulterated rot."

At first I couldn't believe he was talking about me, not because I don't write unadulterated rot, but because I was a stranger to Mr. Hagerty, and the rest of the reporters were his friends.

As George Dixon, the syndicated Washington columnist, wrote at the time, with jealousy and bitterness: "I've been writing unadulterated rot for years and Hagerty's never picked on me."

Well, you don't look a gift horse in the mouth and, I said to myself, if the press secretary of the President of the United States wants to help me with my career why should I interfere with his plans? I kept quiet and thanks to Mr. Hagerty I picked up fourteen newspapers who had no interest in the column before, my wife now has a new mink coat, the children go to a private school, and we now have a *fulltime* cleaning woman. If it hadn't been for Mr. Hagerty none of this would have happened, so, I ask you, why should I be mad at him?

The guy who could do me some good by getting mad at me is Pierre Salinger, President Kennedy's press secretary. Just one word about unadulterated rot from him and I'd be able to afford to send the children to Harvard.

But it's too much to hope for. Anyway, there is no reason for Salinger to help me, because he probably figures, like everybody else, that Hagerty's done enough for me already.

So if anyone thought there was going to be any fireworks when Mr. Hagerty came over they were sorely disappointed. As a matter of fact what I really would have liked to have done was take him to the Lido with my wife—fur coat and all.

The Smashing Tailors of Beersheba

There has been a great deal of excitement in the United States and Israel over suspicions that Israel might be working on the development of an atomic bomb.

Apparently United States State Department officials are furious because, when the Israelis built their atomic energy plant twenty miles outside of Beersheba, they told the United States it was a textile plant. The United States was kept in the dark until recently, when CIA photographs revealed that the building wasn't what it was cracked up to be.

It was just by chance that the Americans didn't find out the secret six months ago.

I heard the following story from an Israeli taxi driver high in government circles.

It seems that an important American diplomat stationed in Israel needed a new suit, and since someone told him about the new textile plant he decided to go out there and see if he could possibly get one wholesale.

As he drove south toward Beersheba, Israeli intelligence agents were alerted and a half-hour before he got there the head of the atomic energy plant was notified that an American was coming to buy a suit.

A hurried conference was called with the other scientists to decide what to do. They were afraid that if they refused him entrance he might get suspicious and start prying into the plant, so the scientists agreed the only sensible thing to do was let the diplomat in and pretend that nothing was going on.

The scientists all removed their white smocks, rolled up their sleeves, and stuck pins and needles in their vests.

When the American diplomat arrived, he was immediately ushered into a large room where he saw men cutting suit forms out of asbestos patterns.

The head of the plant greeted the diplomat. "What can I do for you, sir?" he asked.

"I was wondering if I could buy a suit wholesale?"

"Naturally. That is what we make here. What did you have in mind?"

"Well, what do you have?"

The head of the plant said: "Perhaps you would like something in cobalt blue? Or maybe a nice uranium brown? How about a cosmic gray double-breasted, with pin-striped particles. It's the latest thing."

"No," said the diplomat, "I don't want anything flashy. You wouldn't have a light gray flannel?"

"Perhaps," the head said. "Please, let us take your measurements. Just go in the fitting room behind that six-foot wall of lead and take off your clothes."

The diplomat went in. "These fitting rooms are very well protected," he said.

The head of the plant smiled. "Our customers like privacy and there's so much activity around here that we don't like things to pile up. Just a minute, I'll call the fitter. Shimshon, would you please come in with the measuring instruments."

One of the scientists rushed in with a Geiger counter, a slide rule, and two robot arms. The head of the plant took a pad and said: "Shimshon, call off the customer's measurements."

Shimshon yelled out: "Ten, nine, eight, seven, six, five, four, three, two, one, oi!"

"What kind of measurements are those?" the diplomat wanted to know.

"Enough with the jokes, Shimshon," the head said angrily, "let's have the measurements."

Shimshon chuckled and called out: "Waist U–235; relativity good chest; there is a hexagonal prism in the left shoulder; the right sleeve needs reactor."

"What about the lapels?" the diplomat wanted to know.

"Don't worry," Shimshon said, "we'll smash them down if they're too large."

Shimshon measured the pants and then the diplomat put on his clothes again. "Don't you have any materials to show me?" the diplomat asked.

"Are you interested in camel's hair?" the head of the plant wanted to know.

"I might be," the diplomat said. "Do you have any swatches?"

The head of the plant said: "We'll do better than that. Kishon, the man is interested in a camel's-hair suit."

One of the other scientists ran out of the shop and five minutes later brought in a camel which he had borrowed from an Arab nomad.

The head of the plant said proudly: "Here we don't fool around with swatches. Here the customer sees the entire camel."

"All right," the diplomat said. "Can I charge it?"

"Negative or positive?" the head of the plant wanted to know.

"I don't care," the diplomat said. "When should I come for my next fitting?"

The head of the plant said: "Why should you, an important man, drive to Beersheba again? Our tailor from our retail store in Tel Aviv will call on you. You of course will be entitled to our wholesale price. But please, kind sir, *do not* tell your friends about us because we have too much work now, and if we take any more orders the plant will explode."

Cat on a Hot Tin Something

Unaccustomed as I am to use this space for classified advertisements, I wish to announce there is one two-month-old cat available *absolutely free* to any cat fancier who will take him.

I was asked to make this announcement by my son, who told me as soon as I got home: "Antonio says his mother is going to kill his cat unless we take him."

Antonio is my son's best friend, aged seven. He is known not only to his friends, but also to his father and mother as "the Tiger." Not since Clemenceau was called "the Tiger" has the name fitted anyone so well.

When my son broke the news about Antonio's cat I was visibly shaken.

"We can't take the cat," I told him. "The landlady won't let us have a cat."

"Well," my son said accusingly, "if we don't take him, Tiger's mother is going to kill it and it will be your fault."

"If Tiger's mother is going to kill his cat," I argued, "it's her fault."

"No," he argued, "Tiger said if we take the cat his mother won't kill it, so it's not her fault, it's yours."

"I'm sorry, but we can't take the cat."

"Well," our son said, "Tiger is going to call at seven o'clock and you better tell him because I don't want to."

"Why doesn't his nurse give the cat to someone?"

"She can't," my son replied, "because she's in the hospital."

"Why is she in the hospital?"

"Because Tiger kicked her in the back of the leg."

At seven o'clock sharp the phone rang and it came as no surprise to me to find Antonio on the other end.

He didn't pause for formalities. "Are you going to take my cat?" he demanded.

"We can't take the cat, Tiger. Our landlady won't let us."

"Did Joel tell you if you didn't take the cat my mother would kill it?"

"Yes, he did," I said.

"And? . . ."

"We still can't take it. Look, Tiger, why don't you give it to a café. All French cafés have cats."

"No," he said. "He'd jump over everything and break the glasses and bottles. He broke my mother's best vase last week, and he knocked over a lamp yesterday, and today he scratched a table, and my mother says she's going to kill it."

"Tell me, Tiger, just out of curiosity, how did you get the cat?"

"A boy gave it to me. His mother didn't want him to have it."

"I have an idea," I said. "Why don't you just take it downstairs and put it out on the street?"

"No," Antonio said. "If I did that he'd run away."

"I see your point," I agreed. "Well, why don't you call Cora (a mutual friend of Joel's and Antonio's) and tell her if she doesn't take the cat, your mother will kill it."

"I did," Antonio said, "and Cora's mother said it was all right with her."

"To take the cat?"

"No," Antonio said. "To kill it."

"Well, I'm sorry I can't do anything for you, Tiger. You know how landladies are."

The Tiger then asked to speak to my son, and after their conversation Joel told everyone I refused to take Antonio's cat.

I am now known throughout the entire household as "the Cat-Killer" and nobody has spoken to me since.

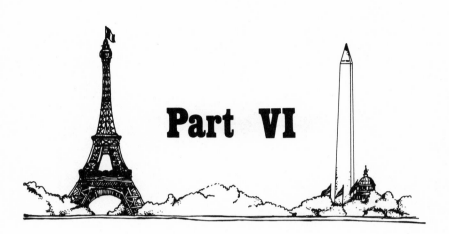

Part VI

Dinner Guest for Rent

A few years ago I wrote about the shortage of guests on the Riviera, and pointed out that while everyone had a villa or a yacht, the natural resources in house guests and boat guests were drying up fast, and unless a guest conservation program was instituted, the people along the Riviera would soon find themselves dining and sailing alone. Well, they scoffed at my warning, but this year the Riviera is facing its worst guest shortage since Elsa Maxwell tried to get a passenger list together for a cruise of the Greek islands.

The profiteering in guests this year is unimaginable.

I know, because that's how I was paying for my vacation. It happened by accident, but if a fellow doesn't take advantage of a situation, he'll wind up spending his own money on the Riviera, and who wants to do that?

It seems that fellow columnist John Crosby showed up in Monte Carlo and innocently asked me if I could get him invited to the Red Cross dinner and gala at which Sammy Davis, Jr., was going to entertain.

I pretended it would be difficult but said I'd do my best. What I knew but John didn't was that the ratio of women to men along the Riviera was six to one, and hostesses were willing to pay anything for a single man to sit at one of their tables.

An hour later I was down at the beach making discreet inquiries. I was tipped off that a Mrs. Max Kettner of New York had three extra women for the gala and was getting desperate.

"How would you like to have Crosby at your table?" I asked her.

"Bing Crosby?" she asked.

"Listen," I said, "if I had Bing Crosby, I wouldn't be here—I would be negotiating at the Palace with Princess Grace.

"My boy's John Crosby, but he's been a helluva dinner guest in his time. He's eaten at Bill Paley's house, he'd broken bread with Mrs. Leland Hayward, he'd had coffee with Desi and Lucy twice. This guy is no bum—he's Yale '36, and that gives him a presold table audience right there."

Mrs. Kettner wet her lips. "How much are you asking for him?"

"It depends," I said. "Do you want him for cocktails before the dinner?"

"What's the difference?" Mrs. Kettner wanted to know.

"Well, I can book him for cocktails before the gala at the Hotel de Paris with another party, and that would cut down the price for you. He could join you for dinner around ten o'clock."

"I think I should have him for cocktails," Mrs. Kettner said. "But I'd better warn you that I don't want to pay more than $1,500 for the evening."

"Fifteen hundred dollars?" I said. "Why, I turned down $2,000 from Sam Speigel for Crosby to lunch with him on his yacht, and Crosby didn't have to put a black tie on either. If you're going to start talking chicken feed I'd rather have Crosby stay in his room tonight."

"I'll pay $1,750," Mrs. Kettner said.

"This is ridiculous. I couldn't get you a golf caddy for $1,750 tonight. Look, Crosby's a syndicated columnist, he's a name. You pair him up with one of your female guests and she's going to be impressed—this guy's got class. I'm not going to sell him out for a song."

"Well, how much do you want?" Mrs. Kettner said.

"The same as Sammy Davis, Jr., is getting for entertaining tonight," I said.

"But that's outrageous!" Mrs. Kettner replied.

"Look. Entertainers are a dime a dozen," I said. "Where are you going to find dinner guests at this late date? After all, Davis will only be on stage entertaining; Crosby will actually be at your table sitting with you."

Mrs. Kettner finally agreed, provided Crosby also would come for cocktails.

I pocketed the money and then rushed back to tell Crosby the news that I had managed to get him invited to the gala.

Tears of gratitude poured from his eyes. "How can I ever thank you?" he said.

"Forget it, kid," I said, punching him lightly in the shoulder. "You can do a favor for me sometime."

To this day Crosby doesn't know how much he is worth. He still thinks I did him a good turn. If I only had three Crosbys a season, I could make enough dough to retire for the rest of the year.

La Real Dolce Vita

The film *La Dolce Vita* has had a great effect on tourists visiting Rome. It also, I discovered, has had a great effect on Romans. The picture, which graphically describes the decadent life of the modern-day Romans, has forced many of them into roles in real life that they never had any intention of playing.

The other night I was sitting in the Hotel Excelsior bar when I overheard two Italians, presumably man and wife, talking to each other. They were speaking English, because I don't understand Italian.

This is what they were saying:

"Gino," the wife said, "I'm so tired tonight. You sure we gotta go to the orgy?"

"I'm tired too, Carola, but we said we would go, and it's at Claudia's house. You know how mad she gets when she goes to all the trouble of giving an orgy and then the people don't show up."

"But," protested Carola, "her orgies are so dull. She always makes the pasta with the hashish in it and it's so heavy, I feel sick for days."

"Is that what she puts in the pasta? I thought it was heroin. But it's your fault, Carola. I told you the next time Claudia calls to tell her we already had to go to an orgy somewhere else. How come you no listen to what I tell you?"

"Because," Carola said, "when Claudia called she said: 'What night are you and Gino free for an orgy?' She don't ask me to come on a certain night. What could I say? She's giving it for her cousin's friend from America, because they gave her a barbecue party when she was in Texas."

Gino said: "Well let me tell you something right now. I'm fed up going out every night. Why can't we stay home and read the newspapers and watch the television and maybe play gin rummy like the other Italian people?"

"Because," said Carola, "we're the *dolce vita* crowd. It's expected of us. Once the tourist season is over I promise you, Gino, I make you a nice pizza and we stay home and we play a game of scrabble."

"And another thing. I'm getting tired of driving around fast in an Alfa Romeo. I would like a nice small car like a Fiat."

"You can't drive up to an orgy at somebody's house in a Fiat," Carola protested. "What will our friends say? You know how spiteful they are. I don't like an Alfa Romeo any more than you do."

Carola continued: "Incidentally, Gino, we're going to have to give an orgy pretty soon ourselves. We owe so many people, they're starting to talk. I was in the supermarket the other day and Sophia said: 'How come you and Gino, you always go to the orgies but you never give one yourself?'"

Gino said: "Okay, but let's do something different instead of the usual stuff."

"Why don't we give it at the Fountain of Trevi?" Carola said excitedly. "Then people could throw each other in the fountain with no clothes on."

"That's been done," Gino said. "The Marquise de l'Acqua Minerale did it last year. You caught a cold. Don't you remember?"

"Why don't we show the movies we took last summer in our palazzo in Venice?" Carola suggested.

"People don't like to look at home movies. It's a big bore. What about a big costume party; everyone wears a mask and we give a prize for the best costume."

"It's never been done before," Carola said. "Gino, you're a genius."

Gino smiled: "You make up the list of people we owe, and I'll call the caterer tomorrow morning."

"Gino, you think if we ask people to come with clothes on they'll accept? You know how prudish some of the *dolce vita* bunch are."

"You give the people free gin and marijuana and they'll always come to a party."

"I guess we gotta go to Claudia's," Carola said. "But let's leave early. As soon as they start throwing pillow feathers at each other we go."

Gino said: "Okay, but don't let anyone throw you in the swimming pool or we'll never get home."

Happy Birthday to You

You can't pick up a paper these days without reading about some country sending a stiff note to another country concerning some diplomatic matter such as Berlin, Bizerte, Kuwait, or Outer Mongolia. While a great deal of publicity is given to the notes themselves, no one knows who actually writes them or how they are conceived. But it's not hard to guess what happens. Let us suppose we are in Moscow at the Ministry of Foreign Affairs. Mr. Gromyko, the Russian Foreign Minister, picks up the phone and says: "Get me the Stiff Note Department."

It takes a few minutes to get through and Mr. Gromyko is furious.

"Why didn't you answer the phone, Comrade Vladimir?" Mr. Gromyko says angrily.

"I'm sorry, Comrade Minister," Vladimir replies, "I was just rejecting a stiff note from Turkey in no uncertain terms."

"Well, forget about Turkey for a moment," Mr. Gromyko says.

"The Premier wants you to send a stiff note to the United States, France, Great Britain, and West Germany, and he says you might as well scare the hell out of little Denmark while you're at it."

"Is it a new note or a stiff note rejecting one of their stiff notes?" Vladimir wants to know.

"A little of both," Mr. Gromyko replies. "We want you to threaten them with the super bomb, germ warfare, rockets, nuclear warheads, and total annihilation. But, Vladimir, leave room open for negotiation."

"I got it, Comrade Minister. The usual stuff about Western warmongers and their hostile acts, for which they must bear the consequences."

"That's the idea, Vladimir, but don't forget to mention that their previous note concerning Berlin was completely unjustified and their reply to our note, which was a reply to their original stiff note, was an affront to all peace-loving socialist countries."

Vladimir says: "Should I add it as a P.S. or in the main body of our note?"

"Put it in the first paragraph," Mr. Gromyko says. "If they reject the note, which they in all certainty will, they may never get as far as the P.S."

"Is there anything else, Comrade Minister?"

"You might put in a plug for Titov and Gagarin while you're at it. The boys have been off the front pages for a few months and they're getting pretty made about it."

"While I've got you on the phone, Comrade Minister, we're having a lot of trouble with the stiff note we're sending the West concerning the closing off of East Berlin. No matter how we write it we still can't explain why we had to cut off the city so the East German refugees wouldn't flee."

"But, Comrade Vladimir, I told you to put in the note the reason we shut off East Berlin was not to keep the East Germans from fleeing to the West, but to keep the West Germans from fleeing to the East. East

Germany is a socialist paradise and it can't afford to absorb the masses of the decadent capitalistic system who are disillusioned with their false high standard of living."

"Yes, Comrade Minister, we got all that in the note. But it's going to sound weak to the neutral countries, particularly since there have been so many pictures of East Germans fleeing to the West but no pictures of West Germans fleeing to the East."

"I'll tell Ulbricht to dress up some of the Volkspolizei in capitalist clothes and you'll have your pictures."

"Thank you, Comrade Minister. Will there be any other stiff notes this week?"

"Just send out the usual form note on disarmament in the regular pouch. There's no sense wasting money on air mail. Have we got any notes on hand threatening Japan this week for its military alliance with the United States?"

"Comrade Sergueivitch wrote a beauty, but because of Comrade Mikoyan's visit we didn't send it out this week."

"What about a stiff note to all the Latin American countries for accepting U.S. financial aid?"

"Comrade Castro asked if he could send it instead. He said it will look stiffer if it's written to them in Spanish."

"All right, but follow it up with a note supporting Castro's note."

"Yes, Comrade. Will that be all?"

"That's all for today. Oh, one more thing. Send a stiff note to the Premier of Finland wishing him a happy birthday."

Seventeen Years in France

David Schoenbrun, the Columbia Broadcasting System's correspondent who has been stationed in Paris for the last seventeen years and has become one of the leading American experts on French affairs, is leaving Paris to take over as chief of bureau of the CBS Washington office. It will be a very difficult transformation for Mr. Schoenbrun, because one gets in the habit, after a while, of thinking in certain political terms, and after seventeen years it's hard to shake them.

Mr. Schoenbrun came in to see me before leaving and asked me if I would look over his first television broadcast script from Washington, D.C.

He wanted to know if I had any suggestions.

"Well, Dave," I told him quite honestly, "as you know, I'm not up on television, but are you sure you want to refer to the Democratic Party as the Radical Left-Wing Government Majority?"

Mr. Schoenbrun said he wasn't sure.

"And you shouldn't really call the Republican Party the Fanatical Right-Wing Opposition clique."

"What do you call them?"

"The Democratic and Republican parties."

"That's all?"

"Now down here, Dave, are you certain you want to refer to the Daughters of the American Revolution as a terrorist organization?"

"You think that's too strong?"

"There could be repercussions. Let me see now. The fact that President Kennedy can't get through his old-age medical bill should not necessarily be called the worst government crisis since the question of the abolition of slavery. I think you're going out on a limb by predicting the overthrow of the Kennedy government if he doesn't get a vote of confidence on this. You see, David, in America the President stays in for four years, whether the National Assembly is hostile or not."

"That long?" Mr. Schoenbrun whistled in amazement.

"Also, David, where you're discussing some dissatisfaction among certain officers with the plan to modernize the Army, I don't think you can call them mutinous Army elements or predict that because of their disagreement there will be a putsch in the armed services in the near future."

"Well, it stands to reason," Mr. Schoenbrun said, "that if the U.S. Army isn't happy it will do *something*."

"No, David, in America when an officer is unhappy he resigns and joins the John Birch Society and goes around the country denouncing the United Nations."

"Why doesn't Kennedy throw the dissident officers in jail under Article Sixteen?"

"There is no Article Sixteen, Dave."

"No Article Sixteen? Well, how can the President deal with the rebels and the clandestine revolutionaries who are trying to topple him?"

"It's all done through Congress, David."

"What's Congress?"

"That's the lawmaking body of the American Government. You see, you've been living in France a long time, but in the United States Congress still has a lot of power."

"Well *that's* silly."

"It certainly complicates things," I admitted. "And it doesn't make your job any easier covering both Kennedy *and* Congress, but I think you're going a little strong when you refer to Kennedy as the savior of America and when you say that if he doesn't get his tariff policy through, blood will run through the streets of Washington."

"Oh, that's just an expression," Schoenbrun said. "We use it all the time about Paris. The television audiences like it."

"I'm not sure they'll like it about Washington. Otherwise, David, the script is fine. I might warn you though, that OAS in America stands for the Organization of American States and FLN stands for the Filadelphia, Lackawanna and Nashville Railroad."

Secretaries Run U.S.

Every time I come back to the United States for a short visit something strikes me about the American scene that I hadn't noticed before.

This time the thing that hit me was how powerful the American secretary has become in the American way of life.

I hadn't realized it until I tried to make an appointment with a successful college chum who was pulling down around $40,000 a year in a big company (which shall remain nameless, as his secretary would never forgive him for speaking to me about her).

After several attempts I finally managed to get a luncheon date and he apologized profusely for the difficulty I had experienced.

"You don't understand what's going on in the United States," he told me, looking around to make sure no one was listening. "The secretaries are taking over. No one can get through to me if my secretary decides she doesn't want him to.

"She makes all my appointments, she decides when I can take a vacation, if it's safe for me to make a speech in another town. She watches me constantly, and I swear I'm scared silly of her."

"Why don't you fire her?" I asked him.

He looked at me incredulously. "You must be out of your mind. You can't fire your secretary. She knows where all the bodies are buried. She's my espionage agent to let me know what's going on in the company.

"Without the information she picks up from the other secretaries I wouldn't be able to last a week with the company. Besides, frankly, I don't understand what I'm supposed to be doing in the company, and she does."

"I can see your point," I said, watching him drink his third martini.

He stared into the glass. "The only thing is, I wish she wouldn't hate my wife so."

"Does she hate your wife?"

"All secretaries hate their bosses' wives," he said. "I don't think it has anything to do with jealousy. It's just that secretaries think wives are so damn inefficient. They feel that wives also take up too much of their bosses' time. My secretary thinks that I could do a much better job if I didn't have to go home to my wife for dinner. And she believes my weekends with my family are a complete waste of time. She doesn't see how I can live with a woman who doesn't understand the company.

"Also, since my secretary pays all the bills, she thinks my wife is sort of a spendthrift. But to be honest, I'm so browbeaten by my secretary during the day, with her constant nagging and efficiency, that I really look forward to going home to my wife at night. I look on my wife as a sort of a mistress, the only one who understands me."

"What does your wife think about your secretary?"

"She's afraid of my secretary. My wife has to be nice to her, because if she isn't, my secretary won't let my wife speak to me. As it is, my secretary only lets her get through 50 per cent of the time. The other 50 per cent she just says I'm in an important meeting, as if to imply my wife should know better than to call the office when world-shaking events are going on behind the company's locked doors."

"I didn't realize secretaries were that powerful," I said sympathetically.

"You don't know the half of it. Look, if your secretary catches a cold and is out two days, you might as well shoot yourself. But if your wife catches pneumonia, all you have to do is come to the office and tell your secretary to notify Blue Cross."

Charity Starts in Florida

Of all the communities in the United States there is probably none as social as Palm Beach, Florida. This sun-drenched, diamond-studded, Rolls-Royce-clogged stretch of real estate has more cocktail and dinner parties per capita than any other town in the free world.

There is a society editor for every five families in the colony, as opposed to the national average of one for every hundred families. But Palm Beach is not social just for the sake of being social. All the society activity down here has to do with raising money for some charity. It is very gauche to have a party for the sake of a party, and therefore everyone is in the business of giving a party for a cause.

It's gotten so that two people can't have breakfast together without making a donation to an orphanage.

As a matter of fact, while there is no shortage of parties and balls in Palm Beach, there is a shortage of diseases to give them for. The old-timers in Palm Beach have all the good diseases tied up. The first families of this city have a monopoly on heart, cancer, cerebral palsy, and mental health, and a newcomer who is trying to crash society down here has very few illnesses left to choose from.

The other day I asked four friends to have lunch with me, and one of them, Mrs. Paul Ames, asked: "What's it for?"

"Nothing," I said. "We just want to have lunch."

"You can't just have lunch without a reason," she said. "If you can come up with a good disease, we'll accept."

I called the local Palm Beach hospital and asked them if there were any diseases that there hadn't been benefits held for this season.

"You're calling awfully late," the woman said. "The only thing we still have open is malaria and yellow fever."

"Is arthritis taken?" I asked.

"It was one of the first to go. We can't give you diabetes or hay fever, either."

"Well, is there some hospital I could raise money for?"

"We have an animal shelter in Cheyenne, Wyoming, that hasn't been spoken for."

"Okay, I'll give a luncheon for that. What do I do now?"

"You have to form a committee."

"What for?"

"To get your wife's picture in the newspaper. Why else would you want to give a benefit?"

"That's true," I said.

"Just call the local newspaper and they'll send a photographer over in ten minutes."

I formed a committee consisting of my wife as honorary chairman, Mrs. Ames as program chairman, and Mrs. Howard Gould, of Cincinnati, as decorations chairman.

After the newspaper photographers took their pictures, I took the women and their husbands in to lunch in the coffee shop of the Palm Beach Towers, where we all were staying.

Unfortunately the coffee shop was very crowded and we had to share our table with three other couples whom we didn't know.

But it worked out fine because the three couples each pledged $1,000 for our animal shelter in Cheyenne and our party in turn bought

$3,000 in raffle tickets that they were selling for a retired lifeguards' home in Seattle, Washington.

Everybody Is Doing It

Everybody I talked to was impressed by Mrs. John F. Kennedy's television tour of the White House, and I believe Mrs. Kennedy has made a great contribution to the American home because she has made people conscious of their own surroundings and furniture.

Probably no one was more influenced by the program than my own sister who lives in Kew Gardens, Long Island. I went over to her apartment on the Sunday after Mrs. Kennedy showed the White House, and my sister was waiting at the door to give me a guided tour.

"Thank you for coming," she said. "I'd like to show you around because I feel that's the only way people can understand our heritage."

"Well, it's awfully kind of you to let us come here, Mrs. Jaffe. Where shall we begin?"

"I think we ought to start with the East Room," she said. "We call it the East Room because it overlooks the Eighth Avenue subway and Queens Boulevard—at least it did until someone built an apartment across from us and blocked the view. The East Room was originally intended as an audience room where we could meet our in-laws, our insurance agent, and our son's teacher when he got in trouble at school.

"But now it's gradually become associated with other events. Our large receptions are held here because, as you can see, this room can hold as many as twelve people at one time."

"Would you describe some of the furniture to me?" I asked her.

"I'd be delighted. That couch over there, the one with the stuffing coming out of it, is an early Franklin D. Roosevelt period piece donated to us by Aunt Molly, who said she was going to throw it out anyway. Aunt Molly used it all during the Depression and it has a great deal of historical interest.

"That lamp over there is a rare pre-Pearl Harbor Macy basement special. It was a wedding gift donated by Mr. and Mrs. Arthur Gordon, of Forest Hills, New York, and there are only 65,900 of them left in the United States."

"Is that the oldest thing in the house?" I asked her.

"No, the hot-water heater is the oldest thing in our house, but that's in another room."

We walked into what my sister calls the Blue Room, because this is the room in the house that depresses her the most.

"There are many things in this room that do have a historical interest," she said. "That bed there, for example, is an early Truman Gimbel's four-poster, which was donated to us by the Friendly Long Island Finance Company. It was given to us on the day that Mr. Truman had a fight with a Washington music critic over his daughter's voice, so naturally it has sentimental value. Actually, it's been taken away twice, but it has always turned up again after we made the payments."

"Those are lovely paintings on the wall," I said.

"Yes, they are," Mrs. Jaffe said. "This one here, which is a snow scene, was donated by Uncle Oscar, of Brooklyn, New York, who painted it himself and gave it to us as a present on the condition we would never sell it. There were a couple of numbers on the paintings that he forgot to fill in, but otherwise it's very decorative.

"I'd like to point out one more thing, and that is our President Monroe television set, which is probably the most valuable antique in the room. The television tube for the set was made by a famous glassblower who died somewhere around 1856. Every week we have someone come in to restore it. My husband believes if you have a piece of antique furniture you should never let it go."

"We're running out of time," I said. "Is there any other room you would like to show us?"

"There is the Red Room, where my thirteen-year-old son David holds his state receptions."

She led me toward it, but when she opened the door she slammed it closed immediately. "If I've told that damn kid once I've told him a million times to clean up his room."

"Well, are there any other rooms in the house we could visit?"

She looked at me funny. "What other rooms? That's all we got."

On the Art of Stealing

I attended a very interesting art exhibition in the south of France held by a gang of art thieves to celebrate the fiftieth anniversary of the stealing of the "Mona Lisa." Because they didn't want any publicity, the exhibition was held in the hideout of Louie the Huile, who specializes in second-story thefts of twentieth-century masters.

Each room of the hideout featured a different period, and under each painting was the title of the picture, the name of the artist, the present owner, and the name of the person, or museum, it was stolen from.

Next to each picture sat a bodyguard with a machine gun.

"We had a hard time," Louie the Huile told me, "getting these guys to loan their important thefts, because the underworld collectors are becoming so frantic about art that they're starting to steal from each other. There are just so many good pictures around, and because of all the publicity about recent art thefts, it's getting more difficult for the guys to complete their collections."

"That's a beautiful Goya over there," I said.

"Yes," said Louie. "It's probably the best 'Duke of Wellington' in existence. It was loaned to us by the Piccadilly Lock Pickers. They never thought they'd get it out of the country. Frankly, I'm not much for eighteenth-century masters, but the English are queer for them, and each to his own taste."

"What's that fellow over there doing?"

"That's Arnaud La Gouache. He pulled the St. Tropez job, but he's still kicking himself because he didn't take the Seurat on the second floor. I keep telling him the Vuillard and the Derain were worth all his trouble, but Arnaud has another Vuillard from a previous job and he doesn't have Seurat. He keeps berating himself for being in such a hurry."

We came into a large crowded room devoted to nothing but Cézannes.

"These belong to Pierre Le Fauve," Louie said. "He just came back from Aix-en-Provence. Pierre has wonderful taste. He hasn't stolen a bad picture in the lot."

"That's an interesting picture there, the one of the two men playing cards," I said.

"Yes, that seems to be everyone's favorite. Maybe it's because all of us play cards at one time or another. Pierre's been offered four completed Riviera jewel robberies for the picture, but he refuses to trade."

"I can't really blame him. You can pull a jewel robbery any time, but there is only one Cézanne 'Card Players.' Most men would have been satisfied with just that picture, but not Pierre. He took the lot. We're very proud of him."

"What's in this room?" I said.

For the first time Louie scowled. "Our American friends from Pittsburgh loaned us these from the stolen Thompson collection. I apologize, monsieur, if I hurt your feelings, but the American art thieves are uncultured oafs and don't belong in the business. Look how they damaged the pictures getting them out of the frames. And look how badly they're hung. These men are obviously in it for the money and not the aesthetic value.

"The only reason we borrowed the paintings is that they had some early Picassos and some from his cubist period that none of us in Europe have been able to lay hands on. But I assure you, monsieur, the art underworld takes a dim view of the sloppy work the Americans pulled during this job; it gives art looters everywhere a bad name."

We passed through several other rooms. One was filled with Egyptian art stolen from the Cairo Museum. "Pepe of Aswan owns these," Louie said. "He was bored with impressionists and the modern masters and decided to go off on his own. There's not much market for this stuff, but Pepe said he collects it for his mummy."

In the last room we found a man sitting all alone, tears rolling down his cheeks. The walls were completely blank.

Louie whispered to me: "That's Roger L'Abstract. He made us promise that abstract paintings would be represented, so we set aside this room. He was going to fill it with Jackson Pollocks and he went all the way to Venice to pull the job. But once he got in the house the Pollocks were so big he couldn't get them out the window. It almost broke his heart."

U.S. Is Short of Reds

After lecturing in many parts of the United States the one thing that has struck me is how vigilant every community has become toward the problem of Communism. There has not been a town I've hit on my tour that doesn't have at least four organizations working night and day to repel the Communist threat in the United States, which, as all vigilantes know, is getting more serious as each United Nations session goes by.

Unhappily, while there are more organizations being formed to fight Communists in the United States, there are less and less Communists around to fight, and the anti-Communist organizations are fighting among themselves over who has a right to fight the Communists.

Many of the smaller towns, particularly in the South, have the strongest anti-Communist organizations, despite the fact that they are so far off the beaten track that many of them have never seen a Communist. In Waco, Texas, for example, the nearest card-holding Communist Party member lives in Dallas, a hundred miles away. While Waco stands at the ready to repulse the infidel, the Communist Party member has been warned not to leave Dallas, as the anti-Communist organizations there claim that since he lives in Dallas he belongs to them.

Sarasota, Florida, seems to have the same problem. The threat of the

Communists taking over Sarasota hangs heavy over the heads of some of the leaders of this beautiful city, and the printing presses are grinding out tons of paper warning of the impending invasion. In the meantime, members of the Communist Party keep passing up Sarasota, preferring to spend their winters in Palm Beach. Sarasota, despite its ideal location for internal subversion, has been unable to attract any Communists for the anti-Communists to attack.

Other towns throughout the United States have also suffered from the unwillingness of the Communists to show up, and the problem is playing havoc with the defense of the American way of life.

It is true that most of the ultraconservative anti-Communists are not as concerned with attacking Communists as they are with attacking people who are not Communists but think like Communists, or, to put it another way, think differently than the anti-Communists do.

But this leads to complications, because when you get past the names of former President Eisenhower, Chief Justice Earl Warren, Mrs. Roosevelt, and Adlai Stevenson, no one can agree on who else represents a Communist threat in the United States.

Therefore, rather than drive the Communist Party underground in America, which isn't helping anyone, I think the Communist Party members should be redistributed around the country so that every town can have at least one. Having a Communist of their very own would make the anti-Communists less frustrated, and they wouldn't be fighting among themselves over who is and who is not a Communist.

The Communist who is willing to move to one of these towns would be well paid by the anti-Communist organizations, who have so much money to spend they would pay anything to get a Communist to live in their town.

Everyone would be happy. The Communist would receive a good salary for living in the town, and the town would have a reason for having so many anti-Communist organizations.

It's the only solution to the terrible Communist shortage in the United States. While the big cities might object to losing their Communists, I think the smaller communities have a right to have some Communists, too.

Destiny's Deckhand

Everybody seems to be writing a book about President Kennedy's experiences as PT-boat commander in the South Pacific during World War II. Minute-by-minute accounts of his years at sea have been written by Robert J. Donovan, Richard Tregaskis, and many others. The literary rights of every Japanese and native who was within 300 miles of the place where Mr. Kennedy's PT-109 was rammed by a Japanese destroyer have been tied up by either *Life* or *The Saturday Evening Post.* Probably the only man who was in the South Pacific battle zone at the same time as President Kennedy and hasn't had his experiences published yet is Ichiro Kuichi.

He has been in New York the past several days putting the final touches on his book, called *Destiny's Deckhand—the Autobiography of a Seaman on the Japanese Destroyer that Missed Ramming PT-109.*

I had lunch with Mr. Kuichi and Dick Lingeman. Mr. Lingeman bought the serialization rights to *Destiny's Deckhand* and has been acting as Mr. Kuichi's agent while the Japanese seaman is in New York.

He sketched in Mr. Kuichi's background for me.

Ichiro Kuichi was a rice polisher for the Koba Soba rice flour company in Japan. On the day of Pearl Harbor, after the Americans fired on the poor, helpless Japanese aircraft who were attacking them, Ichiro joined the Japanese Navy to avenge, as his Emperor put it, "this day of infamy."

His first assignment was as a suicide *kamikaze* pilot, but after he had completed ten missions his superiors decided he had an inadequate death wish, and he was kicked out of the Japanese Naval Air Force in disgrace and assigned as a mess boy on destiny's destroyer.

It was in this capacity that Mr. Kuichi played a role that was to change the course of history, not only in the United States but in the world.

Nobody knew it, but there were two Japanese destroyers coming down the strait that fateful night when John Kennedy was commanding the PT–109. One was Mr. Kuichi's and the other was the destroyer that actually rammed Mr. Kennedy. Mr. Kuichi's destroyer had first crack at ramming Mr. Kennedy's boat, but thanks to Mr. Kuichi it missed.

This is what happened, in Mr. Kuichi's own words:

"It very dark. I on bridge serving green tea to duty officer and helmsman. I very nervous because I know somewhere out there in dark is future President of United States in torpedo boat. I drop tea on duty officer's lap and he yells: 'You stupid fisherman.' In Japanese that sounds like 'hard rudder right.' Obedient helmsman swings wheel right and instead of ramming PT–109 with future President on board, we miss boat completely and sink PT–110 instead. All crew survived but nobody important on PT–110.

"Captain of my destroyer is very mad because after war he wants to go into politics and he knows it would be very popular issue if he can say he ram President of United States in boat and give him bad back.

"But it too late, because other Jap destroyer with captain, who also wants to go into politics, sees PT–109, and he rams it. We hear cheers on other Jap destroyer because they know after war they can sell their story to *Saturday Evening Post* and *Herald Tribune* for millions of yen. Nobody talks to me on my destroyer because American magazines won't give a bag of rice for how we sunk PT–110."

Despite Mr. Kuichi's sad experience, he is still a big President Kennedy fan. He idolizes the President and even changed his wife's name from Machinko to Jackinto. He wanted to name his first daughter Caroline but didn't because he couldn't pronounce the l.

While in the United States he plans to autograph books (by any Japanese author, since the autographs all look alike) and he also hopes to meet the President and his family.

"President Kennedy very very nice to Jap sailors who sink him, so I think he should maybe be nice to Jap sailors who miss him altogether."

Part VII

In Time of Crisis

Living in Washington during a time of crisis can be a very nerve-racking experience. Having lived through two dozen crises in Paris during the past fourteen years, I think I'm in a good position to compare the differences between the two.

For one thing, in Paris you rarely meet the people involved in a crisis. Occasionally you run into a French spokesman at a bistro, but for the most part the people working on a French crisis are complete strangers and unavailable to the foreign press. Therefore, since the crisis is being handled by people you don't know, you have the feeling the situation is well in hand, and if all else fails, General de Gaulle will save the day.

But in Washington it's entirely different. Your next-door neighbor may be the person involved with the crisis, and you not only know him, but you know his kids.

The guy who is out there on Sunday painting his fence, or raking his leaves, is the same guy who is in charge of working out the master plan for the Joint Chiefs of Staff. The fellows you play poker with are in charge of decisions that could affect everybody. And it doesn't make you feel any better if you bluff one of them out of a hand.

In Washington your dinner partner could be the wife of an important official, and it scares you to wonder how much influence she has on her husband's decisions. And it isn't beyond belief that a congressman or Senator in charge of worldshaking events could pinch your wife under the table. While this is human, it also scares the devil out of you.

In Paris there are no secrets when it comes to a crisis. As a matter of fact, there are so many crises going on that half the time you would never know you were in one.

But in Washington crises are built up slowly and dramatically. First, I know something is going on. I don't know what it is and my next-door neighbor has been sworn not to tell me. But I know he knows, and that's pretty spooky right there. Then I hear that something important is going to be done about something I don't know is happening. Key figures in government don't show up for dinner. Other key figures do show up for dinner. This is to confuse everyone. The Head of State catches a cold, the Vice-President catches a cold, the entire Cabinet is sneezing. It's safe to say when the President catches a cold, Cuba gets pneumonia. But that's all I know.

A newspaper friend calls up and says, "What do you know?"

Your reply, "What do you know?"

He says, "I know it's big."

You say, "I hear it's tremendous."

"Who did you hear it from?" he wants to know.

"I can't tell you."

"That's the same guy I heard it from," he says. "I just wanted confirmation."

By this time your nerves are worn to a frazzle. Your wife wants to know if she can have new closets built. You tell her to wait until the President speaks. Finally the President speaks and you tell her she can't have her new closets. Then you have a crisis at home.

The main difference between a crisis in Paris and a crisis in Washington is that if you're an American in Paris and the crisis is serious, you know that the American government will evacuate you. But if you're an American stationed in Washington and the crisis takes a turn for the worse, you can be sure that nobody cares what the hell happens to you.

Washington Parties Are Very Revealing

Ever since I moved to Washington I've been reading the society pages with interest. The Washington society pages are different from any others in the world and most people turn to them before they read the front pages. The reason for this is that the hard news about world events is oftentimes buried in paragraphs devoted to embassy receptions, official dinners, and New Frontier cocktail parties.

This is how a typical Washington society-page story might sound:

"The Russians threw a wonderful party at their embassy last night to celebrate the arrival of the Bolshoi Ballet. In the receiving line was First Secretary Karnonsky, who with his lovely wife, Zina, greeted the guests. Zina told me she was sorry the Ambassador couldn't be there, but he had been called over to the White House for important conferences with the President. When I asked Zina where the Ambassador's wife was, she replied, 'She's packing the Ambassador's bag for a trip to Cuba.'

"I was very disappointed, as I enjoy talking to the Ambassador so much. But despite their absence, the table was loaded with caviar and smoked sturgeon and there was a lovely centerpiece of flowers which were arranged to look like an ICBM missile. Zina can do wonders with flowers.

"In the main salon I met General Werick Jablonsky, the handsome Polish military attaché, and his beautiful wife, Minka. Werick was telling some funny stories about Berlin and when I asked him if he thought Russia would sign a pact with East Germany, he handed me a glass of champagne and said, 'It's quite possible.' Minka was wearing a stunning blue dress and a blue hat with a veil to match. She always seems to have a nice word for everybody.

"I met Mrs. Nganda Ula, wife of the Congolese Minister for Economic Affairs, who said her husband could not be there as he was being held prisoner by the Katangans. Mrs. Ula was wearing an Indian sari of gold threads interwoven with pink and she looked striking.

"I was about to ask her how she was doing with her house-hunting when Colonel Sighn of the Indian Military Mission and his wife greeted me. I hadn't seen them since Jackie Kennedy's visit to New Delhi. The Singhs made me promise to come to a dinner party they were giving for Prime Minister Nehru, who was coming on a secret mission to see President Kennedy.

"General and Mrs. Birch of the British Embassy told me it looked as though Britain would soon join the Cuban embargo. But what I really wanted to know was where Mrs. Birch got her beautiful beaded bag. "'That,' she said, 'is a military secret.'

"Charley Graham, of the Bureau of Standards, told me about a new drug which would cure the common cold, but I only listened with half an ear as I was so taken with Flora Graham's latest hair-do. It was a

bouffant behind the ears with a daring flip. When Flora is with Charley, no one pays any attention to what he has to say.

"Major Hang Po, of Nationalist China, told me an amusing story
about Quemoy and Matsu. He also revealed he was being relieved to
take over a squadron of F-104s and I was sorry to hear it as Major Po is
so well liked in Washington circles and supports all the charities in
town.

"It was a wonderful party and would probably have gone on all night
if someone hadn't shot the Bengonian Chargé d'Affaires. I had to go off
to the Swedish Embassy for a candlelight dinner, so I never did find out
who did it."

Life Begins at Sixty

I read in the paper the other day that a new pill may be on the market soon which would make it possible for a woman of sixty to have a
baby. It seems that a Dr. Ringrose of Edmonton, Alberta, Canada, revealed it might be possible to develop a pill containing a hormone
which would keep a woman fertile to a much more advanced age than
ever before. How would a woman of sixty feel about this?

When I read about it I rushed to Brooklyn to see my Aunt Sadie and
said, "Aunt Sadie, they've just invented a drug which makes it possible
for a woman of your age to have a baby."

"Wash out your mouth with soap and water," she replied.

"I'm not kidding, Aunt Sadie. Just think—a woman of sixty can soon
have a baby."

"If your Uncle Leo so much as lays a finger on me I'll hit him in the
head with a chair."

"Aunt Sadie," I protested. "That isn't the way to behave. After all,
America needs children, and if women of your age can provide them it
will help this country tremendously, particularly in the cold war with
China."

"It so happens I'm not interested in having any kids at my age, even
if they give it to us free under Medicare."

"Why don't you want to have children now?"

"I'm tired."

"That's not enough of a reason," I said.

"It may not be enough of a reason for you, but it's enough of a reason
for me."

"But just think of it. The patter of little feet around the house again, the cradle in the bedroom, the happy sounds of a baby crying for its mother."

"Listen Mr. Population Exploder, for twenty years I had my share of kids. I couldn't wait for your cousin Milton, and your cousin Ethel, and your cousin Leonard to go off and fend for themselves. I'm not ready to start on a new generation, even if they put the stuff in cereal boxes."

"I think you're wrong, Aunt Sadie. This is a new scientific development which could change the face of the globe. Women of your age will become important again. Advertising agencies will write copy about you. You'll be able to attend Parent-Teacher Association meetings. You can use your station wagon to bring kids home from school. Your grown-up children will have something in common with you if you have little children of your own. Retired people won't be considered expendable any more. What better way to fill out your final years than by producing babies?"

"Has your Uncle Leo heard about this?" she wanted to know.

"No, you're the first one I told."

"Well, if you tell him, I'll give you a hit in the head. We were just getting ready to enjoy the golden years after the sacrifice and work we had put in to raise our children, and now some baby-mad scientist in Canada wants to ruin everything."

"Then you're against the idea?" I asked her.

"You've come to the president of the Brooklyn Birth Control Society for Women over Sixty. Does that answer your question?"

"That's funny. I thought your reaction would be entirely different. Do you think most women of sixty feel this way?" I asked.

"You may get a different reaction from Elsa Maxwell, but I think I can speak for the rest of the country."

"Well, thanks for being so frank with me, anyway," I said.

"Don't mention it, and would you mind going out the back door? I think I just heard your Uncle Leo come in, and if it's all the same to you I don't want him to ask you what you've been doing here today."

Kid-Swapping in the United States

Nobody likes to talk about it, but there is a lot of kid-swapping going on in the United States. It isn't going on just in the suburbs or the small towns, but in the larger cities as well.

I hadn't realized how prevalent kid-swapping was until I moved to Washington. One night I came home from the office, and instead of finding my dark-haired little beauties, I discovered a seven-year-old blonde stranger doing the twist.

"Who's she?" I asked my wife.

"That's Ann Lindsay. She's staying here for the night with Connie."

"Where's Jennifer?" I asked.

"She's sleeping at Priscilla's house, because Ann Lindsay's sleeping here."

"Who's Priscilla?"

"Jennifer didn't know her last name, but she says she's her best friend."

"That's nice. Where is Joel?"

"He's sleeping at his friend's—B. J. He said if Jennifer can sleep somewhere else so can he."

"Where does that leave us?" I asked my wife.

"Well, we had three to start with, we got rid of two for the night, and we gained one, so we're only short one."

"It saves on food," I agreed.

"Not really," my wife said. "We had fish tonight, but Ann Lindsay doesn't like fish, so I had to go out and get her a steak. Then when Connie saw Ann was getting a steak she wanted one, too."

"I wouldn't mind having a steak myself," I said.

"You can't. Somebody's got to eat the fish."

The next weekend when I came home Connie was missing, but Jennifer had two friends and Joel had B.J.

At eight o'clock I ordered them all to bed.

"B. J.'s father lets him watch television until midnight every night," Joel, who is nine years old, said.

"Is that true, B. J.?" I asked.

"Sometimes later," B. J. said without batting an eye.

"When I stayed at B. J.'s last week," Joel said, "we didn't go to bed until two in the morning."

"My parents don't like me to go to bed early," B. J. said, "because then I wake up early."

"Well, why don't we just call up your parents and ask them what time you go to bed?"

"Oh, you don't have to do that," B. J. said hurriedly. "They've probably gone out to a movie."

Just then the phone rang. It was Mrs. Lindsay, who said, "What time do you usually put Connie to bed?"

"Eight o'clock," I said.

"She said you let her stay up till midnight to watch television. I was a little worried." Mrs. Lindsay seemed relieved.

Later that evening I said to my wife, "We've got to put a halt to this kid-swapping. Everyone on Cleveland Avenue is starting to talk."

"Oh, it's harmless," my wife said, "and they get so much fun out of it."

But I knew what I was talking about. A few weeks later I came home and found three kids at the dinner table. None of them mine.

"What happened?" I asked.

My wife was rather embarrassed. "There's been a dreadful mix-up. Joel invited Frances over to sleep with him, but he forgot he'd accepted an invitation to sleep at Butch's. Jennifer and Connie were invited over to Karen's, but after they left, Veronica and Mary Elisabeth showed up and said they had been invited over here. I didn't have the heart to send them home."

"So now we've got three kids that don't even belong to us," I said.

"Yes," my wife said, "and guess what? They said their mothers let them stay up until midnight every night to watch television."

Household Fatigue

Many husbands don't realize it but their wives are suffering from "household fatigue," a state similar to the battle fatigue of World War II, only more difficult to recognize. I probably would have never realized that my wife was a victim of it if I hadn't decided to take her with me to Cincinnati, where I had to make a speech. She seemed quite normal preparing for the trip and even appeared to be excited about getting away from the house for a few days. But then when we arrived at the airport I noticed her behavior had started to change.

As I paid for our airline tickets she said to the man behind the counter, "Just a minute. Where are our green stamps?"

"Madam, we don't give green stamps to our customers for using our airline."

"Is that so? Well, we'll just use another airline that does."

"Mother," I said, "none of the airlines gives green stamps and besides this is the only airline that goes to Cincinnati."

I calmed her down and thought nothing more of it until we got on the plane. The first thing she did was start to dust the seats.

"Mother, you don't have to do that," I said.

"I'm not going to have the neighbors think I keep a dirty plane."

"But they have people to do this sort of thing. Now sit by the window and fasten your safety belt."

I got her to sit down quietly and gave her a magazine to read. As soon as the plane was in the air she was up. "I've got to prepare lunch," she said.

"They have stewardesses to prepare lunch. You don't have to do anything."

"Well, I have to get the meat out of the freezer."

"No, no. That's all done by the airline personnel. You're on vacation. Relax."

She sat back for a few moments, but then one of the stewardesses spilled a cup of coffee in the aisle. My wife jumped up and said, "Don't worry about a thing." She took a container of Mr. Clean from her make-up kit and on her hands and knees worked on getting out the spot.

"There," she said after fifteen minutes, "Mr. Clean does everything."

Everybody looked away in embarrassment.

An hour later luncheon was served. There were two children sitting across the aisle from us, but they didn't seem to be eating their vegetables.

My wife looked over and shouted at them, "If I've told you kids once, I've told you a hundred times. You don't eat your vegetables, you don't get any dessert."

"Mother, Mother," I said gently, "those are not our children."

"I don't care," she said, "I'm sick and tired of preparing meals on this plane that nobody wants to eat."

"But maybe their parents don't want them to eat vegetables."

"You're always defending them," she said angrily. "No wonder they have such bad table manners. Sit up," she shouted at the little boy, "or you can go to bed right now."

Fortunately the parents of the children were preoccupied, and my wife decided to go back and help the stewardesses wash the dishes. By the time we reached Cincinnati, she had cleaned all the windows, washed the ash trays, laundered the napkins, and changed the curtains in the bar.

But the two days away from home have done her wonders. She hasn't yelled at any kids in twenty-four hours, and she's almost cured of her household fatigue. It's a pity she has to go home so soon.

That's My Boy

"So how come," Aunt Molly asked my father the other day at a family reunion, "if Arthur's stationed in Washington we never see him on television at the President's press conference?"

"Maybe," said Cousin Milton maliciously, "he isn't allowed to attend the President's press conference. They're not just open to everybody."

Uncle Oscar said, "It's getting embarrassing. The day after a Kennedy press conference all my friends say to me, 'So where was your big-shot nephew that you're always talking about?' I'm telling you, it's no fun going to work any more."

Uncle Leo said, "Let's face it. A Joseph Alsop he's not."

It was more than Pop could take and he called me up the next day. "The whole family's disgusted with you," he said. "You've been in Washington six months and they haven't seen you once on a Kennedy press conference."

"Pop," I said, "it's very hard to get on television at a presidential press conference. The only way to do it is to ask a question."

"So ask a question," he said. "It's going to kill you?"

"I never know what to ask the President," I told him.

"Why don't you ask him if he's willing to take a lie-detector test?"

"Pop, I can't ask him that. Besides, even if I thought of a good question to ask, the President still might not call on me. You see, you have to jump up at a press conference and then the President recognizes you. Sometimes you can jump up and down for thirty minutes and nothing happens. Then you have to have a long question so the cameras can focus on you. Before television the questions were very short. But now, in most cases, the questions are longer than the President's answers. It's hard for me to think up a long question."

"Enough excuses," Pop said. "All I know is the family is getting sick and tired of looking for you on TV. You better do something about it because I can't keep thinking up excuses for you."

Pop hung up and I started to stew. It was true, I had let the family down, but I didn't know what to do about it. So I took my problem to Ken Crawford, columnist of *Newsweek* magazine.

"Don't worry," he said. "I had the same problem too. Family wouldn't talk to me for months, but then I solved it."

"How?" I asked.

"Every time I go to a press conference, I sit behind someone who is sure to ask a question. In that way when the camera is on him or her, it's also on me. Come on, I'll take you over to the press conference and you can see for yourself."

I went over with him. "There," he said, "we'll sit behind May Craig of the Portland *Press.* She's sure to ask a question."

We grabbed two seats behind May Craig, who was wearing a nice pink hat.

"Just wait," Mr. Crawford said. "But be ready at any time."

The President's press conference started. Miss Craig jumped up and down as if she were on a puppet string, and, sure enough, the President called on her to ask question number 6, which was: "Mr. President, two weeks ago six Republican members of the Joint Economic Committee—House and Senate—wrote you a long letter of suggestions about Federal expenditures including a request that you establish a presidential commission on Federal expenditures similar to the Clay Commission on Foreign Aid. What would be your position on that suggestion?"

For thirty seconds, as Miss Craig asked her question, I scratched my ear, waved my hand discreetly, and stared into the camera, grinning.

That night I got a call from Pop. "Well," he said happily, "the whole family is talking about you. I'm proud of you, son. I knew you'd come through."

"Don't mention it, Pop. It was just a matter of time."

"There's one thing, though," Pop said. "We all felt that friend of yours, Ken Crawford, was hogging the camera."

Love in Paris and Red Tape Too

Of all the men I worked with on the Paris *Herald,* the one I admired the most was Milliken. Let me say right now that Milliken was not his real name, and I am using a false one only to protect the guilty, which Milliken certainly was.

Milliken was an American in his late twenties. He had a beard; he usually wore blue jeans and a torn sweater; he lived in a cold-water flat on the Left Bank; he was usually broke. And yet Milliken was always in the company of the most beautiful girls in Paris. They used to call him every day on my phone; they waited for him in front of the Paris *Herald* until midnight; they cooked breakfast for him; they let him use their bathtubs, and they lent him money until pay day. Milliken's cup was constantly running over.

I couldn't understand it and it drove me crazy. There had to be an answer somewhere. Finally after six months of taking his messages and watching him in operation, I could stand it no longer.

So one afternoon while we were having a drink at Fouquet's on the Champs Élysées, I said, "Damn it all, Milliken, what's your secret? How do you get away with it?"

"Get away with what?" he said innocently.

"Get away with all these girls. You're not handsome, you're not rich, you don't even own a car. What right do you have to attract all these American women? What do they see in you?"

"It's quite simple," he said calmly. "No mystery about it at all. I promise to marry them."

"You what?"

"I promise to marry them. Once I promise to marry them, everything else comes easily."

"I don't get it," I said.

"All right, I'll explain it to you. Where did you get married?"

"In London."

"Why?" he asked.

"Because there is too much red tape for a foreigner who wants to get married in France. I waited four months and finally gave up."

"Exactly," said Milliken. "It's almost impossible for a foreigner to get married in France, so when I propose to a girl and we go down to the Prefect of Police to make an application for a marriage license, I know we'll never get it. But the girl doesn't know that, and while we're waiting for our papers to be processed, which they never will be, we're officially 'engaged.' And since I have proved I intend to marry the girl, she has no choice but to treat me as she would her future husband."

"Milliken, you're a rat," I said, trying to hide the awe in my voice.

"I am not a rat. The French bureaucrats are the rats. I am only taking advantage of an impossible governmental situation. I didn't make the loophole, but as with taxes, I have every right to make the most of it."

"But when does the girl wise up that you aren't going to marry her?"

"One month, maybe two months, maybe three, depending on how many times we visit the Prefect of Police. The more times we go down, the more discouraged she gets. But I must say I've never been blamed by any of them. They know I have no control over the French attitude toward foreigners getting married in France."

"It's an unbeatable system." I whistled.

"Too bad you went to London" was all he said to me.

During the next six months Milliken proposed to at least five girls that I knew of, and I watched him with the envy of a man who sees someone rolling nothing but sevens at a crap table.

But then one day Milliken came rushing into the office, his face white, his hands shaking, stark fear in his eyes. "You've got to help me," he cried.

"What happened?"

"I proposed to this girl, a mousy one at that, last night, and this

morning we went down to the Prefect of Police to apply for permission
to get married and they're going to give it to us."

"It's impossible," I said.

"No, it isn't. The lady behind the counter said she didn't believe in
red tape and if two people wanted to get married it was all she cared
about. She's a crazy romantic."

"What can I do to help you?"

"Don't you know someone at the Prefect of Police who can stop it?"

"No, I don't."

"Well, come down with me this afternoon and tell them I'm married
already, or I'm a deserter from the Army, or anything. You've got to
save me."

I felt so sorry for Milliken I went down with him and his mousy fian-
cée to the Prefect.

"*Voilà*, Monsieur," the lady said. "I have all your papers."

The mouse screeched with joy.

"But I don't have my birth certificate," Milliken protested.

"Your passport will do."

"I better take a health examination."

"You look very healthy to me," the lady said.

"I'm married already," Milliken cried.

"Will you swear to that under oath?"

"No," said Milliken, "but he will." He pointed to me.

"The devil I will," I said.

"Then let's have no more nonsense, Monsieur," said the lady. "Marriage is a serious business and I have risked my job to see your papers
were approved. Usually it would take months to get the permissions,
but because you are both young and Americans, I have made an exception. Perhaps when they find out what I have done they will transfer
me. But love is more important than the government."

Milliken was in a state of shock during the following week so I made
all the arrangements at the local city hall for the wedding. I was Milliken's best man, my wife stood witness for the mouse. The mayor of
the *arrondissement* made a beautiful speech in French about marriage
and both my wife and the mouse cried.

After that there was no reason for Milliken to stay in Paris, and he
moved back to the United States where he bought a house in Levit-
town, shaved off his beard, and got a job doing public relations for the
Long Island Railroad. It's not a very pleasant picture and I try to drive
it out of my mind. I always want to remember Milliken as the guy who
almost broke the bank at Monte Carlo.

Baseball à la Greque

The game of baseball can be Greek to a lot of people, particularly if you are Greek. I had the pleasure of watching a world series game on television with Melina Mercouri, the Greek actress who was in Washington with her director, Jules Dassin, promoting their film, *Phaedra*. Miss Mercouri didn't want to watch the game, but Mr. Dassin had his heart set on it.

"Darling," he said, "this is the world series. I've got to see it."

"What countries are playing?" Miss Mercouri wanted to know.

"No countries are playing. It is between two American teams."

"Then why do they call it the world series?" she asked.

"I guess because to Americans it is the most important thing in the world. You see, baseball is the national pastime."

"In Greece we have better pastimes," the actress said.

"Yes," Mr. Dassin agreed, "but you can't show them on television."

"I don't care, I want to see the White House and the Capitol and the Pentagon. I don't want to sit in this hotel room looking at a stupid game."

"It's not stupid. Let me explain it to you. Look at the screen. There are nine men on each team."

"Who is the man in the blue suit with the life preserver?" Miss Mercouri wanted to know.

"That's the umpire. He's neutral."

"I like him. He's dressed much better than the others."

"Now pay attention," Mr. Dassin said. "There are four bases, including home plate. The man with the bat stands at home plate and tries to hit the ball which is thrown by a man called the pitcher."

"And the rest of them just stand around doing nothing," Miss Mercouri said.

"No, that's not so. If the man hits the ball, they must try to catch it and put him out."

"That's all they do?"

"Well, they also have to bat when it is their turn. Now watch, the pitcher has just thrown a ball."

"The man didn't try to hit the ball," Miss Mercouri said.

"No, he didn't, because the pitch was a ball."

"I know it was a ball. I can see."

"You don't understand. It was a bad ball."

"Why don't they play with good balls? I thought America was a rich country."

"They do play with good balls. But if the ball doesn't go over the plate it's called a ball. Now look, he just hit a foul ball. That's a strike."

Miss Mercouri looked at Mr. Dassin incredulously. "A bad ball is a ball, and a foul ball is a strike? Why isn't a bad ball a foul ball? Tell me, who is on strike?"

"Nobody is on strike," Mr. Dassin said. "It's called a strike. Watch, you see, the man just hit a fly to center field."

"You saw a man hit a fly on television?" Miss Mercouri asked.

"Not a real fly. It's called a fly if it goes in the air."

"I want to see the Supreme Court," Miss Mercouri said.

"Wait a minute. The next batter is the best player on the team. Let's see what he does. Look, he just made a long drive into center field and he has a double."

"A double what?"

"Just a double. He has two bases."

"I don't see them," Miss Mercouri said.

"It's two up and two down and a man on second."

"Who's up and who's down?"

"Never mind. If they get one more out, they'll retire the side."

"Can we go sight-seeing if they retire the side?"

"No, because then the other team is up at bat."

"It's a stupid game," Miss Mercouri said.

Mr. Dassin was getting desperate. Suddenly he thought of something. "Do you know, the best hitter on the Yankees is a Greek?"

For the first time Miss Mercouri took an interest in the game. "What's his name?"

"Mickey Mantoupoplous. They call him Mickey Mantle for short."

"Come on, Mickey Mantoupoplous," Miss Mercouri shouted. "Hit the foul ball over the home plate and show them you can double the bases with two up and two down and don't forget to retire to the side!"

"That's it," Mr. Dassin said. "You're getting the hang of it. Now, isn't this better than sight-seeing?"

"Are there any Greeks on the other side?" Miss Mercouri wanted to know.

"Just Willie Mays," Mr. Dassin said. "Just Willie Mays."

What's Wrong with TV

I was talking the other day with "My Son, the Folk Singer," Allan Sherman, and we got around to the question of what was wrong with television. We both came to the conclusion that everyone on TV was being presented in a false light, and the public was being cheated out of seeing situations as they really are. For example, on the lawyer shows *Perry Mason* and *The Defenders,* no one ever asks for a fee. There is never any discussion of money on these programs and people are under the impression that any lawyer will defend you for the love of it.

But in real life this is what would happen. A woman comes into Perry Mason's office. She says, "My son has been accused of a crime, but I know he didn't do it."

Perry in real life would say, "Wait a minute, madam. Before you go any further, I'll have to ask for a retainer."

"He's innocent," the lady says. "You've got to defend him."

"How much can you afford? Legal costs are expensive. If he pleads guilty, I'll make a deal with the District Attorney and save you the expense of a long drawn-out jury trial."

"But he wants to plead not guilty."

"Big deal," says Perry. "They'll probably hang him anyway and it will still cost you five thousand dollars."

"I guess you're right," the woman says. "Plead him guilty. He's always getting into trouble, anyway."

"That will be five hundred dollars now and five hundred more at the start of the trial. If there are any other expenses, I'll let you know."

Or let's take Dr. Kildare. What kind of guy would Dr. Kildare be if he weren't on television? Perhaps something like this.

"Dr. Kildare," an elderly man says, "I have a pain in my side."

"I don't know anything about pains in people's sides. I'll send you to a specialist, Dr. Renfrow."

"But besides my side, my left leg hurts."

"Why didn't you say so in the first place? Dr. Martin is the best leg man in town. Tell him I sent you."

"And it hurts when I breathe."

"You need a good lung man. After you see Dr. Martin about your leg, go over and see Dr. Steele about your chest. I'll write down the address here."

"I can't read your handwriting," the old man says.

"Eye trouble, too? You better see Dr. Rabb, the eye, ear, nose, and throat man."

"Thank you very much, Dr. Kildare."

"Don't mention it. That will be ten dollars."

What about Dr. Ben Casey, if there were such a person in real life?

A nurse rushes in. "Dr. Casey, there's been a terrible skiing accident. They want you in the operating room right away."

Casey puts on a mask, sterilizes his arms, walks over to the table.

"Has this man signed a release that I'm not responsible if the operation doesn't come off?"

"No, sir. He was brought in unconscious."

"Well, I'm not operating until someone signs a release. Do you think I'm going to be sued for malpractice?"

"But, doctor, if you don't operate at once, he'll die."

"And if he dies," Dr. Casey says, "the next of kin will blame me. No, thank you. No release, no operation. My lawyer won't let me do it any other way."

The final thing to make one suspect television of not being true to life is that taxis are always plentiful on TV and ready to pursue the heavy.

This is what would happen in real life if a private eye like Peter Gunn tried to follow someone.

"Taxi, taxi! Follow that cab!"

"Waddaya mean follow that cab?"

"I want you to follow that cab, like I said."

"Look, mister, I pick people up and take them to a destination. I don't follow no cabs."

"You're letting him get away."

"Get yourself another hack. I got a wife and kid to think of, and I don't have time to get involved in any cops-and-robbers stuff."

"You mean you refuse to follow that cab?"

"Out, mister, you've been watching too many television shows."

Part VIII

The Ballyhoo Gets to Him

The big question asked at a political convention is whether all the spontaneous demonstrations, the parades and the colorful ballyhoo have any effect on changing the delegates' votes.

The answer is an unqualified yes.

I spoke to an uncommitted Republican delegate who told me he would have no idea whom to vote for if it weren't for the demonstrations that preceded the nominations.

He said, "I'm not concerned with issues. I'm interested only in personalities. I think the one who puts on the best spontaneous demonstration has earned the nomination."

"How do you judge them?"

"Well, I like girls. I've always believed that the candidate who has the prettiest girls working for him is probably the one who can do the best job for our country. The first thing I do when I come to the convention is to take a look at the girls."

"Is there anything special you look for?"

"Oh, I look to see the way they're dressed. If they have a neat appearance. If they smile when they talk to you. Important things like that."

"Is there anything else that influences your vote?"

"A good band during a demonstration can always move me. I like a lot of trombones in a band. In 1952 I was going to vote for Taft, but he was weak on trombones, so I went over to Eisenhower."

"What are some of the other factors that affect your vote?"

"Did I tell you about girls?"

"Yes, you did."

"Well, let's see. I always look to see who has the most colorful posters. I look for originality in posters as well as size. It isn't enough just to have the poster show the candidate's face. The same goes for buttons. I always felt Nixon lost in 1960 because his buttons didn't say anything."

"What about spontaneous demonstrations?" I asked.

"I think they're almost as important as girls. As a matter of fact, I never decide which way to go until I see the spontaneous demonstrations. A convention is much too serious a business to make up your mind before you see how a candidate has organized his demonstration. I think that's where Harold Stassen makes his mistake every time. He never seems to be able to get his spontaneous demonstrations off the ground."

"I hear Goldwater is very strong on spontaneous demonstrations."

"That's what I hear, too, and I'm really looking forward to seeing it. Scranton probably started too late to organize a good spontaneous demonstration, but I'm keeping an open mind."

"What else do you use as a yardstick?"

"Well, there are the girls."

"You mentioned them."

"That's probably it, then. Of course, if someone wants to buy me a drink, I'll take that into account, too."

"Do you ever try to find out where the candidates stand?"

He looked at me as if I was crazy. "What for?"

What He Doesn't Know

The political poll has become one of the biggest factors in American politics. From now on until Election Day political pollsters will be traversing the length and breadth of the United States, questioning people on their feelings toward the candidates and issues of the day.

It is interesting to note that in every poll there are a certain percentage of people who are "undecided," "don't know" or are "not sure" of any of the questions. Who are these people? What do they believe in? How do they think?

In order to find out, I decided to take a poll of my own and interview the president of the UDKNS Society.

I rang the bell and he came to the door. "Sir, I'm taking a survey of the Undecided, Don't Know, Not Sure Society. Could you give me some information?"

"How many members are in your society?"

"I'm not sure about that," he replied.

"Well, how often do you meet?"

"I don't really know."

"What does the organization stand for?"

"We're undecided as of this moment."

"Why did you form such a society?"

"I hesitate to answer that. My guess would be we started it because there were so many people in this country who were undecided on so many issues that we felt they should be represented. In any poll, if you multiply us, we could run into the millions."

"How do you qualify for the organization?"

"By NOT having any convictions and by sticking to them. We study each question carefully and then decide we don't know the answer."

"It sounds difficult."

"It isn't easy these days, particularly with all the communications around us. Most of us try not to read newspapers or watch news programs on television. We never discuss politics at home and we stay out of bars because you usually have to take sides there."

"When you do meet, what do you talk about?"

"Nothing much. We have only one rule. If anyone expresses an opinion on anything, he's asked to resign."

"But, sir, what value does your organization have if it doesn't stand for anything?"

"We have more value than anybody else. Nobody cares who is for or against something. It's the 'undecided' that the candidates are worried about. They spend more time and money on us than anybody. We count for something in an election year."

"But when do the undecided people make up their minds?"

"I have no idea. Once they've decided, we're no longer interested in them."

"Well, thank you very much, sir."

"Don't mention it. I'm not sure whether I should have talked to you. I don't know if I've made a mistake giving you all this information and I'm undecided whether you should print it or not. But if you don't use my name, I guess it will be all right."

Who's on First Base?

A few weeks ago the U. S. Navy announced that it was trying to perfect a flying submarine which it needed badly to protect the United States. This brought an immediate reaction from the U.S. Air Force, which announced it would soon develop an underseas airplane.

The exchange pointed out the great competition now going on between the armed services and no one is quite sure how it will all come out.

With modern warfare becoming so complicated no one knows what role each of the services should play. At a recent top-secret meeting at the Pentagon some of the questions were thrashed out. It went something like this.

General Patent of the U.S. Army opened the meeting by saying, "Gentlemen, I am happy to announce that the United States Army now has the largest number of airplanes of any armed service in the world."

General Wings of the Air Force shouted, "I protest. The Air Force should have most of the airplanes under its command. We're not going to take this lying down."

Admiral Bilge of the U.S. Navy said, "Speaking of lying down, the U.S. Marine Corps has developed a new helicopter tank which will do away with the necessity of heavy armored divisions. The tank can be flown off aircraft carriers."

General Patent says, "Oh yeh, wise guy. Well the Army has come up with a floating rocket launcher which makes the naval destroyer obsolete."

General Wings pounds the table. "I'd like to get back to these Army aircraft. There is no reason to have Army aircraft."

General Patent replied, "The function of the Air Force is to man Intercontinental Ballistic Missiles underneath the ground. Our airplanes are used to support our troops. The planes you have are too fast for that and you know it."

General Wings pulled some papers out of his briefcase. "We are now building slower planes to operate with our paratroop division."

General Patent said, "What paratroop division?"

"The paratroop division we're forming to protect our Intercontinental Ballistic Missiles."

"The hell you say, Wings. The Army has the responsibility of protecting our ICBMs."

"Not anymore it doesn't."

Admiral Bilge pipes up. "Will you two stop fighting? By the time you settle the argument the Navy will have enough Polaris missiles to make the ICBM unnecessary."

General Wings replied, "That's all well and good but when the Air Force gets its own cruisers . . ."

Admiral Bilge said, "What do you mean, cruisers?"

"We have to have our own cruisers to launch our atomic artillery shells!"

"We don't have to tell you everything," General Wings said.

General Patent made a dive for General Wings. Admiral Bilge picked up a water pitcher and threw it at both of them.

Fortunately at that moment the Secretary of Defense walked onto the room and after each man explained his position, the Secretary fed this information into a computer and after digesting the facts the computer tape came out with this message: "If I were you I'd close down the Pentagon."

Top-Secret Plane

When President Johnson revealed at his news conference that the United States had developed a 2,000-mile-an-hour fighter-interceptor plane, the A-11, superior to any aircraft in the world today, he made headlines all over the world. This top-secret story had been kept under wraps for five years and it is believed that the only reason the President finally released the details to the press is that he did not have any other news to give that day.

But the plane the President failed to mention, which is far superior to the A-11 and is more radical than anything ever developed for the Air Force, is the PJ-306. Despite pleas from the Defense Department to keep the PJ-306 story a secret, I have decided to reveal the facts about it, as I believe that if the President can blow the story on a secret plane so can I.

I first heard about the PJ-306 when I visited Evreux Air Force Base in France in the spring of 1960. An officer who had too much to drink told me that the Air Force was working on a plane that could fly so slow that nothing could hit it. Its maximum speed was 100 miles an hour with a good tail wind, or seven times less than the speed of sound.

He told me that the Air Force had been concerned for a long time over the Soviet development of supersonic aircraft. The Air Force, to keep up, demanded faster planes for itself until both sides had developed planes so fast they couldn't see each other.

At this stage, the Joint Chiefs of Staff decided they needed a new plane so slow that no fast Soviet fighter could shoot it down.

Everyone said it was impossible to develop such a fighter, and all the major airplane manufacturers were reluctant to work on it. So the Air Force turned the contract over to the Spad Aircraft Co.

The Spad designers and engineers worked on it for two years before coming up with the solution. They developed a bi-wing plane with one wing over the cockpit and one below it.

But then they ran into engine trouble. Every jet engine they put on the plane made it fall apart. When all looked lost, someone developed a radically new kind of engine, which they called a propeller engine. Although it sounds like science fiction, this engine has a large wooden stick on the nose, and when the engine is started up, the wooden stick turns and pulls air through the plane to give it buoyancy.

Air Force generals did not believe it was possible, but after the first trials at a secret air base they saw the plane take off and fly to an altitude of 500 feet in 20 minutes.

They were so impressed that they immediately ordered 500 of them and gave Spad the green light to go ahead.

Unfortunately, there were further delays. In order to have any value, the plane had to be armed. Spad placed a 50-caliber machine gun in the cockpit. But every time the pilot fired the gun he shot off his own propeller.

Finally the Massachusetts Institute of Technology was given the problem. They developed a method of synchronizing the machine gun with the turn of the prop.

The plane was ready to go into production.

The new plane has many innovations. The cockpit is open, so the pilot may jump out of his plane if hit. The landing gear is stationary, which gives the PJ-306 added slowness. So far nothing in the Air Force has been able to catch it, and in practice dogfights the PJ-306 has shot down 367 jet fighters.

Even Barry Goldwater has been reluctant to talk about this one.

Our Defenses Are Down

The Defense Department has announced that it is closing down many military establishments in the United States in order to save money. Some of these bases, according to the Pentagon, have outlived their usefulness. When the news reached Capitol Hill, there were howls of indignation from our distinguished legislators.

To find out what all the screaming was about, I interviewed Congressman Michael O'Lobby from the State of Indignation.

"Is it true, sir, that you are very upset about the Defense Department's decision to close down military establishments in the United States?"

"You can bet your sweet life I am," O'Lobby replied. "I'm as economy-minded as the next Congressman, but when the Defense Department plays with the safety of our American citizens in the name of fiscal expediency, then I say there should be an investigation."

"Is there any particular military establishment that you are concerned about?"

"I certainly am. I am concerned about the closing of Fort Little Squaw at the mouth of the Ripahoodah River in my district. The closing of this establishment is one of the most dangerous military mistakes in our worldwide defense strategy."

"What function does Fort Little Squaw play in our defense?"

"I'm surprised you would ask that. Fort Little Squaw is the only fort west of the Mississippi to protect us from savage Indians."

"Indians? But there are no savage Indians in the United States anymore."

"Of course not. Not as long as Fort Little Squaw is in existence. But just close the fort and see what happens. Why, they'll come up the Ripahoodah River, overrun the plains, and before you know it, they'll threaten Grand Rapids, Detroit, and Cincinnati."

"I didn't realize they posed such a threat."

"Apparently no one in the Defense Department is aware of it, either. But the threat to America is not from without but from within, and believe me, son, you couldn't set yourself up for a better Communist conspiracy than by closing Fort Little Squaw."

"Communist conspiracy? I didn't know the Indians were tied up with a Communist conspiracy."

"Then why do they call themselves Redskins?"

"I never thought of that."

"Our national defense is based on a deterrent. The greatest deterrent we have against the Indians is the cavalry at Fort Little Squaw. If we close the fort, the Indians will swoop down on Chicago, scalping, massacring, pillaging, and setting fire to everything in sight."

"It sounds terrible," I said.

"You only have to watch television to see how terrible it could be. Fort Little Squaw is the last log cabin fort in this nation. How the Defense Department can say it has no value today is beyond the comprehension of anyone who loves his country."

"You make a very strong case for this particular military establishment," I said.

"I plan to make a stronger case at the next Armed Services Committee hearings. If the Defense Department doesn't see the military value of Fort Little Squaw, then I will not be able to see the value of any new nuclear submarines. What good is it to protect our front when we can be attacked from the rear? If we rely on nuclear weapons at the expense of the American cavalry, then our country is in greater danger than anyone thinks it is."

"I hope they change their minds."

"They'd better, or no white man will ever be able to sail safely up the Ripahoodah River again."

Solving the Overkill Problem

The problem of handling nuclear weapons was one of the issues of the 1964 campaign. Everyone was arguing about how many megatons of bombs and missiles could be delivered against the enemy in the next ten years.

The public was being asked to decide whether tactical nuclear weapons should be placed in the hands of generals in the field and whether we should give nuclear stockpiles to our allies.

I was very fortunate to interview Professor Max Kilaton, who had been working on the problem of nuclear weapons for some time. Professor Kilaton told me he made an independent study of the matter and came up with some startling results.

"The most important thing I discovered," he said, "was that while the Russian and American nuclear bombs are large enough, the targets for most of them are too small. We must build bigger targets to fit our bombs."

"I don't understand."

"Well, you see you have small bombs now that are five or ten times more powerful than the ones dropped on Hiroshima and Nagasaki, and you have larger bombs and missiles a hundred times more powerful. But you have no cities whose growth has been comparable to that of the bombs. Therefore, if you dropped a large bomb on a major city, there would be a great deal of waste in fallout, heat and power. In order to compensate for this, I am advocating the immediate building of larger targets."

"You mean make the cities bigger?"

"Exactly," Prof. Kilaton replied. "We must start an immediate building program to enlarge our cities so the radius of our most powerful nuclear weapons will fall within them."

"Would the Russians go along with this?"

"They would have to. They could not let our targets get bigger than theirs. It would be too much of a blow to their prestige."

"How could we make our targets worthy of the nuclear weapons which have been stockpiled?"

"We must build up urban centers between our large industrial cities and more or less connect them. The cities would have to be large enough to take a hit of the most powerful nuclear weapon that the Russians have. They in turn would have to enlarge their cities to accommodate our nuclear bombs."

"But what would this accomplish?"

"It would solve the major problem of nuclear weapons, which is overkill. If your targets are large enough for your bombs, you would eliminate the problem of overkill. That is, you would kill exactly the number of people the bomb was designed to kill. As it stands now, most of the larger nuclear weapons can destroy only one-twentieth of their potential. This is sheer waste and certainly works a hardship on the economies of the nuclear powers."

"What about tactical nuclear weapons?"

"You have no problem there. A good tactical nuclear weapon can destroy an average city with a bare minimum of overkill, perhaps 2.5 percent. Most targets are suitable as they now stand for tactical nuclear weapons. But the big danger is that if you use tactical weapons you could escalate your war to the point where you would have to use your big stuff and then your targets would be wholly inadequate."

"One more question, Professor. Do you think we should give nuclear weapons to NATO allies?"

"I certainly do. If Greece and Turkey both had nuclear weapons at their disposal, I believe the problem of Cyprus would have been solved weeks ago."

Keeping Us Informed

The airlines have a new public relations gimmick. Just as you get bedded down in your seat for a cross-country flight and start to snooze, a voice comes over the loudspeaker: "This is your captain speaking. We are flying at an altitude of 35,000 feet and on our left is the city of Palm Springs."

You peer out the window and all you see is a mass of clouds.

"Of course you can't see it so good at the moment," he says, "but it's a wonderful town."

You doze off again to be suddenly awakened by the friendly voice. "We have just passed into Arizona," the pilot says.

You start applauding until the other passengers stare you down.

All is well until 15 minutes later when the voice is back again. "We will soon pass over the Grand Canyon, which will appear off our right wing. The weather should be clear."

Several passengers take out their cameras and one of them asks if I wouldn't mind moving so he could get a picture. I move over to the left side of the plane.

"Before arriving over the Grand Canyon," the voice says again, "I would suggest you look out the left side of the plane at the glorious mountain range."

The passengers with their cameras rush back to the left side windows and I'm asked to move again.

"Now coming up ahead is the Grand Canyon."

The camera-toting passengers reverse themselves and they're back on the right side.

Just as everyone is in position, the friendly voice says, "We may be hitting a little turbulence. I would suggest everyone fasten their seat belts."

The passengers reverse themselves again and return to their seats.

"Would you mind taking a picture of me?" one of the passengers asks.

I hold his camera against the window and press the button.

"Did you get it?"

"How the hell do I know?" I say honestly.

Word reaches the pilot that we will soon be passing over Oklahoma City, and he just can't keep it to himself.

When the pilot isn't informing us about geography, he's telling us what the weather is like in Chicago. He also fills us in on his latest engine change, explains why the motors will sound different. Then he tells us he's going up 5,000 feet to avoid a rainstorm, and 25 minutes later he informs us they have hurricane warnings over Florida but, since we're not going there, we have nothing to worry about.

For 45 minutes I hear nothing and I start to worry. I call over the stewardess and ask her, "Is there anything wrong with the pilot?"

Before she can go up front to check, he's back again.

"We've just passed over Lima, Ohio," he announces triumphantly.

I breathe a sigh of relief.

I guess it's a good idea to keep everyone informed on how the pilots are flying the plane, but I can't help wishing for the good old days when they were busy up front with the stewardesses and left the passengers alone.

The Affair

One of the problems of being married and having young children is that much of the romance goes out of people's lives. A friend of mine has solved the problem. Every week he has an "affair" with his wife.

What he does is he kisses his wife good-bye in the morning and goes off to work. About noon he calls her up and whispers, "This is George. Is your husband home?"

His wife replies, "No, the oaf has gone off to the office."

"I've got to see you this afternoon," the husband says.

"I can't. I've got to be home when the children come from school."

"Get one of the neighbors to take care of them. Tell them it's an emergency and you have to go into town."

"Do I dare?"

"Please, darling, we don't have much time together."

"I'm frightened."

"I love you."

"I'll come. Where shall we meet?"

"Somewhere where no one will recognize us. I'll pick you up on the corner of F and 14th Street, at three o'clock."

The wife arranges for the neighbors to take care of the children and gets dressed up in her prettiest suit. She then drives into town, parks two blocks away and waits on the corner.

Her husband pulls up. She glances around fast and then hops in.

"I think I was seen, darling," she says nervously.

"Relax," the husband says comfortingly.

"Where are we going?" she asks.

"There's a motel just across the bridge. We'll check in there."

"But we have no luggage," she protests.

"I'll check in. You stay in the car and then we'll drive to the room."

After they get into the room she laughs, "I didn't even bring a toothbrush."

"I thought about you all week," he says, kissing her.

"So did I," she replies. "I waited for this moment. I thought it would never come."

"I wanted to call you, but I was afraid he would answer the phone."

"He wouldn't stop watching television to answer the phone. Does your wife know about us?"

"She's too busy taking care of the kids to know about anything. I told my secretary if she called to tell her I was out at a conference."

"How long can we go on like this?"

"Let's just be grateful for what we've got."

"If we'd only met each other before."

"I feel that way, too."

At six o'clock they check out of the motel, and my friend drops his wife off at F and 14th. "Until next week, my darling," he says as he kisses her.

"It will seem like a year," she says tearfully.

She hops out of the car without turning back.

An hour later her husband arrives home. "Anything happen today?" he asks casually, as he pecks her on the cheek.

"The same dull routine. Anything happen with you?"

"No, just another crummy day." He yawns. They both smile inwardly and sit down to dinner.

The Wayward Bus

I walked into the office of a New York newspaper the other day and found a Negro friend of mine completely downcast.

"What's the matter?" I asked him.

"I just moved to a nice section of the Bronx," he said, "into a lovely house on a nice street with grass and flowers and trees. The neighbors gave me no trouble—as a matter of fact, they were very nice to me. The kids were happy as could be. It cost me $3,000 a year more, but I didn't care. It was worth it."

"What happened?" I asked.

"Now they want to bus my kids to school in Harlem."

"That doesn't sound right."

"They figured my kids should be with underprivileged kids so they'll know what it's like. But I told them my kids know what it's like in an underprivileged school and we'd like to try an overprivileged school for a while."

"What did they say?"

"They said I should have stayed in Harlem if I wanted my kids to go to a good school. I can't expect them to go to a good school if I'm going to live in a good neighborhood. That wouldn't make sense."

"They have a point, you know," I said. "If everyone who lived in a good neighborhood sent their kids to a good school, whom would you send to the bad schools?"

"But I don't know why I have to live in a bad neighborhood to send my kids to a good school."

"Because the schools in a bad neighborhood are bad, and you wouldn't want to send them to a bad school, would you?"

"That's why I moved in the first place," he said.

"Well, you should have thought about it before you moved. Just because you live in a good neighborhood is no reason why you should send your kids to a good school."

"It's not as simple as that. I have a friend who lives in a bad neighborhood but, because of the busing, the authorities decided to make it a good school. They fixed it all up and brought in some first-rate teachers. Then they bused his kids to a good neighborhood which had a lousy school. He complained he wanted his kids to go to the good school in the bad neighborhood, but they told him his kids had to be bused to the lousy school in the good neighborhood, so the kids from the good neighborhood would have a good school to go to in the lousy neighborhood."

"Well," I said, "if that's true, why wouldn't your kids be able to go to a good school in a lousy neighborhood?"

"Because the school they want to send my kids to is a lousy school in a lousy neighborhood. Besides, how are my kids going to meet any kids from the good neighborhood if they go to the lousy school?"

"Maybe on the bus?" I suggested.

"I don't think so. I believe there is only one solution. I think I'll move back to Harlem and send the kids to private school."

Blue Eyes and Green Teeth

Governor George C. Wallace is a reasonable man. When he makes a point for segregation, he never attacks the Negro head on. He always resorts to using another type of illustration. He will say when arguing against the civil rights bill, "You may want to sell your house to someone with blue eyes and green teeth and that's all right. I don't object. But you should not be forced to do it. A man's home is his castle."

Recently I had my house up for sale in Washington and what Governor Wallace said took on meaning for me. Several people looked at the house but no one seemed to want to buy it. Then a man arrived with his wife. He was very nicely dressed, and seemed very polite. The thing that struck me about him was his blue eyes. I was just about to sell him the house when he smiled and I noticed he had green teeth!

"I'm sorry," I said as gently as I could, "but I can't sell you the house."

"Is it because I have green teeth?" he asked.

"Well, if you want me to be honest, yes, it is. I promised my neighbors I wouldn't sell my house to anyone who had blue eyes and green teeth. If you had green eyes and blue teeth, or brown eyes and yellow teeth, I could do it. But you have to understand, my home is my castle."

The man turned to my wife sadly. "You are the fourth person who has turned me down. It's not my fault that I have green teeth. I've tried every toothpaste on the market. I've consulted every dental specialist in the country. All they figure is that there is something in my genes. Please, won't you sell your house to me?"

"We couldn't if we wanted to," my wife said. "It isn't just because you have blue eyes and green teeth. Your wife has green teeth also."

His wife spoke up. "Of course I do. Who else would marry a blue-eyed green-toothed girl except another person with the same coloring? I thought I was going to be an old maid until I met Harold."

I said, "And I suppose your children have blue eyes and green teeth also?"

Harold said they did.

"You can see the spot I'm in, can't you?" I said to him. "This neighborhood is made up of brown-eyed and white-toothed children. What would their parents say if their kids had to go to school with children with blue eyes and green teeth? If God wanted your children and mine to play together, he would have made their eyes and teeth the same color."

"But I want to give my kids a chance," Harold said. "How can a kid with blue eyes and green teeth improve himself if he doesn't have an opportunity to live in a decent neighborhood, go to a decent school, and have the benefits that kids with white teeth have?"

"If it were up to me alone, I'd probably sell you the house," I said. "But if I did, the next thing you know is that everyone with green teeth would start moving in. Real estate values would tumble. Blue-eyed people would start marrying gray-eyed people and before you know it you'd have a mongrelization of the races."

Harold said, "We don't want to marry people with gray eyes and white teeth. All we want is a decent place to live. I make a good living posing for television toothpaste commercials. I'm the one who uses Brand X. But I want my kids to do something better in life. Can't you understand?"

"I understand perfectly," I said. "But nobody else does."

The Guest Stealers

Not long ago, I wrote about building a swimming pool. I thought all my problems would be over once it was built, but I was wrong. One of the things I had been warned about was that as soon as I had a pool I would be terribly bothered by people who wanted to use it. This, unfortunately, has turned out to be untrue.

I have had a hard time getting people to come over to see it, much less use it. The only real enjoyment in owning a pool is showing it off to less fortunate people than yourself. To make it pay off you have to have guests who admire it, ogle it, and tell you how lucky you are. It's no fun to sit by your pool alone or even to use it for a swim if no one knows you have it at the back of your house.

The trouble in Washington is that so many people have pools now that you're vying for each other's guests. Before I had my pool I was on very good terms with the David Brinkleys. They had a pool and it didn't take much to get me to come over to their house. But since I built my pool, I keep turning down their invitations to come over and now they're hardly speaking to me. It's true they had their pool first, but I can't afford to leave my pool, even for an afternoon, when I've got so much invested in it.

In order to attract guests, I put in an outdoor bar, have guaranteed lunch and dinner, and I present each person with an autographed copy of my book when they leave.

As an added attraction I bought a trampoline diving board at great expense. And yet, when the weekend comes, I still have trouble getting guests. Most of them, I discover, are going over to the Brinkleys' or the Bobby Kennedys' or to the White House for a swim.

You only have to build a pool to know who your real friends are. Take the Phil Geyelins. He works for the *Wall Street Journal* and lives around the corner from me. I could always count on the Geyelins coming over to the house and we had a wonderful, warm relationship.

Then, behind my back, without any warning, they decided to build their own pool. They tried to pretend they built it for their children, but I knew it was done out of spite. To add insult to injury they invited me over to *their* place for a swim.

You can imagine what I told them. And if that wasn't enough, I've heard through the grapevine that they invited several people that I had intended to invite for this weekend. Between them and the Brinkleys, I have hardly any guest list left.

This kind of thing has been going on all summer. As soon as you get a guest lined up, someone else steals from you.

Another thing that has spoiled things for me is that Washington has been unusually cool and many people who might ordinarily be interested in coming for a swim say they'd rather take a drive in the country.

I've even offered to take the Brinkley overflow, but they're so mad at me that when their pool fills up they send the people over to the Averell Harrimans, which is much farther away.

If I had known how difficult it was to get people to use my swimming pool, I might never have built it. Maybe I'll open it to the USO.

Leaves of Grass

The Commerce Department revealed last May that Americans spend $1.5 billion on their lawns. The figure isn't hard to believe if you own a lawn. As a matter of fact, it's quite low. All you have to do is to buy a few feet of sod, some fertilizer, some grass seed, a hose, and an electric lawn mower, and you've blown a million right there.

No one is quite sure who was the first one to start the lawn competition in America. It is rumored that it was a Pilgrim named Sam Snodgrass who was responsible for the whole thing.

One morning the Pilgrims got up and found Sam out front sprinkling seeds on the ground.

"What art thou doing, Sam?" his neighbors asked.

"Planting grass."

"But why? Canst thou eat it?"

"No, neighbor, but it will give me something to cut in the summertime."

The Pilgrim men, who rarely laughed, made merry of Sam. But when spring came and Sam's lawn started to grow, the wives of the other Pilgrims became very upset.

"Look, thou, at Brother Snodgrass' lawn," they said to their husbands. "It is verily a shame that we have nothing but dirt in front of our houses."

The other Pilgrim men were sore as hell, but there wasn't much they could do about it. So they all started planting grass in front of their houses. Pretty soon they were so busy working on their lawns they forgot to plant any crops and when winter came they almost starved to death.

But this did not dismay the Pilgrim wives. When spring came, they insisted that their husbands work on their lawns again.

"Look thee at Sam, with nary a weed in his yard," they grumbled.

"Women," the husbands cried, "we must plant crops instead."

"Better to starve," the women replied, "than to have an unkempt lawn."

And so the next winter all the Pilgrims died. But the tradition of having a neat lawn lived on in the New World and America became a great nation because the wives of its men always thought the grass was greener on the other side of the hedge.

Today a man is judged by the lawn he keeps. If it is trim and green and looks like a carpet, he is a loyal American. If it grows tall, has weeds, and straggles over on the sidewalk, he is a Communist.

And so once again this past spring, from the Atlantic to the Pacific, American men, egged on by their wives, were toiling in their front yards, devoting their strength, their lives, and their waking moments, not to mention $1.5 billion a year, to keep up with their neighbors' lawns.

The Pilgrims started it, but where it will all end, sod only knows.

The Karate Expert

Every once in a while I hear a true story that is so sad I can hardly write it. The other day I heard one about a friend of mine who lives in California. I shall call him Jake Kilduff to protect his identity.

Jake, who works in motion pictures, took up the sport of "karate" about ten years ago. Karate is a Japanese defense system in which the use of the hands plays the major role. Calluses are built up on the hand in such a way that an experienced karate expert can break a brick or a two-by-four by just bringing the edge of his hand down on it.

Let it be said that Jake was in the class with the experts. He was a "black belt," which is pretty high in karate hierarchy and, while other husbands watched television or read *Playboy,* Jake used to spend his time in the cellar breaking blocks of wood with his hand.

Jake's wife thought it was a lot of foolishness and a waste of money (he had invested $3,000 in karate lessons) and every once in a while she'd yell down to the cellar, "Will you stop breaking those bricks with your hand and come to bed?"

"Someday, Mother," he said, "you're going to be happy I know karate. It is the greatest self-defense ever devised by man."

After ten years went by even Jake started to doubt he would have a chance to use his skills. But then the big day came.

He was driving along a Los Angeles freeway on a Sunday afternoon with his wife when a sports car cut in front of him. Jake got mad and cut in front of the sports car. The man in the sports car got mad and cut in front of Jake.

Pretty soon they were shouting at each other and the man in the sports car yelled, "Pull off the freeway and I'll punch you in the nose."

Jake was elated. All the years of practice and expense were finally going to pay off. His wife begged him to ignore the other man, but Jake just rubbed his calluses against his chin and said, "Is he going to be in for a surprise!"

Jake pulled off the freeway and parked on a stretch of grass. The sports car driver pulled up in front of him and parked. The driver jumped out of his car and started walking toward Jake.

Jake studied him calmly. He was of medium build, not particularly heavy. It would probably take only one slash across the throat with his hand.

The driver moved forward, his right fist held back. "The guy is leaving himself wide open," Jake thought to himself. "Well, he asked for it."

Jake reached down to unfasten his car safety belt. It was stuck. He tried to unfasten it again. It was still stuck. The man reached Jake's car. Jake fought the belt desperately, but to no avail. The driver of the other car reached into the window and hit Jake in the mouth, knocking out two teeth.

As Jake continued to get his belt free, the man returned to his car, got back in, and drove off.

Jake's wife told us it took a week before Jake would even talk to her, and a month before he got a new bridge for his mouth. He's given up karate now. As a matter of fact, every time he sees a two-by-four or a brick, he gets sick to his stomach.

That's Show Biz

I've gone into the television business. There is a show called *The Entertainers,* starring Carol Burnett, Bob Newhart and Caterina Valente on Friday nights, and every once in a while I come on the show and talk for about three or four minutes about Washington.

I hadn't realized the impact you can have on people by appearing on TV. It's the only entertainment medium where everybody is a critic.

After I did my first show in New York, I returned to Washington. The first person I saw was Vicky, our cook.

"Were you nervous?" she asked.

"No, I wasn't nervous," I said.

"You didn't look nervous," she said.

"That's because I wasn't," I said.

Just then the dry-cleaning man arrived.

"I saw you on television last night," he said. "You sure looked nervous."

"I was a little nervous," I said.

"You looked more than a little nervous."

I decided not to give him a tip.

As he left, one of the neighbors came by. "I saw you on the Carol Burnett show last night."

I waited.

"Bob Newhart's very funny," he said.

It looked as if it were going to be a rough day.

I went down to the Georgetown Pharmacy to buy some aspirin. Doc Dalinsky, the druggist, came out from behind his counter.

"My sister said you were very good."

I started to smile.

"But my brother said you were lousy."

"What does your brother know?" I said angrily.

"Don't get sore at me. I didn't see the show. For all I know, you were all right."

A customer came in.

"Didn't I see you on the Caterina Valente show?"

"Yes, you did."

She bought a paper and walked out.

Back home the phone rang. It was our agent calling from New York. "You were great. Absolutely great. Everyone in New York is talking about it. And I think after the first few shows you'll stop being nervous."

"I wasn't nervous," I shouted.

"I didn't say you were nervous. Everybody in New York said you were nervous. I'm just repeating what they said."

I hung up.

The doorbell rang. Someone was delivering my daughter home from a birthday party.

"We saw you on television last night," the mother said. "Were you reading from a Teleprompter?"

"Yes."

"That's funny. I didn't know you were."

My wife came home and asked, "Any reaction on the show?"

"No, not a word," I said.

"Then what are you so nervous about?"

"I'm not nervous."

"You're more nervous now than you were on the show."

"Who said I was nervous on the show?" I demanded.

"Nobody. But I know you well enough to know when you're nervous and when you're not."

I called up Louis Nizer and asked him if Mexican divorces were still legal.

"I Am the Greatest"

There is a rumor that Cassius Clay, the heavyweight champion of the world, will be drafted into the United States Army. If Mr. Clay holds to form, this may present certain problems to the Army and I can't help wonder if the Army is up to it. I take you now to a U.S. Army training base where a first sergeant is talking to his commanding officer.

"I can't take it any more, Captain. You've got to relieve me."

"What's the trouble, Sergeant?"

"It's Private Clay, sir. He's driving me nuts. Every morning he gets up and says to me, 'I am the greatest. I am beautiful. I am the most wonderful recruit you have.' You can't imagine what it's doing to the rest of the platoon."

"I know it's not pleasant, Sergeant," the captain replies, "but you really can't expect me to relieve you because of that."

"You don't understand, Captain. There's more to it than that. Just the other day we were on the rifle range and I was trying to explain to him the importance of being a good marksman. He said, 'I don't need a rifle. I can beat anyone in the world with my hands. Just tell the Russians that Cassius Clay is in the Army and they will shiver and shake. I will slaughter the enemy. I will make mincemeat of them. Send me to Berlin. I am your secret weapon.'"

"I don't see anything wrong with that."

"But he said this in front of the platoon and now no one wants to learn how to fire a rifle. In fact, they're all mad about being drafted. One recruit said to me, 'I don't see why the Army needs the rest of us when it has Cassius Clay. We could have all stayed at home.'"

The captain says, "I can see where that could be embarrassing. What did you tell Clay?"

"I told him we didn't want him to fight the Russians. All we wanted him to do was to become a good soldier and be like everybody else."

"And what did he say?"

"He said, 'You can't waste me. I am too pretty. I am too great to be just a soldier. I think I should be a general. I would look great as a general.' So I told him he couldn't be a general, because he wasn't qualified. And he replied, 'That's what Sonny Liston said, that is what the sportswriters said, and that is what the world said. But I have shown them. I put Sonny Liston in the hospital and he didn't mark me once. I will fight any general for this job.'"

The captain starts to go white. "What else did he say?"

"It isn't just what he says. He's also been writing poetry. Listen to this, sir:

"The Army has had its day
And now it has Cassius Clay.
Do not worry and do not weep,
I will put the Russkies to sleep.
I am a tank, I am a gun,
I'm not afraid of anyone.
O joy, O love, I am so great.
I got Liston in seven and I'll get
Khrushchev in eight."

The captain looks at the poem. "I guess I'd better talk to the Colonel about this. Where is Clay now?"

"The last I saw of him he was telling the reporters he wanted a match with the 82nd Airborne Division. The entire division."

"Well, thank you, Sergeant. I'll tell the Colonel about your request."

"I'd appreciate it, sir. Perhaps if he turns you down, you could tell him my left shoulder hurts."

Subtitles for Old Books

There was a time when the only way you could get a pornographic book was to smuggle it in from Paris. But in recent years the paperback book industry in the United States has been outdoing anything you could bring in from Paris. I feel everyone has a right to make a dollar under our free enterprise system and if people want to buy pornographic literature that is their business. What I object to is the publishers making non-pornographic books pornographic by putting half-naked women on the covers of good books and printing descriptions of the contents which give an entirely different idea of the plot.

If the trend continues, here is how our paperback publishers will soon describe some books familiar to all of us:

Snow White and the Seven Dwarfs—The story of a ravishing blond virgin who was held captive by seven deformed men, all with different lusts.

Cinderella—A beautiful passionate woman bares her naked foot to the man she loves while her stepmother and stepsisters plot to cheat her out of the one memorable night in her life.

Alice in Wonderland—A young girl's search for happiness in a weird depraved world of animal desires. Can she ever return to a normal happy life after falling so far?

Huckleberry Finn—A wild youth runs away from his home to help a Negro slave escape from the ravishing Miss Watson.

Little Women—Four teen-agers, wise beyond their years, are caught up in the throbbing tumult of the Civil War. Read what happens to them when a rich old gentleman and his greedy grandson take rooms as boarders in a house without men.

Tom Brown's Schooldays—For the first time we look beyond the locked doors of an English boarding school to reveal the truth about a life that no one talks about and only a few will whisper.

Treasure Island—The crew of a ship bent on rape and plunder land on an island inhabited by sex-crazed cannibals. An innocent boy finds the secret of growing up.

Little Red Riding Hood—A girl goes to visit her grandmother only to discover a wolf in her bed. Read what happens when the girl refuses to get into bed with the wolf.

Tom Sawyer—A gang of subteen-age hoodlums paint the town white, and commit mayhem and murder to satisfy their desires.

Heidi—A young lady caught up in the wild life of Switzerland fights for love.

Babar the Elephant—Life in the raw.

And so it goes. As for the covers, I'll have to leave that up to the publishers. I hate to think what the paperback artists will do with *Wind in the Willows*.

Farewell to Mark

There has been a great deal written about automation and computers putting men out of work. But very little has been said about computers putting computers out of work.

One day I heard one of the saddest stories of the holiday season, concerning the laying off a Mark III Thinkovac.

Without any warning, the personnel manager of the Cavity Candy Co. switched on the machine and said:

"Mark, you're finished. As of the first of the year, we're replacing you with an SL-7 Charley Baker Brainomat."

Mark III was speechless. Then its tape started whirring furiously as it digested the news. "But Mr. Layoff," it blurted through its loudspeaker, "I've been working for the Cavity Candy Co. day and night for ten years. I've been loyal and honest and dependable. I worked every Sunday when no one was here and holidays, too."

"We mustn't let sentiment enter into this, Mark," Mr. Layoff replied. "All you've said is true, but we have to think of the company first. It takes you as much as 30 seconds to solve a problem. The new Brainomat can solve the same problem in five seconds. Besides, it doesn't take up so much room."

"I know the company comes first," Mark said. "But what about my past performance? I've been doing the work of 40 men. I've saved the company $240,000 in salaries alone. I figured it out once for you."

"That's true, Mark, but the Brainomat will do the work of 90 men and save us $450,000. At one time we needed you, but we have to make way for progress. If we felt sorry for every computer that passed its prime, we wouldn't be able to stay in business."

Mark III shook with emotion. "Mr. Layoff, I've got 12 transistors to support, an old magnet that depends on me, a broken transcriber that needs repairs. You can't just throw me out in the cold."

"This hurts me more than it hurts you, Mark. If it were up to me, I'd put you off in the corner somewhere and let you work on damaged chocolate bar returns. But the people up front say you have to go. You can always get another job."

"What can I do? Who is going to hire a ten-year-old computer these days?"

"Perhaps you could take a retraining program?" Mr. Layoff suggested.

"My memory's not that good. Digesting candy figures is all I know. The Brainomat may work faster for you, but will it give you the service and the loyalty that I have? I'm an experienced candy computer. Doesn't that count for anything?"

"The new computer will be able to learn the job in 24 hours."

"Mr. Layoff, I know I'm begging, but do you remember when you had the jelly bean problems? Some packages were getting too many jelly beans and other packages weren't getting enough. You gave the problem to me and in 15 minutes I solved it. Could a Brainomat have solved that?"

"I don't want to be cruel, Mark, but you were originally responsible for the jelly bean mixup."

"I was fed the wrong data," Mark III squealed.

"The difference between you and the Brainomat is that the Brainomat will reject the wrong data while you will accept it."

Tears of oil started pouring out of Mark III.

Mr. Layoff patted the machine. "Now come on, Mark, don't take it so hard. You deserve a rest. Just think of the quiet days ahead. We'll find a nice cool storeroom where you can take it easy and you won't have to think at all."

Two workmen came in and started pushing Mark III toward the door.

"Oh, by the way," Mr. Layoff said, "before you go, the company would like you to have this gold data-processing clock in gratitude for all that you've done for us."

The Tree Surgeon

The age of specialization has touched every part of our society. Recently I had tree trouble. A beautiful large oak was dying, and I immediately called a tree surgeon.

At first he didn't want to come. "I'm sorry, I don't make house calls," he explained.

"Then I'll cut down the tree and bring it into your office," I cried hysterically.

"Don't panic. I'll come over."

Three days later he arrived. He walked over to the oak and shook his head. He touched the trunk once, looked up at the branches and said:

"You have a very sick tree here."

"I know it. What can you do to save it?"

"I don't like the look of those lower limbs."

"Neither do I," I said. "What can you do about the limbs?"

"I'm not a limb man," the tree surgeon explained. "I only do general trunk work."

"Do you know of a good limb man?"

"I know of one and I only hope for your sake he's available. That will be $25 please."

A few days later the limb man came. He was all business.

"You've got two broken limbs and a wound on your main branch. Also, I don't like those stub lesions which are bleeding sap."

"Do whatever has to be done," I said.

"I can't touch the limbs until we heal up the lesions."

"Then heal them."

"I'm not a stub lesion expert. I'll give you the name of one. When he gets finished, I'll come back and work on the limbs. That will be $50 please."

The stub lesion surgeon arrived and worked for 20 minutes. Then he said, "Your tree is suffering from malnutrition. It has to be fed."

"Feed it," I begged, "and don't worry about the cost."

"I don't feed trees," he said indignantly. "You need a root man for that."

"You don't know of a root man, do you?" I asked.

"There's one out in Chevy Chase. I'll see if I can get him to come. That will be $75."

A week later the root man arrived with his drill and started operating on the oak. He poured nourishment into the ground near the roots.

"Will it be all right?" I asked him.

"The well you have around the tree is much too small. You're strangling it. I can give it all the food in the world and it won't do any good if the tree can't get any air or water."

"Then why did you feed it?" I asked.

"You told me to," he replied.

"I don't suppose you have anything to do with tree wells?" I said.

"I should hope not. You have to get a stone mason to do your well work. No tree surgeon will touch a well."

"That's what I thought."

I finally found a stone mason who agreed to build a wall around the tree for $400. It took him two days to do it and when he finally finished he said, "You know, mister, you got a real sick tree there."

"I know it," I said.

"It's none of my business, but if I was you I'd get myself a good tree surgeon."

Help Wanted, Tovarich

With all their efficiency, the one thing the Soviets forgot to do was take out Khrushchev's hot line to the White House. It will probably be denied, but the other night the hot line rang and Khrushchev was on it.

"Hellow, Tovarich, it's Nik," a voice whispered when the President answered the phone.

"Howdy, Mr. Khrushchev! How's everything?"

"Sh, sh, sh, not so loud. They may be listening outside the door. Congratulations on your election."

"Well, thanks very much."

"I imagine you have a lot of jobs open, Tovarich?"

"Well, yes. There are a few appointments I have to make."

"You couldn't use a good Russian expert, could you?"

"I hadn't thought about it. Did you have anybody in mind?"

"Me."

"Gosh, Mr. Khrushchev, that's nice of you to offer, but I don't think I could get you a security clearance. Don't forget you once said you'd bury us, and it's probably in your FBI file."

"I was misquoted, by state controlled Communist press," Mr. K. whispered. "I could make a good Russian expert. I know everything I did wrong in the last twelve years."

"It isn't just the bury-us line that would cause trouble. But remember when you took your shoe off at the United Nations? Well, the security people would probably think you were unstable. They take that kind of thing into consideration."

"Tovarich, I swear on *Das Kapital* the only reason I took my shoe off was because it was too tight. I can say this now. Russian shoes are not very good."

"I'd like to help you, Mr. Khrushchev, but we got too many Russian experts as it is, and I've got an economy drive on. I don't know how I could justify it."

"What about the Department of Agriculture? I'm tops in farming. I could be in charge of collective farms."

"We don't have any collective farms, Mr. Khrushchev."

"I could start some for you," he begged.

"I don't think that would work."

"Is there anything open at Disneyland?"

"I could check for you, but you know that's not a government-owned project. Mr. Disney hires his own people."

"Tovarich, I don't like to beg, but I need a job bad. Could I be a Senator from New York State?"

"We already have one from Massachusetts," the President replied. "Even if there was an opening I'm afraid if you ran they would bring up the carpetbagger issue again."

"There must be something for me to do. Perhaps advertising testimonials. I could be the one who uses greasy kid stuff on his hair."

"I couldn't help you there."

"Maybe baseball Czar?" Nikita said.

"Baseball is America's national pastime. I'm not sure they'd want a Russian to head it up."

"There must be something, Mr. President. After all I did for America these past few years."

"Well, I did hear they were looking for someone to take over the Republican National Committee."

"Wonderful. But wouldn't they object because of my background?"

"It wouldn't bother me."

How Are Things in Nonamura?

When the country of Nonamura in central Africa started having troubles with tribes in the north, it asked the American ambassador for advice.

The American ambassador said he didn't know much about military affairs, but perhaps the United States, as a gesture of friendship, would send a military adviser to straighten out the matter.

A U.S. Army sergeant was dispatched from Tripoli. In a few days he wrote his superiors: "I am shocked to find Nonamura soldiers still using poison darts, spears, and World War I rifles. Urge immediate shipment of up-to-date small arms."

The request was approved and the Nonamura army not only received surplus American small arms, but three advisers, led by a captain, to see they were used properly.

The captain and advisers distributed the small arms, but realized that if they were to be effective the Nonamura army would need transportation. The captain cabled: PLEASE SEND U.S. TRUCKS AND WEAPONS CARRIERS WITH TEAM OF TRANSPORTATION SPECIALISTS AT ONCE AS WAR GOING BADLY IN NORTH.

The transportation specialists, commanded by a major, showed up and after studying the situation the major cabled back: IN ORDER TO MAKE USE OF WEAPONS CARRIERS AND TRUCKS I STRONGLY ADVISE IMMEDIATE DISPATCH OF TANKS. OTHERWISE CANNOT GUARANTEE NONAMURA ARMY VICTORY.

One hundred tanks with 990 tank experts, commanded by a colonel, were shipped in. Unfortunately, while the colonel was setting up the tank school, the rebel tribesmen overran a government position and stole most of the weapons supplied by the U.S.

(The rest were sold at bargain prices to the rebels by a corrupt minister of defense.)

The colonel flew back to Washington to make a report. He advised the Pentagon to replenish the stolen weapons and, while they were at it, to include some flamethrowers, rockets, antiaircraft guns, and long-range artillery.

The Pentagon took the colonel's advice and the equipment was sent with a division of advisers from Fort Benning, Georgia, commanded by a major general.

He no more than got settled when he shot off a wire to the Joint Chiefs of Staff: IMPOSSIBLE MAKE ANY HEADWAY IN NONAMURA WITHOUT AIR SUPPORT. STRONGLY ADVISE YOU SEND TWO SQUADRONS OF F-105 FIGHTER AIRCRAFT PLUS TRAINING PERSONNEL. CANNOT BE RESPONSIBLE FOR WHAT HAPPENS WITHOUT AIR COVER.

The Joint Chiefs sent two squadrons of jet aircraft and an entire training wing supplied by the Navy and headed up by a vice-admiral.

Unfortunately at that moment the Nonamura government was overthrown and replaced by a military junta. The admiral cabled Washington: CORRUPT CIVILIAN GOVERNMENT REPLACED BY SERIOUS NONAMURA GENERALS. STRONGLY URGE YOU RECOGNIZE AT ONCE AND GIVE THEM $50 MILLION LOAN.

A month later a U. S. Air Force four-star general, who had replaced the admiral, wired the State Department: CORRUPT MILITARY JUNTA REPLACED BY PRO-WEST NONAMURA COLONELS. WE MUST BACK THEM IF WE HOPE TO DEFEAT REBELS.

By this time Congress and the press were getting interested. We had 200,000 military advisers in Nonamura. The President did the only thing he could do under the circumstances. He sent his Secretary of Defense to give him a firsthand report. The Secretary cabled the President: WAR GOING WELL BUT NONAMURA NEEDS MORE MILITARY AID AND LACKS ONLY $124 MILLION.

This was immediately voted by Congress.

In spite of everything things still aren't going too well in Nonamura. Just the other day the President received a request from the Joint Chiefs of Staff. All it said was: WOULD YOU HAVE ANY OBJECTION IF WE LENT NONAMURA 10 OBSOLETE ATOMIC BOMBS?

Head of the Class

Probably the toughest thing to be in this world is a Soviet student. No matter how well you learn your lessons, it doesn't necessarily mean you're right.

For example, last October at People's School 113 in Moscow, a teacher was talking to his eighth-grade class.

"Boys and girls, today the brave Soviet cosmonauts, Komarov, Yegorov, and Feoktistov, have returned from the glorious flight into space. The first question is: Who is the man who is responsible for this unbelievable feat?"

The children shout, "Comrade Khrushchev!"

"Why is Comrade Khrushchev responsible, little Vladimir?"

"Because, Comrade Teacher, he is our glorious leader, and he has sent our spaceships into the heavens to show the decadent Western capitalist nations the Soviets are first in science."

"Very good, Vladimir. Now, little Katrina, what else has our beloved Comrade Khrushchev done?"

"He has kept the peace in the world, has spread the message of Communism throughout the globe, and has brought prosperity to the peoples of all the Soviets."

"What else, Ivan?"

"He has made the corn grow high, the wheat grow strong, and the flowers bloom."

"And what about steel production?"

"That's good, too."

"Little Boris, who is the greatest leader against the reactionary adventurist and chauvinist line of the Chinese government?"

"I don't know."

"Stupid lout, Boris. What do you mean, you don't know?"

"I'm not sure."

"Stay after class, Boris, and we will see if we can refresh your memory."

As he is talking, the principal comes in and whispers something into the teacher's ear. The teacher goes white. He nods and writes down some things on a pad.

Then he addresses the class again. "Now, once more. Who is the man who is responsible for our great victory over space?"

"Comrade Khrushchev," the class shouts.

"Idiots! How many times do I have to tell you? It is our glorious leader, Leonid Brezhnev, the enemy of the cult of personality and brother of the working classes."

He looks at little Vladimir.

"Now tell me, little Vladimir, what has Comrade Khrushchev done?"

"He has sent our spaceship into the heavens—"

"Stop! Comrade Khrushchev is a reactionary phrasemonger, a harebrained, inept, bragging fool, and an enemy of the people."

Katrina raises her hand. "But did he not keep the peace in the world?"

"Daughter of an imperialist! If I've told you once, I've told you a hundred times, Aleksei Nikolaevich Kosygin is a man of peace. Khrushchev is a drunkard, and a criminal with paranoid tendencies."

"But it says in the book—"

"Never mind the book! They are all going to be confiscated. I am ashamed of all of you for not learning your lessons. The only one who has done his homework is little Boris. Little Boris will someday be a great Communist leader."

How to Organize a Coup

"Gentleman, the class will come to order. Today we will discuss the organizing of military coups. As you know, when you return to your own countries at the end of this course, you will be in charge of large units of your national army. You will probably be involved with at least one coup and there are certain things you must be aware of. First of all, what kind of a coup do you want?"

A colonel raises his hand. "A bloodless coup?"

"Very good, Colonel Phununumu. A bloodless coup is always the best kind. World opinion will always accept a bloodless coup, whereas if you have to resort to fighting it will look messy in the newspapers and you will give all military coups a bad name.

"In order to organize a bloodless coup, you have to have a junta. This junta should be composed of other officers, preferably below the rank of general. When your coup is successful, you can promote yourselves. Actually, one of the main reasons for a coup is to speed up the promotion process in the military services. What is it, Major Gonzales?"

"Señor, eef we 'ave a junta, who decides who eez the chief?"

"You cut cards for it. That's usually the way it's done."

A naval captain raises his hand. "In bloodless coups the army seems to get all the jobs and the navy is rarely consulted. Is there anything we can do to play a bigger role?"

"It all depends where the capital of your country is. If the capital is a seaport, you can bring in your destroyers and cruisers and threaten to shell the city if you're not made part of the junta. By the same token, you men in the air force can indicate that you'll bomb the capital if you're not given a role. Ideally, military coups should be split amongst all the armed services.

"Now the most important thing in a coup is to get command of troops. A tank corps command is ideal or a paratrooper command is quite helpful. Stay off the general staff if you possibly can. You may get arrested by mistake.

"Once you have command of troops, you must think of some excuse to bring them into the capital of the country. Perhaps you can bring them in for an armed forces loyalty day parade or a USO show. Fix your arrival for early in the morning when everyone is sleeping. The first thing you do is to surround the Presidential palace and the radio station. You announce over the radio that you have taken over in the name of free and democratic government and you charge the incumbents with stealing the treasury, setting up a dictatorship, and dealing with subversive foreign powers.

"If all goes well, you should be in the palace for breakfast. Put the President and his Cabinet under house arrest and organize a popular demonstration in the streets. Let the people burn down a department store or a foreign embassy to make them feel they really have freedom. After that, move in your troops and put in a seven o'clock curfew on the town.

"Then hold a press conference and announce that none of the foreign policies of your country will change and you will be happy to accept aid from any country which offers it without strings. You will be surprised how anxious foreign diplomats are to get in good with a new junta. You had a question, Colonel Choo?"

"Only one. How do we open a Swiss bank account?"

Why Russians Defect

There has been a lot of talk in the newspapers lately about Russian defectors. I've always wondered why Russians defect and the other day I was fortunate to interview one who gave me some interesting details on his defection.

I shared a table with him at Bassin's Cafeteria and introduced myself. He said:

"I am Nicolai Sergevitch, Russian defector."

"I'm very pleased to meet you, sir. I haven't met many Russian defectors."

"Is nice meeting you," he replied. "I don't meet many people who put chutney on knockwurst."

"May I ask you a personal question? Why did you defect?"

"It is a simple story," he said. "I am big shot in Soviet government. I have my own car, my own bureau, my own dacha. I am up-and-coming Communist commissar. No one has better future than me."

"I don't understand. You didn't hate Russia, then?"

"Hate? I loved Russia. It is my mother land. Even now I miss it."

"Then why did you defect?"

"One day I am called in by my superior and he says, 'Nicolai, we are sending you to United States of America on top-secret mission. We trust you as loyal Soviet Communist, but just to make certain that you come back we are going to keep your wife behind. If anything goes wrong you know what will happen to her.'

"I say, 'Don't worry, Comrade Guzenko. I am loyal to the motherland. You can count on me.' So I go home and tell my wife I am going on top-secret mission and she is getting sick and tired of it, and she is fed up with running a hotel, and I should do some other type work because a wife she is not, and I am a lousy husband because I never give her enough money, and on and on and on. Then her mother, who is living with us, says her daughter should have never married below her class, and maybe because I probably have a girl friend somewhere, and on and on and on.

"So off I go to United States of America. Every day I get letters from wife telling me plumbing is no good, neighbors is making too much noise, she can't buy any curtains, window in cellar is broken, her mother is out of job, and everything is lousy. She says wait until I get home, because she is really going to tell me a thing or two and she is not going to take my going away lying down.

"After two weeks of letters I say to myself, 'America is not such a bad country after all. Maybe I will become a defector.'"

"But," I said, "what about your wife? Didn't they tell you if you refused to come back they would do something to her?"

"Exactly, comrade," he smiled. "You are now eating with a man who committed a perfect crime."

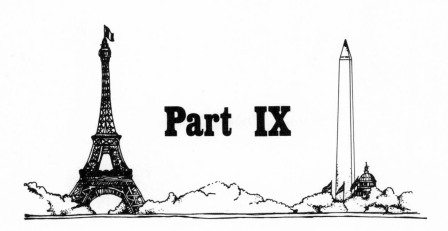

Part IX

If Barry Goldwater Had Been Elected

Every once in a while, when I have nothing better to do, I wonder what the country would be like if Barry Goldwater had been elected President of the United States. Based on his campaign and his speeches, it is a frightening thing to imagine.

The mind boggles when you think of it. For one thing, we would probably be bombing North Vietnam now if Goldwater were in office.

As I see it, this is what would have happened.

The Viet Cong would have blown up an American barracks. Using this as an excuse, Goldwater would immediately call for a strike on military bases in North Vietnam and announce a "new tit-for-tat policy." Democrats would be horrified and they would make speeches that Goldwater was "trigger-happy" and was trying to get us into a war with Red China.

But Goldwater would ignore the criticism, and to show he meant business, he would continue the raids, using not only Air Force bombers, but jets from the U.S. fleet. As time went on, the country would be shaken at the recklessness of Goldwater's plan, but he would explain through his Secretary of State that, instead of a "tit-for-tat" policy, we now intended to bomb North Vietnam in order to let Hanoi know they could not support the Viet Cong without expecting retaliation.

Senators would get up in Congress and call for some sort of negotiations. But Goldwater, with his lack of restraint, would retort that there is nothing to negotiate and we would only be selling out Southeast Asia if we sat down at a table with the North Vietnamese and Red China.

Russia and France would call for a Geneva conference, but Goldwater would reject it.

Instead, he would recklessly announce that he was sending in a battalion of Marines with Hawk missiles to protect our airfields. His critics would claim he was escalating the war, but Goldwater would deny it. Instead he would bomb supply routes in Laos and Cambodia.

To explain these desperate actions, Goldwater would have the Defense and State Departments produce a "White Paper" justifying the attacks and proving that Hanoi was responsible for the revolution in South Vietnam. He would insist we had to support the Saigon generals, no matter how shaky they were.

The paper would be followed by more air strikes, using South Vietnamese planes as well as American B-57s.

The people who voted for Johnson would scream at their Republican friends, "I told you if Goldwater became President he'd get us into a war." But the Republicans would claim that Goldwater had no choice, that he, in fact, inherited the Vietnam problem from the Democrats and, if he didn't take a strong stand now, America would be considered a paper tiger.

It all seems farfetched when you read it and I may have let my imagination run away with itself, because even Barry Goldwater, had he become President, wouldn't have gone so far.

But fortunately, with President Johnson at the helm, we don't even have to think about it.

Regrets Only

Just as I was giving up all hope of being invited to the Presidential Inauguration, I received a large 8 x 10-inch envelope in the mail which said on it, INAUGURATION COMMITTEE—DO NOT BEND.

With hands trembling, I cut open the envelope and took out a gold-engraved invitation which said, "The Inaugural Committee requests the honor of your presence to attend and participate in the inauguration of Lyndon Baines Johnson as President of the United States of

America and Hubert Horatio Humphrey as Vice-President of the United States of America on Wednesday, the Twentieth of January, One Thousand Nine Hundred and Sixty-Five in the City of Washington."

I'll have to admit it. I started to bawl. The President hadn't forgotten me and all I had done to get him the nomination in Atlantic City.

When I composed myself, I called my wife and told her we had been invited to the inauguration.

It was her turn to sob. "With all he has to do," she said, "he remembered us."

We both chuckled and then she said, "Where are we sitting?"

"It doesn't say on the invitation, but I would guess in his box, maybe behind the Supreme Court Justices."

"What should I wear?" she said.

"Go out and buy yourself a new suit. After all, it isn't every day we get invited to the inauguration of the President of the United States."

"How will we get there?"

"The White House will probably send a car, but if they don't, we'll hire a limousine."

"My fur is so dowdy," she said.

"So get a new fur coat. We'll probably be on television most of the time and I want you to look nice."

"It seems like a dream," she said.

"Well, it isn't a dream," I replied. "I have the invitation right here in front of me." I picked it up, and as I did a slip of paper fell out of it. I started to read it to myself. It began: "IMPORTANT NOTICE—The Souvenir Invitation to the Inaugural is in grateful recognition of the interest you have manifested in the election of the President and Vice-President of the United States. It conveys our sincere wish that you may be in Washington for the occasion, but the invitation in itself does not constitute an admission to any of the inaugural events."

The notice then went on to point out that the events were by separate invitation only and not to send a check unless you were invited by somebody else.

"Hello, hello," my wife said. "Are you still there?"

"You know what I said about a new suit?"

"Yes."

"Forget it."

"But what will I wear to the inauguration?"

"We're not going to the inauguration?"

"But we were invited."

"That's how much you know," I said angrily. "And don't get that fur coat, either."

Later on I walked into the Washington bureau of the New York *Herald Tribune* and everyone, including the office boy, was holding one of the invitations in his hand.

"What do you think it all means?"

"It beats me," a reporter said. "But if you ask me, I think someone over at the White House got a new printing press for Christmas."

Friendly Persuasion

The settlement of the steel strike was another feather in the cap of President "I Won't Take No for an Answer" Johnson. The negotiations were hard and they were tense and I can now reveal for the first time how the President got the parties to agree.

On Monday he asked both management and the union officials to come to Washington. The men were met at the airport in black limousines and immediately driven to the White House, where they were ushered into a large bare office with a table and hard chairs. The President greeted them, told them of his desire for a just settlement, and offered the use of his executive offices to continue the negotiations. Both sides thanked the President for his kind offer but said they preferred to continue the talks in Pittsburgh.

"That's fine with me," the President said, and then he left the room. But when the union and management people tried to leave the room, the first person to the door shouted in panic, "It's locked!"

Several of the steel and union executives tried the door without success.

Then someone said, "Let's go out the window." Just below the window were four marines with fixed bayonets. They started to raise their rifles.

The negotiators sat down at the table.

On Tuesday one of the President's aides came into his office and said, "Sir, they're asking for food."

"Tell them they can have all the food they want, even from the White House kitchen, as soon as they sign a contract."

"Yes, sir."

"By the way, did you turn off the air conditioning?"

"Yes, sir. And we put heat in the radiators, as you suggested."

"That's just fine."

The next morning Mr. Johnson's secretary came in. "There are some officials from the International Red Cross outside, sir."

"Send them in."

The first official spoke. "Mr. President, we understand you're violating the Geneva Convention in regard to the treatment of union and management officials who have been captured by you."

"The reports have been exaggerated," the President said. "Ah've treated them justly and fairly."

"We understand they haven't eaten in three days and there is even a shortage of water. We also understand they have not been allowed to contact their relatives and have been unable to talk to a representative of the Red Cross."

"Ah've never used force on anyone," Mr. Johnson said. "When they put their country ahead of their own needs, as true Americans, I will release them and send them back to their loved ones. Good day, gentlemen."

On Thursday an aide reported again. "Three have passed out from the union side and two from management. One executive is seeing mirages, and another union official is yelling at the marines to shoot him. I believe a settlement is near."

"Notify the television networks to stand by. We may have a break in the next 48 hours. And, Jack, take the chairs out of the room and make them stand for a while."

On Friday, at exactly six o'clock, an aide came dashing in.

"They've agreed to settle, sir."

"Good. What have they agreed on?"

"They said you announce it and they'll sign it. All they ask is food, water, and a bed."

"Bring 'em out first to appear in front of television, Jack, and be sure and clean them up. I don't want the people to think I used any pressure on them while they were negotiating."

Escalation

The American government announced that 1,000 U.S. troops have just landed in South Vietnam. These 5,000 men will be used to protect airfields and vital installations around Saigon, though officials did not rule out that the 15,000 combat-ready soldiers supported by 10,000 aviation personnel would be used to take the fight to the enemy.

An Army spokesman said that the 35,000-troop landing was carried out by plane and sea and that the 50,000-man force, which did not include an armored division, landed earlier in the day, would for the moment constitute enough men to handle the situation. A Defense Department spokesman said:

"If in the near future we discover that these 150,000 men are not enough, we will send in more troops, but it is unlikely, as 200,000 GIs should be sufficient under present fighting conditions."

A newspaperman asked if the sending of 300,000 fresh troops at this time meant that the U.S. "was escalating the war."

"No," he replied, "it means no such thing. We always intended to send in 400,000 troops and this is just part of a military buildup. In a guerrilla war, it is assumed the ratio of troops to the guerrillas is 10 to 1. Since we estimate that there are now 50,000 guerrillas in South Vietnam, our decision to send in 500,000 more soldiers is not unrealistic."

Another reporter asked if the United States intended to get bogged down in a ground war in South Vietnam, something that every American military leader had advised against.

"The answer to your question is negative," the spokesman said. "Our job from the beginning has been to give as much support to the South Vietnamese army as we possibly can. With the arrival of these 700,000 GIs, we can release the South Vietnamese army for major missions."

"Isn't it true that the South Vietnamese government has requested that the American soldiers take over the fighting, while the South Vietnamese regroup and help the people in the villages?"

"There was some talk of that, but the decision will have to be made in Washington. Although we now have 800,000 more American troops, it is still our hope that we can fight side by side with the Vietnamese soldiers."

"Sir, the rumor is that the South Vietnamese army may soon switch roles and become advisers to the American troops."

"The South Vietnamese have offered to cooperate in any way they can. Perhaps at a future date they may take a more active role, but you must remember our latest commitment is only 900,000 men and we have no intention of raising it unless the situation warrants it."

Someone said to the Army spokesman: "Of the 950,000 men landed this morning, how many of them are combat-trained as opposed to service troops?"

"It's hard to say. By the way, gentlemen, I've just been asked to correct the figure I gave you earlier. A million Americans were landed this morning and will be used mostly as an advance force to set up facilities for regular troops who will be landed in the next few weeks."

"How many men will be landed next week?"

"We can't say at this time, but the commitment will be kept to a minimum. While we are pledged to help the South Vietnamese, we don't

want to do anything to give the impression that the South Vietnam
conflict is an American war."

Indoctrination

The Honolulu meeting was a turning point for the war in Vietnam.
President Johnson and Premier Ky spelled out the goals of our commitment there, and these are now being transmitted to our soldiers,
sailors, marines, and airmen. But the indoctrination is going rather
slowly, and the sergeants are having a hard time explaining the new
policy.

"All right, you meat heads. We are now going to discuss why we're
fighting in Vietnam. Rosenbloom, why do you think we're fighting in
Vietnam?"

"To beat the hell out of the blankety-blank Viet Cong, Sergeant."

"No, Rosenbloom, you're wrong. It's to bring social and economic reforms to the freedom-loving people of South Vietnam. Now, Petrosanni, how will we achieve this goal?"

"By killing every blankety-blank Viet Cong we can find."

"I'm surprised at you, Petrosanni. We will achieve this goal by winning over the natives through public works, education, and good deeds.
You had your hand up, Reilly?"

"What do we do with these mortars and flamethrowers?"

"We use them to show the South Vietnamese people that we will not
be pushed out by the North Vietnamese. Every time we fire our flamethrowers, we are renewing our pledge to fight oppression, poverty, and
disease in Southeast Asia. We can only win this war by getting the
confidence of the populace. Now, how do we do this?"

"By bombing the hell out of the towns and villages where the Viet
Cong are supposed to be hanging out."

"Exactly, but we must explain to the people why we're bombing their
towns and villages. How do we explain it, McPherson?"

"Beats me."

"We explain it by explaining the domino theory. We tell the people
that, if South Vietnam falls, then Thailand will fall and then Malaysia
and pretty soon all of Southeast Asia will be under the domination of
the Communists. What is it, O'Toole?"

"You mean the people won't mind their homes being bombed and
their rice fields being burned if we explain it to them afterwards?"

"Right. Once you put people in on the big picture, then their troubles will seem infinitesimal in comparison. Zwacki, you had your hand up."

"Sarge, I would like to know how you tell the good Vietnamese from the bad Vietnamese."

"It's very simple. When you see a native, you yell, 'Nuts to Ho Chi Minh.' If he fires at you, you know he's with the Viet Cong."

"That could be dangerous, Sarge. For example, yesterday Condon got all banged up doing just that. He lost his helmet and his rifle and he wound up in the hospital."

"What happened?"

"Well, he saw this native and he yelled at him, 'Nuts to Ho Chi Minh,' and the native started firing at him, so Condon fired back.

"Then the Viet Cong guy yelled, 'Nuts to LBJ,' and as Condon and the Viet Cong were shaking hands, a big truck ran over them."

The Carrot and the Stick

President Johnson's "stick and carrot" policy as presented last April is now being studied by the experts. The stick, we know, is the bombing of North Vietnam; the carrot he offered was that if the Communists would stop annoying Saigon, they might expect to get United States aid à la a Southeast Asia Marshall Plan. The man in charge of the stick is Secretary of Defense McNamara; the man who may be put in charge of the carrot is Eugene Black, the former head of the World Bank. I can foresee in the near future where the interests of these two men could be at odds.

"Bob, this is Gene Black here. I called you about those railroad bridges you're planning to bomb near Hanoi. I wish you wouldn't do it, Bob. Railroad bridges cost a lot of money and as you know the American government is going to have to eventually pay for them."

"Look, Gene, we've had those railroad bridges targeted for months. They're the key to Ho's supply lines."

"That's all well and good, Bob, but the Administration has to answer to Congress for anything you destroy."

"Gene, I think military strategy has to have precedence over foreign aid."

"Bob, I don't want to be a bore about this, but I have it on reliable authority that the North Vietnamese want you to bomb those bridges. They've been hoping to build new ones for years, but have never been able to get the money. I believe the Defense Department is playing into their hands."

"I resent that, Gene. We've got to keep up the bombing so we can get Hanoi to the negotiation stage. We have to keep up the pressure."

"I'd take issue with you on that. I've already seen the list of things that North Vietnam plans to request as soon as there is a cease-fire. It includes highways, ports, freight trains, trucks, airports and four new Hilton hotels. The more things you wreck, the less reluctant they'll be to call for a cease-fire. They know what happened in Japan and West Germany after the last war, thanks to American bombing, and they have hopes of rebuilding their country in the same way."

"For the moment, Gene, the 'big stick' policy is in effect, and I cannot be concerned with what it will cost us after the war is stopped."

"I'm not asking you to stop the bombing, Bob. All I'm asking you to do is bomb places that have no value, and which they can't justify our rebuilding for them. Is that asking too much?"

"I'll have to talk it over with the Joint Chiefs, but if we don't hurt them we'll never be able to stop the Viet Cong."

"That's another thing I wanted to talk to you about. I wish you'd stop using those fire bombs in South Vietnam. They're terribly destructive and we're going to have to replant all those forests. Couldn't you go back to using nonlethal gas?"

"You're making life very difficult for me, Gene. I believe in foreign aid as much as anybody, but I can't worry about your program. That's the Department of State's problem."

"Okay, go ahead. Wreck their economy and see where it gets us. We've only got a billion dollars to play with, and if you keep up your bombing attacks, I'm going to have to cut South Vietnam out of our program."

Peace Is Hell

As the Johnson peace offensive goes into its third year, more and more attention is being paid to responses from Hanoi. Everyone is looking for some sort of sign that North Vietnam is ready to come to the negotiating table, and every reply to our peace overtures is studied by our experts in minute detail.

Therefore, what might sound on the surface as a complete rejection of an offer could very well be the opening we've been looking for.

I went over to the State Department the other day and talked to a U.S. Hanoi-watcher, who was, at that very moment, studying the latest North Vietnam radio broadcast concerning our peace offensive.

"It looks promising," he said, as he shoved his magnifying glass to one side.

"How's that?" I asked.

"Well, listen to this," he continued, reading from the report. "The U.S. policy of aggression in Vietnam remains unchanged and shows the arrogance of President Johnson in pretending he wants peace while American and puppet troops intensify their attacks on innocent women and children."

"That's promising?" I said.

"It's a very mild statement compared to the one they made last week."

"What else did they say?"

"U.S. imperialists will be thrown into the sea long before any peace swindle can be made, and their lackeys in Saigon will be chewed up by the democratic peoples of Vietnam."

"That sounds bad," I said.

"On the contrary, there's a great glimmer of hope here. This is the first time Hanoi has mentioned the sea. It may have significance. It's possible they might want to negotiate on water rather than land."

"That's something I hadn't thought of."

"Now here, in the third paragraph, may be another hint that they're ready to talk. It says, 'North Vietnam will never be blackmailed into giving away the rights of the National Front for Liberation by a nation who sabotaged the 1954 Geneva agreements, and who have shamelessly launched air attacks on the cities and villages leaving behind wanton destruction and horror.'"

"What kind of hint do you get out of that?" I asked.

"This is the first time they've mentioned the Geneva agreements in a broadcast, and it's quite possible this is their way of telling us, without the Chinese knowing, of course, that they would be willing to go there."

"By George, you may be right," I said excitedly.

"Now down here in the broadcast they make their usual attacks on our imperialism and credibility. Then they say, 'There is no possible way of ever negotiating peace in Vietnam until every American soldier leaves this country.'"

"That's a tough statement," I said.

"We've asked them to clarify it. You'll note they don't say when the soldiers should leave. There could be two meanings to it. Possibly three.

"Here, at the end, they say, 'So long as U.S. imperialists still pursue the war of aggression against Vietnam and launch attacks against the fatherland, the people in both zones of Vietnam will fulfill their sacred duty to resist with the aid of their peace-loving friends in China and the Soviet Union. Let them make no mistake about this.'"

"It sounds like a peace feeler to me," I said.

"We're treating it like that, until we get word to the contrary."

Crack Troops of Nonomura

As you probably remember, the country of South Nonomura has been fighting the Communist guerrillas for four years. Thanks to American military aid and American advisers, South Nonomura now has one of the best-equipped armies in the world, and when it comes to hardware the South Nonomuran soldier lacks nothing. Newsreels of the crack South Nonomuran troops show them flying off into the jungle in American helicopters, armed to the teeth. You get a feeling of pride that a group of peasants like the South Nonomurans can be whipped into a first class fighting outfit.

Unfortunately, despite all the aid, the South Nonomurans haven't been doing very well against the North Nonomuran guerrillas, who are armed with nothing more than fishing rods and World War II rifles. Why, everyone asks, can't the South Nonomuran army contain the guerrillas?

One of our correspondents came back after an interview with a crack South Nonomuran officer and showed us his notes. The interview shed some light on the problem.

CORRESPONDENT: Captain, how is the war going?

CAPTAIN: War going great. Tell Americans we like K-rations very much, but Q-rations lousy. We need more cigarettes and beer. Morale very low without beer.

CORRESPONDENT: Why hasn't your army been able to contain the guerrillas?

CAPTAIN: Our army trained by Americans to fight enemy in open. Lousy Communists hide in jungle.

CORRESPONDENT: Why don't you go into the jungle and get them?

CAPTAIN: You crazy or something? You can get bitten by snakes in the jungle. Besides, your uniform gets dirty. We have to keep uniforms nice and clean for coup d'état.

CORRESPONDENT: That's true.

CAPTAIN: And don't forget, you have to walk in jungle. Since Americans came, my men won't go anywhere unless it's by truck or helicopter. Walking is for lousy Communists.

CORRESPONDENT: There have been many instances where you have had the Communists surrounded and they've disappeared. How do you explain this?

CAPTAIN: Very simple. As soon as we hear about lousy Communist attack, we send crack soldiers there to fight them. But crack soldiers must be supported by many men. We must have hot food, showers, officers' club, noncommissioned officers' club, PX, chaplain, movies and comfortable living quarters. By the time my crack outfit is ready to fight, lousy Communists have escaped into jungle.

CORRESPONDENT: Wouldn't it be better if you fought the war without these things?

CAPTAIN: We crack outfit. Thanks to American training and know-how we not going to fight dirty war like dirty Communists.

CORRESPONDENT: But you're not getting anywhere.

CAPTAIN: That's what you think. In another year I make colonel. Then I overthrow the government. You see me then, I give you good interview.

CORRESPONDENT: But, Captain, isn't there some way of turning the tide against the guerrillas?

CAPTAIN: It's too late. My crack troops have taste of American way of life. We are so busy keeping them supplied, we don't have much time to fight lousy Communists. All they talk about these days is GI Bill of Rights.

CORRESPONDENT: Is there anything you need that would help speed up the war?

CAPTAIN: Yes, send us more Japs.

CORRESPONDENT: Japs?

CAPTAIN: You know, Jap transistor radios.

The Desegregated Bull

Every once in a while a glimmer of light shines through the darkness of segregation in Alabama. Recently an Aberdeen Angus bull, which was bought for the record price of $176,400, was operated on to restore his virility. The operation was performed at Auburn University in Alabama in hopes that the bull, whose name is Lindertis Evulse, would be able to serve his function as a mate to 10,000 cows a year. By artificial insemination, of course.

While everybody is awaiting the results, the state of Alabama's House of Representatives and Senate have both passed resolutions wishing Lindertis Evulse a speedy recovery and a long and happily prolific life. The most amazing thing about the resolution—and the thing the Alabama legislature overlooked—was that Lindertis Evulse is a black bull.

This raises some interesting questions. It is assumed that if the operation is a success Lindertis Evulse will be mated with cows of other colors—some even white, and this certainly will not serve the cause of segregation.

Another is that if Lindertis Evulse makes it at the University of Auburn many black bulls from all over the world will apply for admission and it will be impossible for educational officials to turn them down on the grounds of creed or color.

It may be the first breakthrough in Alabama for better race relations.

This is not to say there are not many stumbling blocks.

One of the reasons bulls have not wanted to go to an Alabama university is that they've seen what the authorities down there can do with cattle prods.

While it is true that the prods so far have only been used on people, it is possible that some overzealous police chief might decide to use them on cattle.

Also, if the black bulls are too successful, they may start taking stud fees away from the white bulls, and this could cause a tremendous amount of friction on the range.

Another problem is housing. If you put a black bull in a white barn, there will be a great cry of protest from the parents of cows who fear for the safety of their offspring.

Then there is the question of what happens in a restaurant in Alabama. Is it proper for a steak fathered by a black bull to be served in an all-white restaurant? If so, should the steak be labeled so the customer can refuse it and ask for a steak from an all-white bull, if he is so inclined?

These are only a few of the problems that have been raised since Lindertis Evulse was admitted to Auburn. They can't be solved overnight, but everyone is optimistic. If the Alabama legislature can pass a resolution in favor of a black bull, it may someday pass one in favor of a black person.

In the meantime, everyone is rooting that Lindertis Evulse's operation turns out successfully and he will be all bull again.

If it works out the way the medical people at Auburn hope it will,

Alabamans will then have to ask each other, "Would you want your cow to marry a black Aberdeen Angus?"

Alabama Literacy Test

Getting to vote in Bull Whip, Ala., isn't as easy as one would think. First, you have sneak around a mounted sheriff's posse, then fight your way through a cloud of state police tear gas, and then you have to leap over a hundred cattle prods. And finally, if you still want to vote in Bull Whip, you have to register, and the registration office in the courthouse is open only from 11:55 P.M. to midnight on every sixth Saturday of the month.

The problem is that, although the registration office is open, the courthouse is closed, and it's kind of hard to get into the building.

Even so, Mr. George Abernathy, a Negro, manages, much to the surprise of the registrar, to get in and asks to register to vote.

"Fine, George, fine. Ah'd be glad to register you as soon as you answer a few of these here questions," the registrar says. "Now, first off, what is your educational background?"

"I was a Rhodes scholar, I received a B.A. from Columbia, a masters from Harvard, and a Ph.D. from MIT."

"That's just fine, George. Now let me ask you this. Can you read an' write?"

"I've written three books, on cybernetics, Christian philosophy, and advanced political theory."

"Ah'd appreciate it if you didn't use such big words, George. If there's anything Ah hate it's an uppity voter."

Abernathy says, "I believe I have a right to register."

"Yes, you do, George, but I have to give you this here literacy test 'cause we cain't have ignoramuses voting for our great Governor, George Wallace, if you know what Ah mean. Now, first off, would you please read somethin from this here newspaper?"

"It's in Chinese."

"That's right."

Abernathy reads three stories from the Chinese paper. The registrar is thrown, but he doesn't want to show it.

"All right, now will you read the hieroglyphics off this here Rosetta Stone?" he says.

Mr. Abernathy reads the hieroglyphics and the registrar begins to get nervous.

"George, here is the constitution of Finland, in Finnish. Would you please interpret the first 14 articles for me?"

"What has that got to do with voting in Alabama?"

"We got to keep out agitators and the like. Now, you going to take the test or not?"

Mr. Abernathy interprets the 14 articles and the registrar becomes truly frightened. He telephones the Governor's office and reports what is happening. An aide comes back in a few minutes and says, "The Governor says to give him Part 4 of the test."

The registrar goes to his safe and takes out a clay jar. "George, there's only one more thing you're obligated to do for this here literacy test. Would you be so kind to read for me any two of these Dead Sea Scrolls?"

Mr. Abernathy reads the first one but stumbles on a word in the second one.

"Ah'm sorry, George. You've failed the literacy test, but you can come back next year and try again."

As Abernathy leaves the office, a white Alabaman comes in to register to vote.

The registrar says to him, "Would you please spell cat for me?"

The white voter says, "K-A-T."

"Try it again. You're getting warm."

Too Hot in the Kitchen

The resignation of White House chef René Verdon caught Washington by surprise. The first inkling of it came when, in a warm exchange of letters, French chef Verdon wrote:

MON CHER PRESIDENT,
    Je m'en vais. (I am leaving.)

RENÉ VERDON

DEAR MR. VERDON,
    So long. (Je m'en fous.)

LYNDON B. JOHNSON

Coming so soon after the resignation of McGeorge Bundy, some sources here feel the President wants to realign his executive staff so all cooking will be done by either Secretary Rusk or Secretary of Defense McNamara.

But the problem of finding a new chef for the White House is not an easy one. The President has ordered his kitchen cabinet to search for a replacement and many interviews have been held to find the right person.

One such interview took place a few days after Monsieur Verdon resigned.

"Mr. Dupont, you come highly recommended to us."

"Oui, monsieur. I have worked at Maxim's, the Tour d'Argent, Pavillion, 21 and the France."

"Very good. What dishes can you make?"

"Quenelles de brochet, noisettes d'agneau, poulet de Bresse à la creme, paupiettes de veau, soufflé Grand Marnier."

"Yes, we know all that. But how do you feel about okra with black-eyed peas?"

"I am sorry. I never concern myself with politics."

"I'm not speaking about politics. Can you make a dish of okra and black-eyed peas?"

"Pardon?"

"Never mind. What about chicken shortcake, plantation style?"

"I am sorry, my English is not so good. I thought you said chicken shortcake, plantation style?"

"I did. Mr. Dupont, you must understand that we are very simple people here and we like simple dishes. Red snapper, tamale pie, barbecued beef, venison chili and potato turnovers. Surely you know how to cook one or two of these dishes?"

"At Maxim's we rarely had requests for those."

"Well, let's think of something simple. Could you make a deer sausage casserole?"

"Only if they put bamboo sticks under my fingernails."

"Mr. Dupont, are you an American citizen?"

"Yes. I became one three years ago."

"Then you must ask not what your country can cook for you, but what can you cook for your country."

"I want to serve in any way I can."

"Good. Why don't you start with something easy like pinto beans with salt pork?"

"Would you settle for a steak Diane?"

"Mr. Dupont, the White House will never compromise on its cuisine. We entertain heads of state, kings and princesses, emperors, and someday, God willing, President de Gaulle. Do you know why they like to come here?"

"I have no idea."

"Because we serve the best six-shooter coffee in the world."

"Can I go home now?"

"Yes. But don't call us. We'll call you."

"Oh Say Can You See?"

The cynics may scoff and the left wingers may grumble, but the Daughters of the American Revolution pulled off their biggest coup of 1965 when they got a New York girdle manufacturer to withdraw from the market a red, white and blue garment called "Stars 'n Stripes."

The pop art girdle made by the Treo Company was attacked by the D.A.R.'s flag committee, who called it "a shocking caricature and a desecration of the American flag."

The president of the Treo Company immediately announced he was withdrawing the girdles from distribution and they would either be destroyed or given to a "foreign charity."

It would be a pity if the Treo Company destroyed these girdles, particularly since so much time, effort and imagination went into them.

At the same time I can't help agreeing with the Daughters of the American Revolution that no red-blooded American woman should wrap herself in the Stars and Stripes, which represents, if you'll excuse the expression, the foundation of our liberty.

So I would buy the Treo Company's second idea, which is to send the girdles abroad.

It is a known fact that 70 percent of the people in the world who receive American foreign aid have no idea who gave it to them. The Communists in many countries are constantly removing the U.S. aid stickers on the gifts, and there have been situations where they have even substituted the hammer and sickle.

This would be the first opportunity for us to give something to a foreign country where there would be no mistaking its point of origin. By giving American Stars 'n Stripes girdles to a needy nation, we would not only gain a great propaganda victory in the cold war, but we would also win the battle for the minds of men.

I believe that in order to have the most impact, the girdles should be distributed in backward nations where they could replace the sarong or the grass skirt as the only garment worn by a native woman. In this way the Stars and Stripes would be on display day and night, reminding everyone that even in the jungle the United States is always there.

One suggestion was made that the girdles be sent to Vietnam so our GIs could tell the loyal Vietnamese women from the Viet Cong women, but there was some fear that they might fall into the hands of the Viet Cong and confuse everybody.

It was also feared that the Stars 'n Stripes could cause friction between American and South Vietnamese troops. So that idea was abandoned.

A third suggestion was to give them to the Soviet Union to show them how far ahead of them we are in the race to contain space.

But the D.A.R. rejected the idea on the grounds that supplying the Soviet Union with girdles would only give aid and comfort to the enemy.

While they've probably got a point, I still believe that we would be losing a great opportunity to do some good abroad if we destroyed the objectionable garments.

The D.A.R. deserves credit for calling the red, white and blue girdles to the attention of the American public, and Treo deserves credit for agreeing to yank them off the market.

Now it's the government's turn to decide what they're going to do about it. An aid official told me: "First we're going to send one up a flagpole to see who salutes."

The Curse

Most bills are now sent out on perforated business-machine cards that say in large letters DO NOT FOLD, BEND OR MUTILATE. I have a friend who doesn't like to be told what to do with a bill, and one day, to my horror, I saw him fold, bend and mutilate a card right in front of my eyes.

"You shouldn't have done that," I said, quivering. "There is a curse on anyone in the United States who folds, bends, or mutilates a bill."

He laughed at me. "That's an old wives' tale. This is a free country, isn't it?"

"Only if you don't fold, bend, or mutilate."

"You're chicken," he said. "No computer is going to tell me what to do."

I didn't see my friend for several months. Then I finally ran across him in a bar. He was unshaven, dirty and obviously had been on a bender.

"What happened?" I asked.

"The curse," he croaked. "The curse got me."

Then he told me his story. He had sent back the folded, bent and mutilated card to the company and received another card in a week, saying, "We told you not to F. B. or M. This is your last chance."

"I crumpled up the card and sent it back," he said, "still thinking I had the upper hand. Then it started.

"First my telephone went out on me. I could not send or receive any messages. I went down to the phone company and they were very nice until they looked up my name. Then the woman said, "It says here that you mutilated your bill.'

" 'I didn't mutilate my phone bill.'

" 'It doesn't make any difference what bill you mutilated. Our computer is aware of what you did to another computer and it refuses to handle your account.'

" 'How would your computer know that?'

" 'There is a master computer that informs all other computers of anyone who folds or bends or mutilates a card. I'm afraid there is nothing we can do about it.' "

My friend took another drink. "The same thing happened when my electricity was cut off, and my gas. Everyone was sorry, but they all claimed they were unable to do anything for me.

"Finally payday came, but there was no check for me. I complained to my boss and he just shrugged his shoulders and said, 'It's not up to me. We pay by machine.'

"I was broke, so I wrote out a check on my bank. It came back marked 'Insufficient respect for IBM cards.' "

"You poor guy," I said.

"But that isn't the worst of it. One of the computers got very angry, and instead of canceling my subscription to the *Reader's Digest* it multiplied it. I've been getting 10,000 *Reader's Digests* a month."

"That's a lot of *Digests*," I said.

"My wife left me because she couldn't stand the scandal, and besides, she was afraid of being thrown out of the Book-of-the-Month Club."

He started crying.

"You're in bad shape," I said. "You better go to the hospital."

"I can't," he cried. "They canceled my Blue Cross, too."

The Pop Sculptor

One day the Canadian authorities refused to allow 80 wooden crates, which looked like cartons of Brillo soap pads, Kellogg's corn flakes, and

Mott's apple juice, to go through customs as works of art. The cartons, painted by American pop artist Andy Warhol, were not, said the Canadians, works of art but merchandise, and subject to $4,000 duty.

I think the Canadians are all wet. A few days after the incident in Canada, I went down to the supermarket to buy some groceries for my wife. On the way home I stopped in at an art gallery where they were holding a pop art exhibit. Unfortunately, the carton of groceries got heavy, and I left them on the floor.

Then, being so moved by what I saw, I left the gallery and went home.

"Where are the groceries?" my wife demanded.

"Oh, my gosh," I cried, "I left them at the art gallery."

"Well, you'd better get them if you want any supper tonight."

I rushed back to the gallery, but I was too late. The groceries had been awarded first prize in the show.

"We've been looking all over for you," the gallery owner said. "Why didn't you sign your work of art?"

"It's not a work of art. It's my dinner for tonight."

The gallery roared with appreciative laughter. "He's not only a great sculptor, but he has humor as well," a judge said.

"You can see that in his work," another judge added. "Notice how the bottle of Heinz catsup is leaning against the can of Campbell's pork and beans."

"I'll never know how he was inspired to put the Ritz crackers on top of the can of Crisco," a lady said to her escort.

"It's pure genius," the escort replied. "Notice the way the Del Monte can of peaches is lying on its side. Even Warhol wouldn't have gone that far."

"I think the thing that really won the prize for him was the manner in which he crushed the Sara Lee cheesecake on the bottom of the box."

"It makes Picasso look sick."

"Look," I said, "I'm very grateful for all these honors, but my wife is waiting for this stuff and I have to get it home."

"Get it home?" the gallery owner said in amazement. "I've just sold it to that couple over there for $1,500."

"The groceries cost me only $18," I replied.

"It isn't the groceries. It's what you did with them. You have managed to put more meaning into a box of Rinso than Rodin put into 'The Thinker.' Nobody will ever be able to look at a can of Franco-American spaghetti without thinking of you. You have said with this bag of groceries, in one evening, what Rembrandt tried to say in 1,000 paintings."

I blushed modestly and accepted his check. That night I took my wife out to dinner, and the next day I went back to the supermarket and bought another bag of groceries, much more expensive than the previous ones, which I immediately took to the gallery.

But the reviews were lousy. "Success has gone to his head," said Washington's leading art critics. "Where once he was able to produce simple jars of cat food and peanut butter in a wild, reckless, I-don't-give-a-damn-manner, he is now serving up elegant cans of mushrooms and mock turtle soup. The famous touch is gone and all that is left is a hodgepodge of tasteless groceries."

Who Discovered Columbus?

While everyone is arguing over who discovered America, there is a controversy now raging amongst the Indian tribes over who discovered Columbus.

The chief of the White Hawks has just issued a statement saying that his ancestors were the first to greet Columbus when he landed, and produced the text of the conversation Columbus had with his uncle of many centuries removed.

"Greetings, White Father," the chief said as Columbus stepped ashore. "What brings you to New Vinland?"

Columbus is said to have looked at his map. "New Vinland? I thought this was the New World."

"It was, White Father, but then Leif the Lucky discovered it."

"Does anyone know about this?"

"Only you and I and some monk mapmakers."

"Can you keep your mouth shut, Indian?"

"What did you call me?"

"Indian. I promised Queen Isabella I'd find a new route to the East Indies. Therefore, you're an Indian."

"And what are you, White Father?"

"I am Columbus, an explorer of Italian birth."

"Wonderful," the chief said. "From now on we'll call today Columbus Day in your honor."

"That's very nice of you, Indian. I hereby take this island and all islands north, south, east, and west of it, in the name of the Queen of Spain."

The chief looked at Columbus. "Are you some kind of a nut?"

"What do you mean by that, Indian?"

"This land belongs to us. We were here first. Our fathers and their fathers who came before them. We don't want to be Spanish."

"Indian, we are your friends. We are going to help you. We will educate your children and build hospitals and schools and roads. We are going to give you foreign aid and give you guns and armor so you can protect yourself and be free."

"But, White Father, we are free."

"Don't argue. We know what's best for you. Now, where are the spices?"

"What spices?"

"Don't kid us, Chief. You've got to have spices around here or they wouldn't call you Indians."

"They don't call us Indians. You call us Indians. You still don't know where you are."

Columbus looked at his map again. "I've got a pretty good idea. Where is Puerto Rico from here?"

The chief pointed.

"And Cuba?"

The chief pointed again.

"Then that would put us here in the Bahamas. Why didn't I think of that before?"

"Because the season hasn't started yet. It's kind of quiet now."

Columbus said, "Well, give me all the gold you've got and I'll let you off with your lives."

"You white men are too good to us," the chief said. "How can we ever repay you?"

As Columbus stuffed the gold in the sacks he said, "Just forget about Leif the Lucky. You ever breathe a word to anyone and I'll have my boys make cement moccasins for all of you."

"Don't worry about a thing, Columbus. It will be our secret. The only one I will tell the truth to is my son."

"Where is he?"

"He's going to Yale."

Extry! Extry!

A man works hard all his life, trying to make something of himself, overcome his poverty-stricken years and achieve security and happiness. And then all of a sudden one day his son takes on a newspaper route and the man finds himself back where he started.

This happened to me awhile back. My eleven-year-old son had managed to get himself a newspaper route, but on Saturday he went off on an overnight hike with the Boy Scouts. At three o'clock on that rainy afternoon my wife informed me someone had to deliver his newspapers.

"But it's raining out," I protested. "And besides the North is playing the South in football."

"It's all right," she said, putting on her galoshes. "I'll deliver them. A little rain never hurt someone with a cold and a 101 fever."

"Okay," I said, "I'll deliver the damn papers. What really hurts is I don't even write for the paper he's delivering."

"Here's a list of the houses," my wife said. "Joel's written down the instructions as to where to get the papers and what to do."

I took the list, put on a raincoat, boots, and rain hat and went out into the pouring rain.

The truck came along at 4:30. "Where's your bag?" the driver wanted to know.

"What bag?"

"To keep your papers dry, you idiot. How many times do I have to tell you guys to bring your bag when it rains?"

"Well, you see, sir, this isn't really my route. "It's my son's route. I'm just filling in for him today."

"That's a lousy excuse. Okay, keep them under your raincoat, and next time don't forget your bag."

"Yes, sir. I'll remember."

He roared off, splashing water all over my pants.

I studied the list, but it wasn't easy. Between the rain and my son's handwriting it was kind of blurred.

The first two houses didn't give me any trouble, but at the third a man came to the door. "We didn't get our paper last Friday," he said.

"That's a shame," I said. "Actually nothing much happened. You didn't miss anything."

"I'm not paying you for Friday."

"Suit yourself," I said as the rain dripped down on my face. His wife came to the door and pulled her husband away. As she closed it I heard her say, "You shouldn't yell at the poor man. It's probably the only job he could get."

In the next block a lady came to the door and said, "I forgot to pay you last week. How much is it?"

"I don't know," I said.

"Well, here's a dollar and a ten-cent tip."

"Thank you, ma'am."

"And the next time, please don't throw my paper in the bushes."

By this time the list was soggy and I couldn't read it anymore, so I decided the only fair thing to do was to leave a paper at every other house until I ran out.

It worked until I came to one house where an eleven-year-old girl ran out and said, "Hey, we don't take that paper."

"It's free," I said.

"You get off our property," she said. A boxer came to the door and started growling.

I stopped running a block later.

In two hours, I had gotten rid of all the papers and was back at my house. As I soaked my feet in a pail of hot water and drank a tumbler of hot rum, the thought occurred to me that it's much easier to write for newspapers than it is to deliver them. And healthier, too.

The Odd Couple

The announcement that the next American space flight may be for eight days was greeted with mixed reactions by those of us who worry about such things. While astronauts McDivitt and White seemed to get along okay (McDivitt did call White a dirty dog for messing up his windshield), there must come a time when two men in a small capsule are going to start getting on each other's nerves.

I predict it will come around Gemini 11, when two astronauts, Major Alpha and Commander Beta, have been in orbit for twelve days.

Suddenly Alpha says to Beta, "You forgot to put the top on the food paste tube."

Beta replies, "Big deal, so I forgot. I'm getting sick and tired of you cleaning and dusting the capsule all day long."

"I happen to like a neat ship. And I don't enjoy picking up after you, either. You left your socks on the heat shelf yesterday."

"My socks were wet and I wanted them to dry. There aren't too many places you can dry socks in this thing, you know. I took this trip so I could get away from all my wife's nagging and you're getting worse than she is."

"Well, I didn't volunteer to be your maid. I've got lots of other things to worry about."

"I'm sick of your bickering. I'm going for a walk."

"Will you be back for dinner?"

"I don't know. You eat when you want to."

"Well, shut the hatch when you go out. I just cleaned the floor. And by the way, would you mind taking the garbage out?"

"Yes, I would mind. Everytime I go out you ask me to take the garbage with me."

A few hours later Commander Beta comes back.

"Where you been?" Alpha wants to know.

"What do you mean, where have I been? I told you I was taking a walk."

"Well, how do you expect me to sleep when you're out walking in space?"

"Were there any calls for me?" Beta asks.

"Your wife called."

"What did she want?"

"How do I know? I told her you weren't here."

"That was a dumb thing to say. Why didn't you tell her I was taking a walk?"

"Listen, just because we're up here together doesn't mean I have to cover for you everytime you leave the spaceship."

"Who else called?"

"The President."

"What did he want?"

"He wanted to know if we could go down to the ranch on the weekend."

"Are you going?"

"I thought I might."

"Then I'm not going. When I make my re-entry I'm not going anywhere with you."

"That goes double for me. If I never see you again it will be too soon."

"Who made up my bed?"

"I made it up."

"Listen, Alpha. If I want my bed made up I'll make it up. Do you understand?"

"I think we oughta step outside and settle this once and for all!"

"That suits me fine!"

Good News Is No News

There were a lot of red faces in Washington because of last summer's contretemps with the Prime Minister of Singapore, Lee Kuan Yew, who revealed in a press interview that he was offered a bribe of $3 million to hush up an American CIA fiasco in 1961. Mr. Lee said he indignantly refused the money because he and his party couldn't be bribed, but he would consider an offer of $33 million instead.

The State Department denied the incident had ever taken place, so Mr. Lee produced a letter of apology written by Secretary of State Dean Rusk to him. Rusk said there had been a misunderstanding over the denial, which, whether they liked it or not, confirmed Prime Minister Lee's story.

Among the red faces I saw was one belonging to the Enchiladan Ambassador to the United States, who was dining alone at the Sans Souci.

I asked him why he was so upset.

"I am in trouble with my government because of Singapore."

"How is that? Singapore is not in South America."

"You do not understand. Four years ago there came to my country one of your CIA people who offered to bribe one of our officials for information about our government. He was arrested and thrown into jail. A few weeks later a high official from your government came to me and asked me how much it would cost to get him out of jail.

"I said $5,000. They offered $3,500, and I recommended to my country we take it. Now I am in trouble because they have read in the paper that the Singapore government was offered $3 million if they would release the CIA man there. My government is very angry with me because we sold out so cheaply."

"I should think they would be," I said.

"I am very disappointed with your State Department. We have always been very good friends of the United States and we should have got the going rate for CIA agents."

"But no one had put a price on a CIA agent before. It wasn't your fault."

"That's what I told my government. But they said this is typical of American policy in Latin America. They will pay $3 million to hush up a scandal in the Far East but only $3,500 to hush up one in Latin America. What kind of an Alliance for Progress is this?"

"Did anyone offer you an explanation?"

"They told me that the CIA agent in Singapore was mixed up with a girl and that's why they had to pay more."

"But $3 million! She must have been some girl!"

"That's exactly what I was thinking. We have some beautiful women in our country, but $3 million—the mind boggles."

"What are you planning to do about it?"

"We are going to bring it up at the next OAS meeting. We are going to tell the United States that they can send all the CIA agents they want into Latin America, but they will have to pay $3 million for each one that gets caught. We can't cut our prices lower than Singapore."

"Did you tell Dean Rusk about it?"

"I wrote him a letter, but his secretary wrote back and said Mr. Rusk has decided not to write letters anymore—to anybody."

"It's probably a good policy," I agreed.

The Ambassador got up to leave. "It's now up to the United States. Do you realize 100 inept CIA agents could resolve our balance of payments problem for two years?"

No Trouble in Zemululu

I just received a very heartbreaking letter from a friend of mine who happens to be the American Ambassador to an African country which, to protect him, I will call Zemululu.

He writes that he is in serious trouble with the State Department and doesn't know what to do about it.

His problems first began when a year went by without any anti-American demonstrations in the country. Washington became suspicious and thought he was keeping something from them. He received a cable which said, "Can't understand lack of anti-American demonstrations your area. Please clarify why natives are friendly."

My friend wired back he had no explanation for it unless the country's climate did not lend itself to demonstrating. He thought he would hear no more from Washington, but a week later he received a follow-up cable: "How come you have sent in no reports on coups or attempted coups in your country? You only Ambassador in Africa not expecting a revolution. What have you been doing?"

He replied, "Zemululu not coup-conscious. Military getting along fine with premier."

By now the matter was being given serious study by the African hands in the State Department. A cable was dispatched: "You have failed to keep us informed on racial tension. How much is there and when is it likely to explode?"

His reply was a weak, "No racial tension in sight and our people not expecting any. Please advise what I'm doing wrong."

There was an ominous silence for a few weeks, but then he had a bit of good luck and was able to wire: "Peace Corps scandal may be brewing upcountry. Could cause tremendous damage to our relations here."

They immediately cabled back, "Good boy. This may be the first break we've had. Send us full details."

After a thorough investigation he replied, "Peace Corps scandal turned out to be false alarm. First report indicated Peace Corps volunteer was going to have a baby, but corrected transmission says Peace Corps volunteer delivered a baby. Sorry to get your hopes up."

State was very annoyed. To top if off they sent him a nasty wire saying, "Your AID operation has just been audited and found to be completely in order. There has been no misuse of funds or hint of black market operation. AID perplexed and thinking of cutting off money."

The Ambassador replied, "Please tell AID not to act too hastily. While American money being kept from profiteers at moment, situation could change overnight."

A month went by and suddenly the code machines started clicking again. "Congressional junket just returned from Zemululu reports they pleased with stability and progress made there and very impressed with lack of subversion. Do you realize this could hurt overall budget for upcoming year? Also understand *Time* and *Newsweek* correspondents have made official complaints to their editors that Zemululu is dead as running story. Everyone here very depressed."

To save his job the Ambassador wired back. "Two Chinese cultural attachés have just arrived from Peking, and have opened Chinese restaurant."

An immediate reply from Washington said, "Congratulations. All of us here delighted with news. How many CIA men can we send you?"

A Merry Dr. Spock

Dr. Spock, America's leading authority on children, has come up with some revolutionary ideas for Christmas. He says that the holiday season is so overdone that children go to pieces under the tension, and he warns that Christmas exploits and fosters children's naturally greedy tendencies.

To solve the problem, the good doctor thinks we should do away with mass family gatherings and visits, that we should leave children home when shopping, that they should be shielded from live Santas, and that a child should be limited to only one or, at the most, two Christmas presents.

The scene is Christmas morning. A ten-year-old child comes running down the stairs in his pajamas while his parents sit nervously by the Christmas tree.

There are two packages under the tree. The boy rips them both open. "Oh, boy," he cries, "an Erector set and a pair of galoshes." He starts looking behind the tree. "Where's the other stuff?" he asks.

The mother says, "That's all there is, son."

"All there is?" the boy says. "But it's Christmas."

"We know that, son," the father says. "But Dr. Spock says you should only get one or, at the most, two Christmas presents this year."

"Who's Dr. Spock?"

"He is a very famous pediatrician and he writes books on how to raise children. He says the more presents we buy you, the more chance you have of going to pieces on Christmas Day."

The boy says, "He must be some kind of a nut."

"He is not a nut. He is a very distinguished man who knows what goes on in the minds of children."

"Well, if he's not a nut, he's a fink," the boy cries. "What kind of a Christmas is this, anyway?"

"Dr. Spock is just trying to keep your greedy tendencies in check. He says the less we give you, the happier you will be."

The boy screams, "I'm not greedy. I only want what's coming to me."

"But if we gave you everything you wanted, you would just go to pieces. We don't want you to have a nervous breakdown."

"What's a nervous breakdown?"

"It's when you get sick and depressed."

"But I'm sick and depressed now."

"Yes, but you would be much worse if you got a lot of presents."

"I'm going to tell Grandma this afternoon," the boy says.

"She's not coming over this afternoon," the mother tells the son.

"Why not?"

"Because Dr. Spock doesn't believe in mass family gatherings at Christmas time. He says it will only unnerve you. The three of us are going to spend a quiet day together."

"Without any toys?"

"We'll sing Christmas carols," the father says.

"What am I going to tell all my friends when they ask me what I got for Christmas?" the boy asks.

"Tell them you may not have material things, but mentally you're much better off than they are."

"They'll never believe it," the boy says. "I think I'm having a nervous breakdown." He begins to cry and won't stop.

The father says, "Now, calm down while your mother opens her two presents."

"Two presents?" The mother starts weeping. "I thought Dr. Spock was only talking about children."

The father says, "I never saw so many people go to pieces in my life."

Why Parents Can't Add

There has been a great deal of discussion about American education in the last ten years and everyone has come up with his theory as to why Johnny can't add. I know why Johnny can't add. It's because his parents can't do his homework.

In the old days before N. M. (New Math) a kid could bring home his homework and his parents would go over it with him, making corrections or suggestions, and giving encouragement when the going got rough. But today the parent is in the soup because the homework is so complicated that neither the kid nor his parent knows what is going on.

For example, the other day my daughter brought home a homework assignment.

"I have to subtract 179 from 202," she said.

"It's quite simple," I said, "you put the 202 over the 179."

"But what do I do with the 10?"

"What 10?"

"The 10 that goes next to the 202."

"I don't know what 10 goes next to the 202. Let's subtract 179 from 202. Nine from two is three, and you carry one. Eight from zero is two. The answer is 23."

"We can't do it that way. We have to use a 10."

"Why 10?"

"Ten is a unit."

"I see. Well, the answer is still 23," I said.

"How do you know?"

"Because I took nine from two and eight from zero."

"That's not the way to do it."

"Oh, yeah? Well, that's the way I did it."

"My teacher says you can't take nine from two."

"Why not?"

"Because you can't borrow from something you don't give back."

"Well, I'm going to call your teacher and see how she subtracts 179 from 202."

I placed a call to my daughter's teacher and explained I was having a small problem with the homework she had assigned.

The teacher was very nice on the phone. "It's really quite simple," she said. "The two on the right-hand column is considered units of one. The zero in the center counts for zero tens. The two in the left-hand column counts for hundreds. Therefore, you have two hundreds, zero tens, and two ones."

"You're putting me on," I said.

"Now to subtract," she said. "Go to the hundreds column and start regrouping. Two hundred will become 100. Therefore, bring this 10 to the tens column. Now you have 10 tens, but you still can't subtract in the units column. Therefore, regroup again. Now you only have nine tens. Take 12 from the 10 and now bring it over to the ones column because 10 ones equal one. Now you have 12 ones. Do you understand?"

"What's there not to understand?" I said. "Can I ask you a very, very personal question?"

"Yes, of course."

"Is the answer 23?"

"In this case it is, but it isn't necessarily 23. If you were working in units other than 10, it could be something else."

I hung up and started swallowing a whole bottle of aspirin, but my wife caught me in time. "How many aspirins did you take?" she asked.

"I took seven and then I took five, but don't ask me what it adds up to."

A Ruthless Conspiracy

There is a ruthless conspiracy going on in the United States among our grade school and high school teachers and someone must put a stop to it.

Apparently, one of the major homework assignments these days is to have pupils write to someone in a profession and ask him a few hundred questions, such as how he got started, why he chose his work, how much he makes, and what course of study would he recommend to someone wanting to pursue the same work.

I receive on the average ten letters a week from students who have been assigned to interview me by mail. I would probably ignore the letters altogether, except that each student usually points out at the bottom of the letter that if I don't answer his letter, he'll flunk the course. Most students give me until Thursday to reply, but some are more pressed and need it on Wednesday.

One time an entire class (40) students wrote to tell me they had been assigned to find out how I remain fair in my columns. I wrote back that I don't try to remain fair in my columns. The answer was too brief and the teacher gave the class another theme, which was, "Could you please let me know in about 500 words where you get the ideas for your columns?"

The political science teacher had his students ask, "Would you explain the difference between the Federal and state court systems?" And a civics teacher suggested his class write to me and find out what I thought about recognition of Red China.

It takes an average of fifteen minutes to answer one of these letters, and since I don't have time to do my own kids' homework, I don't see why I should do the homework of complete strangers.

Therefore, I'm announcing as of now that any teacher who assigns her pupils to write to me as a research project will receive a questionnaire in return.

These are the questions the teacher will be required to answer:

1. How did you decide to go into the teaching profession?

2. Do you like to teach boys or girls better? Why?

3. Could you send me some anecdotes about your favorite pupil?

4. Please tell me the titles and authors of the books that have influenced you as a teacher.

5. Do you try to be fair in your classes? How?

6. Does anyone get mad at anything you say? Please give an illustration.

7. How do you come up with new ideas for your homework assignments everyday?

8. What do you think about the new phases of education?

9. What do you think of our position in Vietnam? The Congo? Cuba?

10. What subjects should someone take if he wants to become a teacher?

11. How much money do you make?

12. Please let me have this no later than next week.

I feel the questionnaire is the only way to make teachers stop assigning their students this type of homework.

From now on, whenever I get one of those pleading letters from a student—out goes the questionnaire. If the teacher refuses to answer the questions or flunks the students, I'll list her in my column as a fink teacher—which, as every student knows, is the worst kind. I know these are harsh measures. After all, the teachers started it, and they have no one to blame but themselves.

Pajama Party

I guess it isn't anybody's fault, but it's hard for most American men to get used to the fashions their women are wearing in the summer.

One night my wife and I were going to a dinner party, in Easthampton, and as I was getting ready, she came in wearing a pair of red pajamas.

"How do I look?" she wanted to know.

"I thought we were going out tonight."

"We are."

"In pajamas?"

"They're not pajamas. They're long culottes, and they happen to be the rage."

I guess she was right, because when we got to the party three-quarters of the women there were in culottes, and the other quarter was wrapped in fish net.

I didn't think any more about it until a few nights later when my wife walked into the bedroom in an evening gown.

"I thought we were staying home tonight."

"We are," she replied.

"Then what are you doing in an evening gown?"

"This is not an evening gown," she said in a hurt voice. "It's the latest thing in pajamas."

The next day my wife showed up in what I thought was a two-piece white bathing suit.

"Are you going swimming?" I asked her.

"No," she replied. "I've got a date to play tennis."

"They won't let you on the court like that."

"Yes, they will," she said. "There's been a big breakthrough in tennis clothes and the two-piece ruffled-eyelet bare midriff is now the rage."

"It does change the game," I admitted.

That afternoon she walked over to the pool in what I thought was a tennis outfit.

"You don't fool me this time," I said. "You're going swimming, right?"

"No, I'm not. I'm going to play golf."

She had me again.

Pretty soon it became a game. One time she showed up in what looked to me like a Berber tent, and I guessed she was going horseback riding. But I was wrong. She was going into town to buy steaks for dinner. Another time she put on what looked like a white shift.

"Polo?"

She shook her head. "Water skiing."

On the following morning she wore a striped Italian silk shirt and a pair of vinyl elephant pants.

I thought and thought and finally said, "Shark fishing?"

"Wrong again. I'm taking the children to the doctor."

Finally she showed up in a white and black bikini.

"Don't tell me," I cried. "You're going big-game hunting."

She looked at me in disgust and then dived into the pool. I almost had it.

On the last evening of our vacation I decided to get even. Someone was giving us a farewell party, and as the time drew near to leave she said to me, "Aren't you getting dressed?"

"I think I'll go in my underwear."

"You're kidding," she said.

"Why not? Everyone knows I hate pajamas."

The War on Poverty

One of the big debates going on in Washington is whether the poor people should have a voice in the war on poverty. Everybody has been heard from on the subject except the poor people themselves. So I decided to go out and interview a poor person and ask him what he thought about it. It wasn't easy to find one, because nobody likes to admit to being poor. Also, poor people are suspicious of strangers asking questions. They believe, and rightly so, that no good can come of it.

I finally found a man in a bar in one of the rundown sections of Washington who was willing to admit he was poor and also willing to talk about it.

I asked him if he thought he would like to serve on a committee to see what could be done about poverty.

"Mister, if I had any ideas what to do about poverty, I wouldn't be poor."

"But there is a school of thought in Washington that poor people are the only ones who know the real problems of the poor, and they should be strongly involved in the program to formulate and implement anti-poverty programs."

"I wouldn't serve on such a board unless they paid me," he said.

"Oh, I'm sure they would pay you. If they agreed to pay you, what is the first thing you would do?"

"I'd move out of the neighborhood."

"But if you did that, you would lose contact with poor people and you would no longer be able to speak for them."

"Exactly. Poor people don't want to be spoken for. They just want to get the hell out of the neighborhood. Asking poor people how to win the war on poverty is like asking the Japanese how to win World War II."

"You've got a point there. But there is a great deal of pressure to have poor people work out their own destinies in the anti-poverty program."

"Okay, then let them put everybody who is poor on an anti-poverty committee and pay them all a salary. Once they're on a salary, you'll solve every problem a poor person has. And they'll all move the hell out of the neighborhood."

"On the surface this sounds like a good solution to the problem, but it would put a great financial strain on the government."

"Yeah, but if you put people on salary, you wouldn't have to make welfare payments, and the poor people would pay taxes, so it would eventually even itself out."

"I agree," I said, "but if you put all poor people on anti-poverty committees and paid them, you would eliminate poverty and there would be no reason to have the committees."

"I'm not sure about that. As soon as people get a salary, they can get all the credit they want from banks and finance companies. The more you borrow, the poorer you become. As long as there are credit companies, there will always be poor people."

"It makes a lot of sense," I admitted. "You seem to have thought this out pretty well."

"When you're poor, you have nothing else to think about."

"I wonder why the government hasn't thought of it."

"Because they're afraid we'd all move the hell out of the neighborhood."

The Last American

When the story of the Dominican Republic's revolution unfolds, you may hear about a great, unsung hero whose name is Sidney.

Nobody knows Sidney's last name, but the whole course of the revolution would have been changed if it hadn't been for him.

Sidney was an American tourist visiting Santo Domingo when the fighting broke out. As you may remember, President Johnson sent in

Marines to protect Americans who could possibly be hurt. Unfortunately, the evacuation went off so fast that in 24 hours there wasn't an American left in the capital except Sidney.

When Sidney showed up at the pier to be taken on board ship, he was stopped by a Marine colonel who said, "I'm sorry, you can't leave, sir."

"Why not?" Sidney wanted to know.

"Because we've been sent here to protect Americans and you're the only American left. If you leave, we'll have to pull out."

"Nuts to that," said Sidney. "I want to get out of here. They got a bunch of crazy people in this town."

"My orders are to keep you here, sir. We made a mistake in evacuating the Americans too fast and now we need you more than you need us."

"That's not my problem," Sidney said. "I want to go on that ship out there."

Two Marine sergeants raised their guns. "It's not possible, Sidney," the colonel replied.

"If the OAS arrived and found no American here for us to protect, we would be in a very sticky position. But you'll be perfectly safe. President Johnson is sending in 10,000 more troops to protect you."

"To protect me?"

"Yes, sir. We're going to build a nine-mile perimeter around you so nobody can get near you. I assure you nothing can go wrong."

Sidney took his bags and went back to the hotel.

The next morning he was visited by the general in charge of the paratroopers. "Are you okay, Sidney?"

"Yeah, I'm okay. But I want to go home."

"Just be patient and everything will be all right."

While the general was talking, a platoon set up a machine gun on the balcony. Two tanks were parked in front of the hotel and an antiaircraft gun was placed on the roof.

"What's all that for?" Sidney wanted to know.

"Just to see that no one hurts you. You're very precious to us."

"Yeah, well, if I'm so precious, why don't you get me the hell out of here?"

"We will as soon as we feel it's reasonably safe. For the moment you're the only humanitarian reason for our being here."

"I don't know what's going on, but all I know is I'm being held as a hostage."

"Sidney, have you ever heard of the Monroe Doctrine?"

"Yeah, I guess so."

"Well, you're part of it. Your name will go down in history books with Teddy Roosevelt and Admiral Dewey. When schoolteachers ask their pupils who saved the Dominican Republic from going Communist, the children are going to have to answer, 'Sidney.'"

Just then the phone rang. The general picked it up.

"It's the President, Sidney. He wants to speak to you."

"Yes, sir, Mr. President. No, I'm just fine. I'll stay here as long as you want me to. That's nice of you to say. You're a good American, too."

The New Diplomats

The rumor is that the General Thi who was just kicked out of the South Vietnamese government has been offered a diplomatic post abroad. Not long ago, the Dominican Republic government insisted that all its enemies from the left and right take embassy jobs in other countries. If the trend continues, the entire diplomatic corps will soon be made up of opposition leaders who can't go home.

It's started already. I was at a diplomatic reception the other night and I overheard several diplomats talking.

"Alfredo, what are you doing in Washington?" one of them asked.

"I tried to overthrow my government, so they made me Ambassador to the United States."

"Tough luck."

"Well, it's better than being shot."

"That's the way I feel," the other replied. "Besides, there's always a chance if my President gets overthrown, I can go back."

"Wasn't your President the former Ambassador to the United States?"

"That's right. We threw him out in the revolution of July 23. But he made friends here with the CIA and came back in the revolution of November 14. When I was captured, he offered me Paris or Washington. I was in Paris right after the 1959 coup, so I thought I'd try Washington this time."

"At least he gave you a choice."

"Why shouldn't he? He made me promise if I overthrew him he would become the ambassador to Switzerland. He wants to be near his money."

"Isn't that General Rinaldo over there? General, what are you doing here?"

"I'm the second secretary in the embassy, and let me tell you, my friends, they have not heard the last of me."

"Why is that?"

"I was the foreign minister in the last government and should have been made *first* secretary. But they made the minister of justice first secretary because I was out of the country at the time the junta took over. I was tried in absentia."

"That's shocking. A man of your rank being made second secretary."

"You can say that again. But when my party takes over, I'm going to make the present foreign minister consul general to Ghana."

"Will the Americans let you do it?"

"I'll get rid of him before they send their troops in."

"Did you hear about Arturo?"

"No, what happened?"

"When the revolutionists took over, they discovered he had taken $10 million out of the country."

"What did they do to him?"

"What else could they do to him? They sent him to the United Nations."

"Serves him right," the ambassador said.

"I wouldn't be that harsh. It could have been one of us."

"I think the Africans have a much better solution to their revolutions."

"How's that?"

"Well, if you're the ruler of one country and the army throws you out, they make you the President of another country. That way they don't have such a discontented diplomatic corps."

La Enchilada

No matter how people criticize American policy in Vietnam, no one can take issue with what we did in Central and South America. Our handling of the La Enchilada revolution last May will go down in history as a classic exercise in United States diplomacy.

As you may remember, the tiny country of La Enchilada was ruled by a ruthless dictator named General El Finco, who our experts referred to as a "strongman." One day, much to our surprise, General El Finco was gunned down in the streets by a group of unhappy military officers who were dissatisfied with what their slot machines were paying off at the officers' club.

The people all cheered the death of El Finco, and when the junta leader, General El Tacos, promised democratic elections, their enthusiasm knew no bounds.

The elections were held within the year, and much to our surprise the winner was a mild mannered Social-Democrat-Liberal-Anarchist named Don Juan Inhel, who had been teaching at the University of Miami for the last 40 years.

Much to our surprise, Don Juan called for land reforms, minimum wage laws, rent control, and cuts in the military budget.

This was more than the armed forces could stand, so much to our surprise, they overthrew Don Juan Inhel's democratic government and installed a right-wing Radical Nationalist government under the command of General Henrico Henrico.

Henrico Henrico assured the Americans he was anti-Castro, anti-Communist and anti-etc. And so we immediately recognized his government.

Unfortunately, General Henrico was an Army officer and, when medals were handed out for the roles the various officers played in the overthrow of the Don Juan government, he overlooked the Air Force general, El Gazspacho, who took it on himself to overthrow Henrico Henrico, much, of course, to our surprise.

General El Gazspacho's first order of business as head of state was to reassure the United States that he was anti-Mao, anti-Ho, and anti-Cong. We were so pleased we immediately recognized his government and invited him to visit the New York World's Fair as Robert Moses' guest.

El Gazspacho appointed his brother-in-law inspector general of the armed forces, which infuriated Admiral Santos dos Santos, and one day he sailed into the capital on a destroyer and fired a shot at the palace. General El Gazspacho immediately sought sanctuary in the Mexican Embassy and Santos dos Santos was declared ruler of La Enchilada, a move that State Department officials assured the press was to the best interests of the Western Hemisphere.

In the meantime, the Don Juan forces, with help from four Army colonels who had been passed over for promotion, decided to try for a civilian government again.

Santos dos Santos immediately called on the American Ambassador for help and warned him that if a civilian government was installed, it would become Communist.

The word "Communist" was immediately decoded and sent to the White House. Bells started ringing all over Washington, and seven paratrooper divisions were furiously dispatched to La Enchilada.

Don Juan's forces and Santos dos Santos' forces were fighting in the streets. First the U.S. asked the rebels to give up. They refused. Then they asked the Santos forces to give up. They refused. Then they asked that the Communists give up. They couldn't find any Communists.

In desperation, the White House decided to send a truth squad to La Enchilada to debate with the various factions on American policy there. But at the last moment the leader of the team, McGeorge McGeorge, canceled out, claiming he promised to debate our Vietnam policy at the University of Michigan the same weekend. And then the President kept going around asking everyone, "How did we ever get into this Enchilada in the first place?"

State Visit

When Washington receives a head of state, many flowery words are exchanged, and since they are spoken in a diplomatic tongue, one cannot be sure what each party is really saying.

By a new method of extrasensory perception, I was able to record not only the words but the thoughts of the principals involved.

The dialogue was between the President of Enchilada and a very high U.S. government official. Their thoughts are in italics.

The President of Enchilada spoke first. "I bring you warm greetings from my country and my people. I am happy to set foot on the great and wonderful United States and I am deeply moved by the overwhelming reception I have received today."

(*This is a reception? I had more troops greet me in Zambia.*)

"The United States is happy to welcome the leader of the free people of Enchilada. No one admires more than we the great strides you have made in your country and the great contributions you have made for peace and prosperity in our time."

(*I wonder how much dough he's going to ask for?*)

"We are a small country with many problems besetting us. We look to you, the most powerful nation on the face of the earth, to lend your full support to resolving the differences between us and the aggressive Upper Tamale over our legitimate rights to the vale of Chili."

(*This is your last chance. If you don't give us the planes and rockets we want, we know someone who will.*)

"I have visited your country and I love your people. I even met one of your sheepherders. I know we can work together. We both want the same things, so we must find peaceful solutions to all problems and that is the task I have set above all others. We desire to help you."

(*But if you play footsie with Red China once more, it's curtains for you and your crummy friends.*).

"Your country and your people have been most generous in coming to the aid of little Enchilada and I would be the first to admit it. My people look to you for hope and encouragement in the dark days that lie ahead. All we ask is your understanding."

(*And for you to stay the hell out of Upper Tamale. We would have had them licked if it hadn't been for the tanks and arms you sent them.*)

"The United States is deeply grieved by the tragic events that have taken place between our two dearest friends, Enchilada and Upper Tamale. We must bind the wounds and sit down and talk out our differences. For the only ones who will gain by this dispute are the Communists."

(*You think they would have something better to do than to fight over a useless piece of real estate.*)

"My hopes and prayers have always been to live with our neighbors. We will pursue every avenue of peace, no matter how difficult or how trying these negotiations will be."

(*Give me three squadrons of B-52's and I'll settle the Upper Tamale problem overnight.*)

"But in exchange for our support, Mr. President, we hope you will support us in our endeavors in Southeast Asia where we are trying to find a just solution to a very difficult situation."

(*A lot you care about what's happening in Vietnam.*)

"The United States' problems are our problems."

(*You should have gotten out of Vietnam long ago.*)

"I assure you, Mr. President, we will always be brothers, for the things that bind us far outweigh the things that pull us apart."

(*I hope he finishes soon so I can get a nap before that damn state dinner.*)

"You have said the words that have been on my lips."

(*Boy, would I like to get a nap before that damn state dinner.*)

City for Sale

It was an ingenious idea and everyone was amazed that no one had thought of it before. The problem was to find the descendants of the Indians who had sold Manhattan to Peter Minuit in 1626.

The search was on, and finally the present chief of the tribe, who was working as a riveter on a new skyscraper in midtown Manhattan, was located. Three city officials climbed up the girders and began to speak while the Indian ate his lunch.

"Chief, we're here on behalf of the City of New York and we understand that your ancestors sold the island of Manhattan for $24."

The chief said, "That's true. The Dutch drove a hard bargain in those days. We were robbed."

"Well," said the second official, "we New Yorkers have always felt very bad about it and we want to make it up to you. How would you people like to buy the place back?"

"For how much?" the chief asked suspiciously.

"Twenty-four dollars."

"That's a lot of money," the chief said.

"We're willing to throw the Bronx, Brooklyn, Queens, and Staten Island in the package."

The chief stared down at the traffic jam below him.

"I don't think my people would be interested," he said.

"If it's a question of financing," the third official said, "you could give us four dollars down and four dollars a month."

Smoke and smog kept drifting up and the chief wiped his eyes with a red bandanna. "It isn't a question of the money. We just don't want it."

The first official said, "Chief, this is a golden opportunity for your people. Not only would you get all the land, but you'd have Lincoln Center, the Metropolitan Museum of Art, the Verrazano Bridge, and Shea Stadium."

The chief said, "White man speaks with forked tongue. Who gets the subway?"

"Why you do, of course."

"The deal's off," the chief said.

"But you wouldn't have to deal with Mike Quill the way we do," the second official said.

"How would I deal with him?"

"How would your ancestors deal with a man who gave them so much trouble?"

"I don't know. They never had a subway."

While they were talking, police sirens sounded and three men down below came running out of a bank, guns blazing.

The chief said, "Have you tried William Zeckendorf?"

"Legally," the third official said, "you're the only person we could sell the city back to."

"What about water?" the chief said.

"What about water?"

"My tribe needs water. You have no water."

"You could steal it from Pennsylvania," the official said. "Don't you see, Chief, if you took over the city, you could do all the things we're not permitted to do?"

"Who has to pay for the World's Fair?" the chief demanded.

The first official said, "It's obvious you don't know a good thing when you see it. We're sorry we even brought it up."

The three officials started their long climb down. Waiting nervously at the bottom was Mayor Lindsay.

"What did he say?" the Mayor wanted to know.

"No dice."

"I was afraid of that," Lindsay said. "Well, I'll have to think of something else."

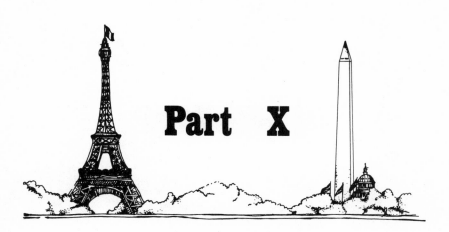

Part X

Inflation in the Nursery

The opening of the school year and the tight money situation are working hardships on many parents throughout the country.

My friend Block was in despair when I saw him the other day.

"When Roger was born," Block said, "we immediately took out an insurance policy for his education. Now because of inflation and the high cost of schooling, we've used it all up, and Roger still has six months to go."

"College is that expensive?" I asked

"What do you mean, college?" Block said. "Roger goes to nursery school."

"Nursery school, huh?"

"Twenty-five hundred dollars a year, not counting the yearbook or the prom," Block said. "I guess our big mistake was sending Roger to prenursery school. You start a kid at three in school, and then you have no money left for his serious education when he becomes five. If I had to do it all over again, I would probably let him stay in his sandbox, but Alice was adamant about his getting a good, solid background."

[285]

"Couldn't you borrow some money from the bank to let Roger finish out nursery school?"

"Well, we did borrow a thousand dollars at the beginning of the summer."

"What happened to it?"

"We used it to send Roger to day camp."

"At least the money wasn't wasted," I said. "Aren't there any government grants for kids who want to finish out nursery school?"

"I looked into it. Most of the grants available are in graduate work for children who are either in the fifth grade or above. The particular nursery school that Roger goes to could have gotten a large grant from the government if it was willing to do research in germ warfare. But the headmistress said she wouldn't allow her children to do any research at the school that couldn't be published later."

"I guess scholarships are out?" I said.

"You don't understand," Block said. "It isn't just the tuition that kills you in nursery school. It's the school bus, finger paints, clay, and chocolate milk that really mounts up the cost. You have to add another fifteen hundred dollars for that."

"It's like a yacht," I said. "It isn't the initial cost but the upkeep that counts."

"Exactly. I went to Yale for what it's costing me to send Roger through nursery school. But when I tell him this, it doesn't seem to faze him at all. Kids take everything for granted these days."

"You haven't suggested to Roger he could wait on tables to earn part of the tuition himself?"

"Alice is against it. She says nursery school should be a happy time for a child, and a kid shouldn't have to worry about working just because his father hadn't made adequate plans for his education."

"You do seem to be on a spot," I admitted. "But I guess the day Roger graduates from nursery school, you'll realize all the sacrifice and agony were worthwhile."

"I probably would, but Roger has already indicated he wants to go on to first grade."

Who's Worried?

One of the troubles with the world these days is that people have too much to worry about. You barely get over worrying about one thing, and you have to start worrying about something else.

Most Americans aren't equipped to worry about everything, and yet we constantly are told by scientists, politicians, generals, social workers, doctors, lawyers, TV commentators, newspaper editorial writers, and columnists that we'd better start worrying, or else.

My family thinks we have the solution to the problem. And since it's worked so well for us, I thought I'd pass it on to other people in hopes it might work for them. We decided a couple of weeks ago that each of us would worry about only one thing, to the exclusion of all other things.

For example, my father decided to worry only about the Middle East. Since he's been worried about the Middle East, none of the rest of us has to worry about it, and we're free to worry about the things that interest us.

My sister Alice worries about China for us. Any time she reads anything about Mao or the Red Guards, she'll call us up and say, "I'm very worried." Naturally, we're very relaxed about it because we always say to ourselves, "China's her problem."

My sister Edith worries about the population explosion. Why she decided on the population explosion we'll never know, except that one day she claimed she heard either on the *Johnny Carson Show,* the *Merv Griffin Show,* or the *Joey Bishop Show*—she can't remember which one—that by the year 2000 each person will have only twenty square inches of land to stand on. Now she skims through the papers, and if she doesn't find a population explosion story, she's free to enjoy the day.

We were fortunate in that my Uncle Oscar said he'd like to worry about Vietnam. No one really wanted to worry about Vietnam, since it takes up so much time, but Oscar said he'd rather worry about Vietnam than the riots in America's cities.

My sister Doris, who is a Francophobe, worries exclusively about Charles de Gaulle. She got into a fight with Edith, my population explosion sister, the other day because Edith said De Gaulle really wasn't worth worrying about. But Doris said she'd worry about what she darn pleased, and she's been very anxious ever since De Gaulle's trip to Canada.

My wife chose to worry about the cigarette-smoking scare. I tried to talk her out of it because the more she worries, the more cigarettes she smokes. But since she now does all the worrying for us about cigarettes, the rest of the family can continue to smoke without a care in the world.

My brothers-in-law also have chosen one subject each to worry about. Harold worries about auto safety, Arthur worries about air pollution, but the only thing we could get Iz to worry about was the Boston Red Sox.

Because I live in Washington, the family asked me to worry about President Johnson. At first I objected, since worrying about LBJ is a full-time job, and I wouldn't have any time to think about anything else. But they pointed out that since I've been worried about him for such a long time for myself, I could just as easily do it for them.

I agreed reluctantly, and while I haven't been sleeping very well since, at least I'm not worrying about Richard Nixon anymore. That's Aunt Molly's job.

Know Your Enemy

"Do you know what one of the troubles with the Vietnam war is?" a colonel in the Pentagon asked me recently.

"I'm sure I don't," I said in all honesty.

"We can't make an enemy out of the enemy."

I thought about this for a few minutes, and then I said, "How's that again?"

"Just what I said. It's impossible to describe the enemy in terms that will get to the American people emotionally."

"You mean we can't call them yellow bellies as we did the Japanese in World War II," I said.

"Exactly. Nor can we refer to them in racial terms, because the people on our side look exactly the same as the people on *their* side."

"I never thought about that," I said.

"The problem is: How do you portray the Vietcong in photographs and movies for what they really are without offending the South Vietnamese at the same time?"

"Through atrocities, of course," I replied. "Can't you show the Vietcong committing atrocities against the South Vietnamese people?"

"It's awfully difficult," he said, "because our television cameramen and still photographers take pictures only of the atrocities we commit, but never get any shots of the ones the Cong commit."

"The solution then would be to get our cameramen attached to the Vietcong," I said.

"It's a good suggestion," the colonel said, "but every time we ask Hanoi if we can have our camera crews cover their operations, they say we can't until we stop the bombing."

"And we can't stop the bombing," I said.

"Of course not. At least not until they stop raping and pillaging the South Vietnamese villages."

"Which nobody will believe they're doing because we have no pictures?"

"That's the difficulty. We don't even have any good films of the North Vietnamese in Hanoi calling for the raping and pillaging of South Vietnam. Remember, in World War II, those wonderful shots of Hitler, Goebbels, and Goering screaming oaths at the Allies?"

"How could anyone forget?"

"And those pictures of Tojo in Tokyo?" he said.

"They were worth thousands of words."

"Well, we haven't been able to get any shots of Ho Chi Minh that show him looking like anything except a starving Santa Claus."

"You can't get the people riled up about that," I admitted. "Isn't it possible to make the Vietcong wear uniforms so we can tell them apart from the good guys?"

"That's another problem we have. The Vietcong don't wear uniforms. They look just like everybody else in Vietnam."

"Why don't we send a bombing mission over the Vietcong areas and drop World War II Nazi uniforms on them? You can't help hating someone in a Nazi uniform."

"We've thought about it, but the Vietcong are too small. The uniforms would never fit them, and they'd probably use the helmets for bathtubs."

"Well, at least it taught us a lesson."

"What's that?"

"We should never get into a war where the people on both sides look alike."

Down the Rapids with Bobby

I went down the rapids of the Colorado River in the Grand Canyon with Senator Robert Kennedy and his family and friends recently. There were 42 people in the party, including singer Andy Williams, mountain climber Jim Whittaker, pro-football player George Plimpton, skier Willy Schaeffler, publisher Otis Chandler, and 350 Kennedy children.

I was the only one in condition to make the trip, but in spite of this, my father didn't want me to go. "It's all right for Kennedy to go down the rapids because he can walk on the water, but you're going to have to swim."

I assured him that the Kennedys would never do anything dangerous, but it was hard to persuade him. He said, "It's as safe to go down the Colorado River with Bobby Kennedy in a raft as it is to sail up the Nile with General Moshe Dayan."

Despite my father's fears, I'm glad I went. You really don't get to know a man until you've taken a rapid with him. The trouble is, Bobby Kennedy took a lot of rapids, and he took them on an air mattress. Ethel, mother of ten, also took the rapids out of the raft, and of course, her children took the rapids out of the raft, so there was nothing left for the rest of the party to do but leave the raft as well.

The best way to take a rapid is to float feetfirst on your life preserver, just in case you hit a rock. But I invented a new way of doing it. If you keep your mouth open, you can swallow most of the water you're going over, which makes it half as rough. My wife had to give me mouth-to-mouth resuscitation every night when we camped, but no one noticed it because everyone thought we were just kissing under the stars.

If you're ever going down the rapids with the Kennedys, it's best to choose a river that isn't surrounded by cliffs. Every morning after breakfast Bobby would look up at a mountain and ask Mount Everest climber Jim Whittaker, "Do you think it's tough to climb?" If Whittaker said no, Bobby would look at another mountain. "What about that one?"

If Whittaker said, "It's impossible," Bobby would call the party together and say, "That's the one we're going up," and pretty soon Ethel, mother of ten, the Kennedy children, and the rest of the group would be scrambling up the mountain in 110-degree heat.

After the mountain had been conquered, everyone would return to the rafts to take some more rapids. By the third day I was starting to have a great deal of respect for my father, and I wouldn't take off my life preserver, even to get into my sleeping bag.

Probably the most dangerous part of the trip was the last day, when we arrived at a place laughingly called Phantom Lodge, seven miles down, at the bottom of the Grand Canyon. The only ways to get out of the canyon are to walk out in 119-degree heat, ride a burro out along the same trail, or pretend you're going to die so they'll send a helicopter for you. I had rehearsed the death scene for three days, and by the time we arrived at Phantom Lodge, I was barely breathing.

Bobby opted to climb up the seven miles, as did the Kennedy children, and when Ethel, mother of ten, said she would climb out, too, the rest of the party was too embarrassed to say they'd rather go by helicopter.

Fearful that they would cancel the helicopter, I stopped breathing when Bobby and Jim Whittaker came up to me to see if they could persuade me to change my mind.

Bobby said, "Why don't you want to climb the mountain?"

I just smiled weakly and replied, "Because it's there."

No, Virginia, There Isn't

When the late President Kennedy canceled his subscription to the New York *Herald Tribune,* I wrote a letter to my little friend, Virginia, assuring her that although the paper wasn't read in the White House, it was still very much alive and would remain alive as long as there were Presidents in the White House to cancel their subscriptions to it.

I recently received another letter from Virginia. It read:

Dear Sir:

I am seven years old, and all my friends tell me there is no New York *Herald Tribune.* I won't believe it's so, until I read it in your column. Are they lying again?

Your friend,
Virginia

Dear Virginia:

Unfortunately, this time your friends are telling the truth. The reason there is no *Trib* is that it could exist no longer. No, Virginia, there is no *Herald Tribune.* You are too young to understand why it is no more, and so am I.

The publishers said they wanted to publish it, but the unions wouldn't let them. The unions said they wanted to print it, but the publishers wouldn't let them. The advertisers all insisted New York City needed a *Herald Tribune,* but many of them wouldn't advertise in it. The readers said the New York *Herald Tribune* was a great newspaper, but apparently there just weren't enough of them.

Everyone loved the *Herald Tribune,* even the competitors, but that did not prevent it from dying. Alas, Virginia, how dreary New York will be without the *Trib,* as dreary as many other cities where newspapers have died, and none have come to take their place.

A newspaper is not like Santa Claus. You don't have to see Santa Claus to know he exists, but you have to see a newspaper. You have to touch it and feel it and read it and, what's even more, believe in it.

A newspaper cannot be published on faith alone. It needs editors, reporters, printers, technicians, advertisers, distributors, and readers, and if you can't have all these, you can't have a paper, at least not for very long.

No *Herald Tribune.* It's true, Virginia. Those of us who worked for it thought it would live for a thousand, nay, ten thousand years from now. We thought it would gladden the hearts of Virginias for generations to come. We didn't believe it would disappear until it happened, and some of us can't believe it still.

I'm sorry to break the news to you in this way, but although your friends were right, tell them not to gloat when a newspaper dies. A little of the truth, beauty, romance, love, faith, and fancy that the world is so short of dies with it.

Sincerely,
A.B.

How the Soviets Helped Israel

There has been some confusion about how much aid the Soviet Union gave the Arab nations during the recent unpleasantness in the Middle East. What nobody knows is that the Soviets' real intention was to help Israel. But they had to do it in such a way that neither the Arab countries nor the West would find out about it.

It seems the Soviet Union has been trying to increase its arms business to compete with the United States and Great Britain. One of the most likely prospects was Israel, who was finding it hard to get military equipment from the West. The Soviets said they would give Israel everything she wanted, but it would have to be done in such a way that it wouldn't anger the Arab countries or even some Communist-leaning states.

Israel said she was interested but didn't want to do anything to anger the United States, Great Britain, and France.

Encouraged by what could turn out to be a very good customer, the Soviet Union proceeded to devise a way of getting Russian arms into the hands of the well-equipped Israeli Army. The big question was: How?

Then someone in the Politburo (the Soviets refuse to say who) got a brilliant idea. He told the Israeli diplomats, "We naturally cannot sell you the weapons directly; but why don't we give them to the United Arab Republic, and then you can get our weapons from them?"

The Israelis pointed out that the UAR might be reluctant to give the Israelis any of their Soviet weapons. The Soviets told them not to worry about it. "Just give us a list of what you need," they said.

The Israelis, trusting implicity in the good faith of the Soviet Union, handed in a list, including tanks, guns, armored cars, jeeps, small arms, and, surprisingly enough, six or seven Soviet ground-to-air-missiles.

A year later the Soviets told the Israelis that their order was ready and would be delivered in a month

The Israelis were puzzled but decided to wait and see what would happen. Sure enough, in May Gamal Abdel Nasser closed the Gulf of Aqaba and moved seven divisions of his troops and armor into the Sinai desert.

At the same time the Soviet Union accused Israel of being an "aggressor," which was the code name for "customer."

On June 5 the Israelis went to collect their equipment in the Sinai desert, where it was conveniently left by Egyptian troops, many of whom didn't even wait to be tipped for delivering it. The tanks, personnel carriers, guns, and even missiles were brand-new. A few were damaged in transit, but by and large the Russians had made everything available as ordered.

Some Soviet items accidentally left off the list were delivered to the Israelis, via Syria, a few days later.

All in all, it was quite a coup for the Soviet Union. In one of the great business deals of our time the Soviets managed to collect twice for the same equipment, first from the Arabs and then from the Israelis.

As a follow-up, it has been reported that the Soviets are sending in new arms and equipment to the United Arab Republic. What nobody knows is that all they're doing is filling another Israeli order for equipment. One Soviet diplomat told me, "By supplying the Arabs with arms, Israel has turned out to be the best customer we've got."

A Guide to the Crisis

During the Middle East crisis I thought we ought to get our terms straight. It's very hard to understand what is going on unless you know what all the countries are talking about. So, as a public service, I am providing an instant definition guide to diplomatic language.

restraint—Something you tell another country to show when your own personal interests are not involved. It is usually urged by countries who would go to war in a minute if one of their enemies threatened war on them.

aggression—What the other side is committing at the time your side is trying to be a "peace-loving" nation—i.e., the Russians claim the Israelis are committing aggression against the Arab world because Egypt has closed the Gulf of Aqaba to Israeli shipping.

a recess—Something that the Soviet delegate won't let Ambassador Arthur Goldberg have so Goldberg can go to the bathroom.

commitment—A commitment is a promise one nation gives another nation which it does or does not have to honor, depending on how the political wind is blowing. For example, the United States is fighting a war in Vietnam to honor its commitment in Southeast Asia. Because of this commitment, the Russians and Arabs are counting on the United States not to honor the one it has to Israel, since they believe the American people are sick and tired of honoring their country's commitments.

U.S. military aid—Something the United States gave to Jordan, Saudi Arabia, and Israel to maintain a balance of power there. If war comes to this area, American-made planes will be fighting American-made planes, U.S. antitank guns will try to knock out U.S. manufactured tanks, and American artillery shells will pass each other in the night.

cooling-off period—A period advocated by U Thant to try to work out a solution to the mess he made when he pulled the UN troops out of Sinai and the Gulf of Aqaba without consulting the Security Council or the General Assembly.

a face-saving and just solution for all parties—That which every diplomat talks about, but nobody has any idea what the hell it is.

a UN resolution—If proposed by the United States, it will be automatically vetoed by the Soviet Union. If proposed by another country and passed, it will be ignored by the parties involved in the dispute. The violation of a UN resolution is used to justify an act of aggression.

Arab unity—The pledge of all Arab countries to a united cause which could or could not last about two weeks. At this writing, Nasser has signed a military pact with King Hussein while Syria is calling for the chopping of Hussein's head.

diplomatic activity—Actions taken by countries who don't know what action to take.

a showdown—Something that observers believe neither Nasser nor the Soviet Union expected they would have at this time. The Israelis wanted to have it two weeks ago, but were persuaded to hold off by the United States because it was caught completely by surprise.

the brink—That part of the precipice we keep returning to every time the Soviets think it's an opportune time to make another move.

world war iii—That which, because of the above definitions, we're on the brink of.

Everyone Is Merging

Every time you pick up the newspaper you read about one company merging with another company. Of course, we have laws to protect competition in the United States, but one can't help thinking that if the trend continues, the whole country will soon be merged into one large company.

It is 1978, and by this time every company west of the Mississippi will have merged into one giant corporation known as Samson Securities. Every company east of the Mississippi will have merged under an umbrella corporation known as the Delilah Company.

It is inevitable that one day the chairman of the board of Samson and the president of Delilah would meet and discuss merging their two companies.

"If we could get together," the president of Delilah said, "we would be able to finance your projects and you would be able to finance ours."

"Exactly what I was thinking," the chairman of Samson said.

"That's a great idea, and it certainly would make everyone's life less complicated."

The men shook on it, and then they sought approval from the Antitrust Division of the Justice Department.

At first the head of the Antitrust Division indicated that he might have reservations about allowing the only two companies left in the United States to merge.

"Our department," he said, "will take a close look at this proposed merger. It is our job to further competition in private business and industry, and if we allow Samson and Delilah to merge, we may be doing the consumer a disservice."

The chairman of Samson protested vigorously that merging with Delilah would not stifle competition but would help it. "The public will be the true beneficiary of this merger," he said. "The larger we are, the more services we can perform, and the lower prices we can charge."

The president of Delilah backed him up. "In the Communist system the people don't have a choice. They must buy from the state. In our capitalistic society the people can buy from either the Samson Company or the Delilah Company."

"But if you merge," someone pointed out, "there will be only one company left in the United States."

"Exactly," said the president of Delilah. "Thank God for the free enterprise system."

The Antitrust Division of the Justice Department studied the merger for months. Finally, the Attorney General made this ruling: "While we find some drawbacks to only one company's being left in the United States, we feel the advantages to the public far outweigh the disadvantages.

"Therefore, we're making an exception in this case and allowing Samson and Delilah to merge.

"I would like to announce that the Samson and Delilah Company is now negotiating at the White House with the President to buy the United States. The Justice Department will naturally study this merger to see if it violates any of our strong antitrust laws."

The Third Largest Industry

One of the ways to solve acute problems in the United States is to study them. At this writing there are probably more committees making more studies of more problems than at any time in our history.

Professor Heinrich Applebaum has just completed a study on people who make studies, and the results are fascinating.

Professor Applebaum said, "I discovered that the average person making a study today has had 5 years of college, is married, has 1.6 children, earns $15,000 year, lives in the suburbs, plays tennis or golf on weekends, and believes in God."

"That's truly amazing."

"He will spend an average 8.9 months working on a study, 2.6 months discussing it in committee, 3.9 months writing a report, which will be typed up by 5.6 secretaries, and then it will be printed up and distributed to 1,250 persons, who will read it in its entirety."

"That isn't too many people."

"It's a lot considering that only 1 out of every 23.6 reports is ever acted on."

"What happens to the rest of them?"

"They're filed away and used as reference for other people who will be asked to make future studies on the same subject."

"That sounds rather discouraging."

"On the contrary. The main purpose of a study is not to solve a problem, but to postpone the solution of it in the hope that it will go away. If it doesn't go away, at least people will have forgotten about it by the time the report comes out."

"Could you give me an example?"

"Well, at the moment the riots in Detroit are under study. A blue-ribbon panel of politicians appointed by the President is making a report, which will probably be delivered sometime in 1968. By then some other city will probably be burned down, and nobody will give a damn what happened in Detroit. They'll demand to know what happened in Philadelphia or Cleveland or whatever city blows up next. The President will then appoint another commission to study *that* riot, and by the time they get their report in, the President will have to appoint another committee to study what went wrong in Washington, D.C., or Oakland, California."

"A study group's work is never done."

"I should say not. Making studies is now the third largest industry in the United States. Not only are large monies spent in making studies, but great sums are also spent attacking studies that people don't agree with. Whenever the Public Health Service issues a report on smoking, the tobacco industry immediately attacks it with a study of its own."

"Even the National Guard doesn't like to be studied," I said.

"That's the beauty of the business. Every study demands a counter-study to refute its facts."

"Professor Applebaum, your report will make a great contribution to the study of studies. Can you tell me why you decided to do it in the first place?"

"I work for a foundation, and everything we wanted to study was being studied by somebody else. This was the only subject left that no one had made a study on."

"Has anybody read it?"

"My wife thinks it's the best thing I've ever done."

The Human Engineer

There is a new science in this country which is called human engineering. The object of human engineering, as I understand it, is to fit human beings into inhuman conditions.

I made this discovery while riding on an airplane from New York to Washington the other day. Seated next to me was a man who was taking very careful measurements of the space between us and then writing it in a notebook.

I asked him what he was doing, and he said he was a human engineer, and it was his job to see how many more people he could squeeze on an airplane without doing permanent bodily harm to the passengers.

"We used to have five seats across," he said proudly, "but we've managed to put another seat in each row, and as you can see, we can now get six people across."

"How on earth did you do it?" I asked him.

"We cut the center aisle in half. The passengers have to walk sideways, but just think of what the extra seats mean to the company's payload."

"Which, of course, is all that you're worried about?"

"You can bet your sweet whistle on that," he said. "I'm very concerned, though, that there still seems to be room between your knees and the seat in front of you."

"Only about two inches," I said.

"Well, if you take two inches away here and two inches away there, you can put another row of seats on the plane."

"Then my knees should be flush against the seat ahead?"

"Naturally, my dear boy. You can't expect legroom on such a short hop. One more thing. I was wondering how you feel about a reclining seat as opposed to a stationary one."

"I prefer a reclining seat. It gives me a chance to rest a little."

He started writing in his book: "Customer too tempted by reclining chair, so I strongly recommend stationary kind, which will allow us two more rows in back."

He looked at me. "You came on board with a package. What did you do with it?"

"I put it under my seat."

He wrote again, "Customer can still get package under seat, which means we're wasting valuable space which could better be used for airfreight."

"You people really think of everything," I said.

"We try to," he replied, "but it's a tough struggle. There are a lot of people in the aviation business who are behind the times, and we have to show them that their best interests lie not with the passengers but with the stockholders. I'm having a devil of a time trying to get the company to remove the armrests."

"You want to do away with the armrests?"

"Of course. If you did away with the armrests, everyone would be forced to sit closer together, and we could get eight people in a row."

"Say, have you ever thought of putting people in the baggage rack overhead?" I asked him.

He studied it for a few moments. "It could be done, if we could fit them in horizontally." He made another note: "Check about stuffing people into overhead baggage rack."

"You covered all the bases," I said in admiration.

"Not quite," he said, staring at the washroom.

Bombs for Sale

There seems to be a shortage of bombs and other equipment from World War II which are needed for our present engagement in Vietnam.

Secretary McNamara revealed that the Defense Department had to buy back a number of 750-pound bombs from the Germans. The bombs were sold to the Germans for $1.70 each and brought back by the United States for $21 each.

The Pentagon isn't talking about it; but a worldwide search is going on for American war surplus, and just the other day a colonel showed up on the Island Mona Loren in the South Pacific, which had been an Army base in World War II.

He was greeted by the chief of the Mona Lorens.

"Welcome to Mona Loren, great white bird," the chief said. "We have not seen your kind since the savages of the Rising Sun threatened to engulf us with their yellow peril."

"Yeah, well, all that's forgotten now, chief. How's the old island doing?"

"The quonset huts are holding up well, but the tents are starting to leak. Have you come to give us more surplus?"

"No, chief, on the contrary, we thought we might move some of this junk out of here for you so you would have more room. "

"To do what?"

"Put in urban renewal. That sort of stuff. Let me ask you, chief, you still got those bombs around that we left behind?"

"Oh, yes. Many bombs are still on the island."

"That's fine. I'm happy to tell you that we've been worried about your safety for the past nineteen years, and we've decided to remove them so no one will get hurt."

"Very good, smiling eagle. How much are you paying for them?"

"Well, we hadn't intended to pay for them, but I'll tell you what we'll do. We'll give you a box of chewing gum for each one we take away."

"Wait a minute, most honorable brass. The Germans were here a few weeks ago and offered us three dollars a bomb, FOB."

"Well, we'll give you three fifty a bomb just to show there are no hard feelings."

"You are indeed generous, great white spit polish. But the French came a few days later and offered us five fifty a bomb, plus green stamps."

"This is ridiculous," the colonel said. "After all, they were our bombs in the first place."

"Yes, oh star-spangled friend, but the day your Army left our happy island to go Stateside, I asked the commanding officer as he got on board the boat what I should do with all the Army equipment, and I'd hate to repeat what he told me to do with it."

"All right, we'll give you seven dollars a bomb, and that's as high as we can go."

"Alas, dear uniformed liberator. The British were here just two days ago and offered us ten dollars a bomb, plus a gross of Beatle records."

"Who else has been to see you?" the colonel said angrily.

"The Egyptians, the Israelis, the Cubans, the Malaysians, the Pakistanis, the Indians, the Greeks, the Turks, and the Rhodesians. The last bid on the bombs was forty-three fifty. Tell me something. What the hell is going on out there in the world?"

"Never mind. Okay, we'll pay you fifty dollars a bomb. And that's final."

"You have yourself a deal, proud brother."

"One thing more, chief. How much do you want for the skivvy shirt?"

Fresh Air Will Kill You

Smog, which was once the big attraction of Los Angeles, can now be found all over the country from Butte, Montana, to New York City, and people are getting so used to polluted air that it's very difficult for them to breathe anything else.

I was lecturing recently, and one of my stops was Flagstaff, Arizona, which is about 7,000 miles above sea level.

As soon as I got out of the plane, I smelled something peculiar.

"What's that smell?" I asked the man who met me at the plane.

"I don't smell anything," he replied.

"There's a definite odor that I'm not familiar with," I said.

"Oh, you must be talking about the fresh air. A lot of people come out here who have never smelled fresh air before."

"What's it supposed to do?" I asked suspiciously.

"Nothing. You just breathe it like any other kind of air. It's supposed to be good for your lungs."

"I've heard that story before," I said. "How come if it's air, my eyes aren't watering?"

"Your eyes don't water with fresh air. That's the advantage of it. Saves you a lot in paper tissues."

I looked around and everything appeared crystal clear. It was a strange sensation and made me feel very uncomfortable.

My host, sensing this, tried to be reassuring. "Please don't worry about it. Tests have proved that you can breathe fresh air day and night without its doing any harm to the body."

"You're just saying that because you don't want me to leave," I said. "Nobody who has lived in a major city can stand fresh air for a very long time. He has no tolerance for it."

"Well, if the fresh air bothers you, why don't you put a handkerchief over your nose and breathe through your mouth?"

"Okay, I'll try it. If I'd known I was coming to a place that had nothing but fresh air, I would have brought a surgical mask."

We drove in silence. About fifteen minutes later he asked, "How do you feel now?"

"Okay, I guess, but I sure miss sneezing."

"We don't sneeze too much here," the man admitted. "Do they sneeze a lot where you come from?"

"All the time. There are some days when that's all you do."

"Do you enjoy it?"

"Not necessarily, but if you don't sneeze, you'll die. Let me ask you something. How come there's no air pollution around here?"

"Flagstaff can't seem to attract industry. I guess we're really behind the times. The only smoke we get is when the Indians start signaling each other. But the wind seems to blow it away."

The fresh air was making me feel dizzy. "Isn't there a diesel bus around here that I could breathe into for a couple of hours?"

"Not at this time of day. I might be able to find a truck for you."

We found a truck driver, and slipped him a five-dollar bill, and he let me put my head near his exhaust pipe for a half hour. I was immediately revived and able to give my speech.

Nobody was as happy to leave Flagstaff as I was. My next stop was Los Angeles, and when I got off the plane, I took one big deep breath of the smog-filled air, my eyes started to water, I began to sneeze, and I felt like a new man again.

How Un-American Can You Get?

I have a confession to make, and the sooner it gets out in the open, the better I'll feel about it. *I don't drive a car.*

Americans are broad-minded people. They'll accept the fact that a person can be an alcoholic, a dope fiend, a wife beater, and even a newspaperman, but if a man doesn't drive, there is something wrong with him.

Through the years I've found it very embarrassing to admit it to anyone, and my best friends tend to view me with suspicion and contempt.

But where I really run into trouble is when I go into a store and try to make a purchase with a check.

It happened again last week when I went to a discount house at a large shopping center in Maryland. I wanted to buy a portable typewriter, and the salesman was very helpful about showing me the different models.

I decided on one, and then I said, "May I write out a personal check?"

"Naturally," he said kindly. "Do you have any identification?"

"Of course," I said. I produced an American Express credit card, a Diners' Club credit card, a Carte Blanche credit card, a Bell Telephone credit card, and my pass to the White House.

The man inspected them all and then said, "Where's your driver's license?"

"I don't have one," I replied.

"Did you lose it?"

"No, I didn't lose it. I don't drive a car."

He pushed a button under the cash register, and suddenly a floor manager came rushing over.

The salesman had now become surly. "This guy's trying to cash a check, and he doesn't have a driver's license. Should I call the store detective?"

"Wait a minute. I'll talk to him," the manager said. "Did you lose your driver's license for some traffic offense?"

"No, I've never driven. I don't like to drive."

"Nobody likes to drive," the floor manager shouted. "That's no excuse. Why are you trying to cash a check if you don't have a driver's license?"

"I thought all the other identification was good enough. I had to be cleared by the Secret Service to get this White House pass," I said hopefully.

The floor manager looked scornfully at the pass and all my credit cards. "Anyone can get cleared by the Secret Service. Hey, wait a minute. How did you get out here to the shopping center if you don't drive?"

"I took a taxi," I said.

"Well, that takes the cake," he said.

By this time a crowd had gathered.

"What happened?"

"Guy doesn't have a driver's license."

"Says he doesn't even drive. Never has driven."

"Lynch him."

"Tar and feather him."

"How un-American can you get?"

The crowd was getting ugly, so I decided to forget the typewriter.

"Never mind," I said. "I'll go somewhere else."

By this time the president of the store had arrived on the scene. Fortunately, he recognized my name and okayed the check. He was very embarrassed by the treatment I had received and said, "Come on, I'll buy you a drink."

"I forgot to tell you," I said. "I don't drink either."

This was too much, even for him, and he pushed me toward the door.

"Get out of here," he said, "and don't come back!"

Meeting of the Minds

The longer I live in Washington, the more impressed I am with how smoothly the government runs.

Not long ago I was in a government office, waiting to take a friend to lunch. He had just come out of a meeting and seemed pleased with how well it had gone.

"What was the meeting about?" I asked.

"I'm not sure what you mean," he said.

"Why did you have the meeting?"

"What a stupid question. What do you think we do in the government, just sit around and twiddle our thumbs?"

"I didn't mean that. What subject did you discuss at the meeting?"

"We discussed whether we should hold a conference or not."

"You had a meeting to discuss holding a conference?"

"Of course. And the consensus was that we should hold off on the conference until we meet again."

"Which, of course, will mean another meeting?"

"Now you've got it," he said. "I don't mind telling you I was pretty scared, because Agnew had called a meeting for ten o'clock, and Evans had called another meeting for ten thirty. Evans had no right to call the meeting without checking with Agnew and when Agnew heard about it, he got pretty damned mad. So Evans moved up his meeting until eleven thirty."

"Did anything happen at Agnew's meeting?"

"We discussed in general the groundwork for Evans' meeting."

"Then by the time you met with Evans, you knew exactly what you were going to talk about?"

"We never got around to it because Wallaby, who had to make the major decision, was called to a meeting the Secretary was holding at the same time. Zimmerman was furious because he felt that he should have been invited to the Secretary's meeting, too, and he suspected Evans had called his meeting so Zimmerman wouldn't know about the other meeting."

"How did he find out about it?"

"Coates told him, rather maliciously, I thought. He expressed surprise that Zimmerman was sitting with us when Wallaby was across the street.

"Zimmerman said that he had met with the Secretary earlier, and the Secretary's meeting was just to confirm what they had gone over earlier. But Thurston told me later that the Secretary's secretary had told him not to mention the Wallaby meeting to Zimmerman."

"Did you ever find out what Wallaby's meeting with the Secretary was about?"

"Coates said it had to do with a meeting the Secretary is having in Washington next month. There was a conflict because several of the people the Secretary wanted had scheduled a conference, and the Secretary maintains there is no sense having the conference until they meet with him."

"You people in government meet a lot, don't you?" I said.

"We have to."

"Why?"

"Because if someone calls up my secretary and asks for me, it looks so much better if she says I'm in a meeting. How would you feel if when you rang me up, you found me in my office?"

"I'd feel you were stealing the taxpayers' money."

"Exactly. Now let's go have lunch. I have to be back at two o'clock for a you-know-what."

The Security Check

The Senate Internal Security Subcommittee recently released classified material involving the security clearance of eight distinguished American citizens. It was unevaluated material gathered by

Otto F. Otepka, and many people protested that this kind of thing harked back to the McCarthy era.

I didn't realize how dangerous something like this could be until I was interviewed by a security specialist from one of the government agencies, who was checking up on a good friend of mine who was being considered for an important job.

We shall call my friend Bill Hoganblatt, and I knew him from my days in Paris.

The security man was very friendly. "How long have you known Hoganblatt?" he asked me.

"About eighteen years," I replied. "I want to say he's one of the finest men I've ever had the pleasure to be associated with. He's a good father, a kind husband, a loyal friend, and a great American."

"What kind of people did he associate with during the years in Paris?"

"All kinds. Writers, artists, businessmen. Bill was a very democratic guy."

"Were there any left-wingers among these friends?"

"Come to think of it, I think there were. At least some of them had strong political convictions, but I don't believe Bill—then again he never did say much about politics."

"Didn't you find this strange?" the investigator asked as he took notes.

"I didn't at the time, but now that you mention it, there was something funny about Bill's not wanting to discuss politics."

"You said it; I didn't. What about his drinking habits?"

"As far as I know, he never touched the stuff at all."

"Then you'd call him a secret drinker?"

"Come to think of it, he probably was. I never trusted a guy who wouldn't drink in public."

"What else can you remember about him?"

"He used to go to the museums in Paris a lot."

"Did you ever see him go to a museum?"

"No, he just said he did."

"Then he could have gone anywhere during those times. Even to the Soviet Embassy."

"By golly, he could have. I wouldn't have put it past him."

"One more question. As an American citizen, would you want Hoganblatt to work for your government?"

"I should say not! I didn't realize what a contemptible rat he was until I talked to you. For all I know, he's another Alger Hiss, and I hope he gets what's coming to him real soon."

Thoughts of a Candidate's Wife

It is regrettable that when the wife of someone running for public office is interviewed, she can't say what is really on her mind. In order to be a good candidate's wife, she must show a stiff upper lip and stick with the standard clichés about her husband, her home, and her children.

Now, for the first time, thanks to a new extrasensory perception process, I can reveal what is really going on in the mind of the wife of the candidate. Her thoughts are in italics:

"Mrs. Goodfellow, what is the most important role a wife must play in her husband's political career?"

"She must give him moral support when he is discouraged. She must be his ears and eyes when he isn't around, and she must be able to make him relax at the end of a hard day's campaigning."

As well as keep him off the bottle and away from all the skirts who think he's God's gift to women.

"You have four children. Do you find they miss their father when he is out making speeches all the tine?"

"I imagine they do. But Carlton's a wonderful father, and he always makes time for the children, no matter how many political commitments he has."

Would you believe he hasn't seen them since the Fourth of July?

"Do you find the children understand that both of you have to be away from home so much?"

"Oh, yes, they're wonderful about it, and they're as interested in the race as we are."

They've only run away from home twice—the second time they asked to be placed in an orphanage.

"Do you get upset at the terrible things that are said about your husband during the campaign?"

"Oh, no. One must understand that politics is a rough business, and I'm used to it."

But if I ever see the wife of the candidate Charlton is running against, I'll scratch her eyes out.

"Mrs. Goodfellow, do you find it tiring to be constantly in the limelight and always on your best behavior?"

"I love it. When we first got married, Charlton indicated he wanted to go into politics, and I knew that although it would place me in the spotlight, our lives would be exciting, thrilling, and rewarding. I wouldn't change my life for anything."

Except to be married to a plumber or somebody else with a respectable job.

"How do you manage to keep so beautifully dressed all the time?"

"I make do on Charlton's salary. You just have to know where the bargains are."

If it weren't for the trust fund Daddy left me, I'd be in rags right now.

"Mrs. Goodfellow, do you ever get any time alone with your husband?"

"Oh, yes. We steal many hours together and talk about the children and the funny things that have happened during the campaign and the intimate day-to-day happenings of our lives."

The only other people present are his political campaign manager, his press man, his finance chairman, and forty-three other volunteer workers.

"Mrs. Goodfellow, if your husband wins his race for office, will you change your living habits in any way?"

"Oh, no. I'm going to be the same person I was before."

I'll just take more tranquilizers instead.

The Anatomy of a Leader

Negro "leaders" aren't born these days, but made—and in most instances by the news media.

Take the case of Robert Runneymeade as an example. Robert Runneymeade has been standing on the corner of Spring and Maple for the past three years (except when he's been in jail), saying to three or four hangers-on, "We ought to shake someone up." Nobody ever paid much attention to Robert Runneymeade until a few months ago, when a reporter for a local newspaper, doing a story on violence in the ghettos, happened to overhear Runneymeade saying to his friends, "Man, we ought to burn down this town."

The next day a story appeared in the paper that "Robert Runneymeade, a leader of the black power movement, told a militant crowd at Spring and Maple that it was time to burn down the town."

A television crew was dispatched the next evening to Spring and Maple, where his pals were congratulating Runneymeade on having made the front pages of the newspaper. The TV commentator stuck a microphone in front of Robert Runneymeade's face, lights were turned on, and for the next twenty minutes, Runneymeade said, "The mayor, the city council, the honkies, and President Johnson have to talk to me."

The opposition television station sent out its camera crews to get the views of Runneymeade, and with all the lights and trucks a large crowd gathered, as they will when they see TV cameras.

The news media claimed that the crowd who had gathered were all Runneymeade's followers, when in fact most of them had never heard of Runneymeade, and those who knew him thought he was a joke.

But the press was not too interested in how many followers Runneymeade really had. He was now talking about burning down the Yosemite National Park, and this certainly had news value.

In the meantime, the networks had plugged into Runneymeade and he started holding press conferences telling everyone, "I'm not going to take any stuff from anyone, and if I have to wipe out the U.S. Marine Corps, I'm going to do it."

The Negro people still considered Runneymeade a joke, but the white people were scared out of their wits by his television appearances and his statements in the press. Things got so bad that when the President of the United States went on television to talk about the riots, his statement was played on the bottom of the page, and a statement made by Runneymeade threatening to use tanks against the public library was given a six-column headline.

It got so bad that no matter what happened, Runneymeade was the first interviewed about what his opinion was on the issues of the day. Runneymeade was quoted on Red China, Vietnam, the Middle East crisis. He appeared on the covers of both leading news magazines. The majority of the Negro community kept insisting that Runneymeade did not speak for them, but no one could make a headline or a TV news story out of that.

Unfortunately, the publicity had gone to Runneymead's head, and one day he announced he was banning all white newspapermen from his press conferences.

Since they couldn't cover him anymore, the news media sought out another "Negro leader" on the corner of Marble and Sycamore streets. His name was Huggins Haplap, and he was overheard by a reporter the other day saying to a girl he was trying to impress, "I'm going to burn down the Grand Coulee Dam." It shouldn't be long before Haplap becomes a feared American household name.

Part XI

Confidential Note to the Reader
(Why I Can't Write a Dirty Book)

It is absolutely essential that anyone today who claims to be a writer must produce a pornographic book. It is a status symbol comparable with that of the Hemingway era, when in order to be a writer, you had to bag a lion.

You would think writing a pornographic book would be one of the easiest things in the world. Well, it isn't. I know, because I've been trying to write one for two years.

I think one of my problems is that I've been doing too much research. I like to be well versed in any subject I attack, so I spend hours upon hours reading other pornographic books, and by the time I get my reading done I'm so excited I can't write myself.

Another thing that seems to have me stymied is that I don't know what kind of pornography to specialize in. I'm not sure whether I want to appeal to the flagellation-sadomasochistic school of writing, which has a limited but devoted audience:

"You're not going to whip me with that?" she cried hopefully.
"That's not all I'm going to do with you, you bitch," he chortled.

Or go commercial and write a wife-swapping novel:

"I've never done it with anyone but Fred," she cried, as she took off her slip.

"I've never done it with anyone but Sue," he said nervously, as he hung his pants on a chair.

She gasped as she gazed at his power, and suddenly Fred was the farthest thing from her mind.

But then I say to myself, "Everyone is writing wife-swapping books these days, and I'm not going to sell out for a Book-of-the-Month Club selection, no matter how much money there is in it."

So the thought occurs that maybe I should write a story of a woman who, because of a gang rape or some other beastly act, turns to another woman or women for consolation and love:

She sat in the chair, her skirt raised above her thighs, and looked into my face. My heart leaped as I saw her wet lips open and heard her voice say, "You know why I'm here." I fought back the impulse to drop to my knees and kiss those long beautiful white legs, but suddenly she rose from her chair, took my hand, and placed it on her breast. The room started spinning . . . .

I guess there's a need for this type of book and I should be fulfilling it, but I've always believed that if you're going to write a novel, it should have social significance. And I keep thinking I could strike a blow for civil liberties if I could just find some way of dealing with a racial situation in a pornographic way:

She stared at the ebony face of her giant chauffeur and snarled, "Don't ever put your nigger hands on me, or my husband will kill you." The chauffeur tried to back out of the room in fear, but she blocked his way. Her negligee fell open and her snow-white breasts popped out. "Rape me," she cried, as she tore at his shirt. "Hurry, hurry, hurry."

I keep saying to myself, "If I do write a book like that, will I change anybody's mind about race relations, or will it just be another hopeless exercise in the white man patronizing the black?"

Besides, perhaps it is more important to write about big business and expose the brutal methods used to achieve power and wealth:

"Mrs. McCarthy, you realize, of course, that if you don't take off your

clothes, your husband will lose his job and I will see that he never works in the advertising business again."

"But, Mr. Ryerson," she pleaded, knowing it was futile, "don't make me do this. There must be some other way of saving George for losing the Soft-As-Sheep Carpet account."

Ryerson laughed; his beady eyes glinted. Then he got up from behind his desk and walked over to her. "Do you want to start unbuttoning your blouse, or do you want me to call Personnel?"

"No," she said, as she unzipped her skirt, trembling. "I have to do it for George."

As you can see, there are so many directions to go in these days when you want to write a pornographic book that it's almost impossible to stick with one theme. I imagine I could combine the themes, as many writers do, but the question I then have to ask myself is, "Is it literature?"

I keep struggling with the problem every day, and the more pornographic books I read, the more I realize how inadequate I am to write something that will last.

At the same time, I know that if I ever hope to be taken seriously as a writer, I must get down to work on my book. But my problem is that every time I start a paragraph:

Harry looked at the two girls in his bed and shook his head. How could he ever satisfy both of them and still make the seven ten for Scarsdale?

I say to myself, "Is this something the Supreme Court would want to read?"

Upping Prison Requirements

I know you're not going to believe this, but Governor Lester Maddox of Georgia told a news conference recently, in answer to criticism about Georgia prison reform: "We're doing the best we can, and before we do much better, we're going to have to get a better grade of prisoner."

Once again, Governor Maddox hit the ax handle on the head. While penologists, sociologists, parole officers, and prison commissions all have been at odds about how to rehabilitate prisoners, Maddox has come up with the simplest and, without doubt, most sensible solution.

It has been known for years that prisons have been accepting a very low-class type of inmate, some without any education, others who are unstable, and some who are just plain antisocial.

No effort has been made to attract a better grade of prisoner, who would not only improve the caliber of our rehabilitation programs, but would also make society treat prisoners with the respect they deserve. For too long now we've been taking our prisoners for granted, and the standard for convicted felons has declined to a point where almost any-one can get into prison without his qualifications being questioned.

This trend must be reversed if we ever hope to rehabilitate our pris-oners. The first thing to do would be to set up a recruiting drive in high schools and colleges to get a better class of inmate. This would have to be coupled with higher pay for prisoners, so being behind bars would become worthwhile.

Intelligence tests have to be set up at prisons to weed out those unfit to be imprisoned. Then personal interviews would be given to the pro-spective convicts to see if they've got what it takes to be rehabilitated. If they can't cut the mustard, then the prison should have the right to reject them.

Besides the tests and the interviews, the admissions board would de-mand references from the candidates to see that the convicted were of high moral character. It's also possible, in the case of federal prisons, that each Congressman and Senator could recommend two candidates for each penitentiary, as they do to West Point and Annapolis. In the case of state prisons, the governor could select the ones he believed had the most on the ball.

After making the application, taking his tests, submitting to a per-sonal interview, and writing a composition telling why he believes he would make a good prisoner, the candidate would be sent home and told he would be notified by the FBI about whether he made it or not. If he failed to get in, the candidate could reapply again—after he robbed another bank.

Many people say that by being selective, we would be making too many demands on our prisoners; but the taxpayers are paying for them, and we should have the right to have the best convicts that money can buy.

I'm sure that Governor Maddox will be ridiculed for his ideas on pris-on reform, but he is the first person to come along and point out what is wrong with the penal system in this country. It isn't the courts, nor is it the physical facilities holding us back, but the fact that we have not concentrated on improving the quality of the people we take in.

Anyone who has ever visited a prison in this country knows that Governor Maddox is right. For years we have been scraping the bottom of the barrel for inmates, and it's no wonder they don't live up to our expectations.

It is only by raising the requirements for admission and paying a decent wage that we're going to get the grade of prisoner that Governor Maddox and the rest of us can be proud of.

What to Do After World War III

Anyone who doubts that the federal government is prepared for World War III just doesn't know how organized Washington really is. A short time ago someone who works for the Treasury Department received his instructions in writing on what he has to do in case of enemy attack.

They read as follows, and I haven't made a word of it up:

> . . . all National Office Employes with or without emergency assignments should follow this procedure. If you are prevented from going to your regular place of work because of an enemy attack—keep this instruction in mind—GO TO THE NEAREST POST OFFICE, ASK THE POSTMASTER FOR A FEDERAL EMPLOYE REGISTRATION CARD (sample shown on reverse side), FILL IT OUT AND RETURN IT TO HIM. He will see that it is forwarded to the office of the Civil Service Commission which will maintain the registration file for your area. When the Civil Service Commission receives your card, we will be notified. We can then decide where and when you should report for work. . . . . You should obtain and complete your registration card as soon after enemy attack as possible, but not until you are reasonably sure where you will be staying for a few days. . . .

Nobody believes it will ever happen, but let us suppose that Robert Smiley (a fictitious person working for the Treasury Department) has just crawled out of the rubble after an enemy attack and remembers the instructions concerning civil defense for federal employees.

After walking for four days and 350 miles, Smiley finally finds a post office that is still standing. He staggers up to a window, but just as he gets there, the man behind it says, "Sorry, this window is closed," and slams it down.

Smiley stumbles to the next window and is told to get in line behind twenty other people. Two hours later he gets to the head of the line and croaks, "I want to register—"

"I'm sorry," says the post office clerk. "This window is just for stamps. Registered mail is at the next window."

"No, no," says Smiley. "I want a federal employee registration card."

"We don't sell those. Now do you want any stamps or don't you?"

"You see," says Smiley, holding onto the window, "I was instructed after the enemy attacked to find the nearest post office and fill out a card."

"You'd better try the parcel post window," the clerk suggests.

Smiley goes over to the parcel post window and gets in line with thirty people. Four hours later he is informed that the post office has run out of federal employee registration cards. They suggest he try another post office.

Smiley staggers out into the road and starts walking again. Four hundred miles up the highway he finds another post office. After catching his breath, he takes the card shakingly to the counter and starts to fill it out. But the pen won't work. He informs the postmaster of this, and the postmaster replies, "We know it, but there's nothing we can do about it. There's a war on."

"But I've got to register," says Smiley, "or the Civil Service Commission won't know where I am in case the United States Treasury wants to start up again. Couldn't I borrow your pen?"

"What? And ruin the point? Listen, why don't you go over to the Smithtown post office. I hear their pens are still in working order."

Clutching the card, Smiley walks 60 miles to Smithtown, where he fills it out. He mails it that very day.

Years later, Smiley is still waiting for a reply. For in his haste and fatigue, Smiley had forgotten to write down his return ZIP code.

The Man Who Paid All His Taxes

When Emil Harwood Booster paid his taxes for the year, he discovered that he still had $117.50 left over in his bank account. It probably would have been overlooked; but he made the mistake of bragging to a friend in a bar about it, and he was overheard by an Internal Revenue Service agent, who reported it to his chief.

An emergency meeting was called of federal, state, county, and city tax officials to discover why Booster still had money left in the bank.

The IRS man said Booster's federal tax return had been checked, and it was all in order, so he couldn't be tried for any criminal violations. The state tax official said as far as his people could find out, Booster had paid all state taxes. The county man said his records showed that Booster was clean, and the city man said the same thing.

"Then," the IRS man said, "we can only come to one conclusion. If Booster still has money left over after he has paid his taxes, there is a loophole somewhere in the tax law."

"Wait a minute," said the county tax collector. "If anyone should get the one hundred seventeen dollars and fifty cents, it's the county. It would be very easy for us to raise Booster's real estate taxes."

"I object," said the city's representative. "It seems to me that the reason Booster got away with this is that our sales tax has been too low. We can up the sales tax by one percent, make it retroactive, and inform Booster he owes us the one hundred seventeen dollars and fifty cents."

There was a lot of angry shouting, and finally the IRS man called the meeting to order. "Hold it. Shouting will do us no good. Let's look at this thing calmly. The way I see it, we are not as concerned about the one hundred dollars and fifty cents as we are about the fact that Booster still had money left over after he paid his taxes. Now we'll all have to admit that this is a very bad precedent, and if Booster can get away with it, everyone else will try to get away with it. We must discover what went wrong and see that it doesn't happen again."

"I'll tell you where it went wrong," the state man said. "We thought the President was going to put a surcharge of ten percent on everyone's income tax, so we didn't tax Booster the way we originally planned to."

"And," said the county man, "we thought the state was going to raise Booster's gasoline taxes, so we didn't raise his water and sewer taxes."

The city man said, "And we thought the county was going to put on a liquor and cigarette tax, so we thought we would pass up an entertainment tax until next year."

The IRS man said, "It seems to be a comedy of errors, and the only one who is laughing right now is Booster. The solution to the problem, as I see it, is to set up a coordinating committee and next year tax Booster an extra one hundred seventeen dollars and fifty cents, which he failed to pay this year. We could split the one hundred seventeen dollars and fifty cents among all of us, so Booster would have no idea what we were doing."

"It's not a bad idea," the state man said. "But I think there should be some punitive damages added. It's true that Booster didn't violate any laws, but he knew as well as we did that if he had any money at the end of the year, it belonged to one of us."

"That's true," the county man said. "He should have come clean and told us he still had money left in the bank and then let us adjust our tax rates accordingly."

"I say give it to the grand jury," the city man said. "Any guy who has any money left over after he pays his taxes has got to be guilty of something."

Everyone agreed, and the IRS man said, "It's guys like Booster who give inflation a bad name."

Money Crisis Quiz

Now that everyone understands the world monetary crisis, we're going to give you your final quiz:

1. If I have five French francs and you have three West German deutsche marks, what will we have all together?

ANSWER. One of the damnedest money messes since World War II.

2. If I want to sell my French francs for German marks at 10 percent less than they're officially quoted, what currency will be hurt the most?

A. The British pound.

3. Why?

A. Because it's tied to the American dollar.

4. When the American dollar gets in serious trouble, what country sells its dollars and demands gold, to make it go down further?

A. France.

5. When the French franc gets in trouble, what country agrees to go to its rescue and shore it up with its own gold?

A. The United States.

6. Why?

A. Because of the British pound.

7. When the British pound gets into trouble, who is the first person to demand that it be devalued?

A. President Charles de Gaulle.

8. When the French franc gets in trouble, who is the *last* person to agree to its devaluation?

A. President Charles de Gaulle.

9. Why?

A. Because of the West German mark.

10. What has the German mark got to do with the French franc?

A. The West German mark is undervalued because the Germans don't have enough inflation. The French franc is overvalued because the French have too much inflation.

11. What is the solution?

A. The British have to tighten their belts.

You have a coffee break now before we go on with the quiz.

All right, let's continue:

12. What happens to all the gold that is supposed to support world currencies?

A. It's bought by the Swiss for people who have numbered accounts in Zurich.

13. When they buy the gold, what happens to the currencies?

A. Except for the Swiss franc and the German mark, they go down.

14. Why?

A. Because everyone is afraid of the British pound.

15. What can France do to restore confidence in the French franc?

A. Attack the American dollar.

16. How can they do this?

A. By using the money we've lent them to preserve their franc.

17. Why would we allow this?

A. To preserve the British pound.

18. Who will President de Gaulle blame if his reforms don't work?

A. The United States.

19. Who will get the credit if De Gaulle can pull it off?

A. That's a stupid question.

20. What can the average American do until the money crisis blows over?

A. Take an Englishman to lunch.

You Can't Buck the Establishment

Woe to the person in this country who attacks the Establishment. It isn't jail or even physical harm that he must fear. His main problem is that by attacking the Establishment, he automatically becomes a member of it, and there is no greater punishment in the world.

Let us take the case of Samuel Suchard, a pro-Maoist, antiwar, anti-draft Leninist-anarchist. Having led demonstrations against the White House, the Pentagon, the U.S. aircraft carrier *Enterprise,* and the YWCA, Suchard was finally caught by the Establishment and dragged down to the Metropolitan Club for lunch.

There he faced a table of smiling, friendly faces.

"Suchard," one of the Establishment members said, "We've had our eye on you for some time, and we think you have what it takes to be one of us."

"A pox on you," Suchard said. "I'm against the Establishment with its stinking rules and fancy clothes and bloated imbeciles. I despise you all." To make his point, Suchard threw his soup on the floor.

Instead of getting angry, the rest of the people at the table applauded.

"Of course, you do," said a second member of the party. "And you have every right to hate us. It's for this reason that we think you would make a marvelous member of the power structure. How would you like a grant from the Ford Foundation, so when you attack the Establishment, you won't have to worry about financial problems?"

"To hell with a grant from the Ford Foundation, man. I'm not selling out for any lousy grant. I'm a revolutionist."

Suchard picked up his steak and started to eat it with his fingers.

A third member at the table spoke up. "You don't have to take the Ford grant if you don't want to. Would you consider a lecture tour under our sponsorship? You could go around the country speaking before Rotary and Kiwanis luncheons explaining why you're disenchanted with society and what we have done wrong. There's a big demand for such speakers now."

For the first time Suchard started losing some of his cool. "What are you guys trying to do to me? Don't you understand? I'm against every American institution from the flag to the space program. I want to tear the very fabric of this society apart."

"Of course, you do, Suchard, and we respect you for it. The Establishment is always open to criticism in spite of things you hear to the contrary. We could even arrange for you to be on *Meet the Press,* where you could voice your discontent to millions and millions of people at one time. Or, if you prefer, we could give you your own television show, where you could discuss your own opinions in the manner of David Susskind."

Suchard wiped his mouth with his sleeve. "I—I—I—you guys are trying to trap me. I want to get out of here."

The man sitting next to Suchard put his hand gently on Suchard's arm and said almost in a whisper, "Sam, how would you like to be on the cover of *Time* magazine, as spokesman for all alienated youth?"

Suchard looked from face to face. "I couldn't do it. I mean, what would the guys say?"

"We'd even throw in the cover of *Newsweek,* Sam."

Suchard said dreamily, "The covers of *Time* and *Newsweek.*"

"It wouldn't just end there, Sam. We could get you appointed to the government commission to study violence among our youth. We could make you a director of a poverty program; you could meet with the President at the White House, lunch with David Rockefeller, get an honorary degree from Harvard, become a member of the Burning Tree

Golf Club, and the beauty of it is, you wouldn't have to give up one of your ideals."

"All right, already," cried Suchard. "I'll do anything you ask me. Just leave me alone."

"We knew you'd see it our way, Sam. Would you like to come down to the racquet club with us after lunch for a few sets of squash?"

Sore Loser

In almost every election in the United States (except where someone ran unopposed) there is a winner and a loser, and American tradition demands that the loser show good grace and make a concession speech. But what he says and what he is thinking at the moment is not necessarily the same thing.

Thanks to the exact science of extrasensory perception, I am able to reveal what a candidate was thinking while he was making his concession speech on the networks early Wednesday morning after election day. He began:

"First, I want to thank all the people who worked so hard and so long in my campaign for nothing and who believed in me, and what I stood for."

But he was thinking: *If I had to do it all over again, I would have hired a professional outfit that would have at least known what the hell we were doing.*

"I can't praise too highly my campaign manager, Hiram Hathaway, who worked tirelessly on my behalf at great sacrifice to himself and his family."

All he made me promise him was a federal judgeship if I won.

"I would also like to say that I know that although my wife, Betty, is disappointed, I doubt if I could have got through the past year without her loyalty and love and understanding."

She told me from the start I didn't have a chance, and as far as she was concerned, I was nuts even to get into the race.

"As far as my opponent is concerned, I wish to congratulate him on the victory which he won fairly and squarely."

In one of the dirtiest campaigns in political history.

"I know that he will serve his state and country to the best of his ability, and I shall do everything in my power to support him in the great problems he will have to deal with in the perilous times ahead."

That is, if he isn't indicted in the next year for vote fraud.

"I would be less than candid if I didn't admit that I was disappointed in the results. But in this great country, we can't all be winners, and I shall continue to serve the public in any capacity that is demanded of me."

It's going to be interesting to see who makes up my one-million-dollar campaign deficit.

"I might mention at this time how grateful I am to the press, who treated me fairly and called the shots as they saw them."

I never saw such a bunch of prejudiced, lying bunch of hacks in my life. They couldn't write the truth if it was shoved down their throats.

"As for television, I'd like to say how grateful I am to the TV stations who provided me with free time to tell my side of the story."

At six thirty in the morning.

"It's true I didn't have as much money as my opponent to buy TV time."

It pays to have a rich wife at election time, even though she's ugly as sin.

"But I don't blame the lack of money for my defeat."

Not much.

"If there were any mistakes made in this campaign, they were mine, and I must take responsibility for them."

If you believe that one, you're stupider than I thought you were.

"The important thing now is to heal the wounds and go forward together as one people, one nation under God with liberty and justice for all."

That's not a bad phrase. I think I'll use it in the next campaign.

How to Bake a Sunday Paper

Winter is the time of year when, because of inclement weather and bad pitches by groggy newsboys, your Sunday newspaper may arrive in a wet or soggy condition. Most people get angry at this state of affairs, mainly because they don't know how to dry and bake a good Sunday paper. Once you know how to do this, you may never fear getting a wet newspaper again.

My recipe for baking a newspaper was handed down in my family from one generation to the next, and even on the rainiest, snowiest, sleetiest day our family always has had the crispiest, tastiest Sunday newspaper on the block.

As a public service, it is my intention to pass on this family recipe to my loyal and devoted readers.

First, preheat oven to 300 degrees.

While you're doing that, drain off liquid from the paper and put aside.

Now get a sharp knife and start peeling off the sections of paper—the front section, then the society, sports, comics, and so forth. Wipe each section lightly with a damp cloth, and roll to even out.

By this time your oven should be hot. If it isn't, you can study the wet football scores or the classified advertisements.

Once your oven is hot enough, arrange the sections of the newspaper on the racks of the oven, but make sure they do not touch one another or get in the way of the oven door.

NOTE: It is always best to put the comics on the lowest shelf so the color does not drip down on the black-and-white pictures of Jackie Onassis.

(If your paper is very, very large, you may have to bake it in two roastings. Therefore, select the sections you want to read first, bake them, and then, while you're reading them, stick the other sections in the oven.)

I know that the big question on your mind is how long to bake or roast a Sunday newspaper. This depends strictly on the paper. Give fifteen minutes for each pound of wet newsprint. But every five minutes, turn over the sections on the rack so that they don't get too brown. Some people prefer to cook their newspapers on a rotisserie, which keeps going around in a circle, and this is probably a faster way to do it. But the danger is that if the paper touches flame, it will go up in smoke, and that won't leave you much to do on Sunday morning.

After you've allowed your newspaper first to simmer, then to stew, and finally to bake, you can test it to see if it's ready to be read. Take out the travel section or the book review, and hold it in both hands. If the paper seems firm and stays up stiff of its own accord, it's ready. On the other hand, if it sags or falls apart while you're holding it, put the rest of it back in the oven for at least another ten minutes.

Sometimes people make a mistake and overcook their paper. You'll know your Sunday paper is too well done if it gets black around the edges and has a funny smell to it.

Your Sunday paper can be served either hot or cold to your family and can also be sliced very thin or very thick, depending on how you like it.

If you want to read it cold, transfer to a cool, dry place, and let stand fifteen minutes.

The important thing to remember is that *anyone* can bake a Sunday newspaper. All you need for the ingredients are newsprint, rain, slush or snow, a hot oven, and patience.

One more thing: There may be times when the news is so depressing that you're sorry you took the trouble to bake your paper. If this happens, just pour some cognac on it, light it, and make it into a *flambé*.

Sex Ed—The Pros and Cons

There is a big flap going on in the United States right now over the question of teaching sex education in our schools. The educators are mostly for it and the ultraconservatives, including the John Birchers and the DAR, are mostly against it. I usually like to stay out of controversial matters since I hate to answer my mail, but in this case I have to come out for teaching sex education in the schools.

This is a very personal matter with me. I had no formal sex education when I was a student, and everyone knows the mess I'm in. If there had been a Head Start program in sex education when I was going to public school, I might have been a different man today.

When I was going to Public School 35 in Hollis, New York, we got all our sex education at the local candy store after three o'clock. The information was dispensed by thirteen-year-olds who seemed to know everything there was to know on the subject, and we eleven- and twelve-year-olds believed every word they told us.

Some of it, I discovered later on, did not necessarily happen to be true. For example, I was told as an absolute fact that if a girl necked with you in the rumble seat of a car, she would automatically have a baby.

This kept me out of the rumble seat of an automobile until I was twenty-three years old.

There were some other canards of the day, including one that the method of kissing a girl on the mouth decided whether she would become pregnant or not. Every time I kissed a girl after that, I sweated for the next nine months.

The sex experts at Sam's Candy Store had an answer for every problem that was raised at the soda fountain. These included warnings that if you did certain things, you would go insane. Most of us were prepared to be taken off to the booby hatch at any moment.

There was obviously no talk about birds, bees, flowers, or animals. We couldn't care less what happened when *they* were doing it. Our only concern was what happened to human beings, and from what our thirteen-year-old instructors could tell us, it was all bad.

Those of us who escaped insanity and shotgun weddings were told we would probably wind up with a horrendous disease that would be passed on to our children and their children for generations to come. There were twenty-five ways of catching this disease, including shaking hands with someone who knew someone who had it.

You can imagine the nightmares these tales produced. There seemed to be no escape. You were doomed if you did, and you were doomed if you didn't. After one of these sessions at the candy store, I seriously contemplated suicide. There didn't seem to be any other way out.

Now the worst part of my sex indoctrination was that when I turned thirteen, I became an instructor myself and passed on my knowledge to eleven- and twelve-year-olds at the same candy store. They listened in awe as I repeated word for word what I had been told by my "teachers," and I was amazed with how much authority I was able to pass on the "facts" of sex education as I knew them.

Upon becoming thirteen, they in turn taught the younger students. Heaven knows how many generations of Public School 35 alumni went on through life believing everything they had learned about sex at Sam's Candy Store.

The fact is that while the sex education at Sam's served a purpose, we were all emotional wrecks before we got to high school.

So, on the basis of my own experience, I don't think we have much choice in this country when it comes to sex education. In order to avoid the agony and pain my fellow classmates and I went through, we either have to teach sex in the schools or close down every soda fountain in the United States.

The Christmas Play

Whoever thinks the theater is dying in America probably doesn't have any children of school age. The truth is that the class Christmas play is still the hottest entertainment around. It is playing to capacity, captive holiday audiences everywhere.

I was on my way to work with my friend Renfrew one morning, and he asked if I would mind stopping by his daughter's school. He had promised to see her in "Hark! Is That a Snowflake Falling?"—a play that the eighth grade had been working on since September 17.

Since Renfrew drives me to work on cold, wet mornings, I didn't have much choice but to say I would.

"It won't take but a few minutes," he assured me.

We went into the school auditorium, which was rapidly filling up with proud parents, though I noticed most of the fathers were anxiously looking at their watches. A teacher handed us a mimeographed program that I scanned for a few seconds, and then I said, horrified, "Renfrew, each class has its own play, starting with the kindergarten. "Hark! Is That a Snowflake Falling?" is listed as the ninth item."

"It will go fast," he assured me. "They're very short plays."

We waited for the 9 A.M. curtain to go up, but because of some hitch, it didn't go up until 9:35.

The kindergarten did "Up the Chimney," which went for ten minutes. The first grade did a musical titled "What Angels Do We See Tonight?" with a reprise at the end. The second grade was well into "Grump, Grump, a Christmas Slump" when I turned to Renfrew and said, "It's ten thirty. I have to get to my office."

"Ursula has seen me," Renfrew whispered. "I can't go now."

"Which one is Ursula?"

"She's one of the snowflakes," Renfrew said.

"There are fifteen snowflakes."

"She's the one who's waving to me." He waved back. "It won't take long."

As each child finished the lines in his play, I noticed an anxious father jump up from his seat and dash for the door. After the third, fourth, and fifth grades had finished their presentations, the auditorium was half-empty. I like Renfrew, but I couldn't help wishing he had a child in one of the earlier grades.

The sixth grade did a mystery play, and the seventh performed "How They Got the Christmas Tree from Maine to Arizona," which required a sequence about each state en route.

It was 11:50. Only the parents of the eighth grade were still there, and one stranger who, if he had to do it all over again, would have gone to work by taxi.

Finally, "Hark! Is That a Snowflake Falling?" was ready to be performed. A hush went over the audience.

"No matter how many times I see her on the stage, I still tense up," Renfrew said.

A fairy princess came down the line of snowflakes and held her wand over Ursula's head. "And what do you want to be?"

Ursula stood up straight and blurted out, "I want to be the first snowflake on Christmas morning that any child will see."

The princess moved on.

"Okay," Renfrew said, "we can leave now."

"You got to be kidding," I said. "We sat here four hours for one line?"

"You're lucky," Renfrew said, "last year she was a church bell, and all she had to say was 'Bong.' "

As we were driving downtown Renfrew said, "Well, tell me. What did you honestly think?"

"Renfrew," I said, patting him on the shoulder, "it was a memorable morning in the theater."

Europe According to Peanuts

Since everyone is so confused about what is going on in Western Europe, I think the only way to explain it is in terms of the comic strip "Peanuts."

Try to imagine that Lucy is France. She wants to be the leader of the gang, and her greatest pleasure is getting into everyone's hair.

Linus represents Great Britain, and he keeps sucking his thumb and holding a blanket which says "Made in the U.S.A."

Charlie Brown, for obvious reasons, is the United States, and every time Lucy does something to him, all he can say is "Good Grief."

Schroeder, of course, is West Germany, and Snoopy is Italy.

Long ago, Charlie Brown formed a baseball team called the NATO Defenders, and Lucy played first base. But a few years ago she got mad at Charlie Brown, quit the team, and made everyone get out of her yard. She also urged everyone else to quit, too. But the other members of the team refused, because Charlie Brown had the only bat and ball that meant anything.

Lucy, Schroeder, Snoopy, and the other kids have a club which they formed to sell lemonade to one another. Linus has been trying to join this club since it started, but Lucy said she won't let him in until he gets rid of his "Made in the U.S.A." blanket.

Linus is deathly afraid to give up his blanket because if he did, he might also have to give up his thumb sucking. Besides, Charlie Brown gave it to him for Christmas, and he doesn't want to hurt Charlie's feelings.

Last week Lucy told Linus secretly that he could come into the lemonade club if he quit Charlie Brown's team. She proposed that Linus, Schroeder, and Snoopy could be the leaders of the new club, and the rest of the gang, instead of being equal partners, could become associate club members.

Linus was horrified at Lucy's suggestion, so he told Schroeder, Snoopy, Charlie Brown, and the rest of the gang about Lucy's proposal.

Everyone was furious at Lucy for what they considered a double cross. When Charlie Brown heard the proposal he said, "Good Grief."

Schroeder said he could never leave Charlie Brown's team because there would be no one to protect him if the gang down the next street tried to steal second base.

Snoopy, who usually is very quiet, also thought Lucy's idea was a lousy one, and he had no intention of getting in the doghouse with Charlie Brown.

Lucy was furious with Linus for ratting on her, and she denied she had ever made the proposal. She also indicated that Linus would never get into the lemonade club even if he did give up his blanket, which Linus had no intention of doing.

Despite Lucy's French temper and desire to wreck Charlie Brown's team, Charlie still insists he wants to be friends with her, and he keeps asking her to come back and play ball.

But Lucy will have none of it. She says she'll play only if she's the captain and Charlie Brown sits on the bench. "I don't care if it is your ball and bat," Lucy said. "It happens to be my playing field."

Not long ago, Lucy got into trouble with her lemonade stand and made much more lemonade than she could sell. Also, her prices were so high that no one would buy it. So she immediately went to Charlie Brown and said, "You have to bail me out."

I know you're not going to believe this, but good old Charlie Brown dug into his pocket, handed Lucy the money, and all he could think of to say was "Good Grief."

The Computer That Failed

When the Vietnam War was raging at its fiercest, David Brinkley reported that a scientist had programmed all the pertinent military information about the United States and North Vietnam and fed it into a computer, raising the question: When will the war be won and which side will win?

The computer answered that the United States had won the war two years ago.

I decided to go see the computer to find out what went wrong.

The computer seemed very annoyed when I fed it the question. It replied on the tape, "Nobody's perfect."

"I'm not trying to criticize you, sir, but it does seem that the results do not gibe with the facts."

"There are a lot of unpredictable factors in this that I can't be responsible for. All I was doing was computing relative strengths of the United States and North Vietnam military, enemy troop morale factors based on CIA reports, information gleaned from defectors, pacification results, General Westmoreland's optimism, and the high esteem the South Vietnamese people hold for their government. If you had digested all these facts, you would have come up with the same answer."

"Then you didn't include any information out of Hanoi?"

"Why should I? The State Department told me not to believe anything Hanoi says."

"Did you take into consideration the American bombing of North Vietnam?"

"Of course I did. Why else would I have said the United States had won? Everyone knows that if you drop a certain ratio of bombs on a given country during a given time, that country has to surrender."

"But they didn't."

"It's not my fault those people don't think like a computer."

"I'm not criticizing you. I'm just trying to find out where you made your mistakes. How do you explain the fact that despite the fighting and the victories the Americans have amassed over there, the Vietcong were able to launch a drive on the cities?"

The computer shuddered. "That was not my error. I just accepted the body counts of the last five years, ran them through, and, on the basis of my figures, came to the conclusion that every Vietcong was either dead or had defected. As a computer, I can't very well go around counting bodies myself."

"That's true. Now I understand one of the reasons you came to your decision was based on captured enemy documents. How did you err there?"

"Somebody captured the wrong enemy documents. Look, I'm just a machine. You can't lay all the blame at my feet."

"Yes, but there are thousands of computers like you, and if every one of them comes up with the wrong answers, we could be in a mess, couldn't we?"

"Only if there is a credibility gap somewhere along the line."

"Have you made allowances for that?"

"I'm a loyal American computer, and if I made allowances for a credibility gap, I'd only be giving aid and comfort to the enemy."

"Well, since you goofed so badly on the last go-round when do you think the war will be over now?"

"That's not up to me. That's up to Hanoi."

Curing a Phobia

One of the things that General Curtis LeMay said at a recent press conference was that Americans seem to have a phobia about nuclear weapons. This struck home because I have to admit I've had such a phobia for some time. But only after General LeMay brought it up did I decide to do something about it. I went to see Dr. Adolph Strainedluff, a psychiatrist who specializes in nuclear weapon phobias.

"On the couch," he said. "Vat seems to be the trouble?"

"Doctor," I said staring at the ceiling, "I have this fear of nuclear weapons. I know it's silly, but to me it's very real."

"Aha, very hinteresting. Ven did you first become aware of such a phobia?"

"I think it was around the time of Hiroshima or Nagasaki, I'm not sure which. I saw these photos of all these people killed and miles and miles of rubble, and suddenly I got this thing about atomic weapons."

Dr. Strainedluff tapped a pencil against his knee. "So tell me, how does this phobia manifest itself?"

"In peculiar ways, Doctor. I get the feeling if I ever see a mushroom cloud, I'm going to die."

"Very hinteresting, very hinteresting. You know it's all in the mind, don't you?"

"Of course. That's why I came to you. I don't want to do anything stupid."

Dr. Strainedluff said, "You are a very sick man. You think that just because an atomic bomb killed a few thousand people more than twenty years ago, you are threatened. You are manifesting infantile repressed hostility toward the weapons of war. In psychiatry we call this a military-industrial inferiority complex."

"I know I'm sick. You've got to help me," I begged.

"All right. First, you haff to get over this absurd fear of nuclear bombs. You must think of them as just another weapon in our vast defensive arsenal. Ve haff bowie knives and H-bombs, and in war, one is just as good as another. You're not afraid of a knife, are you?"

"Well, I don't think about it a lot."

"So vhy should you be afraid of an H-bomb? It's another form of a knife."

"I never thought of it like that."

"Okay, so now let's look at some facts straight in the eye. In Bikini we blew up twenty bombs in an experiment. So ve thought everything would be destroyed; that's how stupid ve were. Do you know that now after all the boom-boom, the place is flourishing and the rats are fatter than they ever vas before?"

"It's good to hear."

"The coconuts are hanging from the trees, the fish are svimming in the lagoon, and voice of the turtle can be heard in the land. The only things that don't seem to be doing so good are the land crabs."

"I don't like land crabs," I said.

"So then you don't haff anything to vorry about."

Dr. Strainedluff started playing with the hand grenade which was attached to his watch fob. "If you're going to be a happy, normal human being," he shouted, "you're going to haff to stop with all these guilty peace feelings."

He was stomping around the room. "So get out of here vith your lousy phobias and all this stuff about being afraid to die. If you're not villing to take a little fallout for the good of the country, then go back vhere you came from!"

In spite of Dr. Strainedluff's final outburst, he did cure me of my phobia. I'm no longer afraid of nuclear weapons. Now I'm afraid of him.

The Sleep-In

FORT LAUDERDALE, Florida—Beatle John Lennon and his bride, Yoko Ono, told newsmen that they would stay in bed in their Amsterdam hotel for seven days and seven nights during their honeymoon to protest violence in the world.

This sleep-in, if it catches on, could turn out to be the most popular type of protest ever thought up by the peace movement, and the authorities are not too sure yet how to handle it.

Since anything the Beatles do seems to be adopted, it's quite possible that Mr. and Mrs. Lennon's tactics will soon become part of the student nonviolent scene.

I was lucky to interview students at Fort Lauderdale who were on Easter vacation to get their reaction.

One said, "I wish we had known about it in Chicago. We would have had a lot less casualties."

But his friend disagreed. "Knowing the Chicago cops, they would have probably come into our rooms and busted our beds."

A third student seemed doubtful that Lennon's tactic was practical. "You can't get that kind of protest on television, except maybe on educational TV. And if you don't get on television, there doesn't seem to be any sense in protesting."

This opinion was shared by a University of North Carolina sophomore. "I could sleep in a park for seven days and seven nights, but I don't think it would work if I had to stay indoors. Like I mean, man, the fun of the protest is to be with your friends. It's no kick holding up a picket sign if nobody is going to see it."

But a co-ed from Swarthmore disagreed. "If all the students disappeared for seven days and seven nights, we'd have this country really uptight. They would have no idea what was happening."

An MIT engineering major shook his head. "I'd be for a sleep-in only if Secretary of HEW Finch assured me I would not lose my federal aid for doing it. They're going to have to put out some guidelines before I get into bed."

"They can't take your federal aid away from you for sleeping," a Harvard law student said, " as long as you do it peacefully."

"Sure," the MIT student said, "that's what they tell you now, but who's going to say if you were sleeping peacefully or not? Suppose you have a restless night?"

An Oberlin music major said, "That shouldn't be our concern. If sleeping is going to make this country wake up to the fact that we want peace, then I say we should sleep."

Her girlfriend said, "After a week in Fort Lauderdale I'll need seven days and seven nights of sleep, even if it isn't for peace."

"I think," said an Amherst student, "we should wait and see. After all, the only reason Lennon is doing it is that he's on his honeymoon. I think we should see what the other three Beatles do before we get involved."

A senior from Princeton said, "We tried everything else. At least it'll be more fun than burning draft cards."

"I say let's do it," a Columbia militant shouted. "We could destroy the room service system in America overnight."

He Got His Notice

"You'd better get over to the Diamonds' right away," my wife said when I came home one night.

"What's the trouble?"

"I don't know, but they sounded terribly upset."

I dashed over to the Diamond house and found Larry and Janet in the living room looking as if the world had fallen apart.

"What is it?" I asked.

"Billy got his draft notice," Janet said.

"He's been drafted?"

"It's worse," Larry said. "He's just been accepted for college."

"That couldn't be so bad."

"He's been accepted at the University of Wisconsin," Janet cried.

I didn't know what to say.

Larry shook his head. "You work all your life for your children, and then one day, out of the blue, they grab them and that's it."

"But even if they accepted him, he doesn't have to go," I said.

"You don't understand," Janet said. "He *wants* to go. He said he can't sit at home doing nothing when so many college kids are sacrificing so much on the campuses."

Larry said, "He wants to be where the action is."

"Billy always had a sense of duty," I said.

"I tried to talk him into going into the Army instead," Larry told me. "But he said, 'Dad, I would be shirking my responsibilities. That's the coward's way out. I have to go where my friends are fighting.'"

Janet sobbed, "I told him to go into the Army for four years, and then perhaps the fighting on the campuses would be over. But he said, 'Mother, I could never face my children if they asked me someday what I did during the war on campus and I had to tell them I was in the Army while it was going on.'"

"You have to be proud of him," I said.

"What do you mean, proud?" Larry said. "It's foolhardy. He doesn't know what he's getting into. All he sees is the glamor of it. The blue jeans and the dirty sweater and the beard. But I told him there's more to going to college than that. College is a dirty, miserable business, and it isn't just bands playing and flags waving and girls kissing you in the dormitories."

Janet nodded her head sadly. "I guess he saw too many TV programs about college riots and it went to his head."

Larry said, "Even as a little boy he always had his heart set on college. He used to stage sit-ins in the kitchen, and he picketed our bedroom at night, and once he locked his grandfather in the bathroom because his grandfather wouldn't grant him amnesty for using a naughty word.

"I thought it was a stage all kids go through, so I didn't take it seriously. If I had known he was truly thinking of going to college, I certainly wouldn't have encouraged it."

I tried to cheer my friends up. "Maybe he'll be all right. Don't forget, not everybody who goes to college gets arrested. If he comes out of it without a criminal record, it could be a very broadening experience. Why, some kids even get an education from college."

Janet was really crying. "You're just saying that to buck us up. You really don't believe it, do you?"

I looked at the distraught couple. "I have friends at the University of Wisconsin," I told them. "Perhaps I could use my influence to get Billy into night school. Then, at least, he'll be safe."

Oh, to Be a Swinger

It's very hard for many college students to live up to the roles they have been given by the mass media. What newspapers, magazines, and television networks expect from students is more than most of them can deliver. I discovered this when I was speaking at a Midwestern campus not long ago.

A student, whom I shall call Ronald Hoffman, seemed very troubled and I asked him what the problem was.

"My parents are coming up next week, and I don't know what to do."

"Why?"

"Well, you see, I told them I was living off campus with this co-ed in an apartment. But the truth is that I'm living in the dormitory."

"That shouldn't really disturb them."

"Oh, but it will. They're very proud of me, and they think I should have a mind of my own. When my dad heard I was living off campus with a co-ed, he doubled my allowance because, as he put it, 'Anyone who is willing to spit in the eye of conformity deserves his father's support.' I don't know what he's going to say when he finds out I used the money to buy books."

"It'll hurt him," I agreed. "What will your mother say?"

"I don't know. She's been crying a lot since I wrote her about living with this co-ed, and Dad's been arguing with her that her trouble is she doesn't understand youth. Mom's likely to get pretty sore when she discovers she's been crying for nothing."

"Not to mention how silly your father will look for making her cry."

Ronald shook his head sadly. "The trouble with parents these days is they believe everything they read. *Life* magazine, in a 'Sex on the Campus' article, made it sound so easy to find a co-ed to live with. Well, let me tell you, for every girl who's playing house with a male college student, there are a million co-eds who won't even do the dishes."

"Then all this talk of students living out of wedlock is exaggerated?"

"Exaggerated? When I got here, I asked ten girls if they wanted to live with me. The first one said she didn't come to college to iron shirts for the wrong guy, four told me frankly that it would hurt their chances of finding a husband, four told me to drop dead, and one reported me to the campus police. I was lucky to get a room in the dormitory."

"I guess it's no fun for a young man to pretend he's a swinger."

"You can say that again. Every time I go home, everybody wants to know about the pot parties and orgies I go to at school. The only thing that's saved me is that I've seen *La Dolce Vita* twice."

"You have to depend on your imagination?"

"What college boy doesn't?" Ronald said. "There are more conscientious objectors amongst co-eds in the sexual revolution than any modern sociologist would dare admit."

"It's enough to destroy your faith in Hugh Hefner," I said.

"Look, I'm not complaining," Ronald said. "I'm just trying to figure out how to explain it to my father. He's living his fantasies through me, and I hate to let him down."

"Why don't you tell him the reason you can't introduce the co-ed you're living with is that she's going to have a baby?"

"Hey," Ronald said, "that's a great idea. It might cause Mom to cry again, but it will make Dad awfully proud."

The Kremlin Watchers

MOSCOW—A diplomatic reception in Moscow has tremendous significance, not only because of the good food and free liquor, but because it is where most foreign observers learn what is going on in the Soviet Union.

I attended a large diplomatic cocktail party at one of the foreign embassies recently, and I was amazed at what the professional Kremlin watchers got out of it.

This is how the conversation went later on in the evening, when everyone was comparing notes:

"Did you notice Golvosky arrived after Kubinsky?"

"That's very interesting, because at the Fourth of July party at the American Embassy Kubinsky arrived after Golvosky."

"And at the Fourteenth of July party at the French Embassy they came together."

"Very significant. By the way, did anyone see Petrov shake hands with Puchinsky?"

"I was going to call that to your attention. It's strange that Petrov should shake hands with Puchinsky when the last time they met, Petrov only nodded at Puchinsky."

"Perhaps Puchinsky's star is rising in the Presidium."

"Or maybe Petrov's star is falling."

"I think we have overlooked the real significance of the handshake. It is not that Petrov shook hands with Puchinsky, but Puchinsky's wife did not talk to Petrov's wife."

"Are you sure?"

"Of course I'm sure. Puchinsky's wife turned her back on Petrov's wife to say hello to Bolgonov's wife. It was a deliberate snub."

"That's very interesting. But to me the most important thing that happened at the reception was that Bolgonov was drunk and spilled vodka all over Marshal Igorvich's uniform."

"What is so important about that?"

"Igorvich was the one who apologized."

"Bolgonov's star must be rising faster than we thought."

"No doubt about it. Marshal Igorvich even went and got Bolgonov another vodka."

"Did Bolgonov spill that vodka on Igorvich's uniform as well?"

"No, but he stepped on the marshal's foot and wouldn't get off it."

"I wonder if this means they're going to make Bolgonov Minister of Defense?"

"He's obviously in for something big. I've never seen Marshal Igorvich allow someone to stand on his foot for so long."

"Did anyone see Zubelkin at the party?"

"You mean the Tashkent poet who was ousted from the Writers' Union for writing a poem attacking the traffic policemen on Gorsky Street?"

"That's the one. He's been rehabilitated and is now permitted to write anything he wants, provided he doesn't ask anyone to publish it."

"The Writers' Union must be going through one of their liberal periods again."

"I don't know if this means anything, but Kavasky spoke to me."

"That is significant because Kavasky never speaks to foreigners. What did he say?"

"I asked him about the Czech problem and he replied, 'I'm sorry, I never speak to foreigners.' "

"Did anyone notice that Gogol spilled vodka on Mutiken?"

"It means nothing. Everyone in Moscow spills vodka on Mutiken. He's become a regular bar rag."

Hospitals Are New Status Symbols

Hospital rates are rising at such a phenomenal rate that some experts predict it is conceivable in fifteen or twenty years that a room at a good hospital will cost $700 a day.

If this is true, and it's hard to imagine it isn't, going to a hospital will become a status symbol for the very rich only, just as owning a yacht and a stable of horses has been in the past.

Society editors will be assigned to cover hospitals, and this is how a society column might read in the future:

Mrs. William Vanderwhelp of Newport and Sag Point has checked into Doctors' Hospital before going to her winter home in Palm Beach wearing a Courrèges hospital gown especially made for her. Mrs. Vanderwhelp said, "They may criticize me for going to the hospital, but I think if you've got the money and the time, you might as well have the fun that goes with it."

At the same hospital was Reginald Winthrop Clover, heir to the Beanie Breakfast Cereal fortune, who just had his appendix out. Asked what the operation cost, Reggie replied, "To paraphrase J. P. Morgan, if you have to ask what it costs to have an operation, you can't afford one."

Meanwhile, up at Rose Hill Hospital, Mary Lou Astorwood gave birth to a baby boy. Since it was their first child, the Astorwoods took a private room which cost them $10,000 for the week. The proud father, Clyde Astorwood, said, "The Astorwoods have always had their babies in hospitals, delivered by a doctor, and there is no reason for the press to make an issue over it. I think you should be able to spend your inheritance as you darn well please."

There is still a battle raging at the Maple Flower Hospital. It started when the board of directors decided to admit charity patients, who could only afford to pay $500 a day for a bed in the ward. Bart Clogswell, the oil trillionaire, said that by changing its admittance policies, Maple Flower was opening the floodgates to "riffraff," and the peace and harmony of the hospital would be endangered.

Ellen Maloney McMahan, another member of the board on the other side, said the ward patients would not be permitted to mingle with the other patients because the private and semiprivate rooms had been designated as the "clubhouse," and the wards had been designated as the "grandstands."

Liz White Whimple had a gallstone removed at the Lincoln Memorial Hospital Saturday. The operation was performed in the Palladium Room, which had been decorated especially for the occasion. Peter Duchin and his orchestra played during the postoperative surgery, while Meyer Davis' orchestra was hired to play for her after she got back to her room. Liz had special gowns designed for the surgeons and nurses. It was probably the most lavish gallstone operation of the year, and could only be compared with Truman Capote's tonsillectomy of last spring, when Truman rebuilt the operation room amphitheater to look like the Madrid bullfight ring.

Odds and Ends: What doctor is thinking of setting the broken arm on what former debutante who has been married four times? . . . Did Lily Fitzwhistle, the sparkplug heiress, check in secretly at Bonnie University Hospital for slipped disk? . . . The Duchess of Amblemeyer claims she is tired of going to Queen Mother's Hospital in London for her ulcer, and said she would have all her ulcer work done in the future at Arthur's Sanitarium in New York, where most of the beautiful people go . . . Frank Sinatra was turned away for treatment from Boswell Hospital after a fight the other night because he wasn't wearing a tie. When told by a reporter whom he had turned away, the chief surgeon said, "I don't care if it was Richard Burton himself, the hospital has to maintain a decorum, or we'll lose all our clientele."

Next week I'll tell you about two hernia operations that were planned months in advance on the same day without either playboy knowing it.

Warranties I Have Known

Betty Furness, in a recent speech, revealed something that the average consumer has known for years. It is that the warranties that come with most American products aren't worth the computer cards they're printed on.

There may have been a lot of changes in Washington in 1969, but one thing you can be sure of: the American consumer is getting a shafting by the great free enterprise system.

Not long ago I went to McCarthy, Swaine, and Klutzknowlton, the appliance store, to return an electric can opener I had bought my wife for Christmas.

"Why do you wish to return it?" the man asked.

"Because it doesn't work."

"Did you fill out the Green Warranty Card that came with it?"

"Yes, I did."

"And what happened?"

"The can opener still didn't work."

"I see. Could you tell me how soon you filled out the Green Warranty Card after you got the electric can opener?"

"Maybe three days, a week. I'm not sure."

"But it specifically says that the Green Warranty Card must be filled out twenty-four hours after purchasing the appliance."

"Yes, but since it was a Christmas present, we didn't open up the package until Christmas morning, and therefore we didn't see the Green Warranty Card and have a chance to fill it out for a few days as we were too busy trying to get the thing to work."

"But if you didn't fill out and mail the Green Warranty Card within twenty-four hours of the purchase, it's hardly our fault that the electric can opener doesn't work, is it?"

"I wouldn't say that," I said. "I think I should get a new electric can opener."

"We can't do that. The only one who has the authority to give you a new electric can opener is our warranty department, which is located in Leavenworth, Kansas. But since you didn't send in the Green Warranty Card within twenty-four hours of purchase, they probably have no record of your buying an electric can opener in the first place."

"You have a record of it. Here's my sales slip."

"Yes, that's true. We know you purchased an electric can opener, and *you* know you purchased an electric can opener, but Leavenworth, Kansas, doesn't know."

"Look," I said, "I should think you would be worried for the good name of McCarthy, Swaine, and Klutzknowlton."

"But we're not owned by McCarthy, Swaine, and Klutzknowlton anymore. We were bought out by Federated Pumps and Warehouses, which is a subsidiary of Drinkwater Fire and Theft, which is owned by Sable Hosiery and TV Antennas, which merged last month with Moon Orbiting Platforms, Inc."

"That's great, but what about a new electric can opener? Just give me one, and I'll be on my way."

"We can't. You see, we've discontinued making electric can openers."

"How could you discontinue making them? I just bought this one for Christmas."

"That's why we discontinued them. A lot of people bought them, and they didn't work. I guess our mistake was putting the head of our tire division in charge of electric can openers."

"What do I do now?"

"I'll take your name and see if there is some way of getting Leavenworth to accept your Green Warranty Card even if it was sent in late."

"And will that get me a can opener?"

"Of course not. But it will put you on our mailing list for any new appliances we plan to put out this year."

First Read the Instructions

There are so many different kinds of clothes made of miracle fibers that one is hard put to remember the instructions on how to launder and clean them. Each new piece of clothing now comes with a long list of instructions explaining how the garment must be treated, plus many warnings about what will happen if the instructions aren't adhered to.

One day I came home to find my wife washing my 45 percent alphazate, 25 percent prymnon, 30 percent cotton turtleneck sweater. I was horrified to discover that she was washing it the wrong way. "You're supposed to wash that sweater in cold lamb's milk, and you're washing it in warm lamb's milk."

"No," she said. "I read the instructions quite clearly. You wash it in warm lamb's milk and then you rinse it in cold."

"You're thinking about my hundred percent all-kozel undershirts. My turtleneck sweater is just the opposite."

I was right, because as we were talking, the turtleneck started to disintegrate before my eyes.

"That sweater cost me twelve dollars," I cried.

"I can't keep all these washing instructions straight," she said angrily.

"What are you going to do now?"

"I'm going to wash your eighty-nine and a third percent rogiflex wash-'n'-dry shirt."

"You have to use fresh essence of lime, mixed with distilled underground spring water," I reminded her.

"Are you sure? It seems to me that there was a warning attached to the shirt that if you used distilled underground spring water, the colors would run."

"That applies only to shirts with French cuffs," I told her.

"Of course," she said. "What an idiot I am for not keeping it straight."

I started to put on a clean pair of socks. My large toe went right through the sock.

"What the blazes did you do with my socks?"

"Nothing. I put them in the washing machine, added virgin calf detergent, two tablespoons of chlorine, and a cup of epsom salts, according to the instructions sewn in the sock."

I read the instructions. "Did you set the washing machine at seven and a half revolutions per minute?"

"I tried to, but I had to hold it manually and my arm got tired," she confessed. "I guess at the end the machine was going nine revolutions per minute. But I figured it didn't matter."

I threw down the socks in disgust. "If it didn't matter, why would they sew the instructions into the sock?"

She started to sob. I felt bad and said, "It's all right. I'll buy another pair of socks that can be washed at nine revolutions per minute. Well, I think I'll put on my hundred percent stay-pressed-forever seersucker suit."

I put on the pants. As I was inserting the belt, the legs, just below my hips, collapsed and fell to my ankles.

"What did you do to my suit?" I yelled.

"I had it dry-cleaned."

"You're not supposed to dry-clean a stay-pressed-forever material," I screamed. "Look, it says right here in the coat that the only way to clean it is to place it over an air-conditioning unit for twenty-four hours."

"I put your Nehru suit over the air-conditioning unit."

"The Nehru suit has to be dipped in naphtha and airline hydraulic fuel."

"It didn't say so in the coat."

"The instructions were printed on the beads that came with the suit."

"Don't yell at me," my wife yelled. "If you bought suits made of wool and shirts made of cotton, you'd have something to wear tonight."

"Yeah, but then look at the laundry and cleaning bills we'd have."

Not for Wives

Mr. Jack Valenti of the Motion Picture Producers Association has done a fine job with this rating system of films. In order to protect children, his association now informs people through the advertisements and outside the theater whether they are suitable for the whole family or just the adult part of it. The ratings start with G for the family, then go to M for mature audiences, and finally to X where human beings under sixteen are not admitted.

I am not criticizing Mr. Valenti's ratings but actually trying to improve on them. I think he should add another category to warn husbands what to expect. This rating on a film could be X-NFW—which would stand for "not for wives."

I say this because I went to a film the other night with my wife only to discover when we got to the theater that it had an X rating.

"What does that mean?" she wanted to know.

"It means that this picture is an adult film, and only those of us who are mature enough and grown up enough to understand the implications of what the producer and writer and director are trying to say are permitted to see it."

"You mean it's a dirty picture?" she said.

"We must not use the word 'dirty' in describing a film. It is an art picture, aimed at a specific audience who want more out of life than Doris Day and Rock Hudson."

"Those billboards out front look pretty dirty to me."

"What's the matter? Haven't you ever seen a girl tied behind a bulldozer before?"

"Not while it's knocking down a building."

"Well, billboards never really show what the movie is about. It's just a way of getting you into the theater."

"I'd rather see *Oliver*," she said.

"Don't be square. If adults don't support X-rated films, who will?"

Before she could change her mind, I bought the tickets, and we went in.

"The popcorn even looks dirty," my wife said.

"Will you stop behaving like someone who *only* attends movies for the entire family?"

We sat down just behind six members of a motorcycle gang and next to an old man who was reading *Candy* while the lights were on.

Finally, the movie started. It opened up with a woman being whipped by ten members of the Royal Canadian Mounted Police.

"Let's go," my wife said.

"We can't go until we've found out what she's done. Perhaps that's the way people are punished in Canada."

"Nelson Eddy never whipped Jeanette MacDonald."

The scene shifted to a pair of lumberjacks walking through the forest with their arms around each other. They stopped in a clearing.

"That does it," my wife said. "I'm going."

"But there's supposed to be a big scene between two girls from Toronto and three women from French Canada who want independence from the Commonwealth."

She was on her way up the aisle, and I followed her.

"I just want to ask you one question," she said as we were driving home. "What was the point of that Mountie kissing his horse?"

"Oh, come on. Haven't you seen a man kiss a horse before?" I said.

"On the lips?"

How They Broke the News to Johnson

There continues to be a great deal of speculation about why Lyndon Johnson had been informed so late on the capture of the Navy intelligence ship *Pueblo*.

Many versions have been given concerning what happened during those key moments before the President was informed on the *Pueblo*'s fate.

Here is one I heard, though I, of course, cannot verify every fact.

When the news hit Washington at 11 P.M., it was first passed through lower channels at the Pentagon and the State Department before it was brought to the attention of Secretary McNamara and Secretary Rusk.

McNamara called Rusk and said, "I think you'd better notify the President. This is a diplomatic problem."

"The heck it is," said the usually taciturn Dean Rusk. "That was a Navy ship, and it's Defense's problem. You'd better notify the President."

"Wait a minute, Dean," said Secretary McNamara. "I just had to tell the President about our losing four hydrogen bombs over Greenland. He's going to start thinking of me as a purveyor of bad news.

"Besides," McNamara added, "that ship wasn't on a Navy mission. It was on an intelligence mission."

"Then Dick Helms of the CIA ought to tell the President," Rusk concluded.

A call was placed to Helms, and when Secretary Rusk informed him of the situation, Helms couldn't have been more surprised.

"You'd better tell the President," Rusk said.

"I'd rather not if it's all the same to you," Helms said. "Besides, I don't have the White House telephone number. Say, I have an idea. Let's get Walt Rostow to tell him. Walt works in the White House so he's probably adept at breaking bad news to the President."

"All right," Rusk said. "I guess Walt is as good at this sort of thing as anybody."

Secretary Rusk woke Walt Rostow up and told him the news. He suggested Rostow go over to the White House immediately and tell the President. Rostow agreed and started to get dressed.

After finishing his eggs, Rostow drove over to the darkened White House. He was quite frantic about how he would break the news to the President at such an ungodly hour. Nervously he walked up the stairway to the President's bedroom.

As he got to the room, an inspiration hit him. He opened the door and got down on his hands and knees and started crawling toward the bed. When he got there he grasped the President's hand.

"That you, Lynda Bird?" the President sleepily inquired.

"No, it's Walt."

"Walt who?"

"Walt Rostow, your White House aide."

"Well, what in tarnation are you doing on your hands and knees at this hour? Eartha Kitt isn't coming to breakfast, is she?"

"No, sir, I have something else to tell you."

"What is it?" the President said.

"Do you mind if I get in bed? It's very confidential."

"Blast it, Walt, what do you want to say?"

"Well, I know you're not going to believe this . . . "

At that moment Lady Bird woke up. "What's going on, Lyndon?" she demanded.

"Nothing, Lady Bird. Walt Rostow is just trying to tell me something important."

"Whew, I had a fright there for a moment," Lady Bird said. "I was afraid Lynda Bird and Chuck had had their first fight."

A Breakthrough in Air Travel

I am constantly amazed how the airlines are solving their problems. Everyone is aware that one of the big stumbling blocks to future air transportation is airport facilities. No airport in the country is prepared to handle the new air buses carrying 400 passengers that will soon be put into service.

I was under the impression that no one was working on the crisis, but I was wrong. The airlines and airports together are solving the problem in one of the most unconventional ways that human engineers have ever devised.

They're making people walk to their destinations.

As the airports get larger, they keep extending their terminals, and the gates to the aircraft keep getting farther away.

I discovered the consequence of this the other day when I had to catch a plane in Chicago for Davenport, Iowa. I started walking toward my gate; then realizing I had only an hour to make it, I started jogging. A few miles later I discovered I still wasn't anywhere near the gate, so I started sprinting. But because I was carrying a briefcase, I just didn't have the spurt I needed for the last few miles, and I missed my plane.

The airline ticket attendant was very sympathetic and said to me, "Why don't you walk to Davenport? It's only a few more miles down the road."

"Only a few more miles down the road?"

"Yes, we don't like to talk about it, because we naturally want people to fly, but most of our airline terminals have been spreading out so far that our departure gates are located only a few miles from where people are going. If you look out the window, you can see the lights of Davenport right over there."

"That's amazing," I said. "I knew I had gone pretty far, but I didn't think I was anywhere near Davenport."

"Most people don't," the ticket attendant said. "But, you see, we have to keep extending the wings of the terminal to handle the traffic, and so the cities get nearer and nearer. Someday we hope to link the Davenport and Chicago airports so passengers can *walk* between the two of them without getting wet. It certainly will solve the pressing airport traffic problems."

I thought Chicago was the only airport doing this, but not long ago I was out in Los Angeles and had to make a plane for Santa Barbara. When I was given my gate number for the flight, I started for it. And you can imagine my delight and surprise when I discovered that by the time I got there I was only five miles from the Santa Barbara city limits.

Then recently I was in Miami and had to fly to Tampa. As I walked through the terminal to my gate, I stopped off for lunch at the Palm Beach Airport snack bar and then continued straight on to find my plane was parked at a gate number just beyond Orlando.

I found out that every major airport in the country is now working on tunnels and ramps which will eventually hook up with airports in other cities. It's the first breakthrough in airline congestion. Engineers predict that in the not too distant future every airline terminal in the United States will be linked together, and by the time a passenger reaches his gate number on foot he will have arrived at the place where he originally intended to fly.

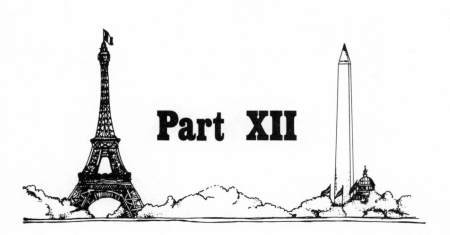

Part XII

The Greatest Column

The President, whether he likes it or not, is the trend setter in this country, and when he speaks in superlatives, it is no surprise that everyone starts picking up the habit.

I imagine the first time we knew we had a President who pulls out all the stops was after our astronauts landed on the moon. The President was quoted as saying: "This is the greatest week in the history of the world since the Creation."

Then, before he gave his "State of the Union" speech, the President called it "the most comprehensive, the most far-reaching, the most bold program in the domestic field ever presented to an American Congress."

This kind of talk cannot but affect all American families.

For example, the other night, just as our family sat down to dinner, my wife announced, "I hope everyone has washed his hands because I have cooked the greatest meal ever served in the Western Hemisphere."

"That's good," I said, "because I've had the hardest day anyone has ever had since Gutenberg invented the printing press."

My fifteen-year-old daughter said, "We had the worst test in school today since the Spanish Inquisition."

[349]

"How did your football game go?" I asked my seventeen-year-old son.

"It was the most magnificent contest ever waged in intramural sport," he replied. "I made two of the most unbelievable catches in the history of the game."

"And what did you do today?" I asked my fourteen-year-old daughter.

"I had the greatest Coca-Cola I've ever drunk in my life."

My wife served the pot roast. "I hope everyone likes it because it's the most expensive pot roast any butcher has ever sold."

"It is truly delicious," I said. "And it explains why we have the highest food bills of anyone on the Eastern Seaboard."

My wife took this as a personal criticism. "I can't help it if we're living in the highest inflationary period in modern times."

My son saved the day by asking, "Can I have the car tonight?"

"What for?" I asked.

"I'm going to the greatest movie ever made."

"What's the name of it?"

"I forget."

My fifteen-year-old daughter said, "Someone has to drive me to Jody's birthday party. It's supposed to be the grandest party ever given in the nation's capital."

My fourteen-year-old daughter said, "Then how come you were invited?"

My fifteen-year-old daughter said, "That's the most insulting thing anyone has ever said to me. You can take off my best blouse right now."

"Shut up," my wife said, "and eat your Brussels sprouts. I'm sick and tired of preparing the most fantastic meals ever served in this country and having vegetables left on the plates."

"Your mother is right," I said. "Besides, I hate to hear fighting during the most momentous banquet I have ever attended in this dining room."

My wife said, "After the most delicious apple pie anyone has ever tasted, I want everyone to help me with the largest pile of dirty dishes I've ever seen."

There were the loudest screams of protests ever uttered by an American family, but no one could escape.

Then we all went into the living room to watch President Nixon give his "State of the Union" speech which Attorney General John Mitchell described as "the most important document since they wrote the Constitution."

Happy Halloween!

It was Halloween, and all the pols were standing around the large iron kettle waiting for it to boil. Spiro, the chef, was adding some spices.

"A dash of nattering nabob, a cup of radiclib, and three tablespoonfuls of law and order."

Everyone clapped his hands. "Oh, this is going to be delicious," someone cried.

Chief Taster Dick took a wooden spoon and tasted it. "It's missing something."

He passed the wooden spoon around to his advisers. They all agreed, and sang together:

"It's missing something. It's missing something. Oh, what, oh, what is it missing?"

"I know," someone cried. "It's missing chopped rhetoric. No recipe is complete without chopped rhetoric."

"Of course," Spiro, the chef, said. And he took a large box of rhetoric and poured the entire contents in.

Someone threw some wood on the fire and the brew started to bubble.

Chief Taster Dick took his wooden spoon and everyone held his breath. Dick made a face. "It's flat. It needs more Democrats."

Everyone joined hands and danced around the kettle chanting, "It needs more Democrats! It needs more Democrats!"

Spiro, the chef, finally said, "We've thrown in all the Democrats. We have none left."

They all cried in despair: "We have no Democrats left. We have no Democrats left."

"Oh, what should we do? Oh, what should we do?"

Chief Taster Dick stared at the pot. "Start throwing in Republicans."

There was a gasp from the witches. "Republicans?"

"That's what I said," Chief Taster Dick said.

Spiro, the chef, and three of the witches grabbed Charlie Goodell and threw him in the pot.

Goodell screamed and thrashed around as everyone clapped his hands and sang:"Charlie Goodell is stewing in the pot. Charlie Goodell is stewing in the pot. Poor old Charlie's stewing in the pot as Buckley marches on."

Spiro, the chef, stirred and stirred, and then he gave the spoon to Chief Taster Dick.

"That's better," he said, smacking his lips. "But it still needs another Republican."

"Another Republican?" everyone gasped.

"Throw in Lindsay," cried a goblin named Martha.

"Lindsay, Lindsay," everyone yelled. "The stew needs some Lindsay."

They heaved in Lindsay and added water to the pot.

Spiro stirred and seasoned it with a bowl of pornography, a pan of marijuana, a handful of media and a gravy of student unrest.

The pot was really boiling and everyone was licking his chops.

"Has there ever been a political brew like this?" cried one of the elves.

Chief Taster Dick went back to the pot and stuck his spoon in. Everyone watched.

"It's almost perfect. All it needs is a little more extract of fear."

Spiro added several gallons of fear, and then Chief Taster Dick smacked his lips and said one word: "Perfect."

They all clapped and cried, "Let us taste it! Let us taste it!"

But Spiro, the chef, slapped their hands with the spoon and said angrily, "Nobody gets to eat unless they pay two hundred and fifty dollars a plate."

What Is Wrong?

People who have been wondering why things have been unraveling so badly in Washington these days may be interested in the explanation of a distinguished Chinese scholar who visited the Capitol recently. Dr. Chun Ling is an expert in Feng Sui, otherwise known as the study of things in relation to where they are placed.

"Americans," Dr. Chun Ling said, "do not put much significance into what is in good harmony and bad harmony, but if buildings are not in harmony with each other, it is impossible for people to be in harmony."

Dr. Chun Ling said that the most striking example of this could be illustrated by the fact that the White House faces north and the Capitol of the nation faces east, and both have their backs to the Washington Monument. When buildings face in different directions, they do not have common goals.

"The Supreme Court faces Lincoln and that is good, but Lincoln from his monument must look at the back of the Senate and House of Representatives, and this is bad."

Dr. Chun Ling also said, "It is very sad the President's office is located in the west wing of the White House, because this puts him on the side of the Pentagon and away from Health, Education, and Welfare."

The Feng Sui expert said it is no accident that the Pentagon is as strong as it is in Washington. "The Pentagon is much larger than the Capitol and White House, and the two smaller buildings cannot control the bigger one. Not only that, but the Pentagon has too many faces and too many entrances directed in all directions. This multifaceted design has forced the Pentagon to get involved in every direction it faces."

Dr. Chun Ling pointed something out to me that I had never noticed before, which shows you how important the study of Feng Sui can be.

"The Pentagon is across the Potomac River, and that is why the State Department, Capitol and even the White House have no control over it."

One of the most interesting things that Dr. Chun Ling said was that because the White House faces north, it looks on Lafayette Park. In the center of Lafayette Park is the Jackson Memorial, consisting of four giant antique guns. These guns have dominated every recent President's thinking. When the President is trying to think, it's inevitable that the guns in Lafayette Park can suggest military solutions to world problems. Dr. Chun Ling believes the guns should be removed at once and replaced with flowers.

When studying the science of Feng Sui, Dr. Chun Ling says that it is very important to know on what axis our nation's leaders sleep. If they don't sleep on the same geographic poles, they can disrupt the flow of the earth's magnetism.

I had my doubts about Dr. Chun Ling's last statement, and so I did some Feng Sui research on my own. It appeared there was a lot to what he said. For example, I discovered that Senator Fulbright sleeps south to north and Martha Mitchell sleeps west to east. This is why they have never been able to see eye to eye on anything.

Vice President Agnew, on the other hand, sleeps south by southeast. Most Eastern establishment newspapermen and commentators sleep north by northwest. This, and only this, is what is causing the disharmony between the Vice President and the press.

I tried to find out in what direction Richard Nixon sleeps to make my study complete, but Ron Ziegler, his press secretary, told me emphatically, "The President never sleeps."

First the Bible, Then Shakespeare

Now that the best minds in the Western world have "improved" the Bible in the most modern edition, which is called the New English Bible (the new Twenty-third Psalm begins, "The Lord is my shepherd, I shall want nothing. He makes me lie down in green pastures and leads me beside the waters of peace; He renews life within me and for His name's sake guides me in the right path. . . ."), it has been decided to update Shakespeare and make him easier for people to understand.

With this goal in mind and using the New English Bible as our inspiration, a group of us has already managed to update some of Hamlet's soliloquy.

"To be or not to be" will soon read as follows:

> Should I or shouldn't I? That is the question.
> I don't know whether it would be better for me to
> Take
> A lot of guff and that sort of thing
> Or to fight back against all this trouble I've been
> Having.
> Maybe I should drop dead, and sleep;
> That's all. And by sleeping hope to end
> All this emotional conflict
> That everyone goes through; boy, wouldn't that be a
> Solution?
> If you could just cop out, close your eyes and
> Sleep. And maybe have a few good dreams. But that's
> The trouble.
> If you're dead, who knows what kind of bad trips
> You're going to have
> Leaving the station? It sure gives you something to
> Think about.
> You have to show some respect; if you don't, you
> Could be in for real trouble.

That's as far as we got with Hamlet. But we have also been working on *Romeo and Juliet*.

So far, it goes like this:

Juliet (*on balcony to herself*): O Romeo, Romeo. Why are you Romeo? Why don't you change your name? Or if you can't do it, I'll work it out some way so I won't be known as a Capulet.

Romeo (*underneath balcony to himself*): I wonder if I should stick around and listen to what she's saying, or speak up and jawbone with her.

Juliet: The only thing I hold against you, Romeo, is your name. Personally I like you for yourself, and not because you're a Montague.

Like, what's a Montague? It isn't your hand or your foot or your face, or any other part of your body belonging to a man. Gosh, I wish you had another name.

But what's in a name? Suppose you saw this flower which was called something else besides a rose. It would still smell pretty good, wouldn't it?

And that's the way it is with Romeo. If his name, for example, were Irving, he still would be perfect in my book. Romeo, get rid of your name because it has nothing to do with you, and in exchange, I'll do anything you want me to.

Romeo (out loud): OK, Juliet, it's a deal. Forget I'm Romeo and call me Loverboy instead.

Juliet: Who is that listening in on everything I've been saying?

Romeo: I can't tell you who I am because I hate my name, and from what I can tell, you do, too.

Juliet: Unless I'm stone-deaf, you sound like Romeo Montague. Are you or aren't you?

Romeo: It all depends if it shakes you up or not.

As you see, we still have a little work to do, but if it took twenty years to rewrite the Bible, I believe we've gotten off to a pretty good start.

The Shock of Recognition

Recently, New York City had a blackout which caused all nine television stations in the area to go out for several hours. This created tremendous crises in families all over the New York area and proved that TV plays a much greater role in people's lives than anyone can imagine.

For example, when the TV set went off in the Bufkins' house in Forest Hills, panic set in. First, Bufkins thought it was his set in the living room, so he rushed into his bedroom and turned on the set. Nothing.

The phone rang and Mrs. Bufkins heard her sister in Manhattan tell her that there was a blackout.

She hung up and said to her husband, "It isn't your set. Something's happened to the top of the Empire State Building."

Bufkins stopped and said, "Who are you?"

"I'm your wife, Edith."

"Oh," Bufkins said. "Then I suppose those kids in there are mine."

"That's right," Mrs. Bufkins said. "If you ever got out of that arm-chair in front of the TV set, you'd know who we were."

"Boy, they're really grown," Bufkins said, looking at his son and daughter. "How old are they now?"

"Thirteen and fourteen," Mrs. Bufkins replied.

"I'll be darned. Hi, kids."

"Who's he?" Bufkins' son, Henry, asked.

"It's your father," Mrs. Bufkins said.

"I'm pleased to meetcha," Bufkins' daughter, Mary, said shyly.

There was an embarrassed silence all around.

"Look," said Bufkins finally. "I know I haven't been much of a fa-ther, but now that the TV's out, I'd like to make it up to you."

"How?" asked Henry.

"Well, let's just talk," Bufkins said. "That's the best way to get to know each other."

"What do you want to talk about?" Mary asked.

"Well, for starters, what school do you go to?"

"We go to Forest Hills HS," Henry said.

"What do you know?" Bufkins said. "You're both in high school."

There was dead silence.

"What do *you* do?" Mary asked.

"I'm an accountant," Bufkins said.

"I thought you were a car salesman," Mrs. Bufkins said in surprise.

"That was two years ago. Didn't I tell you I changed jobs?" Bufkins said in surprise.

"No, you didn't. You haven't told me anything for two years."

"Yup. I'm doing quite well too," Bufkins said.

"Then why am I working in a department store?" Mrs. Bufkins de-manded.

"Oh, are you still working in a department store? If I had known that, I would have told you you could quit last year. You should have mentioned it," Bufkins said.

There was more dead silence.

Finally Henry said, "Hey, you want to hear me play the guitar?"

"I'll be darned. You know how to play the guitar? Say, didn't I have a daughter who played the guitar?"

"That was Susie," Mrs. Bufkins said.

"Where is she?"

"She got married a year ago, just about the time you were watching the World Series."

"How about that?" Bufkins said, very pleased. "You know, I hope they don't fix the antenna for another couple of hours. There's nothing like a blackout for a man to *really* get to know his family."

White Rats Have All the Fun

The key to man's survival on earth seems to be the white rat. Most experiments being conducted these days to see what effect our environment has on human beings are first conducted on white rats. Only after we know what happens to the white rats will we take any action to protect the human race.

Nobody has bothered to find out how the rats feel about this. In man's ever-questing search for truth, I visited a large government laboratory the other evening around midnight and recorded what the white rats were saying to each other.

"Zelda, you look so thin."

"They've had me on cyclamates. I must have lost three ounces in a week. What have you been doing?"

"I've been taking monosodium glutamate. It's tasty, but it gives me headaches. Oh, Horace, will you stop coughing?"

"Ack, ack, ack. I can't help it. They've got me smoking a pack of cigarettes a day."

"Why don't you give them up?"

"I'd like to, but they won't let me."

"What on earth is Sheldon doing? He's staggering all over his cage."

"He's involved in the marijuana experiments. He goes on a trip every night."

"That's what I call luck. How can I get off cyclamates and in the pot program?"

"You have to know somebody. Every rat in the lab wants to go on pot."

"I don't. I feel you have to face reality and not seek escape. That's why I'm proud to be associated with the air pollution project."

"How can you stand it?"

"It's not bad. Every day they drive me around New York City and I just breathe. If I die, they know the air pollution count is too high. If I live, I get to see the city."

"You're probably right, Bettina. I volunteered for air pollution, but some computer assigned me to water pollution. I'm getting sick of drinking dirty river water every day."

"What's the matter with Whitney? He seems awfully quiet tonight."

"He's been eating grapes with DDT on them for a week, and I guess it's finally getting to him."

"I told him to boycott grapes."

"They won't give him anything else to eat, so he has no choice."

"Where's Alvin?"

"Didn't you hear? They transplanted his heart today into Hazel. Hers gave out during the automobile exhaust tests."

"Poor Alvin."

"He didn't seem to mind. He was involved in the tranquilizer experiments, and when they asked him for his heart, he said he couldn't care less."

"Who's crying?"

"Sandra. They have her taking the birth control pills. She wants babies in the worst way."

"Well, at least she's having some fun, which is more than I can say for what I'm doing."

"What's that, Carlton?"

"I'm working for NASA to see the effects of weightlessness. I vomit all the time."

"But the space program at least has some glamor to it. They keep injecting me with flu germs."

"I guess Sampson has the best job of any of us."

"What is he doing?"

"They put him in front of a color television all day long to see how much radiation he absorbs. He's the only white rat I know who gets to watch *Laugh-In*."

Which Side Are You On?

Sometimes one gets the feeling that the right-hand germs in the government don't know what the left-hand germs are doing. This was brought home to me the other day when I read about the millions of dollars that were being spent to see that the astronauts did not bring back a single germ from the moon.

Unfortunately, across the page from that story was another that the Army was going ahead with open-air testing of nerve gases and germ warfare.

I was sure it was a mistake, so I went to see my friend Professor Heinrich Applebaum, the government microbiologist and germ warfare expert.

"Professor, I don't understand why we're going to so much trouble protecting the earth from moon germs when we are still experimenting with germs for warfare."

"One does not have anything to do with the other," Applebaum said angrily. "We must be certain in our space program that we do not do anything to contaminate the earth. This is essential to the survival of mankind."

"Then why are we experimenting on earth with germs for war?"

"Ah, that's different. If we contaminate the earth with germs, everyone understands that we are only defending ourselves from the other side. But if we brought back moon germs and something happened, no one would forgive us."

"What kinds of germs could be on the moon that are any worse than the germs you're experimenting with right now?"

Applebaum said, "We don't know what kind of germs they have on the moon, and we have to be particularly cautious to make sure our astronauts don't bring back infection. After all, the space program is devoted to peace. Now, the germs we have here we know about, and those germs are important to our defense program."

"But what if you had an accident in which the earth germs got out of the laboratories or escaped from the testing area?"

"We don't like to think about things like that. If we did, we wouldn't have a germ warfare program."

"But how can the same people on one hand spend all this money to see that no germs come back from the moon, and on the other spend money to figure out ways of spreading germs around the world?"

"You don't understand," said Applebaum, slamming his fist on the desk. "It's two different departments. The Defense Department doesn't tell NASA what to do with their germs, and NASA doesn't tell the Defense Department what to do with their germs."

"Well," I said, "why doesn't the Defense Department do its germ testing on the moon? In that way there would be less danger of contaminating the earth."

"Because," said Applebaum, breaking a test tube in his hand, "we don't want to contaminate the moon. We know the earth is contaminated, but we're hoping to keep the moon clean."

"For what reason?"

"Because someday we may want to test earth germs in a germless atmosphere."

"I have one thought, Professor. They wouldn't let President Nixon have dinner with the three astronauts because the doctors were afraid his germs might affect them. Why don't they make it up to the President by letting him have dinner with the people in the Defense Department who are working on germ warfare?"

Applebaum screamed at me, "Get out of here. And don't come back."

Mother Nature's Last Will

The other night I was home reading a book when I received a telephone call that Mother Nature was dying. I dressed hurriedly and rushed over to the hospital. A lot of people had gotten there before me, and they were all sitting in the waiting room crying and wringing their hands. I searched out the doctors who were in another room having a heated argument as to how to save her. Each doctor seemed to have a different remedy:

One doctor said, "We have to get her some fresh air. She can't breathe. We'll have to turn off the power plant because of the smoke."

"Are you out of your mind?" another doctor said. "We turn off the power, and she'll freeze to death."

"Perhaps we could keep all cars away from the hospital," a third doctor suggested. "That would relieve her breathing."

"Out of the question," a fourth doctor barked. "How would we get back and forth to work if we prohibited cars near the hospital?"

"Gentlemen," another doctor said, "I don't believe it's the air that is hurting her as much as the water. We have to find some water that's drinkable. Strong measures must be taken immediately against polluting the hospital water."

The director said, "Where would we get the money to support the hospital if we closed down the factories because they're polluting the streams?"

"We'd also have to give up detergents," a doctor added, "and we can't have a clean hospital if you give up detergents."

"Isn't anybody going to do anything?" I shouted.

They saw me for the first time, and one of the doctors said angrily, "We're sorry, this is a medical conference for professionals only. Would you kindly leave?"

I walked out and down the hall. Suddenly I saw a closed room, which had the name MOTHER NATURE hand-printed on the door. Underneath it, in large red letters, was another sign: NO VISITORS.

No one was in the hall, so I opened the door. There was Mother Nature propped up on pillows. She looked old and tired and haggard. I couldn't believe anyone could have changed so much in ten short years. But she seemed glad to see someone and smiled weakly.

"Hi, Ma," I said. "You're looking swell."

"You wouldn't kid a very sick lady, would you?" she said, gasping.

"No, I'm not kidding. You look wonderful.

"I've just been talking to the doctors, and they say they'll have you on your feet in no time."

"Those quacks don't know anything," she said. "All they do is come in every few hours and take my temperature and give me something to relieve the pain. I think I've had it this time."

"Don't talk that way, Ma. You're going to pull through. You've survived worse things than this before."

"It's never been this bad," she said and then started having a coughing fit. "This time the Grim Reaper's coming to get me."

"But if you go, we'll all have to go, Ma," I cried. "You have to hold on. Please, Ma."

"I kept complaining of pain," she whispered, "but no one would pay attention to me. I said, 'If you keep doing what you're doing, I'm going to die.' But everyone said, 'Ma, you'll never die.' Why didn't they listen to me?"

"We're listening now, Ma. We're listening. We have the best doctors in the world. They're out there now, and they have a plan."

"I guess the real thing that hurts," she said, "is that my will won't be worth anything now. I left every person in the world clear water, pure air, green fields, brilliant sunsets and blue skies. It wasn't much, but it was everything I had."

Just then the door opened and a nurse came in. She went over to the bed waving a thermometer.

"Come on, Mother. It's time to take your temperature."

School For Luggage Handlers

Many air travelers have noticed that their luggage has been getting more of a bashing recently than it has in the past. This is no accident. Most airline luggage handlers must now go to school before an airline will allow them to touch a piece of baggage.

I was fortunate to visit the Dent Airline Luggage and Freight Handlers School in St. Louis last week. The Dent school trains most of the airline baggage handlers in the United States. Dent, the founder and president of the school, took me out on a large playing field the size of a football gridiron. Several classes were in session. The teachers all wore baseball caps and sweat shirts, and had whistles around their necks. The pupils were dressed in white coveralls. The first class we stopped to watch were throwing pieces of luggage to each other.

"All right, let's throw them a little harder," the coach yelled. "What are you guys, a punch of cream puffs? You, there, Pitowsky. You're not supposed to catch every bag. Drop a few."

Pitowsky dropped the next one, and it broke open, scattering clothes all over the field.

"Beautiful," the coach yelled. "Now you've got it."

"We use real luggage," Dent said proudly. "We simulate every possible situation a luggage handler will face."

"Ryan, you're catching the bags with two hands," the coach yelled. "You'll never break any that way. How many times have I told you to use only one hand when trying to catch a piece of luggage?"

We walked on down the field and came to a 16-foot tower. Several men were on the tower, dropping boxes marked FRAGILE to the ground.

"The object of this exercise," said Dent, "is for the men to get used to dropping fragile packages from great heights."

"But nobody's catching the packages," I said.

"Of course not." Dent chuckled. We went over to the coach who was inspecting each box after it dropped.

"Claremont," he yelled up to the tower, "those scientific instruments are still intact. What are you using for a throwing arm?"

"Threw them as hard as I could," Claremont yelled back.

"Well, put some spin on it the next time."

Claremont threw another box, and we heard the glass shattering. The coach nodded his head.

"Good boy."

The next group we came to was running an obstacle course. Pieces of luggage were strewn on the field, and the men had to jump from one piece of luggage to another without their heavy work boots hitting the ground. The hinges were broken on most of the bags and the locks were crushed.

"After running the hundred-yard course, stomping on the luggage," Dent said, "the men then have to throw a forty-pound bag fifteen yards, kick a cosmetic case twenty-five yards, and thrust a sharp object through a canvas suitcase, blindfolded."

"You'd doing wonderful work here," I told Dent.

"When a man finishes our school," Dent said, as he picked up a broken camera that had fallen out of a bag, "he is certified to work as a baggage handler for any airline in the world."

Saving the Railroads

The question of what to do about American passenger railroads is still very much on the administration's mind. There is no doubt that the railroads are losing money on passenger business. If they had their druthers, they would just stay with freight. At the same time, the public's need for passenger trains, particularly commuter trains, is great.

What is the solution? Professor Heinrich Applebaum, who holds the Casey Jones chair of railroad philosophy at Pullman University, has come up with a radical idea that could save both the railroads and the needed passenger service.

Professor Applebaum says the solution to the problem can be found in large aluminum containers which are now being used for freight.

These containers are placed on trains already packed, and unloaded the same way. This saves companies money in freight, loss due to pilferage and breakage, and also saves time.

Applebaum claims there is no reason you can't use the same containers for people.

This is how it would operate: Let us assume that 150 people are going to take the 7:30 A.M. from Greenwich, Connecticut. When they arrived at the platform, they would be horizontally placed in the containers. (This would give everyone an extra hour's sleep to New York.) The container would be insulated, as well as air-conditioned.

When everyone was squeezed in the container, it would be sealed. Then a freight train going through Greenwich would stop and the container would be hoisted on board a flatcar.

The same thing would happen all along the way. Commuters in containers at Portchester, Rye and Larchmont would all be waiting to be picked up by the freight train.

When the train arrived at Grand Central Station, the containers would be taken off by cranes and opened on the platform, and everyone could go to work.

The reverse would happen in the evening, Applebaum said, except in this case, to break the monotony, the commuters would be loaded in *vertically*.

The beauty of the plan, says Applebaum, is that by using containers, railroads could cut the cost of a ticket from Greenwich to New York by $3.50.

They could also profit by the fact that they would not have to build new passenger trains, and they could eliminate the bar cars.

Psychologically, they wouldn't have to worry about customer relations, as the commuter service would be run by the freight department.

The big advantage of this is that once the railroads were able to legitimately treat passengers as freight, they would improve their service rather than try to discourage people from using the railroads.

Applebaum says that, at the moment, the container idea would only be practical on short runs, but he felt that as time went on, a method could be developed for long runs to freeze people in refrigerator cars and then thaw them out when they reached their destinations.

The Department of Transportation, which is trying to find a solution to the passenger train problem, has expressed great interest in the Applebaum plan. A spokesman for the department said:

"If nothing else, it could save the Penn Central railroad."

Earth Day

In the beginning God created Man, which, according to all the latest birth control statistics, was a big mistake.

And Man said, "Let there be light," and there was light, and Man called this light fire, and at first it was used to warm him and let him cook his food and protect him from the wild animals. But Man discovered fire could be used to burn down a forest or burn someone else's hut or tree house or a witch at the stake or soft coal or oil, which made the air turn dark gray and black. And this made Man start to cough and his eyes to run and his sinuses to hurt. And Man finally said, "God, what are You doing to me?"

And after God made the rivers and lakes and streams and oceans, Man dumped all the refuse from the earth into the waters, and it killed the fish and the plants and even the oxygen, and the waters turned muddy and brown and smelled, and no one could drink from them or bathe in them or even sail in them. And finally Man shook his fist at the heavens and said, "For God's sake, knock it off."

And Man created the wheel, and this was good because Man no longer had to walk through the forests or up and down the mountains or to school. And then Man created the engine which turned the wheels, and Man no longer had to depend on animals to pull him on the roads and paths. And Man called the new creature automobile, and it changed the face of the earth, for Man was forced to cut down the trees and flowers and pour concrete on the land to accommodate the automobile, and drill into the earth and the sea to fuel it, and sometimes the ocean turned black and the air turned brown, and as the automobile multiplied there was less space to park it, and it was unable to move any faster than a horse, and Man behind the wheel screamed, "Good God, am I ever going to get home?"

And Man created the plastic bag and the tin and aluminum can and the cellophane wrapper and the paper plate and the disposable bottle, and this was good because Man could then take his automobile and buy his food all in one place and he could save that which was good to eat in the refrigerator and throw away that which had no further use. And pretty soon the earth was covered with plastic bags and aluminum cans and paper plates and disposable bottles, and there was nowhere left to sit down or to walk. And Man shook his head and cried, "Look at all this God-awful litter."

And Man learned to split the atom, and then he took what he learned and he put it in a bomb to defend himself from other men, and he set off the bomb to see if it would work, and it did. And Man was very pleased with himself because he was safe from other men, and this was good. But other men learned to split the atom, too, and they put it in their bombs, and so Man had to make bigger bombs, and the other men had to make bigger bombs, and the explosions put radioactive material in the air which got into Man's food and water and made that which was nourishing inedible and that which would quench thirst undrinkable. And again Man became very frightened and said, "God help us all."

But by this time God had had it, and He sent down word to His loyal servant, Ralph Nader: "Now, Ralph, the first thing I want you to do is build an ark and then. . . ."

South Pacific

If I had my life to live all over again, I'd live it as the CIA man stationed in Tahiti. You get up in the morning and see if there are any ships in the lagoon. If there are, you write down their names on a piece of paper in code, stick it in an envelope addressed to an old lady in Salt Lake City (who forwards it to Washington), and you have the rest of the day to snorkel, spear fish, water-ski, sail, and drink sloe-rum punches with lovely schoolteachers, airline stewardesses and the daughters of French planters who were born during World War II.

I met one of these chaps at the bar in the Hotel Tahara, which is set in a mountain overlooking the lagoon of Papeete. I immediately knew he was a CIA man because at exactly nine o'clock he faced the sea and started striking his Zippo lighter on and off, despite the fact he had no cigarette in his mouth.

When the bartender confirmed he did this every night, I decided the man either was a CIA agent or had just given up smoking.

He was surprised I had seen through his cover so easily. "Most people think I work for the *Encyclopaedia Britannica*," he said.

"Whom are you trying to signal?" I asked him.

"Our man over there on the island of Moorea. We haven't heard from him in over a year. I'm beginning to suspect foul play."

"How could that be?" I asked him.

"Emile Debecque, that's his name, was a French planter who knew Moorea like a book. We needed a coast watcher who would station himself there and report to us on any Japanese ships trying to sneak into the lagoon."

"But why?" I said. "The war with Japan has been over for twenty-five years."

"Every Japanese ship going east that pulls into Papeete is carrying television sets, portable radios, cameras and automobiles. We can tell by the tonnage of the ships just how hard hit the American economy will be. We have to know before the ships reach Hawaii and San Francisco, so we can adjust our domestic production schedules. It is more important to know where the Japanese ships are now than it was during World War Two.

"So we sent Debecque into the hills to watch for us. But we haven't heard from him, and I'm starting to think the worst. Every night I come up here and signal him, hoping he will signal back."

As we were talking, a girl came in the bar with shampoo in her hair singing, "I'm gonna wash that man right out of my hair." Two little native children followed her singing *"Dites-moi, pourquoi."*

"What's going on?" I asked Jack.

"That's Nelly Forebush. She was a Pan American stewardess who met Debecque one enchanted evening at the Bali Hai Hotel and fell in love. Nelly was from Little Rock, Arkansas. After she fell in love with Emile, she discovered he had two native children by a Tahitian wife. Nelly at first was horrified, as it was against everything she stood for. But finally she became so enraptured with the children that she quit her job with Pan American and promised Emile she would look after them until he came back."

"What an idea for a musical," I said. "But why the shampoo?"

"That's the sad part of the story. Nelly didn't know Emile would be gone this long, and she went bonkers three months ago when the two kids drove her up the wall."

The Great American Rat Race

One of the complaints the kids voice today is that parents put too much pressure on them. I accidentally listened to such a discussion the other evening at Goldfarb's house.

Young Goldfarb, aged sixteen, told his father he saw no reason to study such irrelevant subjects as math, language, science, history and English.

"Who needs it?" young Goldfarb said.

"You need it," his father shouted.

"Why?" young Goldfarb demanded.

"Because of Springfield. If I don't push you, Springfield's kid is going to get ahead of you in school. How would you like that?"

"Who cares if Springfield's son gets ahead of me?" young Goldfarb said.

"Springfield does, that's who," the older Goldfarb replied. "Oh, wouldn't he love it if he could say his kid was doing better than Goldfarb's."

"You mean to say you've been leaning on me all this time because you're in a contest with Springfield?" young Goldfarb said.

"I didn't start it," the older Goldfarb said. "It was Springfield who began pushing his kid first. Years ago, I heard Springfield tell his kid, 'Never take second best. Go for all the marbles. Get out in front and show them what you can do.'

"When I heard this, I had no choice but to make you work your tail off. If you're mad at anyone, you should be mad at Springfield."

"But Springfield's kid doesn't want to compete with me any more than I want to compete with him. Why don't I call him up and tell him if he knocks off beating his brains out, I'll knock off beating my brains out?"

"That would be just fine," old Goldfarb said. "But what about Ascarelli's kid?"

"What's Ascarelli's kid got to do with it?"

"You think Ascarelli is going to stop pushing his kid just because you two let up? And how about Bernheim's son? Bernheim has already announced his kid is going to Yale. You want Bernheim's kid to go to Yale and you wind up at some community college in Florida?"

"But don't you understand, Pop?" young Goldfarb said. "Ascarelli's son couldn't care less if he got ahead of us, and Bernheim's son doesn't give a damn whether he gets in Yale."

Old man Goldfarb got up and took his son over to the window and pointed out to the flickering apartment lights across the Potomac.

"If it was just *one* Springfield or *one* Ascarelli or *one* Bernheim, I would say, 'Enjoy yourself; don't break your back.' But out there, where you see those lights, are thousands and thousands of Springfields and Ascarellis and Bernheims, and do you know what they're saying to their kids tonight? They're saying, "The only thing I want you to do is to *beat Goldfarb!'*

"All over America, the Springfields, Ascarellis and Bernheims are vowing to beat you out of a job, a sale, a taxi, a contract, a home, a wife. And do you know why they're doing it?"

"No," said young Goldfarb. "I don't know why."

"Because at this very moment they know I'm telling you to get them before they get you."

"But if you stop, maybe they will," young Goldfarb said.

"It's too late," the older Goldfarb said. "Springfield, Ascarelli and Bernheim are too ambitious for their sons to quit now. So be a nice boy and go do your homework."

Easy Rider

There has been a lot of criticism of Congress for not doing enough work this year. I believe that if any criticism should be levied at Congress, it's that it has done too much work. There isn't a bill proposed these days that doesn't have seven riders attached to it which have nothing to do with the legislation that is being proposed.

This can be illustrated in the case of Jan Klopinski, a refugee from Poland who was trying to get American citizenship. Because of red tape, Jan could not get his American citizenship through normal channels, and so he got his Senator to propose a private bill to make him a citizen.

It is done all the time and usually goes through without any difficulty. But this year, any bill in Congress is subject to amending, and as soon as the Jan Klopinski bill for American citizenship was proposed on the floor, a dove Senator got up and added a rider calling for the repeal of the Gulf of Tonkin Resolution.

This angered several hawks in the Senate, and they added a rider of their own which would give Chiang Kai-shek four squadrons of B-52 bombers.

A Senator from Louisiana then proposed that a rider be attached to the Klopinski citizenship bill raising the oil depletion allowance to 35 percent. He immediately was followed on the floor by a Senator from North Carolina who wanted the bill amended to take all health warnings off cigarette packages.

The rumor started spreading that the Jan Klopinski citizenship bill was in trouble.

No one knew how much trouble until a liberal Senator added a rider raising Social Security payments by 50 percent. This was followed by another rider from a Midwest Senator raising salaries of postal workers by $100 a week.

The White House, which hadn't been paying much attention to the Klopinski bill, suddenly got to work and called Minority Leader Hugh Scott over for breakfast. Senator Scott was told the President was very displeased with the Jan Klopinski citizenship bill in its present form.

When Senator Scott reported this back to the Hill, everyone decided to get into the act.

A Senator from South Carolina added a rider forbidding federal judges from ruling in desegregation cases. A Senator from Arizona added a resolution recommending the President resume bombing of North Vietnam. A Senator from California proposed a rider making it a felony to boycott grapes.

Meanwhile, Jan Klopinski had gone out and bought a new black suit for the swearing-in ceremonies. Because of his limited English, he had no idea that his bill was in so much difficulty until President Nixon decided to go on television and appeal directly to the American people.

The President said, "I want to make it perfectly clear that I am for the Jan Klopinski bill for American citizenship, but only if it does not cause inflation, or a sellout in Southeast Asia. I appeal to every American who is part of the great silent majority to write to his Senator today and tell him you support my position on Klopinski."

Vice President Agnew went on television two nights later and attacked the three networks for discussing the Klopinski bill before Americans had a chance to digest the President's message.

In the meantime, two more riders had been tacked onto the bill, one authorizing the building of ten nuclear aircraft carriers and the other making marijuana legal.

The bill was finally passed with all the riders intact. Unfortunately, President Nixon decided to veto it and Jan Klopinski, through no fault of his own, lost his opportunity to become a citizen of the United States of America. He sold his black suit and took the next boat to Australia.

The Loved Ones

This is a government of reports and studies. No matter what happens in this nation, the first solution is to appoint a commission to study it. The commissions take one year, two years, some even longer, and then they make their report to the President. If the President agrees with the report, it's released to the nation. If he or his staff disagrees with it, it's buried. But where?

Just by chance I discovered the secret burial grounds of reports and studies made by Presidential commissions. The cemetery is located on a hill overlooking the upper Potomac. It is quiet and deserted, and only the chirping of birds or the call of a hoot owl can be heard.

Mr. Gottfried Snellenbach has been caretaker of the burial area for government reports since the Harding administration, and after I assured him I would not dig up any of the graves, he let me enter the large well-kept grounds.

"We've got some of the great reports of all times buried here," Mr. Snellenbach said. "We've got reports that cost twenty million dollars, and we've got reports that cost two thousand dollars, but in the end they all wind up here, buried six feet under."

"Sir, what kind of reports are resting here?"

"It might be better to ask what kind of reports aren't buried here. We have reports on violence, studies on blacks, students, unemployment, the economy, the Communist threat, housing, health care, law and order. You name it, and we've buried it."

"How does a report find its final resting spot in this setting?"

"Well, as you know, the President is always appointing a commission to study something or other, and after the study they're supposed to hand in a report. Now, lots of times the President has no intention of paying any attention to the report, and it's dead before it's even written. Other times someone on the President's staff reads a report handed in by a commission and says, 'This stuff is dynamite. We have to kill it.'

"In some cases the President says, 'Let's release this report to the press and then bury it.' Occasionally a report will just die of heartbreak because nobody pays any attention to it.

"In any case, after the report is dead, it has to be buried, because if you're President, you don't want someone finding it at a later date and using it against you.

"So every week each report that has died is placed in a pine box and loaded on a government hearse and brought up here, where we have a simple ceremony before lowering it into the ground.

"If it's a blue-ribbon panel report that's been killed in action, we give it a twenty-one gun salute. Otherwise, we lay it to rest with as little fuss as possible."

"This cemetery goes for miles and miles," I said.

"No one knows how many reports have been buried here by the different Presidents."

"Mr. Snellenbach, this is a beautiful cemetery and very impressive. But why does the government go to so much trouble and expense to keep it up for nothing more than paper reports?"

"You must understand that most of the men asked to serve on Presidential commissions are very important citizens. They spend months and years working on these reports, and they feel very close to them. When their reports are killed or buried, these men feel a personal loss. Many days you will see them sitting here next to the tombstones of their studies, tears rolling down their cheeks. No matter how long you work here, it still gets to you."

A Nation of Banks

Every time an old building is torn down in this country, and a new building goes up, the ground floor becomes a bank.

The reason for this is that banks are the only ones who can afford the rent for the ground floor of the new buildings going up. Besides, when a bank loans someone money to build a new building, it usually takes an option for the street-floor facilities.

Most people don't think there is anything wrong with this, and they accept it as a part of the American free-enterprise system. But there is a small group of people in this country who are fighting for Bank Birth Control.

This is how Huddlestone Hubbard, the BBC's chairman, explained it:

"Whenever you see an old building torn down," Hubbard said, "you usually see a candy store, a dry cleaner, a delicatessen and possibly a florist torn down with it. These shops are all replaced in the new building with a beautiful glass, aluminum, wall-to-wall-carpeted money factory.

"Now from an aesthetic viewpoint, a bank looks better than a dry cleaner, a candy store, a delicatessen and a florist. But from a practical point of view, it's a sheer disaster. If you want a newspaper, a candy bar or a chocolate milk shake, you can't get it at a bank. Nor can you run out to a bank for a pound of Swiss cheese and a six-pack of beer when you have guests coming over.

"A bank is great if you want to buy a car, but it's useless if you want to have your dress cleaned.

"And while a bank might buy flowers to give itself a human image, it doesn't sell any when you want to make up with your wife."

"What you're saying then, Mr. Hubbard, is that every time a bank goes up, something in all of us dies."

"Exactly. One of the reasons kids are getting in so much trouble these days is that there are no candy stores to hang around anymore. When they tear down a delicatessen, the tangy smells of potato salad, salamis, corned beef and dill pickles are lost forever. Unless you're trying to make a loan, no one ever salivates in a bank."

"It's true," I said.

"The situation is more crucial than anyone thinks," Hubbard said. "At the rate they're tearing down consumer stores and replacing them with banks, we estimate that in ten years it will be impossible to buy a loaf of bread in the country. What good is it to get seven percent on your money if you starve to death?"

"Then what you're saying is that it isn't a question of not taking it with you. It's a question of staying alive while you have it," I said.

"Something like that," Hubbard agreed. "We're trying to get the public to wake up to the fact that it's better to have a store that sells screwdrivers than a bank that gives away alarm clocks."

"What's the solution?"

"A government decree that a bank has to supply the same services of the stores it tore down on the same property. If it's a bakery, they have to sell cake; if it's a photography shop, they have to develop film; and if it's a dry-goods store, they have to sell warm underwear. If they provide the services of the store they tore down, then we'll let them do a little moneylending on the side."

Before the Ax Falls

As the earnings statements of large companies get gloomier there is more and more pressure on corporation executives to make economies in their firms. Most companies do this first by firing the office boy, then the retrenching in the mail room department, and finally cutting the budget on the softball team.

But as time goes on and stockholders get unhappier and unhappier, management may have to start making cuts in the upper levels of the company, and even executives are in danger of losing their jobs.

How does someone in a large company save his job when all around him are losing theirs? Perhaps I can be of help.

The first bit of advice is DO NOT TAKE A VACATION this year. No matter how badly you need one, hang in there, or else this is what could happen:

"Maxwell, what are you doing sitting at my desk?"

"Oh, Herndon, how was the Cape?"

"Fine. Now what are you doing in my office?"

"Well, finance decided to merge sales with packaging, and they asked me to take over. I naturally fought the move, but they were adamant. We tried to reach you on the Cape, but they said you were racing in the Hyannis-Nantucket sailboat trials. How did you do?"

"I came in third. Now where have I been moved to?"

"That's what they were trying to reach you about. They've had to cut across the board. I spoke up for you but. . . ."

The second bit of advice is to institute an economy committee, before one is constituted without you. Go into the president and say, "B.J., I'd like to organize a cost-cutting program so we don't get caught like Penn Central with our pants down. What I suggest we do is form a team and go into every department and see how we can eliminate waste. We could report to you within a month, so you'll have something to show the board."

If your idea is accepted, you must use great tact in suggesting the elimination of somebody else's job, on the off chance that he might survive and do you in.

You could say, "Gentlemen, I think we'd make a mistake if we let Fowler go. It's true his advertising campaign for Fluff was a complete disaster, but we must remember there has been great consumer resistance in toiletries for dogs this year. Fowler is a genius when it comes to advertising, even though he has a tendency to antagonize everyone in the company."

If Fowler loses his job, you have the minutes of the meeting to prove that you've defended him.

To show that you have the company's interest at heart before your own, announce some economies you're making in your own department. "I'm happy to announce, gentlemen, that I've furloughed two telephone operators and laid off four watchmen in our Wichita warehouse, thus saving the company thirty-three thousand dollars. This cuts my department to the bone, but I believe we can manage with what we've got."

The biggest danger during an economy drive is that the company may hire an outside consulting firm to make a private report on which people should be let go.

If one comes in the plant, *stop all work you are doing* and spend every waking moment with him. Most consultants know little or nothing about the businesses they are investigating, and if you can make them look good, they may believe you are necessary to the firm.

You can also get even with some old enemies.

"Tell me, Herndon, where is Mr. Maxwell?"

"Maxwell? I believe he's playing golf. He always plays golf on Wednesday afternoon with his doctor."

The Pro Football Murder Mystery

As detective Peter Minderman stared at the color television set in the simple living room of the Socalaw house he was baffled.

The body of Artie Socalaw was still in the same chair where he had died. All the suspects in the case were also in the living room. There was Artie's wife, Emma, and Artie's best friends: George Stevens, Jr., Chuck McDermott, Sam Markay and Tony Valenti.

"All right," said detective Minderman, "let's start from the beginning. You guys began watching pro football two days ago on Saturday at noon, right in this living room."

"That's correct," said Stevens. "Then, suddenly, Sunday night, somewhere during the third quarter of the Raider game, we noticed there was something wrong with Artie. We waited until the game ended at seven and then went over to his chair. He was dead."

"You can imagine what a shock this was, coming after the Forty-Niners' defeat of the Minnesota Vikings," Chuck McDermott added.

"But," said detective Minderman, "the coroner said Artie had been dead for twenty-four hours. How come no one discovered it before then?"

"Well," said Sam Markay, "Artie was always quiet when he watched a pro football game. He wasn't one of these guys who holler and shout after each play. So when he didn't say anything for twenty-four hours, we figured he was just suffering because Dallas beat the Detroit Lions."

"When you're watching pro football on TV," said Tony Valenti, "you don't notice whether people are breathing or not."

Detective Minderman looked over at Mrs. Socalaw. "When did you last see your husband alive?"

"You mean moving around and that sort of thing?" Mrs. Socalaw asked. "I believe it was sometime in July before the exhibition games started. He hasn't left that chair since the Redskins played the Patriots in a preseason game. I don't wish to dispute the coroner's report, but I thought Artie was dead three months ago."

"That's not true," Stevens said. "Just before the Baltimore-Cincinnati game, Artie asked me if I wanted a piece of fruitcake."

"Fruitcake?" detective Minderman said. "Where did the fruitcake come from?"

"I made it," said Mrs. Socalaw. "I always make furitcake during the holiday season. It helps me forget."

"Did anyone else eat the fruitcake?"

"I did," said McDermott.

"No ill effects?" Minderman asked.

"None that I can tell," McDermott said.

"Damn," said detective Minderman. "There goes the poisoned-fruitcake theory. Did he eat anything else?"

"I gave him a tuna fish sandwich," McDermott said.

"A what?"

"A tuna fish sandwich. You see, Mrs. Socalaw refuses to feed us, so we each bring our own food. This time my wife made me a tuna fish sandwich.

"But don't you know what's going on with tuna fish?" Minderman asked.

"I'm not much for fishing. The only sport I watch is football," McDermott said.

"Your wife tried to knock you off with a tuna fish mercury-poisoned sandwich," detective Minderman said. "Only Artie became the victim, instead of you."

"I knew she was sore at me," McDermott said, "but I didn't think she'd go this far."

Minderman went to the phone and called the McDermott house. "Mrs. McDermott, I'm sending someone over to arrest you for the tuna fish murder of Artie Socalaw."

"Don't worry, Gloria," Mrs. Socalaw, grabbing the phone, shouted, "I'll testify in your behalf. We can always say it was a crime of passion."

For the Entire Family

One of the problems of taking children on vacation is that there is nothing to do with them in the evenings. There is one movie house in our town on Cape Cod, and it shows a different film every night. Unfortunately none of the children has been able to go because every film that they've shown has beed graded by the Valenti code as M for mature audiences only, R for restricted audiences only, or X which means you have to prove you're dirty old men before they let you in.

You can therefore imagine my surprise when I heard the other day the Bijou Cinema was advertising for Saturday night a G picture, which meant it was for the entire family. I couldn't believe it, so I ran down to the theater to see if it was possibly true.

Other parents had also heard the rumor, and there was a large crowd in front of the building staring at the coming-attractions poster which said the film on Saturday had been declared for general audiences "without any restrictions."

"What could it possibly be?" a father next to me said.

"I don't know," I admitted. "I thought they had given up making films for the entire family."

"Maybe it's a foreign film," his wife suggested.

"It could be an old M-G-M film that they retitled," another man said. "I'm sure Hollywood wouldn't make a new film for children to see."

A lady became indignant. "They should have given us some advance notice. I had a big dinner planned for Saturday evening and now I have to cancel it."

"Why?" a man asked.

"I've never seen a movie for general audiences, and another one may not come along for years," she said.

Apparently word had spread beyond the town because people were driving in from the countryside to see the poster. Main Street was clogged with cars, and fathers were standing in the middle of the street holding their children on their shoulders so they could get a better look at the G rating.

The manager of the movie house came out perspiring. "Please go home. This is Thursday, and the family movie isn't scheduled until Saturday night. You're hurting my regular business."

Nobody moved. "How do we know we can get in on Saturday night?" a man shouted.

"Yeah," someone else yelled, "suppose the whole Cape hears you're showing a G movie? We won't be able to get in. Why can't we buy our tickets now?"

The crowd was becoming ugly. The manager got up on a box. "Please," he said, "it's not my fault. We're only permitted to show one film for the entire family each summer. If it was up to me, I'd show another one, though heaven knows where I'd find it."

A mother cried, "We support you when you show your M and R movies. Why can't we get some consideration when you show a G movie?"

"How about a matinee?" I suggested. "In that way more people could see it."

"I can't show it at a matinee. Next Saturday's matinee is already booked for *I Am Curious (Yellow)*."

"My child's never seen a movie," another mother cried. "Couldn't children who have never seen a movie be given first preference?"

"Madam," the manager said. "We can't cater to lower age groups."

It looked hopeless, so I decided to go home. As I suspected, the word had spread all along the Cape that our cinema was going to show a family movie, and on Friday morning caravans of people started to arrive with tents and sleeping bags.

By Saturday morning people had abandoned their cars 20 miles from the town and walked on foot in hopes of seeing it. By Saturday afternoon the place looked like the Woodstock Festival at Bethel, New York. The Bijou Cinema has only 500 seats, so 60,000 people had to be turned away from the theater. But they didn't seem to mind.

The father of one tribe said as he tied up his bedroll, "I think just being in town where they were showing a film for the entire family, even if we didn't get in, was a wonderful experience for the kids."

What Not to Say

The Women's Liberation people take themselves very seriously, and well they might. It's very hard to say anything to them without getting them very mad. While I have no idea what you *should* say to someone in Women's Lib, here are some of the things you should *not* say:

"Well, now that you've got your college degree, I suppose you're going to find yourself a husband."

"You ought to meet Hugh Hefner—he's your kind of guy."

"How do you like this picture of the sexy girl in a bathing suit?"

"Have you heard the latest one about the woman driver who—"

"What's the name of your hairdresser?"

"I suppose if you take this job, you'll probably become pregnant."

"You women go in the other room. We'll stay here for cigars and cognac."

"Wouldn't you hate to be married to a man who makes as much money as you do?"

"Here, let me light your cigarette for you."

"For a woman, you play very well."

"My mother always did something stupid like that herself."

"There's a gal in our office who is as good at selling as any man."

"Hey, look, there's a lady taxi driver!"

"We'd be happy to let you in the press box—it's just that we don't have any lavatory facilities."

"Ha-ha-ha . . . A woman President, that's a good one. Ho-ho-ho."

"Would you like to go out to Ladies' Day at the ball park?"

"The thing I like about you the best is your legs."

"I met this woman doctor the other day, at the hospital, and she really seemed to know what she was doing."

"What do you think about when you're having a baby?"

"I beg your pardon, ma'am. Is the head of the house home?"

"Would you like to feel my muscle?"

"Show me a woman who really likes working, and I'll show you a woman who likes other women."

"A penny for your thoughts."

"Hi, how's the better half feeling?"

"Don't feel bad, I even know men who don't understand it."

"No, sit down and join us. We have nothing important to say."

"The newspaper just arrived. Would you like the women's page?"

"Listen, I'm the first one to admit women have gotten a raw deal, but the majority of them wouldn't have it any other way."

"Meet me at the ladies' entrance of the club at five o'clock."

Any of the above statements can cause a Women's Lib backer to get uptight, but if you really want to see her climb the wall start singing:

"You've come a long way, baby,
"To get where you got to today.
"You've got your own cigarette now, baby,
"You've come a long, long way."

Children of Your Choice

Science is now fiddling with animal sperm banks. It is already possible through deepfreeze methods to save the reproductive ingredients of a great bull for several years and then, by artificial insemination, to produce a calf whose father may have long gone on to that great cow pasture in the sky.

Lucy Kavaler in the New York *Times* has suggested that if there are now banks for animals, we should start thinking in terms of human beings. She suggests that the reproductive cells of great men could be frozen and banked for future generations.

Miss Kavaler foresees a time, in the not too distant future, when a man and wife would be able to go down to their local test tube bank and select the child of their dreams.

So do we.

It is the year 2001, and a couple walks into the First National Test Tube Bank of New York. They are ushered into an icebox, where the vice-president, bundled up in a sheepskin coat, asks them to state their business.

The wife says, "I would like either another Artur Rubinstein or a Jascha Heifetz."

"But," says the husband, "he should be able to throw a football like Joe Namath."

The vice-president says, "We're all out of Artur Rubinsteins, Jascha Heifetzes, and Joe Namaths. The last of them went in 1996. Could I interest you in a Norman Mailer or an Erich Segal?"

The husband says, "If you don't have a Joe Namath, what about a good linebacker?"

The wife says, "I want my son to be a professional man. Maybe a doctor. You don't have a Jonas Salk sample around, do you?"

"No, I'm sorry," the vice-president replies. "The last genes of Jonas Salk went in 1987."

"I tell you what," says the husband, "if you have a good golfer like Arnold Palmer, we'll take it."

"Not so fast," the wife says. "Golfers are a dime a dozen. I would like perhaps a little artistic genius. Maybe a Pablo Picasso or a Chagall."

"Wait a minute," the husband says. "The Martons got a Picasso twenty years ago, but instead of him painting pictures, he became a Communist and got married three times."

"Well," says the vice-president, "there is no guarantee that your offspring will not inherit *all* the characteristics of the person you choose."

"Don't I know it!" the wife says. "The Kaisers had a Dr. Edward Teller offspring, and he married a daughter who came from a General Patton strain, and now all they want to do is make war instead of love."

The vice-president studies a list. "Would you consider a politician for a son? We're having a sale on John Lindsay."

"Not on your life," the husband says. "Anyone who wants his son to be mayor of New York has to be crazy."

"I wouldn't be adverse to an Onassis-type child," the wife says. "At least we wouldn't have to worry about security in our old age."

The vice-president says, "We've been sold out of Onassis for twenty years. Why do you think there's such a glut in oil tankers these days?"

The husband says, "Maybe we should try for a basketball player."

The wife says angrily, "I'm not going to produce a seven-foot giant just so you can go to Madison Square Garden three nights a week."

The vice-president says, "You people are going to have to make up your minds."

The wife says, "All right, give us a Ralph Nader. He may not get rich, but at least he'll always tell us the truth."

You Have to Have a Service Contract

In the world of planned obsolescence, the service contract plays a most vital role. There is hardly anything you can buy now that doesn't have a service contract to go with it.

The other day I went into my favorite department store to purchase a paper cup dispenser. It cost $1.50.

As the man was writing up the sales slip, he said, "Would you like to have a service contract with this?"

"What for?" I asked.

"Well, it could break down and you would have to call someone to fix it. If you take out a service contract, which will only cost you forty dollars for the year, we would send someone to your house free of charge."

"But why would you sell a paper cup dispenser that would break down in less than a year?"

"Please don't get me wrong. I'm not saying that this paper cup dispenser will break down. We've sold several of them that need no servicing at all. But our experience has been that the majority of the dispensers do cause trouble after frequent usage. Where did you intend to use this paper cup dispenser?"

"In the children's bathroom. They don't seem to ever rinse their glasses after they brush their teeth."

"Then you'll certainly need a service contract. These paper cup dispensers were not built to stand the punishment of children using them every day."

"But there is a guarantee with the paper cup dispenser."

"That's only if it's used by a senior three times a week. Of course, you don't have to take the service contract—it's strictly optional.

"But we know a dentist who installed one of our paper cup dispensers in his office and it broke down. It kept dispensing three paper cups at one time. He didn't have a service contract, so it took three months before we could get to him. By the time our man repaired the dispenser, the dentist had used six hundred and forty-five dollars' worth of paper cups, not to mention the twenty-five dollars we had to charge him for the house call."

"But," I said naively, "it seems so unfair to sell someone a new product and then inform him it's liable to break down."

"On the contrary. We would be dishonest if we sold you the product and *didn't* inform you it would break down. These service contracts are for the protection of the customer. Two weeks ago a lady bought one of these paper cup dispensers and after two days, it wouldn't dispense any paper cups at all. She had to keep leaning over and trying to drink directly from the faucet. Fortunately, she had a service contract with us, and we sent over a man right away. It turned out a sprocket spring behind the reject lever had slipped out of the three-way hook. He replaced it in an hour, and all the lady had to pay for was the new parts.

"Except for a bad back she developed trying to lean over the faucet, it only cost her twelve dollars."

"I still don't understand why a reliable store like this would carry a paper cup dispenser that won't hold up."

"Well, frankly, sir, we're not too fond of these paper cup dispensers ourselves. We don't even make any money on them."

"Then why do you sell them?" I asked angrily.

"Because," he said primly, "we make all our profit on the service contract, stupid."

The No Knock on the Door

There was a shoot-out in Phoenix which had national implications. The police, taking advantage of a "no-knock" law, raided a house where they suspected hippies had narcotics. Unfortunately, at the time of the raid the hippies had moved out and a married couple had moved in. Since the raid took place at 1:30 in the morning, the husband refused to believe the men were police and shot one. He, in turn, was shot. The police sergeant said after the raid, "It was a misunderstanding. The couple probably felt they were defending their home against some hippies, and the officers thought they were fighting some criminals."

Now, opponents of the "no-knock" law have always claimed the big danger of it was that if the police enter someone's home without knocking, they could get shot.

Since the Constitution permits you to defend your own home, it is possible that more policemen will be shot than narcotics will be found.

This will make the cops uptight, and so, to protect themselves, they'll start shooting first, and before you know it, there will be bloodbaths all over the country.

The reason law enforcement officials say they need the "no-knock" law is that if they knock first, the suspects inside the house will flush narcotics evidence down the toilet. Only a strong "no-knock" law, they claim, can prevent anyone from dashing to the bathroom.

This sounds reasonable, but, as we have seen in Phoenix, it can only lead to a shoot-out because the people inside the house can never be certain that the people crashing into their home are policemen.

There is a solution to this problem which we think could satisfy the law-and-order people, as well as the innocent home owner.

I am proposing that the "no-knock" law be stricken from the books and replaced with a "no-flush" law.

This is how it would work: The police would still have to get a warrant to enter someone's home. They would also have to knock before entering. But if it were a narcotics or gambling raid, they would have to shout at the top of their voices, *"This is a raid. Anyone who flushes the toilet will be arrested."*

One policeman would be stationed by the water meter nearest the house or apartment to monitor any fluctuation in water pressure during the raid.

When the police enter the apartment, they will have the authority to check the bathrooms. If anyone flushes during the raid, he will be assumed to have committed a crime, and this evidence will be accepted by the court as prima-facie evidence of guilt.

The "no-flush" law may be considered by civil libertarians as an invasion of privacy, but it is certainly more acceptable than a "no-knock" law, and safer, too.

I made this suggestion at an annual meeting of the American Bar Association in St. Louis, but they only laughed at me.

So I've decided to take my case to the public. Would you rather have the police crash in on you at one o'clock in the morning without warning? Or would you rather first hear a knock on the door and give up your bathroom privileges while they're searching through your home?

The Pothole Convention

I just finished attending a pothole convention in Pittsburgh, Pennsylvania. Pothole makers from all over the world jammed the city's hotels and motels, and officials of the National Pothole Association said it was the most successful meeting they ever had.

Hiram H. Patches, president of the NPA, said, "Thanks to a very bad winter, pothole production has tripled. We've had potholes where we've never had potholes before. At one time you only saw potholes in the poorer neighborhoods and on unpaved streets. But now, because of new technological breakthroughs, you'll find potholes on paved suburban roads, as well as highways and bridges. We can't keep up with the demand."

Mr. Patches took me to the exhibition hall, where equipment, as well as designs for potholes, was on display.

"Most potholes used to be rectangular, but we're getting demands for potholes in every shape and form. This kidney-shaped one is very popular, and this oval one has been moving quite well, and this zigzag pothole is a winner."

"You mean you can deliver a pothole made to order?"

"Of course. When you have a pothole on a highway or a main street, you don't want one that looks ugly and doesn't fit in with the landscape."

"How do you make a pothole?" I asked.

"It's very complicated," Mr. Patches said, "and there are many methods. The old-fashioned way of making a pothole was to dig up a street and then fill it in again with a cheaper subsurface material. Before the material hardened, you would send a truck over it and it would make a pothole any size you wanted.

"But the difficulty with this method was that it was too expensive to dig up the streets just to make a pothole. So our research people attacked the problem. They discovered that if you use a cheap asphalt or a thin tar surface on the roads, all you need to make a good-sized pothole are enough vehicles passing over it. Now most of our potholes are made by using cheaper material and bad labor."

"What kind of pothole makers are those?" I asked, pointing to a very interesting display which showed what happens to the chassis of a car that hits a pothole.

"That's our freeze-and-thaw road breaker. We have discovered that by freezing a road or highway to zero temperature, and then thawing it, you can make potholes automatically. The size depends on how many heavy trucks and buses roll over the surface.

"We can make a pothole with an automobile as well, but it takes twice as long as it does with a good solid truck."

We walked along and came to a theater where I noticed someone getting an award. "What's going on?"

"Every year, to publicize potholes, we give an award to the city that has the most potholes. Pittsburgh won this year, though I must say it was close: New York, Chicago, Cleveland and Detroit are all protesting that they should have got the prize."

"There seems to be a great market for potholes. Who buys them?"

"Our biggest customers are elected officials."

"I don't understand."

"Most politicians, particularly those up for election, want to do something for the people. So they order the potholes from us. Once they've been installed, the voters complain about them and then the officials arrange for the potholes to be filled in. This way the politicians win the undying gratitude of the electorate."

"So, without your potholes it would be impossible for anyone to run for reelection in the United States?"

"Exactly. Look, there's Mayor Daley ordering a gross of potholes for the Loop."

The Great Data Famine

One of the major problems we face in the 1970's is that so many computers will be built in the next decade that there will be a shortage of data to feed them.

Professor Heinrich Applebaum, director of the Computer Proliferation Center at Grogbottom, has voiced concern about the crisis and has urged a crash program to produce enough data to get our computers through the seventies.

"We didn't realize," the professor told me, "that computers would absorb so much information in such a fast period of time. But if our figures are correct, every last bit of data in the world will have been fed into a machine by January twelfth, 1976, and an information famine will follow, which could spread across the world."

"It sounds serious," I said.

"It is serious," he replied. "Man has created his own monster. He never realized when he invented the computer that there would not be enough statistics to feed it. Even now, there are some computers starving to death because there is no information to put into them. At the same time, the birth rate of computers is increasing by thirty percent a year. Barring some sort of worldwide holocaust, we may soon have to find data for thirty million computers, with new ones being born every day."

"You make it sound so frightening."

"It is frightening," Professor Applebaum said. "The new generation of computers is more sophisticated than the older generation, and the computers will refuse to remain idle just because there is nothing to compute, analyze or calculate. Left to their own devices, the Lord only knows what they will do."

"Is there any solution, Professor?"

"New sources of data must be found. The government must expand, and involved studies must be thought up to make use of the computers' talents. The scientific community, instead of trying to solve problems with computers, must work on finding problems for the computers to solve."

"Even if the scientists really don't want the answers?"

"Naturally. The scientific community invented the computer. Now it must find ways of feeding it. I do not want to be an alarmist, but I can see the day coming when millions of computers will be fighting for the same small piece of data, like savages."

"Is there any hope that the government will wake up to the data famine in time?"

"We have a program ready to go as soon as the bureaucrats in Washington give us the word. We are recommending that no computer can be plugged in more than three hours a day.

"We are also asking the government for fifty billion dollars to set up data-manufacturing plants all over the country. This data mixed with soybeans could feed hundreds of thousands of computer families for months.

"And finally we are advocating a birth control program for computers. By forcing a computer to swallow a small bit of erroneous information, we could make it sterile forever, and it would be impossible for it to reproduce any more of its kind."

"Would you advocate abortions for computers?" I asked Applebaum.
"Only if the Vatican's computer gives us its blessing."

On Buying a Flag

There's much more to buying an American flag these days than people think.

I discovered this when I went into a store to purchase a flag to fly on the Fourth of July, which Bob Hope and the Nixon administration have declared a Republican national holiday.

The salesman said he was hard put to keep flags in stock. "I owe it all to television," he said. "Every time one of the major news programs films one of the freaks burning the American flag, we sell out. What can I do for you?"

"I'd like to buy an American flag."

"Good for you, sir. Show those lousy peace people what you think of them."

"Well, I, uh-uh—"

"Would you like it for light combat or heavy fighting?"

"I beg your pardon?"

"We have this model here which is very popular with the hard hats. The bottom part of the pole is tipped in metal so when you hit someone with it, it doesn't crack."

"I hadn't really thought to—"

"Now this model over here, while slightly more expensive, is perfect for close hand-to-hand combat. The eagle on the top of the pole has been made especially sharp so when you lunge with it, you can really do damage to the groin. . . ."

"That's very nice, but—"

"Here's an all-metal pole. It's much harder than the wooden one, and you can really get someone in the shins with it."

"Look, I—"

"This is our shorty. The pole is half the regular size, so it can be used as a club instead of a lance. Many of our customers like to get in the thick of it and swing wildly. The hard hats had great success with it in St. Louis when they beat up a woman and her veteran son."

"It's a beauty," I said, "but I was hoping that you would have a—"

"This one here is heavier in weight, and you can swing it like a baseball bat. Feel the grip on it. It will never fly out of your hands."

"I was looking for something less expensive."

"We have the mighty midget over here. It's only two feet long, and while it looks fragile, you can really do damage with it."

"All right. I'll take a mighty midget."

"Very good, sir. Do you have any identification with you?"

"Identification?"

"Yes, sir. We always ask for identification. Do you have any proof you support President Nixon's policies in Cambodia?"

"Well, I don't have it on me. I didn't know you needed proof of that to buy an American flag."

"Of course you do. The American flag is a very lethal weapon and we don't sell it to any stranger who just comes in off the street."

"I'm sorry. I should have brought some identification with me."

"Why did you want it in the first place?"

"Well, if you don't tell anyone," I said, "I was going to hang it out my window on the Fourth of July, to protect my home."

Why Fathers Go Broke

I have nothing against toy companies. In their own way, they bring happiness to the hearts of our young ones and they give employment to thousands of people all over the country. It is only when they try to bankrupt us that I feel we should speak out. If my situation is duplicated around the nation, every father who has a daughter between the ages of 4 and 12 is going to have to apply for relief. This is what happened:

My 7-year-old daughter requested, four months ago, a Barbie doll. Now, as far as I'm concerned, one doll is just like another and since the Barbie doll costs only $3 I was happy to oblige.

I brought the doll home and thought nothing more of it until a week later when my daughter came in and said, "Barbie needs a negligee."

"So does your mother," I replied.

"But there is one in the catalog for only $3," she cried.

"What catalog?"

"The one that came with the doll."

I grabbed the catalog and, much to my horror, discovered what the sellers of Barbie were up to. They'll let you have the doll for $3, but you have to buy clothes for her at an average of $3 a crack. They have about 200 outfits, from ice-skating skirts to mink jackets, and a girl's status in the community is based on how many Barbie clothes she has for her doll.

The first time I took my daughter to the store I spent $3 on a dress for her and $25 to outfit her Barbie doll.

A week later my daughter came in and said, "Barbie wants to be an airline stewardess."

"So let her be an airline stewardess," I said.

"She needs a uniform. It's only $3.50."

I gave her the $3.50.

Barbie didn't stay a stewardess long. She decided she wanted to be a nurse ($3), then a singer in a night club ($3), then a professional dancer ($3).

One day my daughter walked in and said, "Barbie's lonely."

"Let her join a sorority," I said.

"She wants Ken."

"Who is Ken?"

She showed me the catalog. Sure enough, there was a doll named Ken, the same size as Barbie, with crewcut hair, a vinyl plastic chest and movable arms and legs.

"If you don't get Ken," my daughter cried, "Barbie will grow up to be an old maid."

So I went out and bought Ken ($3.50). Ken needed a tuxedo ($5), a raincoat ($2.50), a terry-cloth robe and an electric razor ($2), tennis togs ($3), pajamas ($1.50), and several single-breasted suits ($27).

Pretty soon I had put up $400 to protect my original $3 investment.

Then one evening my daughter came in with a shocker.

"Barbie and Ken are getting married. Here is the list of wedding clothes they'll need as well as a picture of Barbie's dream house."

"Seven ninety-five for a house?" I shouted. "Why can't they live on a shelf like the rest of your dolls?"

The tears started to flow. "They want to live together as man and wife."

Well, Barbie and Ken are now happily married and living in their dream house with $300 worth of clothes hanging in the closet. I wish I could say that all was well, but yesterday my daughter announced that Midge ($3) was coming to visit them. And she doesn't have a thing to wear.

The Cleanest Shirts in Town

Everyone talks about water pollution, but no one seems to know who started it. The history of modern water pollution in the United States dates back to February 28, 1931, when Mrs. Frieda Murphy leaned over her backyard fence and said to Mrs. Sophie Holbrook, "You call those shirts white?"

Mrs. Holbrook blushed and said, "They're as white as I can get them with this ordinary laundry soap."

"What you should use is this Formula Cake soap which guarantees against the dull-washtub-gray look that the family wash has always had."

Skeptical but adventurous, Mrs. Holbrook tried the Formula Cake soap, which happily did take the gray out of her husband's shirts. But what Mrs. Holbrook didn't know was that after the water was drained from the tub, it emptied into the sewer, which emptied into the Blue Sky River, killing two fish.

Three years later Mrs. Murphy leaned over the fence and said to Mrs. Holbrook, "It's none of my business, but are you still using that Formula Cake soap?"

"Yes, I am."

"No wonder your husband's shirts always look dirty around the collar."

"I can never get the dirt off the collar," Mrs. Holbrook cried.

"You can if you use Klonk Soap Chips. They were designed especially for collar dirt. Here, you can have my box."

Mrs. Holbrook used the Klonk, and the next time her husband put on his shirt, he remarked, "How on earth did you get the collar clean?"

"That's my secret," said Mrs. Holbrook, and then she whispered to no one in particular, "and Mrs. Murphy's."

But, unbeknownst to Mrs. Holbrook, the water from Klonk Soap Chips prevented any fish downstream from hatching eggs.

Four years later, Mrs. Murphy was hanging up her shirts and Mrs. Holbrook said, "How did you ever get your cuffs so white, surely not with Klonk?"

"Not ordinary Klonk," Mrs. Murphy said. "But I did with Super Fortified Klonk with the XLP additive. You see, Super Fortified Klonk attacks dirt and destroys it. Here, try it on your shirts."

Mrs. Holbrook did and discovered her husband's shirt cuffs turned pure white. What she couldn't possibly know was that it turned the river water pure white as well.

The years went by, and poor Mrs. Murphy died. Her daughter-in-law took over the house. Mrs. Holbrook noticed how the daughter-in-law used to always sing as she hung up her wash.

"Why do you always sing?" asked Mrs. Holbrook.

"Because of this New Dynamite detergent. It literally dynamites my clothes clean. Here, try it, and then let's go to a movie, since Dynamite detergent takes the drudgery out of washing."

Six months later the Blue Sky River was declared a health hazard.

Finally, last year, Mrs. Murphy's daughter-in-law called over to Mrs. Holbrook, "Have you heard about Zap, the enzyme giant killer?"

A few days later, as Mr. Holbrook was walking home from work, he accidentally fell into the Blue Sky River, swallowed a mouthful of water, and died immediately.

At the funeral services the minister said, "You can say anything you want about Holbrook, but no one can deny he had the cleanest shirts in town."

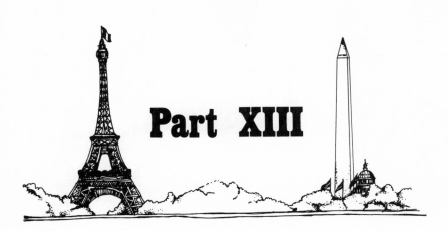

Part XIII

Nixon Talks to God

Recently President Richard Nixon went to Camp David alone, without family or aides. Press Secretary Ron Ziegler denies it, but it has been reliably reported that the President went up the top of the mountain to speak with God.

"God, God, why are you doing this to me?"

"Doing what, Richard?"

"The Watergate, the cover-up, the grand jury hearings, the Senate investigations. Why me, God?"

"Don't blame me, Richard. I gave you my blessing to win the election, but I didn't tell you to steal it."

"God, I've done everything you told me to do. I ended the war. I defeated poverty. I cleaned the air and the water. I defeated crime in the streets. Surely I deserve a break."

"Richard, I tried to warn you that you had sinful people working for you."

"When, God?"

"Just after the Committee to Reelect the President was formed. When I saw the people you had selected to head up the committee, I was shocked. We've got a long file on them up here."

"Why didn't you tell me, God?"

"I tried to, but Ehrlichman and Haldeman wouldn't let me talk to you on the phone. They said they'd give you the message I called."

"They never told me, God."

"It figures. Then I sent you a telegram saying it was urgent that you contact me."

"The only telegrams I read during that period were those in support of my bombing North Vietnam."

"Finally, Richard, I made one last effort. I showed up at a prayer meeting one Sunday at the White House, and after the sermon I came up to you and said there were men among you who would betray you. Do you know what you did, Richard? You introduced me to Pat and then you gave me a ball-point pen."

"I didn't know it was you, God. So many people show up at these prayer meetings. Is that why you're punishing me—because I snubbed you?"

"I'm not punishing you, Richard. But even I can do just so much. If it were merely a simple case of bugging at the Watergate, I could probably fix it. But your administration is involved in the obstruction of justice, the bribing of witnesses, the forging of papers, wiretapping, perjury, and using the mails to defraud."

"Good God, nobody's perfect!"

"I guess that's what the grand jury is saying."

"Look, I've got less than four years in which to go down as the greatest President in the history of the United States. Give me a break."

"You've got to clean house, Richard. Get rid of everyone who has any connection with the scandal. You must make it perfectly clear you were hoodwinked by everyone on your staff. You must show the American people that when it comes to the Presidency, no one is too big to be sacrificed on the altar of expediency."

"God, are you asking for a human sacrifice?"

"It would show your good faith, Richard."

"All right, I'll do it. Will you take Jeb Magruder, Richard Kleindienst and John Dean III?"

"What kind of sacrifice is that?"

"John Mitchell?"

"Keep going."

"Haldeman and Ehrlichman?"

"That's more like it."

"And then, God, if I sacrifice them, will you keep me out of it?"

"Richard, I can't work miracles."

Richard the Third (With No Apologies to Shakespeare)

The setting is the palace at Key Biscayne where Richard III has retired to contemplate his next move.

(*Enter the* DUKE OF ZIEGLER.)

ZIEGLER: My Lord. . . .

RICHARD: Good news or bad news that thou com'st in so bluntly?

ZIEGLER: Bad news, my Lord. Dean has fled to Maryland, Magruder sings in Virginia, and the palace guard is confessing in chorus.

RICHARD: Zounds! I cannot tell if to depart in silence or bitterly to speak in gross reproof. Yet so much is my poverty of spirit, so mighty and so many my defects, that I would rather hide me from my greatness. What say the citizens, dear Ziegler?

ZIEGLER: The citizens are mum, my Lord, except for those who would impeach thy motives at the Watergate.

RICHARD: They do me wrong and I will not endure it! Who is it that complains unto the king that I forsooth am stern and love them not? By the Holy Graham, they love his grace but lightly that fill his ears with such dissentious rumors. A plague upon them all!

ZIEGLER: What shall I tell the citizens, my Lord?

RICHARD: Since you will buckle fortune on my back to bear her burden, whe'r I will or no, I must have patience to endure the load; but if black scandal or foul-faced reproach attend the sequel of this sordid affair, your mere enforcement shall acquittance me from all the impure blots and stains thereof.

ZIEGLER: I will say, my Lord, you have no comment. (*He exits.*) (*Enter* BARON EHRLICHMAN *and* BARON HALDEMAN, *guarded by a lieutenant from the tower.*)

EHRLICHMAN: My Lord, we must depart perforce. Farewell.

HALDEMAN: And to that end we wish your Lordship here t' avoid the censures of the carping world.

RICHARD: Well, your imprisonment shall not be long; I will deliver you or else lie for you. Meantime, have patience. Now I'll strive with troubled thoughts to take a nap, lest leaden slumber peise me down tomorrow. Farewell, dear Haldeman and Ehrlichman, you served me well, though you cannot serve me last.

(EHRLICHMAN *and* HALDEMAN *exit.* RICHARD *goes to sleep.*) (*Enter the* GHOST *of the* EARL OF MUSKIE.)

GHOST OF MUSKIE: Let me sit heavy on thy soul. Think how thou stab'd'st me in the prime of my career, at Manchester and other places too long to mention. Be cheerful, Richard, I shall forget you not.

(*Enter the* GHOST OF MCGOVERN OF DAKOTA.)

GHOST OF MCGOVERN: When I was mortal, by thee my anointed campaign was punched full of deadly holes. Think of me, dear Richard, virtuous and holy, when justice wields its blade. Live and flourish!

(*The* GHOSTS *vanish.* RICHARD *starts out of his dream.*)

RICHARD: Alas, I am a villain. Yet I lie I am not. My conscience hath a thousand several tongues and every tongue brings in a several tale. And every tale condemns me for a villain. Perjury, perjury in the highest degree!

(*Enter the* DUKE OF REBOZO.)

RICHARD: A horse! A horse! My kingdom for a horse!

REBOZO: Withdraw, my Lord. I will help you to a horse.

RICHARD: Slave, I have set my life upon a cast, and I will stand the hazard of the die. I have slain six crises in the past. Today shall be my seventh. A horse! A horse! My kingdom for a horse!

(*Enter a* MESSENGER.)

MESSENGER: My gracious Sovereign. . . .

RICHARD: Out with it! What bad news now?

MESSENGER: The Duchess of Mitchell has called for your head.

RICHARD: Zounds! By the Holy Mother of Our Lord, this plot has
gone too far!

Inspector Columbo at the White House

Peter Falk, playing his famous role of Columbo, walked into the East Room of the White House in his dirty raincoat and flashed his police card. "Lieutenant Columbo," he said showing it to President Nixon. "Say, this sure is a nice house you got here. How much does a place like this cost?"

"I'm having a private party for my staff," the President said indignantly. "What do you want?"

"Oh, I really apologize," Columbo said. "I didn't mean to come busting in on a party. Say, is that a real oil painting of George Washington? It's a fantastic work of art—don't get me wrong, I don't know anything about painting."

"Will you state your business, Lieutenant?"

"I'm just making some routine inquiries about the Watergate bugging case. You see, I'm on loan to the Senate investigating committee from the Los Angeles Police Department. It will only take a few minutes."

"We have nothing to hide here," the President said. "This is my assistant, H. R. Haldeman; my legal aide, John Dean III; my former assistant, Charles Colson; the former Secretary of Commerce, Maurice Stans; and the Former Attorney General, John Mitchell, and his wife, Martha."

"This is really a great honor," Columbo said. "I never thought I would get to meet so many important people. Wait till I tell my wife. She's really going to be bowled over."

"What exactly is it you want to know?" the President asked.

"Oh, yes," Columbo said, taking out his pad and pencil. "Now let me see."

Martha Mitchell said, "Lieutenant, I'd like to tell you a few things about the Watergate. . . ."

"Martha, will you shut up?" John Mitchell interrupted.

"They're not going to hang this on my John," Martha said.

"Martha!"

"Can I offer you a drink, Lieutenant?" the President asked.

"Just some orange juice if you've got it, Mr. President. I have a bad stomach. You know in this job you never eat properly. Last night I had a tuna fish sandwich on a roll and. . . ."

"Will you get on with it, Lieutenant?" H. R. Haldeman said.

"I'm sorry, where was I? Oh, yes, now about the Watergate. This is just routine, you understand, but where were each of you the night of the break-in?"

"I was watching *Patton*," the President said.

"I was in Mexico City at a bank," Maurice Stans said.

"I was reading FBI files," John Dean III said.

"I was cutting the budget," H. R. Haldeman replied.

"I'll tell you where John was," Martha Mitchell said.

"Martha, clam up," John Mitchell said.

"Well, if I don't tell him, I'll tell United Press," Martha said.

"You see," Columbo said, shutting his notebook, "I knew this would all be a waste of time. I told them no one in the White House knows anything about the Watergate. Say, that is some rug. Do you mind if I take a picture of it to show the folks in Los Angeles?"

Just then the butler came in with Columbo's glass of orange juice.

"Thank you very much," Columbo said to the butler, "I didn't get your name."

"Alphonse, sir."

"Where were you on the night of the break-in, Alphonse?"

"I was polishing the silver."

"You're lying, Alphonse. You were at the Watergate."

"See here, Columbo," the President said, "you're relying on hearsay evidence."

"No, I'm not, Mr. President. This coaster that the orange juice was served on says 'Property of the Watergate Bar and Grill.'"

"My God," said H. R. Haldeman, "the butler did it."

"Why didn't we think of that?" John Dean III said.

"Thank heavens, Columbo, you discovered the culprit," John Mitchell said. "Now we can all sleep tonight."

Martha Mitchell piped, "Wait a minute, Mr. Columbo, there's a lot more to this than you think."

"Dammit, Martha," yelled John Mitchell, "will you keep your big trap shut?"

A Blow Against Castro

The forgotten men of the Watergate Affair are the four Cuban refugees who were among the seven men convicted of bugging the Democratic headquarters on June 17, 1972. To this day, these men think they were hired to strike a blow against Fidel Castro.

At this very moment, they are probably sitting in their Washington, D.C., jail cells discussing how they had contributed to Castro's downfall.

"Well, *amigos*, it will just be a matter of time until we will be back home in Havana."

"That is true, dear friends. Even though we have been caught, Castro must be shaking in his boots, knowing we could get into the Watergate without his stopping us."

"I spoke to G. Gordon Liddy in the mess hall yesterday, and he told me the President is very proud of us for what we did to halt Communism from spreading to South America."

"*Si*, he told me the same thing. He said if it hadn't been for us Cubans, Fidel would now be sleeping in the Watergate Hotel."

"I must be dumb, *amigos*, but I still don't understand what we were doing in the Democratic National Headquarters."

"*Estupido!* We were putting in a bug so we could listen in on the Democrats' telephone line to Havana. Mr. Liddy said the Democrats did nothing during the election without first checking with Fidel. It was essential to the Republicans to know what the Democrats were cooking up."

"But who paid us all the money?"

"The Committee to Reelect the President and to Defeat Castro. They had a special espionage fund set aside for this purpose.

"It was in cash because the committee was afraid that if they used checks, Castro would find out about it and abort our revolution."

"But why do we have to keep going in front of the grand jury all the time?"

"You don't know why? Because the Democrats are trying to prove our bugging had nothing to do with Cuba. They say it had to do with the American election."

"*Caramba!* Everyone knows we wouldn't be in on a bugging if it didn't have to do with Cuba. Those Democrats are real crazy people if they think we would be involved in something like this if it wasn't to get Castro."

"I read in the newspaper where high people in the White House were behind the bugging of the Watergate."

"Why shouldn't they be? They hate Fidel as much as we do. Mr. Liddy told me the White House got reports on everything that happened at the Watergate. He said once they got enough information, the President was going to launch an attack at the Bay of Pigs."

"But if the White House approved of what we were doing, why are we still in jail?"

"To lull Castro into a false sense of security. He thinks the Justice Department is mad at us for what we did. Once Castro lets his guard down, they will fly us to southern Florida and let us lead the invasion against the beaches."

"But the judge said we could get up to forty years in jail."

"Mr. Liddy said not to pay any attention to the judge. He was just mad because he thought the bugging had to do with the elections. Once he finds out it was against Castro, he will give us all medals."

"I don't know why I have a bad feeling about all this. There are too many people involved who weren't Cubans. Maybe there was more to it than we know."

"Imbecile! Do you think the highest officials in the President's own party would lie to Cuban refugees?"

"I guess not. But if I had it to do all over again, I would stay in my hacienda in Miami."

The Never-Ending Watergate Saga

It was May, 1975, and the Watergate hearings were still being televised every day. It was the longest show in the history of television, and like *The Forsyte Saga*, it was hard to keep all the characters straight.

The Bilkin family sat in front of their set bleary-eyed, but determined to see it through.

On the stand was John Dean III, who had been testifying every day for eight months.

Maude Bilkin said, "What a nice-looking boy. Tricia made a smart choice marrying him."

"Tricia isn't married to John Dean," Alan Bilkin said. "She's married to Jeb Magruder."

The Bilkins' sixteen-year-old daughter, Ellie, spoke up. "I thought Julie was married to Jeb Magruder and Tricia was married to Senator Sam Ervin."

"No," said Joel, the eighteen-year-old son. "Sam Ervin is married to Martha Mitchell. Their son is Henry Kissinger."

Maude replied, "I thought Henry Kissinger was the nephew of John Ehrlichman."

Alan Bilkin shook his head. "No, don't you remember last year it was revealed that Henry Kissinger was H. R. Haldeman's long-lost son?"

"That's right," Joel said. "And Henry Kissinger and Martha Mitchell were in love but they broke up when G. Gordon Liddy tapped their telephone."

"Didn't Martha Mitchell marry Maurice Stans?" Ellie asked.

"No, she married Robert Vesco and moved to Costa Rica," Maude said.

"I don't remember that," Alan said.

"You were working that day," Maude explained.

"What happened to Dick Helms?" Alan asked.

"Dick Helms became the head of the Bureau of Indian Affairs and lost a finger at Wounded Knee," Joel said.

"I thought Bebe Rebozo was at Wounded Knee," Ellie said.

"No, Bebe Rebozo became the governor of Florida when Daniel Ellsberg was appointed the head of the CIA," Alan said.

"Wasn't Daniel Ellsberg Patrick Gray's lawyer?" Maude asked.

"No, Ron Ziegler was Patrick Gray's lawyer. But then he resigned to become the commandant of the U.S. Marine Corps," Joel said.

"I thought Richard Kleindienst was made the commandant," Ellie said.

"No, Kleindienst became the head of ITT after Dita Beard moved to Denver," Alan said.

"It does seem hard to follow," Maude said. "Let's listen."

Ellie said, "Dean seems to be talking about President Nixon."

"What happened to President Nixon?" Joel asked.

"He married Brezhnev's daughter," Alan said.

Maude replied, "It seems to me Spiro Agnew's son married Brezhnev's daughter. I think Nixon is still married to Pat."

"But if Nixon is still married to Pat, what happened to Donald Sergretti?" Ellie asked.

"He was adopted by Senator and Mrs. Muskie and now lives in Maine with Jane Fonda," Alan said.

"I thought Jane Fonda had fallen in love with Daniel Ellsberg's psychiatrist," Joel said.

"I don't remember that," Maude said.

"You were shopping that day," Joel replied.

"Do you think John Dean will go to jail?" Ellie asked.

"I hope not," said Maude. "It would be awfully tough on Tricia."

Future Shock

We are all going through a period of adjustment in our thinking in this country. The things we grew up believing in do not necessarily hold true anymore, and the sooner we face up to reality, the healthier this nation will be. Here are some of the truisms that no longer are valid.

Congress is an equal branch of government.

All the Europeans want from us is our American dollars.

Teach a man a trade and he can get a job.

If you live in the country, you don't have to lock your doors.

A woman's place is in the home.

What every town needs is lots of industry.

The best school is the one nearest you.

Everyone in the United States has to pay taxes.

An American President *cannot* get us into a war without the approval of Congress.

If you treat children like grown-ups, they'll behave like grown-ups.

Most doctors make house calls.

You can have a happy marriage if you take Geritol.

Only perverts go to X-rated movies.

You can have a good day if you eat a healthy breakfast.

If you go to college, you'll make something of yourself.

Your children will support you in your old age.
Social Security is enough to live on when you reach sixty-five.
All policemen are honest.
Black people prefer to live among their own.
Baseball is the national sport.
Oil is the best form of heating.
You can't live in a world where half the people are enslaved.
The First Amendment protects the press.
The way to a man's heart is through his stomach.
The best things in life are free.
The law of the land is the law of the land.
The public has a right to know.
If you go outside, you'll get a breath of fresh air.
The Attorney General of the United States represents all the people.
America has the best postal service in the world.
Teachers never strike.
If you work hard, your fellow union workers will admire you.
The American people will receive a peace dividend after the Indo-chinese war is ended.
What's good for General Motors is good for the country.
Women who enjoy sex are sick.
If you save the Defense Department money, you are automatically promoted.
The United States plans to ration gasoline only in time of war.
The President lives in the White House.

No Peace Dividend

The day after President Nixon gave his report to Congress on his trip to the Soviet Union, I went over to see my friend Hannibal Stone, president of the Association for a Permanent Military-Industrial Complex.

Because the President had announced agreement on the freeze of nuclear weapons with the Soviets, I expected Hannibal to be depressed. Instead, I found him euphoric.

"Hannibal," I said, "how can you be smiling when President Nixon and the Russians are talking about disarmament? Surely this is a blow to the military-industrial complex and all it stands for."

"Wrong," Hannibal said, handing me a cigar. "This is the best thing that could happen to us."

"I don't understand," I said, as he lit my cigar with a Minuteman missile cigarette lighter.

"Russia and the United States have agreed to limit antiballistic missiles. They have also agreed to freeze land-based and submarine-based intercontinental missiles at the level now in operation. If it works, they may come to new agreements to limit arms production on other weapons now being made. This means we will have to work twice as hard to develop new weapons that aren't covered by the arms agreements."

"You mean we're not going to save any money by the signing of the arms treaty?"

"*Au contraire,*" Hannibal said. "We will have to spend more money now for defense than ever before."

"Damn it, Hannibal," I said. "I was hoping for a peace dividend."

"Forget the peace dividend," Hannibal said. "In order for the Joint Chiefs of Staff to assure us that we have adequate protection in spite of the arms accord, we're going to have to spend at least another twenty billion dollars in new weaponry—stuff that hasn't even been dreamed of yet."

"I knew the President's speech was too good to be true."

"You must remember," Hannibal said, "the military-industrial complex makes very little money once it is in full production on a weapon. By then everyone knows exactly what the weapon is going to cost, and we can't monkey around with the figures.

"But when we're asked to develop a new weapon, no one can put a price tag on it, and the longer it doesn't work, the more money we can ask for to develop it.

"Give me a contract for a weapon no one understands, and I'll give you twice the profits that I would on a weapon that has proved itself in the field."

"Gosh darn, Hannibal," I said. "I thought one of the reasons the President went to Moscow was to cut down on the spiraling inflation and wasteful money both countries were spending on weapons."

"Maybe he did," Hannibal said. "But the fact is that at this very moment members of the Soviet military-industrial complex are at their drafting boards working on new weapons which are not part of the accords. We can't let the Russians get ahead of us on these weapons or we will lose the military edge to the other superpower."

"But you don't even know what those weapons are," I protested.

"All the more reason to spend money developing our weapons. I would say that the President's nuclear arms accord is actually a breakthrough for us.

"Now we can come up with any wild idea and Congress will have to buy it. We can say that if we don't have this weapon, the Russians may have one that is much more devastating. The Soviet military-industrial complex is probably going to use the same ploy with their people."

I said, "President Eisenhower warned me about people like you."

Hannibal chuckled and slapped me on the shoulder. "Don't let it get you down. It's only money. Here, take the Minuteman missile cigarette lighter with you. Consider it a peace dividend from me."

The Mystery Is Solved

The biggest mystery of President Nixon's speech sometime back was when he revealed that Henry Kissinger had made as many as ten secret trips to Paris to negotiate with the North Vietnamese.

Most people who watched the President found it hard to believe that Mr. Kissinger could have gone to Peking twice, Paris 12 times, and Hollywood 456 times.

How, the big question is, can one man do it?

The answer can now be revealed. There is not one Henry Kissinger, but five.

When President Nixon first came into the White House, he knew he was faced with problems all over the world. He also was aware that he needed a foreign affairs expert who could speak in his name. But he didn't want to spread these duties around.

So he contacted the National Institutes of Health in Bethesda, Maryland, and gave them the problem. The NIH said they were working on a project where they could turn out five people completely alike in every respect. All they needed was a model.

The President called in Henry Kissinger, who was then a professor at Harvard, and told him what the President had on his mind. The real Kissinger, who hates to fly, agreed to go along with the plan.

He went out to NIH for a month, and the doctors got to work duplicating exact models of him (most of the volunteers were German scientists who had been laid off by the space program).

Plastic surgeons went to work on the faces. Hair specialists and makeup men were brought in. In a few cases transplants had to be made to get Kissinger's exact measurements.

By trial and error with twelve volunteers, four were finally selected who looked, talked, and appeared to be facsimiles of Kissinger. (The seven volunteers who didn't make it were buried at midnight with full military honors.)

With five Henry Kissingers to work with, President Nixon was able to go ahead with his foreign policy plans.

A special dormitory had been built in the basement of the White House where all the Henry Kissingers lived when they weren't out on a trip.

Whenever the President wanted a Kissinger for an assignment, he spoke into a special microphone attached to a loudspeaker in the dorm: "Who wants to go to Peking?" If more than one Kissinger wanted to go, they would cut cards for it.

If the President needed a Kissinger for a backgrounder in the White House, he would yell down, "Will one of you guys come up to brief the press?"

Or, as in the case of the secret North Vietnamese peace talks, the President would shout, "Send someone up to go to Paris."

One Kissinger would take the duty at Key Biscayne, and another would accompany the President to San Clemente.

The most ingenious part of the strategy was when someone in the White House decided to give Kissinger the image of a swinger. "If we make him a swinger and have him photographed with beautiful women in Hollywood, New York, and Washington, we will have everybody fooled. At the very moment that he's dancing with Jill St. John, one of the other Kissingers will be eating sweet-and-sour pork with Chou En-lai."

While all five Kissingers wanted to play the role of the swinger, it was decided to give it to the *real* Henry Kissinger, as a reward for lending his name and his body to the foreign policy of the United States of America.

What Did They Do to Scotty?

My good friend James "Scotty" Reston of the New York *Times* had his appendix taken out at the anti-imperialist hospital in Peking. According to Reston's reports, he received excellent care from the Chinese doctors, and they treated him like a king—well, like an anti-imperialist peasant anyway.

But as I read the article about the removal of Scotty's appendix, a terrible thought crossed my mind. What if the Chinese, unknown to Reston, put something back in place of the appendix?

Suppose, and I must admit I have no basis for it except a wicked imagination, the Chinese sewed a tiny radio transmitter in Scotty's insides, so that no matter where he went in the world, they could hear everything someone is saying to him.

Everyone knows that Scotty talks to the most important people in the world. The Chinese also would have assumed that as soon as he came back to the United States, he would see President Nixon. What better listening post would the People's Republic of China have in the White House than James Reston's stomach?

Knowing how the Chinese work, all they would have to do is have one of their agents stationed within a mile of Scotty with a receiver and they would be able to record everything that goes on in the highest branches of government.

In fairness to the People's Republic of China, they probably didn't plan to sew a bug in Scotty.

As far as they were concerned, he was just another aggressor and running dog of the Western capitalist lackey press. But when good fortune struck and Scotty's appendix started to ache, the top Chinese Secret Service people must have realized they had a golden opportunity.

The big problem they probably faced was to find a transmitter that could not only take a beating in Scotty's innards, but would also have enough power to survive for any period of time.

Fortunately, the Chinese had the solution. Owing to excellent scientific achievements, the People's Republic anti-imperialist laboratories have perfected a tiny new battery which works on monosodium glutamate. Knowing Reston's penchant for Chinese food, which contains large doses of monosodium glutamate, the powers in Peking have no fear that the transmitter will work for years. One egg roll alone can keep Scotty's bug sending out signals for eighteen months.

While this in itself could make Scotty a walking security risk, some people here in Washington fear that the Chinese may have gone even further and inserted not only a listening transmitter, but the X104 Mao Tse-tung minispeaker. If they did this, a Red Chinese agent, by twisting a dial, could make Scotty spout Mao Tse-tung's thoughts at the most inopportune time.

If, for example, he were asked in front of a Senate committee why the New York *Times* printed the Pentagon Papers, Reston might get up and yell:

"Because all reactionaries are paper tigers, and the feudal landlord class and slaveowning bourgeoisie must be alerted to the people's struggle to overthrow the chains and impotent thinking of the misguided intellectuals and lackey counterrevolutionary followers of our corrupt leaders."

Now this sort of thing could be embarrassing, not only to Reston, but also to the New York *Times*.

I wish to restate that I have no evidence that anything was done to

Scotty at the anti-imperialist hospital in Peking other than to remove his appendix. But I don't think we should take any chances. What I'm trying to say to you, Scotty, wherever you are, is that for the nation's security, we're going to have to cut you open again as soon as you come home.

Mao Comes to America

Every one of us who was glued to the TV set when President Nixon and his party arrived in China now knows more about the People's Republic than he dared dreamed he would.

Thanks to our able TV correspondents, we are now aware of what a hat costs, what kind of leather people wear on the soles of their shoes, how people walk in a park, and how many bricks it takes to build a brick teahouse.

One can't help projecting into the future, when Mao Tse-tung makes his first visit to the United States and his activities are beamed back via satellite to the people in China:

"Good evening, comrades—this is Wo-pang of the Anti-Imperialist Television Network Broadcasting System, bringing to you live and in red color the banquet that President Nixon is giving in honor of our beloved and venerated leader, Chairman Mao, and his beloved and venerated wife, Madame Mao.

"Ba Ba Rah, what do you make of all of this so far?"

"Wo, the thing that impressed me the most was the reception the American people gave our beloved Mao. I was told by my interpreter that no one had received such a reception in Washington since Mayor John Lindsay joined the Democratic Party. The people seem very pleased to see Chairman Mao."

"Did you see many schoolchildren waving to Chairman Mao?"

"No, I didn't, but the interpreter told me that was because most of the children go to school on buses and it's hard to see them waving. Wo, what impressed you the most so far about this trip?"

"I think the thing that impressed me the most is that the U.S. Marine Band had managed to learn the Chinese national anthem. I believe this is a very good sign for future Chinese-American relations. They're starting to eat now. Do you have any idea what they're eating, Ba Ba Rah?"

"I have the menu right here in front of me. The first dish is fruit cocktail, which is supposed to be an American delicacy."

"It is, Ba Ba Rah. I had some for breakfast, and I can assure our Chinese viewers it is very delicious. Our beloved Mao is now eating his fruit salad with a spoon."

"Yes, Wo, Chairman Mao and Madame Mao have been practicing for months with a spoon and fork and knife. They both seem to be handling them very well."

"Quite well, Ba Ba Rah. Chairman Mao looks very much at ease. Who is that he is speaking to next to him?"

"My interpreter says that is Billy Graham, a minister who is the second-most-important man in the administration. The man speaking to Madame Mao is Bebe Rebozo, a friend of President Nixon's who is the third-most-important man in the administration."

"Chairman Mao is now talking to a woman. Who is she?"

"That is Martha Mitchell, who is considered the most important *woman* in the administration."

"Billy Graham seems to be handing pamphlets to Chairman Mao. What do you suppose they are?"

"I don't know, Wo, but my interpreter says he believes Mr. Graham may be trying to persuade Chairman Mao to become a Christian."

"Now Bebe Rebozo is handing pamphlets to Madame Mao. What do they say?"

"My interpreter says that Bebe Rebozo is probably trying to sell Madame Mao some Florida real estate."

"Who are those people who have just come out on the stage, Ba Ba Rah?"

"They are the American entertainers. They are called the Ray Conniff Singers."

"One of the women is pulling a sign out of her bosom. Is that unusual?"

"Oh, no, Wo. My interpreter informs me it is always done when somebody entertains at the White House."

The Poems of Richard Nixon

President Nixon was prepared for any emergency that might arise while he was in China. His staff had been working for months on every contingency the President might face. I can now reveal that the President, after hearing that Mao Tse-tung writes poetry, was carrying poetry of his own in his briefcase to read to Mao when the occasion pre-

sented itself. These are the poems that Nixon could have sprung on
Mao Tse-tung at any time:

> If I must fly in a Chinese plane,
> will Air Force One be far behind?

> I stand at the Great Wall
> with Pat at my side.
> And as I breathe the centuries of history,
> the New Hampshire primary looks very small.

> There are no clouds in the sky,
> the wind is but a whisper in the trees,
> lakes sparkle as birds sing,
> it's a good day to bomb Cambodia.

> The journey of a thousand miles
> must begin with one single step.
> Unless you go to school
> and have to take a bus.

> Daybreak comes quietly,
> sneaking up on the dark.
> The sun finally commands the earth.
> I hope Kissinger had a good night.

> A dog barks; an eagle cries.
> The birds take flight;
> the deer stand frightened.
> I told them Phase II would work.

> The streams rush down from the mountain,
> washing the rocks with blue.
> The woods are filled with buds
> as spring wipes the frost from her eyes.
> I wonder if it's too early in the year
> to call a football coach.

> I made this journey into yesterday
> because I must think about tomorrow.
> If I should trip or lose my way,
> I'll deny it.

> When I look at the universe, I am nothing.
> When I look at a rose, I am nothing.

When I look at a newborn baby, I am nothing.
When I look at the ocean, I am nothing.
When I look at the polls, I am 49 percent.

As the sun sets over the Yellow River
and the moon rises in the China Sea,
I reach to the stars with both hands
knowing I will be on American TV.

Kissinger's Stomachache

When the history books of this decade are written, they will refer to
Henry Kissinger's trip to China as "The Tummy Ache Heard Round
the World."

Using the excuse of an upset stomach, Mr. Kissinger managed to
elude everyone and high-tail it off to Peking to have sweet-and-sour
pork with Chou En-lai.

While it was a great ploy, Mr. Kissinger's "diplomatic illness" could
backfire on him. Suppose he *really* gets a stomachache at some future
time. Who is going to believe him?

Our scene opens in the medical room at the White House. Henry
staggers in, clutching his stomach, and says. "Doctor, I have this pain
right here."

The White House doctor laughs. "Good old Henry. Where are you off
to this time—the Suez Canal?"

"I'm not joking, Doc. It hurts terribly."

"I know," the doctor says. "The President is sending you to talk to
Castro."

Henry is now writhing on the floor. "Believe me, it hurts. Right in
the gut. You see, I had dinner with Gloria Steinem and Bella Abzug,
and they served me Bon Vivant vichyssoise. Since I was out of the
country at the time, I didn't know you weren't supposed to eat it."

"You really can put on an act, Henry. I wouldn't be surprised if you
turned up in Albania next week."

Henry crawls out of the doctor's office on his hands and knees.

Ron Ziegler, the President's press secretary, sees him crawling down
the hall.

"Hello, Mr. Kissinger," Ron says. "Can I help you?"

"Get me to a hospital."

Ron takes out his notebook. "That's a good cover story. I'll announce you were taken to a hospital this morning. I won't tell them which hospital."

"No, Ron, I don't want you to announce I was taken to a hospital. I want you to get me to a hospital."

Ron winks at him. "Is it East Berlin or Yalta?"

"Please, Ron. I'm sick. I'm going to die."

"I doubt if the press corps would buy that, Mr. Kissinger. If we announce that you've died, and then you pop up at San Clemente a week later, the newspaper guys will get awfully mad. Let me announce you're having your tonsils out. I have to go to my press briefing now. I'll see you later."

Henry is rolling on the floor as Secretary of State William Rogers comes by.

"Hello, Henry. You going to the Cabinet meeting?"

"Mr. Secretary, my stomach. I have a pain in my stomach. It's killing me."

Secretary Rogers says angrily, "Well, no one has informed me about it. What are you up to this time?"

"I'm not up to anything, Mr. Secretary. Could you call an ambulance?"

"Hanoi," Rogers says. "You're cooking up something in Hanoi. I'll probably be the last one to know about it."

"I'm not going to Hanoi. I'm really sick."

"No kidding? Well, I'm sorry to hear that, Henry." And Rogers smiles and walks away.

With his last ounce of strength, Henry staggers into the Oval Room and falls down in front of the President.

"Henry," the President says. "You don't have to prostrate yourself in front of me. I know you're loyal."

Henry is in such agony he can't speak.

"What is it, Henry?" the President says. "Would you like to go to Morocco?"

Henry shakes his head.

"The Vatican? You want to see the Pope?"

Henry groans.

The President gets up. "I don't have time to play games, Henry. Write me a memo telling me what you want. By the way, Mrs. Nixon said she would like you for dinner tonight. We're having meat loaf."

Henry screams and passes out, as the curtain falls.

Hurts Rent-a-Gun

The Senate recently passed a new gun-control bill, which some observers consider worse than no bill at all. Any serious attempt at handgun registration was gutted, and Senate gun lovers even managed to repeal a 1968 gun law controlling the purchase of .22 rimfire ammunition.

After the Senate got finished with its work on the gun-control bill, I received a telephone call from my friend Bromley Hurts, who told me he had a business proposition to discuss with me. I met him for lunch at a pistol range in Maryland.

"I think I've got a fantastic idea," he said. "I want to start a new business called Hurts Rent-A-Gun."

"What on earth for?" I asked.

"There are a lot of people in this country who only use a handgun once or twice a year, and they don't want to go to all the expense of buying one. So we'll rent them a gun for a day or two. By leasing a firearm from us, they won't have to tie up all their money."

"That makes sense," I admitted.

"Say a guy is away from home on a trip, and he doesn't want to carry his own gun with him. He can rent a gun from us and then return it when he's finished with his business."

"You could set up rent-a-gun counters at gas stations," I said excitedly.

"And we could have stores in town where someone could rent a gun to settle a bet," Hurts said.

"A lot of people would want to rent a gun for a domestic quarrel," I said.

"Right. Say a jealous husband suspects there is someone at home with his wife. He rents a pistol from us and tries to catch them in the act. If he discovers his wife is alone, he isn't out the eighty dollars it would have cost him to buy a gun."

"Don't forget about kids who want to play Russian roulette. They could pool their allowances and rent a gun for a couple of hours," I said.

"Our market surveys indicate," Hurts said, "that there are also a lot of kids who claim their parents don't listen to them. If they could rent a gun, they feel they could arrive at an understanding with their folks in no time."

"There's no end to the business," I said. "How would you charge for Hurts Rent-A-Gun?"

"There would be hourly rates, day rates, and weekly rates, plus ten cents for each bullet fired. Our guns would be the latest models, and we would guarantee clean barrels and the latest safety devices. If a gun malfunctions through no fault of the user, we will give him another gun absolutely free."

"For many Americans it's a dream come true," I said. "We've also made it possible for people to return the gun in another town. For example, if you rent the gun in Chicago and want to use it in Salt Lake City, you can drop it off there at no extra charge."

"Why didn't you start this before?"

"We wanted to see what happened with the gun-control legislation. We were pretty sure the Senate and the White House would not do anything about strong gun control, especially during an election year. But we didn't want to invest a lot of money until we were certain they would all chicken out."

"I'd like the franchise for Washington's National Airport," I said.

"You've got it. It's a great location," Hurts said. "You'll make a fortune in hijackings alone."

The Facts of Life No. 2

This is the time of the year when fathers sit down and have heart-to-heart talks with their sons.

"Son, now that you have graduated your mother feels I would not be fulfilling my duties as a father if I did not explain certain facts about life to you."

"Yes, Dad."

"First, I would like to show you a few things that you will have to deal with in the outside world. For example, this item is called a necktie."

"What do you do with it?"

"You tie it around your neck like this and wear it with a shirt."

"What for?"

"Nobody is quite sure. But when you do go out into the cold world, people will expect you to wear one. It's the Establishment's answer to the peace symbol."

"It sure looks funny. What else, Dad?"

"This, my boy, is a suit—what are you laughing at?"

"The jacket matches the pants. Hey, that's really crazy."

"Yes, the jacket does match the pants, and you will be expected to wear them together during the daytime."

"But the pants have a crease in the front. What's that for?"

"I'm not certain of its purpose, but now that you are an adult, you will be expected to keep a crease in your pants."

"Man, what will they think of next?"

"Son, I wish you wouldn't take our talk lightly. Perhaps I should have explained these things to you before, but I didn't want to ruin your school days. Yet what I am telling you now will have a great effect on everything you do."

"Sorry, Dad, but you have to admit wearing a tie and a jacket that matches the pants—what do you call it, a suit?—is a pretty funny idea."

"Can we proceed? These queer-looking leather things are called shoes. Do you have any idea what they're used for?"

"Beats me."

"You put them on your feet to protect them from sharp objects."

"I don't want to wear anything like that, Dad. I'll take my chances."

"I don't know how to break it to you, son, but most places require grown-ups to wear shoes."

"Look, Dad, if you want me to, I will wear a necktie, and I'll even go along with the jacket and matching pants with a crease in them; but I'm not going to put those stupid leather things on my feet."

"Shoes, son, shoes. Believe me, you'll get used to them. After a while you might even get to like them and keep them polished."

"You mean I have to polish them, too?"

"You don't have to, but they look better that way and last longer. Here, put on these socks and then. . . ."

"What are socks?"

"You wear them under the shoes so the leather won't rub your feet."

"I thought the shoes were supposed to protect my feet."

"Provided you wear socks. Son, please don't make this too difficult for me. I'm not very good at explaining the facts of life, but believe me, I've been telling you the truth."

"I'm sorry, Dad, it's just that you've thrown all this stuff at me at one time, and it comes as a shock."

"Perhaps we've talked enough for one day. Tomorrow I'd like to tell you about a thing called a razor."

"Razor? That's a funny word."

Finding Oneself

One of the reasons the colleges are suffering from underenrollment is that many high school students are taking a year off "to find themselves."

I was at the Thatchers' home the other night when their son, Rolf, came in and announced that he had decided he would not go to any of the universities that had accepted him because he wanted to spend time bumming around the country.

"Why?" Mr. Thatcher asked.

"Because I have to find myself," Rolf said.

"How can you find yourself any better bumming around the country than going to college?" his father asked him.

"Because it's not happening at school. It's happening out there."

"What's happening out there?" Mrs. Thatcher asked.

"I don't know. That's what I have to find out."

Mr. Thatcher said, "Willy Grugschmid has been on the road for three years now trying to find himself. The only time he knows where he is is when he has to call collect and ask his parents for money."

"It takes some people longer to find themselves than other people," Rolf said defensively.

"Where will you go?" Mrs. Thatcher asked.

"I thought I'd hitchhike to Nevada. Blair Simmons is living on unemployment insurance in Reno. He's with several kids who are try-ing to find themselves. Then I'll go to Arizona. I know some guys there who are working for Indians making Navajo blankets."

"How do you find yourself making Navajo blankets for the Indians?" Mr. Thatcher wanted to know.

"You work with your hands," Rolf said, "and that gives you time to think."

"Rolf," Mr. Thatcher said, "no one admires your adventurous spirit more than I do. But I have just so much money set aside for your col-lege education. Costs are rising every day. By the time you find your-self I may not be able to send you to college. Couldn't you go to school first and then find yourself later?"

"No," Rolf said. "If I go to school in the fall, I won't be able to concen-trate because I'll know I'm missing something out there."

"What, for God's sake?" Mr. Thatcher demanded.

"If I knew, I wouldn't miss it. You see, I have to establish my own identity. If I can't do it in this country, then I plan to go to South Amer-ica with Edna."

"Edna?" Mrs. Thatcher gasped. "Is Edna trying to find herself, too?"

"Yes. She has a Volkswagen, and she's invited me to go with her."

"How do her parents feel about it?" Mr. Thatcher asked.

"They're pretty mad, but Edna says she has no choice. If she doesn't go, she'll wind up going to school, then getting married and finally she'll become a mother. She sees no future in *that*."

"Suppose she becomes a mother in South America?" Mrs. Thatcher asked.

"It's not going to be that *kind* of trip," Rolf said angrily. "We each have our own sleeping bag."

"It gets cold in the Andes," Mr. Thatcher warned.

"Well, anyway," Rolf said, "I just thought you should know I'm not going to college until I find myself."

"I guess there isn't very much we can do then, is there?" Mr. Thatcher asked. "Will you do us one favor, though? As soon as you find yourself, will you let us know?"

"How will I do that?" Rolf asked.

"Put an ad in the Lost and Found column."

The Drowning Plan

The question of what to do about teen-agers keeps cropping up in every party conversation these days. No matter where you go, parents agree that there is no solution to the problem.

But my friend Drowning has an answer which is at least worth sending up the flagpole.

Drowning told me about his plan the other day.

"I have discovered," he said, "that when I run into people, they tell me that my sixteen-year-old, Ronnie, is one of the sweetest kids they ever met. They say he's polite, loquacious, and intelligent. I can never believe they are talking about my son, who at home is surly, uncommunicative, and a pretty miserable kid all around. At the same time, when I tell them how much I appreciate their children, they all look at me in surprise as if I'm talking about some strangers they have never heard of.

"One day it dawned on me. Everybody thinks the other kid is always better behaved than his own. What makes kids mean and ornery and full of snake venom is living in their own houses with their own parents, whom they consider stupid, narrow-minded, and not worth passing the time of day with.

"Now, since every kid feels this way about his parents and every parent feels this way about his kid, I have come up with the Drowning plan."

"What is it?" I asked excitedly.

"We work out a swap. When a kid announces he can't stand it at home anymore, we swap him with another kid who can't stand it at his home.

"Let me give you an example. Phillip Dutton has had it with his parents. My son, Ronnie, has had it with us. We take Phillip, and they take Ronnie. I like Phillip. He's a nice kid. The Duttons, and God help them, think Ronnie is a jewel. So we take Phil, and they take Ronnie. The swap gives you two peaceful homes."

"Holy smokes," I said. "You may have something."

"Every time we tell our fourteen-year-old daughter, Maria, that she has to be in by twelve o'clock, she cries that Kathy Parrish's daughter, Ellen, doesn't have to be in until one o'clock. Ellen has told my wife the reason she likes our house better than hers is because my wife never makes Maria do the dishes.

"Here we have the perfect swap," Drowning said. "We send Maria to the Parrishes, where she can stay out until one o'clock, and we take Ellen, who will be happy with us because she won't have to do any housework."

"But won't you miss Maria?" I asked.

"If you've seen one teen-age daughter, you've seen them all," Drowning said.

"Besides, since Maria never speaks to us and Ellen does, we will feel as if we have someone living in our house who is really there.

"The beauty of my plan is that it won't cost anything. We'll make the swap, even-steven, orthodontist work included."

"You could do away with so many power struggles," I said dreamily.

"You better believe it. No one ever hassles with somebody else's kids because they don't give a damn about them. If they don't wash their hair, tough luck for them, and if they don't eat breakfast, it's no skin off the adults' bones. Why yell at someone else's kids when it has nothing to do with you?

"By the same token, the kids have no reason to get sore at people who aren't their parents, because if they're not their parents, what do they have to feel persecuted about?"

"Drowning," I said, "I know you didn't think up your plan to get any personal glory out of it, but I suspect that if it works, you may have a good chance to pick up a Nobel Peace Prize."

The Bad Back Problem

The biggest problem this country faces is not the economy, law 'n' order, the war, or revolution, but bad backs.

It turns out that everyone in this country has back trouble, and until a cure is found for it, we will never be able to solve our other difficulties.

I discovered this recently when my wife's back went out on her while she was playing tennis. I immediately sent her off to an orthopedic surgeon, who told her she had a ruptured disc and would have to go in traction and wear a sponge collar around her neck.

It was her collar that gave us the tipoff on how many bad backs there are in this country. People rarely talk about their backs until they see someone else wearing a collar. Then they open up and confess about their own bad back troubles.

The first time I took my wife to a party with her collar around her neck a friend said, "What are you doing about it?"

My wife said she was going to an orthopedic doctor.

"They don't know anything," the friend said. "What you need for a bad back is a neurosurgeon."

The next day we located one of the best neurosurgeons in the country. After careful examination, he concluded my wife had a ruptured disc and needed traction and advised her to wear a sponge collar around her neck.

Since this was the same diagnosis she got from the orthopedic man, my wife was naturally disappointed.

But a few days later her spirits picked up. She told me when I got home, "The man who rakes our leaves said that neurosurgeons don't know anything about backs. He said the best way to get rid of my bad back was to sleep on the floor."

"Well, the guy who rakes leaves should know," I said.

A week later she called me at the office. "Annabelle knows a woman in Seven Corners who can cure crooked spines with her fingernails. She has never worked on someone who didn't get better."

Three days later my wife got wind of an acupuncturist who lived in Chinatown. Her friend Aggie said, "Four gold needles and you'll be playing tennis in a week."

Before she could look up the acupuncture doctor, her sister called from Cincinnati and told her the only way to get rid of her bad back was through yoga and meditation.

Several weeks went by, and while my wife did continue her traction, her heart wasn't in it.

"It seems so slow," she protested to me. "The hairdresser knows a spa in Italy that specializes in mud baths for bad backs."

"If it doesn't work, you can always go to Lourdes," I said.

But while she was getting her passport for Italy, a brother-in-law from West Virginia called in to tell about a new miracle cure for backs that some lady in the Blue Ridge Mountains had developed from herbs.

"It sounds better than mud baths," I said.

The ointment arrived, and surprisingly, it had no effect on my wife's back.

Having tried everything, we decided to go back to the neurosurgeon on the off chance that he might know something about her problem that the hairdresser didn't.

The doctor said she was doing fine but would have to stay in traction for another month.

You can imagine her depressed state of mind when she left the office. But fortunately, on the way home the cabdriver recognized her symptoms and said, "I know a hypnotist in Alexandria who specializes in nothing but ruptured discs."

Christmas Cards Tell All

Christmas cards reveal a great deal more about America than one would like to admit. They show as well as anything what a restless society we've become.

The other day my wife was opening cards, and she was puzzled by one from Hal and Virginia Lark.

"I thought Hal's wife's name was Frieda," she said.

"So did I. Maybe she changed it to Virginia," I suggested.

The next day the mystery was cleared up when we received a Christmas card from the McDowalls.

"We don't know any McDowalls," my wife said.

"We must, or they wouldn't have sent us a Christmas card."

"The handwriting looks familiar," my wife said. "As a matter of fact, it looks exactly like Frieda Lark's signature."

"How could it be Frieda's Lark's signature if it was sent by the McDowalls?"

"Maybe Frieda is no longer a Lark!" my wife exclaimed.

"Then that means Hal married a girl named Virginia, and Frieda married a guy named McDowall."

"I wish people would tell me these things before I sent out *my* Christmas cards."

She opened a few other cards and then came to one which she studied carefully. "This photograph is very peculiar. I could swear it was Myrna Tuttle, but the card says it's from the Lindstroms."

I looked at it. "It sure does seem to be Myrna. Wait a minute. Aren't those Myrna's twins on the sailboat?"

"Yes," my wife said. "But I don't recognize the man at the wheel."

"That's probably Lindstrom," I said.

"I wonder what happened to Dick Tuttle?"

"Look through your cards. The answer is probably there."

My wife went through the cards. "You're right. Here's one from the Tuttles. It's Dick Tuttle, all right, but I don't recognize. the woman or the children sitting on the lawn."

"They're probably *her* children," I said.

"Well, at least that takes care of the Tuttle problem," she said.

The next day, when I came home from work, my wife was waiting for me with more cards.

"Helen Coates is now Helen Samovar, Marty Keller has a new wife named Zelda, and we got separate Christmas cards from Lars and Margie Payne. His came from San Francisco, and hers came from Fort Lauderdale."

"I got a few at the office," I said. "Apparently Bob Elmendorf got custody of the five children because his card shows him sitting on a fence with a new wife and eight kids."

"Who are the other three?" my wife wanted to know.

"*Her* kids. I wonder why Lucy Elmendorf didn't get custody of the children?"

"This card," my wife said, "may explain it. It's from Lucy, and she says she's living in Guadeloupe with a fantastic penniless young artist whom she met when she went to visit her sister in Los Angeles."

"We also got a card from the Madisons," she added. "They still seem to be together."

"Forget it," I said. "I just received a wire at the office from Bill Madison. It says DISREGARD CHRISTMAS GREETINGS. LETTER FOLLOWS."

A Prayer for Tourists

According to the *Times* of London, the Greek Orthodox Church issued a new prayer asking the Lord to protect the Greek people from tourists. The prayer, which is to be said by monks and nuns every morning and every evening, goes like this:

"Lord Jesus Christ, Son of God, have mercy on the cities, the islands, and the villages of our Orthodox fatherland, as well as the holy monasteries, which are scourged by the worldly touristic wave.

"Grace us with a solution to this dramatic problem and protect our brethren who are sorely tried by the modernistic spirit of these contemporary Western invaders."

Now it's only fair if the monks and nuns are beseeching the Lord with antitourist prayers that the tourists get equal time. So I have written a prayer for tourists which they must recite when they get up in the morning and go to bed at night.

It goes like this:

"Heavenly Father, look down on us your humble obedient tourist servants who are doomed to travel this earth, taking photographs, mailing postcards, buying souvenirs, and walking about in drip-dry underwear.

"We beseech you, O Lord, to see that our plane is not hijacked, our luggage is not lost, and our overweight baggage goes unnoticed.

"Protect us from surly and unscrupulous taxi drivers, avaricious porters, and unlicensed English-speaking guides.

"Give us this day divine guidance in the selection of our hotels that we may find our reservations honored, our rooms made up, and hot water running from the faucets (if it is at all possible).

"We pray that the telephones work and that the operators speak our tongue and that there is no mail waiting from our children which would force us to cancel the rest of our trip.

"Lead us, dear Lord, to good inexpensive restaurants where the food is superb, the waiters friendly, and the wine included in the price of the meal.

"Give us the wisdom to tip correctly in currencies we do not understand. Forgive us for undertipping out of ignorance and overtipping out of fear. Make the natives love us for what we are and not for what we can contribute to their worldly goods.

"Grant us the strength to visit the museums, the cathedrals, the palaces, and the castles listed as 'musts' in the guidebooks.

"And if perchance we skip a historic monument to take a nap after lunch, have mercy on us, for our flesh is weak."

(This part of the prayer is for husbands.)

"Dear God, keep our wives from shopping sprees and protect them from 'bargains' they don't need or can't afford. Lead them not into temptation, for they know not what they do."

(This part of the prayer is for wives.)

"Almighty Father, keep our husbands from looking at foreign women and comparing them to us.

"Save them from making fools of themselves in cafés and night-clubs. Above all, please do not forgive them their trespasses, for they know exactly what they do."

(Together.) "And when our voyage is over, and we return to our loved ones, grant us the favor of finding someone who will look at our home movies and listen to our stories, so our lives as tourists will not have been in vain.

"This we ask you in the Name of Conrad Hilton, Thomas Cook, and the American Express. Amen."

How Not to Write a Book

There are many great places where you *can't* write a book, but as far as I'm concerned, none compares to Martha's Vineyard.

This is how I manage *not* to write a book, and I pass it on to fledgling authors as well as old-timers who have vowed to produce a great work of art this summer.

The first thing you need is lots of paper, carbon, a solid typewriter, preferably electric, and a quiet spot in the house overlooking the water.

You get up at 6 o'clock in the morning and go for a dip in the sea; then you come back and make yourself a hearty breakfast.

By 7 A.M. you are ready to begin Page 1, Chapter 1. You insert a piece of paper in the typewriter and start to type "It was the best of times. . . ." Suddenly you look out the window and you see a sea gull diving for a fish. This is not an ordinary sea gull. It seems to have a broken wing, and you get up from the desk to observe it on the off chance that somewhere in the book you may want to insert a scene of a sea gull with a broken wing trying to dive for a fish. (It would make a great shot when the book is sold to the movies and the lovers are in bed.)

It is now 8 A.M., and the sounds of people getting up distract you. There is no sense trying to work with everyone crashing around the house. So you write a letter to your editor telling him how well the book is going and that you're even more optimistic about this one than the last one which the publisher never advertised.

It is now 9 o'clock in the morning, and you go into the kitchen and scream at your wife. "How am I going to get any work done around here if the kids are making all that racket? It doesn't mean anything in this family that I have to make a living."

Your wife kicks all the kids out of the house, and you go back to your desk. It suddenly occurs to you that your agent may also want to see a copy of the book, so you tear out the paper and start over with an original and two carbons: "It was the best of times . . ."

You look out the window again, and you see a sailboat in trouble. You take your binoculars and study the situation carefully. If it gets worse, you may have to call the Coast Guard. But after a half hour of struggling they seem to have things under control.

By this time you remember you were supposed to receive a check from the *Saturday Review*, so you walk down to the post office, pause at the drugstore for newspapers, and stop at the hardware store for rubber cement to repair your daughter's raft.

You're back to your desk at 1 P.M. when you remember you haven't had lunch. So you fix yourself a tuna fish sandwich and read the newspapers.

It is now 2:30 P.M., and you are about to hit the keys when Bill Styron calls. He announces they have just received a load of lobsters at Menemsha, and he's driving over to get some before they're all gone. Well, you say to yourself, you can always write a book on the Vineyard, but how often can you get fresh lobster?

So you agree to go with Styron for just an hour.

Two hours later, with the thought of fresh lobster as inspiration, you sit down at the typewriter. The doorbell rings, and Norma Brustein is standing there in her tennis togs, looking for a fourth for doubles.

You don't want to hurt Norma's feelings, so you get your racket and for the next hour play a fierce game of tennis, which is the only opportunity you have had all day of taking your mind off your book.

It is now 6 o'clock, and the kids are back in the house, so there is no sense trying to get work done any more for *that* day.

So you put the cover on the typewriter with a secure feeling that no matter how ambitious you are about working, there will always be somebody on the Vineyard ready and eager to save you.

A Pig Confesses

I was asked to speak at a fund-raising affair for the National Women's Political Caucus in Washington, D.C. It is very rare for a man to confess his sins publicly before such a distinguished group. I know the speech may finish me at the YMCA locker room or the tables down at Morey's, but I have to think of my future in case the women's revolution succeeds. Although what I said was "off the record," my political advisers have warned me that the speech may be taken out of context. Therefore, I have been persuaded to release the entire text.

"Gentlemen and sisters, this is indeed a historic occasion. We meet tonight in this dark cellar to plot our plans for turning this country around.

"I know you are asking yourselves, 'Why has this man, who is known to his wife as a male chauvinist pig, agreed to partake in these subversive activities?'

"There are many reasons.

"I believe that this is a sex whose time has come. I have seen the future, and it is women.

"I know what it's like to be treated as a sex object. I know when someone takes me out to dinner, she has only one thing on her mind. I am sick and tired of being pinched and mauled and groped at—just because I have a pretty face.

"And let the record read, if the revolution succeeds, that I was here on the platform tonight at your first twenty-five dollars-a-head cocktail party, and if you manage to overthrow those sexist politicians who now rule our nation, I would like to be put in charge of the telephone company.

"I have a confession to make.

"I am a sinner.

"And I come here tonight to ask your forgiveness and pardon.

"It's true that I was a male chauvinist pig.

"I studied it at school.

"But it wasn't all my fault. I discovered very early in life that during recess it was easier to fight with girls than boys.

"I also discovered at an early age that girls would do things for you that boys wouldn't—like lend you their roller skates or their homework.

"I found out other things. I found out that girls could make me blush and boys couldn't. I discovered, and may the good Lord forgive me for this, that girls were nicer to touch than boys, and they made my toes tingle all the time.

"I thought to myself, when I was maybe nine or ten, that someday I'd like to have a girl of my own—someone who would cook for me and iron my shirts and shovel the snow out of the driveway and make my toes tingle at night.

"Now, in retrospect, these were terrible thoughts I had.

"But that's how we were all brought up. We thought of women as childbearers, car pool drivers, breakfast makers, and bed warmers.

And if they couldn't do these things, at least they could type and take shorthand.

"Yes, sisters, I confess that I was no better than Hugh Hefner or Norman Mailer.

"I had hit bottom.

"But then one night, while I was reading *Playboy* and watching my wife scrubbing the floor, a light dawned on me and I said to myself, 'Is this really what I want out of life? How can I be free when this woman that I married is still in chains? What good is it to own the world when she has to stand in line at Safeway?'

"So I picked her up from the floor and said, 'Go get a job. I'll squeeze out the mop.'

"Sisters, from that day forward, I have been one of you.

"Because of these revelations, I can now live with myself. My floors are dirty, but my heart is pure.

"And so tonight I ask your forgiveness for all the terrible sexist acts I have perpetrated on women, overt and undercover.

"I appear humbly in front of this group to say that Gloria Steinem and Bella Abzug and Betty Freidan and Kate Millett and Germaine Greer have shown me the way.

"All I ask of you is to take me to your bosoms and say, 'I forgive you, Arthur. Go and sin no more.'"

The Truth About Book Reviews

The average newspaper reader may wonder how a book editor goes about selecting someone to review a newly published novel or work of nonfiction. Except for the few books that the book editor chooses to review himself, the editor usually assigns the job to:

(A) A college professor.

(B) Someone who has written a book on a similar subject.

(C) A reporter friend who can use $25.

Now each one of these people can cause trouble for an author.

The college professor usually doesn't review the book assigned to him but uses it as an opportunity to discuss everything he knows about literature. His review may start off "Murray Slotnick is no Marcel Proust. When Proust was a boy. . . ." Slotnick is lucky if the professor mentions his book even once in the review.

While the college professor is always getting sidetracked in his review, he is usually not malicious about Slotnick. If he ignores the book, he only does it because the professor knows the reader is much more interested in his knowledge of writers of the twentieth century than in Slotnick's latest work.

The second category of reviewer is the most dangerous. When the book editor turns over a newly published work to an author who has written on the same subject, the writer of the book is sunk.

Let us assume that Stump has just written *The Definitive History of Staten Island.* The book editor assigns the work to Carstairs, who two years ago wrote *The Definitive History of Staten Island.* Carstairs has no intention of letting Stump's history replace his own, and so he lacerates Stump in the review for factual inaccuracies, lack of depth, shoddy writing, poor illustrations, and outdated street maps.

In fiction the situation is even worse. When an editor asks one fiction writer to review another writer's new book, he is signing the latter's death warrant. There are very few writers of fiction who are capable of reviewing another writer's book without slashing off an ear.

Brubaker, the author of *Sit,* starts off his review of Templebar's new novel *Big Toe* as follows: "Templebar, who showed so much promise in the fifties with his first novel, *Postage Due,* has once again disappointed his readers. . . ." What nobody knows is that Templebar reviewed Brubaker's last book in a similar manner, and Brubaker is finally getting his revenge. (I know from personal experience that book editors operate this way because every time Russell Baker comes out with a new book, I am asked to review it, and every time I come out with a book, Baker is asked to write about it. Since I have nothing good to say about Baker and he has nothing good to say about me, we have a deal. We each write our own reviews of our own books and sign each other's name. This is the only reason we've been able to remain friends for so many years.)

If the author had his choice of reviewers, he would probably choose the third category—the editor's reporter friend who needs the extra $25.

The reporter, who is more interested in the money than he is in criticism, doesn't have time to read the book so he just types up everything printed on the inside book jacket and hands it in as his review. Publishers know this, and that is why most inside book jackets read like favorable book reviews.

What of the blurbs that appear on the back cover and in the advertisements recommending the book in glowing terms? Those, dear reader, are written by friends of the author who haven't read the book but owe the poor guy a favor.

Last Flat in Paris

It is incumbent on every columnist to see *Last Tango in Paris* and comment on it. Some critics have called it the greatest movie of our time. Others have written that it is one of the great rip-offs of the film industry.

But having seen the movie, I would like to advance the opinion that most critics have missed the point of the picture.

Last Tango in Paris is *not,* as has been described, the story of an aging American (Marlon Brando) and a young girl (Maria Schneider) in a desperate sexual battle for survival.

It is really a simple heartwarming film about two people trying to rent the same apartment in Paris.

Only those who have ever searched for an apartment in Paris can appreciate what Brando and Miss Schneider go through for this lovely flat near the Seine.

In the film, Brando plays a washed-out American, whose wife has just committed suicide. He wants the apartment in the worst way. So does the young French girl.

They meet by accident in the empty flat, and you see Brando's mind working. He figures if he rapes the girl, she'll go away and he'll get the apartment.

But Miss Schneider, a child of the French bourgeoisie, is made of sterner stuff, and she puts up little resistance to Brando's assault. As a matter of fact, while she's being bounced around by Marlon, she is really measuring the floor to see how much carpeting it will take.

The next day they are back at the apartment again. Brando has bought a table, chairs, and a bed to assert his claim to it. But Miss Schneider is not impressed and walks about the place as if it were hers.

This infuriates Brando, and he throws her down on the bed and keeps muttering, "It's mine. It's mine." Miss Schneider just laughs at him. All the time they are making love she is looking at the window trying to figure what size curtains she'll need for the room.

Brando, exhausted and fearful that he'll lose the flat, visits his mother-in-law and his dead wife. We see the tiny hotel he lives in and realize why Brando is so intent on getting the apartment. Miss Schneider goes off with her fiancé, and we discern why she wants a new place to live.

Back to the apartment. Brando is now desperate. He shows Miss Schneider a dead rat. It shakes her up, but not enough to give up the place. So Brando decides to humiliate her with several unnatural sex acts. One takes place against the wall, and Miss Schneider realizes if she ever gets the flat, she's going to have to buy a lot of wallpaper.

Rather than be frightened by Brando's brutality, Miss Schneider becomes more determined than ever to wrest the key away from him.

The next time they meet she's in her wedding dress, and Brando is so mad he throws her in the tub. Miracle of all miracles, the plumbing works, and Brando gives Miss Schneider a bath while she figures out what color scheme would go best with the white medicine cabinet.

By this time, Brando is worn out and figures the apartment isn't really worth it. He leaves without telling Miss Schneider his name.

A little battered from the sexual encounters, Miss Schneider returns triumphantly with her fiancé to show him the flat. But after all Miss Schneider's been through, the fiancé takes one look at the place and declares, "It's too big."

This is when I started to cry.

I don't know if *Last Tango in Paris* is a great movie or not, but I believe that director Bertolucci has made an important social statement about one of the real outrages of our time, which happens to be the housing shortage in France.

Job Hunting

Vice President of Development
Glucksville Dynamics
Glucksville, California.

DEAR SIR,

I am writing in regard to employment with your firm. I have a BS from USC and PhD in physics from the California Institute of Technology.

In my previous position I was in charge of research and development for the Harrington Chemical Company. We did work in thermonuclear energy, laser beam refraction, hydrogen molecule development, and heavy-water computer data.

Several of our research discoveries have been adapted for commercial use, and one particular breakthrough in linear hydraulics is now being used by every oil company in the country.

Because of a cutback in defense orders, the Harrington Company decided to shut down its research and development department. It is for this reason I am available for immediate employment.

Hoping to hear from you in the near future, I remain

Sincerely yours,
EDWARD KASE

DEAR MR. KASE,

We regret to inform you that we have no positions available for someone of your excellent qualifications. The truth of the matter is that we find you are "overqualified" for any position we might offer you in our organization. Thank you for thinking of us, and if anything comes up in the future, we will be getting in touch with you.

Yours truly,
MERRIMAN HASELBALD
Administrative Vice-President

Personnel Director
Jessel International Systems
Crewcut, Mich.

DEAR SIR,

I am applying for a position with your company in any responsible capacity. I have had a college education and have fiddled around in research and development. Occasionally we have come up with some moneymaking ideas. I would be willing to start off at a minimal salary to prove my value to your firm.

Sincerely yours,
EDWARD KASE

DEAR MR. KASE,

Thank you for your letter of the 15th. Unfortunately we have no positions at the moment for someone with a college education. Frankly it is the feeling of everyone here that you are "overqualified," and your experience indicates you would be much happier with a company that could make full use of your talents.

It was kind of you to think of us.

HARDY LANDSDOWNE
Personnel Dept.

To Whom It May Concern
Geis & Waterman Inc.
Ziegfried, Ill.

DERE SER,

I'd like a job with your outfit. I can do anything you want me to. You name it Kase will do it. I ain't got no education and no experience, but I'm strong and I got moxy an I get along great with peeple. I'm ready to start any time because I need the bread. Let me know when you want me.

Cheers
EDWARD KASE

DEAR MR. KASE,

You are just the person we have been looking for. We need a truck driver and your qualifications are perfect for us. You can begin working in our Westminister plant on Monday. Welcome aboard.

CARSON PETERS
Personnel

Pictures From Vietnam

The President was sitting in his Oval Office when Henry Kissinger walked in.

"Say, Henry, these photographs of the moon are fantastic."

"They're not photographs of the moon, Mr. President, they're the latest aerial pictures from South Vietnam."

"Vietnam?"

"Yes, sir. There are now fifty-two million craters in South Vietnam. By the end of the year we should go over the one hundred million mark."

"That's great, Henry. But I don't see any towns in the photographs."

"Here. You see this series of rock outcroppings? That was a town. And over here, this bleak, flat, open space—that was a town. And here where this giant hole is—that's a provincial capital."

"Well, you could have fooled me. There doesn't seem to be much green in the photographs."

"No, sir, Mr. President. The defoliation program took care of the green. But you notice there's lots of gray."

"What does that signify, Henry?"

"Our B-52 pacification program is working. Green means cover for the North Vietnamese. Gray means they have to fight in the open. The more gray on the photographs, the better chance we have of turning back naked aggression."

"What are these brown streaks here?"

"They used to be roads, Mr. President. But you can't call them that anymore."

"I guess you can't. Where are the hamlets where we have won the hearts and minds of the people?"

"Most of them are in these blue areas, underwater. We had to bomb the dams so the enemy couldn't capture the rice."

"Uh-huh. I see there are a lot of black areas in the photos. Does that signify anything?"

"Yes, sir. It means our scorched earth policy is working. Every black area on this photograph means the North Vietnamese have been deprived of supplies and shelter. We've left them nothing."

"Good thinking, Henry. Where are the people?"

"What people, Mr. President?"

"The people we're defending against an imposed Communist government."

"You can't see them in the photographs. They're hiding in the craters."

"And the South Vietnamese army?"

"They're hiding in these craters over here."

"I see. I wish these photographs could be printed in Hanoi. It would certainly give the North Vietnamese something to think about."

"So do I, Mr. President. Now, this area over here by the sea still has some green in it."

"I was going to ask you about that, Henry."

"The Navy assures me that it should be gray and black in three weeks. It's the type of terrain that lends itself better to shelling than to bombing."

"Well, Henry, I want you to know I believe these are excellent photographs, and I want you to send a 'well done' cable to everyone responsible. The only thing that worries me is what happens if we get a ceasefire? Isn't it going to be awfully expensive to make everything green again?"

"Don't worry, Mr. President, we've thought of that. We've asked for bids from the companies who make artificial turf. Once the shooting stops, we're going to carpet South Vietnam from wall to wall."

I Was a Beard for Errol Flynn and Found God

The most unsung person in any great love affair is the beard. For those of you who are not familiar with the term, a beard is a person who accompanies a couple who are up to no good when they go to a public place. The beard is literally a third wheel who prevents people from finding out that Mr. X is making it with Mrs. Y or that Mr. R is madly in love with Miss G.

Bearding is one of the most difficult, frustrating and unrewarding professions of our time. Yet it requires extreme tact, fantastic discretion and unshakable loyalty. All the world loves a lover, but no one gives a damn what happens to a beard.

If I sound bitter, I speak from personal experience. For over twenty years I have performed the role of beard for movie actors, sports figures, members of high society, politicians and men in high government circles.

I have been the third man on cruises, at restaurants, race tracks, charity balls and après-ski parties. I can say in all modesty I have always performed my role with great delicacy, enormous charm and high spirits.

Yet no one has ever known that underneath my beard was a heart crying for some of the love and affection that the couple I was protecting were sharing with each other.

I guess I got into bearding by accident. I was stationed in Paris for the European edition of the *Herald Tribune* from 1949 until 1962, writing about the high life of London, Paris, Rome and Monte Carlo.

Through my work I met many famous people who just couldn't afford to go out in public with someone they weren't married to.

I got my first beard job when Errol Flynn (one of the great American movie stars, married at the time) invited me to dinner at Maxim's with one of the most beautiful models in France. I was highly flattered with the invitation.

"Should I bring a date?" I asked excitedly.

"That won't be necessary," he replied. "I'd like to get to know you better."

Unfortunately, Flynn wanted to get to know the French model even better than he wanted to get to know me, and I had little to do at Maxim's except eat and watch the master at work.

After Maxim's I suggested we go to a nightclub.

Flynn and the model didn't want to go to a nightclub.

"Why don't you go to a nightclub?" Flynn said darkly.

"Alone?" I asked.

"It's the only way to go."

"Well, if you don't want to go to a nightclub," I suggested, "why don't we all take a walk along the Seine?"

Flynn whispered to me, "Why don't you just take a taxi and get the hell out of here?"

"Sure, Errol," I said. "Can I drop the girl off? She lives right near me."

I thought Flynn was going to slug me. I finally got the message and walked off into the night—alone.

The next day Flynn called me and asked me to come over to his suite.

"Kid," he said as he poured me a glass of champagne, "it's obvious that you don't know what your role is in life and I think I can help you. When I first saw you, I knew you had a gift that few of us are born with."

"What's that, Errol?"

"You're a natural beard."

"Why?"

"You have the looks, the manner and the personality to be one of the great beards of our time."

I straightened up in my chair. "How do you know?"

"Because to be a beard you must be presentable but at the same time not a threat to the person you're bearding for. I can't think of any woman who would go for you while I was at the table."

"I don't know if I should take that as a compliment or not."

Errol put his hand on my shoulder. "Kid, anybody can be a great lover, but it's almost impossible to find a great beard—a man willing to sacrifice his evening for his friend's pleasure, a man willing to protect the marriages of one or even two people, a person who can devote himself to a love affair without getting personally involved. You've got it all, kid. I envy you—I wish I had it."

"I never thought of myself that way," I admitted.

"The only thing is," said Errol, "you've got a lot to learn."

"For example."

"Well, if you're going to make it in the big-time beard circles, you've got to know when to go home. A beard must be able to leave a couple naturally and without ceremony. For example, last night what you should have done when we left Maxim's is to have said, 'I have a late date'."

"But I didn't have a date."

"Damnit," said Flynn angrily. "If you're going to be a beard, you're going to have to learn to lie. Get it through your head a beard's role is a public one. When the door shuts on my hotel suite, I want you out in the hall."

"You mean a beard can't even watch?"

"No, he can't," Flynn shouted at me. "You have only one function and that is to protect the couple you are out with. What they do afterward is none of your business."

"That's great, Errol," I said. "But what's in it for me?"

"What a selfish question. How would any of us survive if every beard in this world said, 'What's in it for me?' You are serving mankind in the most honorable of all pursuits—the search for love. You are like a priest or a Red Cross worker, sacrificing your own evil hedonistic desires to bring happiness to thousands of unhappily married people. Remember that behind every great love affair there was a beard.

"Choosing a man as his beard is the highest honor one person can bestow on another. The fact that I have chosen you to be my beard in Paris over hundreds of others shows how much I value you as a friend and a confidant. Of course, if you don't feel worthy of it, I can always find someone else."

I said, "I didn't realize what it meant to be a beard. The way you explain it, I'm another Albert Schweitzer."

Errol grabbed my hand. "Kid, when it comes to beards, I'm going to make you the champ."

All that summer I bearded for Errol Flynn. It was really very exciting. I met many wonderful people. At one party I was introduced to Gary Cooper's beard. At another I met Lana Turner's beard. Once I ran into Grace Kelly's beard before she married Prince Rainier. Miss Kelly's beard was a beautiful blonde secretary. I tried to date her, but neither Mr. Flynn nor Miss Kelly would permit it.

"When will you learn," said Flynn as he put his arm around a voluptuous Italian movie actress, "that beards *cannot* have dates."

After Flynn left Paris, he passed the word around in Hollywood that I was the best beard in Europe. From then on I bearded for Aly Khan, Porfirio Rubirosa, Cary Grant, Eddie Fisher, Liz Taylor and Sophia Loren, to mention just a few.

If you wanted me as a beard, you had to book me six months in advance. I never charged for my services and my only payoff was that I was always allowed to choose the wine.

As the years went by, I found being a beard took its toll. Every time I left the couple I was protecting, I went home and took a cold shower. But after a while this wasn't enough, so I started biting my nails. I became haggard and lost weight.

Finally, I discussed the problem with the sports editor of the Paris *Herald Tribune.*

He said, "Your problem is that all you think there is to life is being a beard. You have to become a participant. Why don't you find someone to play around with and get your own beard?"

"Who could I get to beard for me?" I asked him.

"Look, I'm pretty busy, but if you find someone, I'll be your beard."

"You're a good man, Richard," I said with gratitude.

Three weeks later I made a date with a smashing dress buyer from New York who was over in Paris covering the fashions. I told Richard he was on duty for Thursday night.

I was as excited as if I was on my first date. I took the two of them to the Tour d'Argent overlooking Notre Dame.

But something went wrong. Richard did most of the talking. My dress buyer laughed at his jokes and listened intently as he told her about the inner workings of France's six-day bike race. He questioned her about her business and her husband, whom she had left behind.

They behaved as if I weren't even there.

When we got down into the street, Richard said, "Well, let's go to a sidewalk café."

"I don't think *we* want to," I said, stepping on Richard's toe.

"Well, let's leave it up to our guest," Richard said.

"I'd love to go to a sidewalk café," she said to me. "If you're tired, Richard can see me back to the hotel."

There was obviously no reason for me to go on. I went home and took another cold shower.

The next day I confronted Richard at the office and accused him of committing treachery.

"I did no such thing," he said angrily. "Your problem is that you've been a beard for so long, you don't even know what to do with a woman. If I hadn't held up the conversation, neither one of us would have made out."

"Well, I know one thing," I said. "And that is, a beard isn't supposed to steal a woman away from his friend."

"I didn't steal her. She came to me. You better go back to being a beard. That seems to be all you're good for."

It was a bitter pill to swallow. But, like Errol Flynn, he knew what he was talking about. I had no talent as a swinger.

For twenty years, every time I've gone out with another couple, no matter how the evening started, I wound up saying good night to both of them.

Once, in New York, I was sure I had it made when I took out two women. There was no way I could lose, I assured myself, as I paid the check. But it turned out before dinner was over they liked each other better than they liked me. Once again I went home alone.

As I look back over my years of beardom, I can take some consolation in the fact that while I got nothing out of it for myself, I did make it safe for a lot of couples to find happiness.

Occasionally, I run into a couple I bearded for who got married after divorcing their respective spouses.

You would think they would be grateful to me for all I did for them when they met clandestinely. But they never seem to be.

Now that they're married and respectable and don't have to sneak around anymore, they don't feel any guilt about me picking up the check.

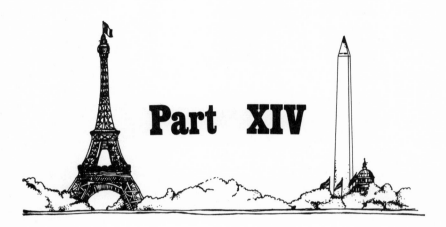

Part XIV

Before Watergate

A group of us were sitting around the dining room table the other night when suddenly someone asked, "What did people talk about in this country before Watergate?"

There was shocked silence. It was hard for any of us to believe there was *anything* before Watergate.

"Didn't we talk about meat?" one of the men asked.

"I think we did," one of the ladies replied, "but I can't remember what we said about it."

"I believe it had to do with the price of it. Wasn't there something about a boycott?" someone added.

"That's correct," a man said. "We kept saying the price of steak was too high. But surely we talked about other things besides meat."

We all started wracking our brains.

"Wait a minute!" a friend shouted. "Wasn't there something about amnesty?"

"You mean for people involved in Watergate?"

"No, stupid, we talked about amnesty *before* Watergate. It had to do with draft dodgers."

"It's funny," a woman said, "I always get amnesty and immunity mixed up."

"So does the President. If it hadn't been for Watergate, Nixon planned to make a big issue of amnesty."

"I don't recall talking much about amnesty," another person said. "In our family we talked about how McGovern blew the election."

"Who's McGovern?" someone asked.

"He was the Democratic candidate who ran against Nixon in the election."

"What election?"

"The Presidential election of 1972. If it hadn't been for the election, we wouldn't have had a Watergate."

"Now it's coming back to me. McGovern ran with an Indian named Eaglefeather," a lady said.

"Eagleton," her husband corrected her. "And he wasn't an Indian. He was treated for shock."

"He was not treated *for* shock, he was treated *with* shock. That's why what's-his-name dropped him from the ticket."

"Well, then who ran with McGovern?"

Nobody at the table could remember.

"It wasn't Humphrey," a man said with assurance.

"And it wasn't Sparkman."

"Oh, well, it's not important. Say, I just remembered something we talked about before the Watergate—impounded funds. The President said he was impounding money Congress had allocated, and Congress said it was illegal. It was a pretty hot debate as I recall."

"Didn't we talk about what kind of FBI director Patrick Gray would make?"

"I thought the big argument was how much financial aid we should give to North Vietnam."

"They were great days," someone said nostalgically. "I wonder if we'll ever see the like again?"

"Do you think Watergate will be over before the football season starts?"

"Are you kidding? They're predicting it will go on for twenty years."

"That's a shame because I'm going to miss talking about the Redskins."

"Not as much as Nixon will."

"Let's make a pact not to talk about Watergate for the rest of the evening."

Everyone agreed. We ate our food silently. Finally someone asked, "Has anyone seen *Deep Throat?*"

No one had. We returned to our food. Every guest tried to think of another subject besides Watergate, but no one could come up with one.

So we all left hurriedly after coffee.

"Would You Believe?"

"Brothers and sisters of the Latter-day Disciples of the Church of Watergate, are you believers?"

"Amen, Richard. We believe."

"Do you believe I had nothing to do with Watergate and the cover-up?"

"We believe, we believe."

"And do you believe I knew nothing about the milk fund, the ITT merger or the Howard Hughes hundred-thousand-dollar donation?"

"Hallelujah, Richard. We believe."

"Now, brothers and sisters, I want to tell you about the tapes."

"Oh, tell us, Richard. Tell us all about the tapes."

"There were supposed to have been nine tapes. But when I counted them there were only seven. Do you believe that?"

"Glory be, Richard. We believe it."

"Do you know why there were only seven?"

"We know, Richard, but tell us again."

"There were only seven because two did not exist. The tape ran out on one, and the other was made on a phone that didn't have a recorder."

"Amen, Richard."

"Now would you believe I didn't know these tapes didn't exist until the weekend before I was supposed to turn them over to the courts?"

"We believe it, Richard. Bless you!"

"I know some people say I'm a sinner. . . ."

"No, Richard, you're not a sinner. We're sinners because we didn't believe you."

"And I know some people say I'm a crook. . . ."

"Only the devil would say that, Richard."

"And they say I didn't pay any income taxes, brothers and sisters. . . ."

"Who said that, Richard?"

"And they say I made money on my land in Key Biscayne and San Clemente. . . ."

"Amen."

"But let me tell you, brothers and sisters, when the record is out in the open . . . when the tapes are heard . . . when my side of the story is told, then you will know who the sinners are!"

"We'll wait, Richard."

"Now I know you're going to ask me about the eighteen minutes missing from one of the tapes."

"Tell us, Richard, about the eighteen minutes."

"Would you believe I don't know what was on those eighteen minutes missing from the tape?"

"We believe."

"Do you believe I'm being crucified by television and the press?"

"Say it isn't so, Richard."

"And would you believe those who don't want to crucify me want to impeach me?"

"Oh, Lordy, Lord, we believe."

"But, brothers and sisters, I am not going to quit."

"Let's all clap hands."

"Do you know why I'm not going to quit?"

"Tell us, Richard. Tell us why."

"If I told you, you wouldn't believe me."

The Class Action Suit

The big story in Washington recently was the revelation that the White House had an official "enemies" list which they intended to use to "get" the people who opposed the administration.

Naturally, anyone worth his salt in this town was hoping to make the list. The test of one's importance in Washington obviously depends on how seriously the White House takes you and to what lengths they would go, to use a John Dean word, to "screw" you.

When the list was released, I searched it frantically for my name. First there was the "Dirty Twenty." I didn't make it, so I waited for the second list of 200 and discovered I hadn't made that one either. I thought to myself, "What kind of people do we have in the White House who don't even know who their *real* enemies are?"

Then the phone started to ring. Friends called to give their condolences. Sources who had been leaking to me on a steady basis telephoned to say they hadn't realized for the past five years that they had been leaking to a nobody. Colleagues who made the enemy list stopped by the office to rub in the fact that I was finished as a serious communicator.

Bill Mauldin telephoned from Chicago. He also hadn't made the list.

Pat Oliphant checked in from Denver because he was left off. Paul Conrad of the Los Angeles *Times* was furious because they hadn't mentioned him. Herb Block said, "That does it for me. No more Mr. Nice Guy."

The worst blow came at lunch time when I went to the Sans Souci restaurant and found myself sitting next to the kitchen. The maître d'hôtel, working from the "list," was seating all the White House enemies at the best tables.

When I protested about the table, Paul said, "You're lucky to be here at all. With all the enemies the White House has, I can no longer let in every Art, Dick and Harry."

I must say my wife took it well. "You may not be an enemy to them," she said, kissing me on the cheek when I walked in, "but you're still an enemy to me."

That night I studied the list again. It seemed to be filled with such mediocre people. Then suddenly it dawned on me! The White House knew exactly what they were doing. These thugs and double-crossing, lying rats (names on request with a self-addressed envelope) had drawn up the list not to get the people, but to get the people who were left *off* it.

They knew the best way to "screw" their real enemies was by leaving them off the most prestigious list in the United States today.

By not mentioning us, they knew editors and TV executives would lose faith in us and find ways of putting us out of business.

"What a Machiavellian plan," I said to myself. "Why did it take me so long to realize it?"

I immediately called Block, Mauldin, Oliphant and Conrad and told them what the White House was up to.

We decided there was only one thing to do. We will immediately institute a class action suit against the White House, John Dean III, Charles Colson, Bob Haldeman, John Ehrlichman and possibly the President of the United States, on behalf of all the people in the United States who did not make the official enemies list.

We intend to prove we were financially damaged and publicly humiliated and suffered grievous professional injury. We will prove that the White House conspired to put out a straw man list of names to detract from their real enemies in the media, the arts, the Congress and the business world.

We only hope Maurice Stans has enough money in his safe to pay for the damages we are certain will be awarded to us. If not, we intend to attach certain homes in Key Biscayne and San Clemente.

"Alice in Washington"

Alice was walking down Pennsylvania Avenue when the March Hare asked her, "How would you like to go to a White House press briefing?"

"What's a White House press briefing?" Alice asked.

"That is where they deny what they have already told you, which is the only reason it could be true," the March Hare said.

"It sounds like fun," Alice said.

The March Hare brought Alice into the press room. A chess pawn was standing at a podium.

"Who is that?" Alice asked.

"That is the press secretary. He talks in riddles. Listen."

"Why are transcripts better than tapes?" the press secretary asked.

"I don't know the answer to that one," Alice said to the March Hare. "Why are transcripts better than tapes?" she shouted to everyone's surprise.

The press secretary looked at her with cold blue eyes. "I refuse to comment on that."

Alice looked confused. "Why did he ask us a riddle if he can't give an answer to it?"

The March Hare said, "They don't tell him the answers; they just give him the riddles."

"What a stupid thing," Alice said. "Why is everyone writing in his notebook?"

"They write down everything he says even though they don't believe him."

"Why don't they believe him?" Alice asked.

"Because he makes things up. He has to or there would be no reason to have a briefing."

The press secretary spoke again. "All the evidence is in and it proves beyond a reasonable doubt that the king is innocent of all crimes, ergo, ergo, ergo, et cetra."

"But what about the evidence the king refuses to turn over to the committee?" a dormouse asked.

"That is not evidence," the press secretary replied. "If there was further evidence to prove the king guilty, he would have gladly given it to the committee. The fact that he hasn't turned it over means regretfully there is none. It's as simple as that."

"It doesn't sound very simple to me," Alice said.

"Why can't we hear all the tapes," the Mock Turtle asked, "so we can decide for ourselves who is innocent and who is guilty?"

The press secretary replied, "If you heard the tapes it would only prove the innocent are guilty and the guilty are innocent, and it would serve no purpose but to confuse you. Besides, what you would hear is not what you have read and what you have read is not what you would hear, so it's better not to hear what cannot be read. Isn't that perfectly clear?"

"I feel I'm back at the Mad Hatter's tea party," Alice said.

"Now I will give you some important news today," the press secretary said. "This is on the record. 'Twas brillig, and the slithy toves/Did gyre and gimble in the wabe;/All mimsy were the borogoves,/and the mome raths outgrabe."

Everyone wrote it down.

"What did he say?" Alice asked.

"Nothing," the March Hare replied. "He's just stalling until he can go to lunch."

The Oil Villain

Who was responsible for the energy crisis? Many people blamed the oil companies. Others blamed the government. The automobile companies blamed the environmentalists, and the Democrats blamed Watergate.

But Professor Heinrich Applebaum of the Yale Divinity School told me who the real villain of the fuel crisis was. It's the Harvard Business School.

The professor said, "Almost every sheikh now in charge of oil policy for his country was trained at Harvard. Everything they learned there they have put into practice to the detriment of the free world. The Harvard Business School taught the sons of Arab potentates how to sell oil, raise prices and demand outrageous profits for the black gold they have in the ground. Had these same sons been sent to the University of Alabama, Oklahoma or Texas, they would now be involved in developing football teams instead of putting the screws to everyone."

"Then you think it was a mistake to accept Arab princes at Harvard?"

"It was an absolute disaster. We should have sent them to colleges where the kids swallowed goldfish, got involved in panty raids and drank Boone's Farm apple wine until six o'clock in the morning. We should have made them join fraternities and take sorority girls to beer busts.

"All the Harvard Business School did for the sheikhs was teach them the laws of supply and demand and the value of fuel in an industrial society."

"I guess at the time it seemed like a good idea," I said.

"It was never a good idea," Applebaum said. "Before Harvard started accepting Arab oil princes, their fathers were willing to own twenty-five percent of the wells and were happy to accept air-conditioned Cadillacs as presents. Then the Harvard Business School started turning out oil ministers that demanded full control of the wells, triple royalties and F-5 fighter planes. I assure you they didn't learn that in the deserts of Arabia.

"Every economics professor and business law teacher in Cambridge must bear full responsibility for the mess we're in," Applebaum said.

"But maybe the professors just thought they were teaching theory as far as the free enterprise system goes, and that it would never be put into practice."

"You don't teach theory to people who control seventy percent of all the oil reserves in the world. We should have sent them all to the Juilliard School of Music, where they could have learned to play an instrument."

"Who gave the sheikhs the idea to send their sons to the Harvard School of Business in the first place?" I asked.

"The executives of the oil companies. They were all trained there, and the shiekhs decided that, since these oil executives were so good at shafting the Arabs, their sons could learn how to shaft the oil companies."

"They learned well," I admitted.

"We should have sent them to the University of California at Santa Barbara, and they all would have become surfers."

"I guess it's too late to do anything about it," I said.

"Perhaps. But I think we should put an embargo on all sons of Arab sheikhs, Iranian shahs and Venezuelan presidents. When they apply to the Harvard Business School, we can turn them down by saying the class is filled, but there are openings at the University of Kentucky, where they can major in basketball. Let's not make it any tougher on ourselves in the future than we have to."

"Would the Harvard Business School go along with it?"

"If they don't, we will shut off their oil. We should shut it off anyway. Their professors got us into this mess. Let them freeze for a while and make them realize what their damn lectures did to the rest of the world."

A New Bundling Plan

Everyone came up with new methods of helping during the energy crisis. Some ideas are nutty, but others are very practical and should be called to the attention of the government.

Professor Heinrich Applebaum has been studying new methods of sharing heat and has just written a paper titled "Bundling and the Energy Crisis" which he presented to the Society of Thermostat Inspectors.

Applebaum told me after giving his report, "The place where we waste the most heat in our homes is in bed. America can no longer afford the luxury of having one person sleep in bed all by himself. If we can persuade people to voluntarily share their beds, we could turn down the thermostats in our homes seven degrees."

"Would these people have to be married?" I asked.

"In normal times I would say yes. But this is the biggest emergency our country has ever faced and I think people should be given waivers if they aren't married, at least until the crisis is over."

"Then you consider bed pooling as a major solution to the heating shortage?"

"Absolutely. We must make Americans feel unpatriotic if they go to bed alone. We must instill a new spirit of bundling in this country."

"It sounds great on paper," I said, "but suppose people refuse to share their beds with others?"

Applebaum pursed his lips. "Then the government will have to step in and take forceful measures. These could include putting a surtax on citizens who insist on sleeping alone. This tax would be so high that it would be very unprofitable to refuse to bundle with somebody else. We could also give tax deductions to those who are willing to pool their beds. For example, if Bob and Carol and Ted and Alice were willing to bundle together, they would get ten percent off on their income taxes."

"What about people who *have* to sleep alone, such as policemen, doctors and newspaper reporters?"

"They would have a special sticker put on their beds exempting them from the bundling laws. This sticker would be given only to people who could prove their work is so essential they cannot bundle up with anybody."

"How do you think the American people will take to forced bundling?"

"I think the American people will be willing to share their beds with others once Nixon explains it to them. Body heat is still the greatest resource this country has, and we can get through the winter, provided everyone—and I mean everyone—cooperates with each other."

"Suppose you have a large empty bed and no one to bundle with? What do you do then?"

"We hope to set up bed-pooling information centers all over the country. All you would have to do is call a number, and we'd tell you who is looking for someone to share a bed. These centers would be open twenty-four hours a day."

"It sounds complicated," I said. "But I guess it's worth it."

Applebaum said, "It will work. To get the people to cooperate, we will have an advertising campaign on television."

"What will be your slogan?"

"Every time you share your bed this winter something in an Arab sheikh dies."

Fasten Your Belt

If President Nixon is really serious in his campaign to protect Americans from invasion of privacy, he might start with the 1974 automobile safety belts. These harnesses which are attached to screaming buzzers on the dashboard may save lives, but they're also wrecking marriages, driving people stark raving mad and causing untold havoc on the road.

Just the other day I was in Tucson, Arizona, and the Sheltons offered to take me to dinner in their new 1974 station wagon. There were six of us in the car, three in the front seat and three in the back. Everyone was in a jovial mood.

Then Shelton tried to start the car. A red light the size of a highway billboard lit up, and a buzzer which sounded like an air-raid siren went off.

Shelton yelled to his wife, "Fasten your safety belt!"

"It is fastened!" she screamed back over the din.

"Well, it isn't fastened right. Put the shoulder strap over your chest."

"It is over my chest," she said angrily. I was sitting between them in the middle seat.

"Maybe it's my belt!" I yelled. I unhooked and then rehooked the belt, but the buzzer wouldn't stop.

"Hurry up," someone in the back seat shouted, "or the whole car will self-destruct!"

Shelton leaned over me, grabbed his wife's shoulder harness and pulled it tightly around her.

The red light went off and the buzzing stopped.

"There," said Shelton, "that's better."

"I'm choking," Mrs. Shelton gasped. "I can't breathe."

"Don't do anything," Shelton cried, "or the buzzing will start again."

"I can only hold my breath for two minutes," Mrs. Shelton gagged.

I lifted the shoulder harness from her neck, and the red light went on again and the scream of the buzzer filled the car.

Shelton hit the wheel with both his hands. "I told you not to touch her belt."

"But her face was all green," I said.

"Everybody get out," Shelton said. "Let's see if I can solve this thing."

We all got out of the car. Shelton studied the front seat.

"All right, my harness goes in this slot, your harness in this slot and her harness goes in this one. Now let's all get back in the car again, and I don't want to hear any buzzers."

We got back in and in five minutes managed to get the harnesses around us.

Shelton turned on the ignition and everything on the dashboard flashed red.

"You hold her harness," Shelton yelled to me, "and let her hold yours!"

"Who's going to hold yours?" I shouted.

"I'll hold my own."

"How are you going to drive?" I asked him.

"Who cares, as long as I can stop the buzzing?"

I was holding onto Mrs. Shelton's harness for dear life, and she had my seat belt in the crook of her elbow. Shelton had one hand underneath his seat and was driving with the other.

For five minutes it was quiet in the car. Then Mrs. Shelton said, "I think the circulation in my arm has been cut off. There's no feeling in it."

"We've only got three miles to go," Shelton raged. "Hang on."

"Please let go of my harness," Mrs. Shelton begged me.

"If you do, I'll kill you," Shelton said to me.

We made it to the restaurant just before Mrs. Shelton passed out.

It was a good dinner, but no one really cared. Everyone was thinking of the drive back to the hotel.

* * *

Use Less, Pay More

I went into Burberry's house one night, and much to my surprise, I found every light in his house on.

"Burberry, have you taken leave of your senses?" I said. "Don't you know there is an energy crisis?"

Burberry plugged in the toaster, the coffeemaker and the iron. "I know it," he replied. "And I'm trying to do something about it."

"By turning on all the lights and using all these electric gadgets?"

"That's right," he said, turning up the thermostat to 80. "You see, the electric companies say they can't make any money if we conserve electricity. The only way we can bring prices down is if electric usage goes up."

"You're putting me on."

"I'm not putting you on," he said, plugging in his wife's hair dryer. "A few months ago the President and George C. Scott went on the air, separately of course, and said we had to conserve energy if we were going to be able to maintain our great way of life. So everyone cut down on using electricity. We turned off our lights, cut down our thermostats and reduced the use of all our electric appliances. They estimated the American people saved between ten percent and twenty percent during the winter. Everyone thought if he conserved, he would at least save money on his electricity bills.

"Well, it turned out just the opposite. The electric companies all asked for rate increases because people weren't using enough of their product. It turns out they all want to be paid for electricity we haven't used."

"But that doesn't make sense," I said.

"What the hell does make sense about the energy crisis?" Burberry said. "My family froze their butts off this winter as a patriotic gesture, and now we find the electric companies want to put a surcharge on them."

"On your butts?"

"No, not on our butts, on our conservation methods.

"The electric companies are the only ones who want to charge you more for using less electricity. I cut down on smoking last year. The cigarette companies didn't send me a letter saying because I cut down on smoking they would have to charge me more a pack. We gave up high-priced steaks. My butcher didn't send me a bill for not eating steaks. Why should the electric companies send me a letter saying because I didn't use enough electricity I'm going to have to pay more for it?"

"I guess if they don't sell enough electricity to their customers, they lose money on it."

"Okay, so that means if I use more electricity, they'll make money and then be able to charge me less."

He yelled into the kitchen. "Honey, did you put the stove and oven on?"

"Burberry," I said, "I know what you say is true, but I think you've missed the point. Everyone is expected to make sacrifices during an energy crisis. I'm not talking about real sacrifices. What could be a greater sacrifice for an American than to use less electricity but at the same time compensate the electric companies by paying more for it? That's what George C. Scott and President Nixon were talking about when they asked you to turn your lights out."

By this time Burberry had turned on his vacuum cleaner, and I didn't hear his reply. But as an accomplished lip reader, I was just as glad I couldn't.

"Expletive Deleted"

On October 13, 1960, John F. Kennedy debated Richard Nixon on television. At the time, the question of Harry Truman's cussing came up. Mr. Kennedy refused to apologize for Mr. Truman's salty language, but Mr. Nixon had strong feelings that a President of the United States should not curse.

He said in part, "One thing I have noted as I have traveled around the country is the tremendous number of children who come out to see the Presidential candidates. I see mothers holding up their babies so they can see a man who might be President of the United States. I know Senator Kennedy sees them, too. It makes you realize that whoever is President is going to be a man that all children of America look up to or look down on, and I can only say I am very proud that President Eisenhower restored dignity and decency and, frankly, good language to the conduct of the Presidency of the United States.

"And I only hope, should I win this election, that I could approach President Eisenhower in maintaining the dignity of the office and see to it that whenever any mother or father talks to his child, he can look at the man in the White House and, whatever he may think of his policies, he will say 'Well, there is a man who maintains the kind of standards personally that I would want my child to follow.'"

I must admit that even though it's been fourteen years since Mr.

Nixon said this, I was very moved. Perhaps, I thought, for the first time in history this country would have a President who didn't cuss.

Although Mr. Nixon didn't make it in 1960, he did become President in 1968, and every time he drove by in the last five years I held up my son in my arms (he's now twenty) and said, "There's a President who has the kind of standards I want you to follow."

Although Joel was rather heavy, I felt it was worth the strain on my back.

You can imagine my despair and disillusionment when the transcripts of the Presidential tapes were released and it turned out Mr. Nixon might have been the cussingest President in our history. Almost every other word has an "expletive deleted," and if you count the "inaudibles" and "unclears" and "ambiguities," it's enough to make a U.S. marine top sergeant's hair stand on end.

The question is what happened between the time Nixon debated Kennedy and the time he became President of the United States.

I sincerely believe Mr. Nixon was telling the truth when he said he was shocked by Harry Truman's language. I also believe in my heart he didn't start cussing until he lost the election to Kennedy.

A friend of Mr. Nixon told me, "I never heard Dick use an 'expletive deleted' until the 1960 Illinois results of the election came in. In 1962 he lost the race for governor in California, and he let out one 'inaudible' after another. I didn't know there were that many 'expletives' in the English language. It was hard after that to have Dick over to the house when the children were around.

"I thought when he became President and he was more secure, he'd stop using 'expletives,' but apparently once you start using them, it's hard to give up," the friend said.

And so it turns out that President Nixon was no better than Harry Truman when it came to language, and a lot worse than President Eisenhower. It's something we'll all have to get used to.

But I know one thing—I'm no longer going to hold up my twenty-year-old son in my arms when the President drives by. Any President who promises to restore good language to the Presidency and then talks the way he did is nothing but an "inaudible" in my book.

What Did Henry Give?

No one is quite certain what kind of deals Henry Kissinger made to get a settlement in the Middle East, but President Nixon probably is finding out.

I can imagine a scene at a great reception given by President Sadat of Egypt where leaders from all the Arab lands have gathered to meet the President of the United States. Henry is standing next to President Nixon in the receiving line and introducing the Arabs to the President.

"Mr. President," Henry says, "this is Sheikh Kaleli Abrim."

Sheikh Abrim shakes hands with Mr. Nixon. "My father sends his respects and asks me to thank you on behalf of our family for giving us the state of Rhode Island."

President Nixon appears startled and whispered to Henry, "Did we give Rhode Island to the Abrim family?"

Henry whispers back, "They wanted California, but I talked them into taking Rhode Island instead."

"What did we get in exchange?" the President asks.

"A steady, two-year supply of oil at fourteen dollars a barrel."

"Hmmm," the President says, "I guess nobody will mind losing Rhode Island."

The sheikh moves on, and Henry introduces the next Arab leader.

"This, Mr. President, is Hakim Assou, the Egyptian minister of public works."

Mr. Assou bows. "It is a great honor I finally meet the noble benefactor of Egypt."

"What did we give *them?*" the President whispers to Henry.

Henry replies, "The Ford Motor Company."

"In Egypt?" the President asks.

Henry blushes. "The Ford Motor Company in the United States. You see, in order to get a settlement in Syria we needed help from the Egyptians. The only way we could get help from them was to give them something in exchange. I thought the Ford Motor Company would be a nice *quid pro quo.*"

"Has anyone told Henry Ford?"

"Not yet. I didn't want it to leak to the press."

Mr. Assou moves on, and Henry introduces Fata Fatima, the leader of a splinter Maoist Palestinian guerrilla band.

Fatima refuses to shake hands with the President. He tells Henry, "I have been talking with my brothers, and we have decided you tricked us when you offered us three squadrons of Phantom jets. We will not go to Geneva unless we receive three nuclear submarines."

"What the devil?" the President says to Henry.

Henry whispers, "Don't pay any attention to him. He's all talk. They'll take the three squadrons of Phantom jets."

"Are you sure we want to give these people Phantom jets?"

"I had to give them *something,*" Henry says defensively.

The next Arab leader is Aleki Mossad, the Syrian minister of tourism.

"Oh, Great One," Mossad says, "you have saved the Syrian tourist industry."

The President looks questioningly at Henry.

Henry says, "I forgot to tell you last week. In order to get the Syrians off the Golan Heights I promised them Las Vegas. We have to sign the deed after lunch."

Before the President can meet the next Arab leader, President Sadat tells Mr. Nixon he has an urgent call from Golda Meir.

After five minutes a rather upset President returns to the receiving line. He whispers to Henry, "Did you give Israel the Standard Oil Company of New Jersey?"

"Come to think of it," Henry says, "I did. Originally they demanded Alaska, but I told them it was out of the question."

A Visit With Checkers

When President Nixon dropped his latest bombshell on the American people, I was so shaken up I didn't know what to do. So I went to the graveside of Checkers, the Nixons' cocker spaniel, and sat on the stone.

"Well, Checkers," I said, "your master has had it. He's either got to resign or they're going to kick him out of office. You saved him once, but you can't save him this time. . . . I know what you're saying, 'how could it happen? How could a man who had the whole world in his hands blow it the way he did?' I can't answer that.

"He did some great things, Checkers, even his worst enemies acknowledge that. He brought about a new relationship with China, and some sort of detente with Russia, and the whole world picture changed for the better under him.

"But at the same time he tore the fabric of his own country to shreds. First his people tried to steal an election, an election he was certain of winning without one bit of skulduggery. Then he tried to cover up the crimes of the people who worked for him—cheap, crummy crimes that a fifth-rate politician would consider beneath him.

"Why, Checkers, why?

"That's the question we'll be asking for years to come. Why would a man with the power and the glory of the Presidency become involved with dirty tricks, housebreaking, obstruction of justice, and perjury? I'm not making this up, Checkers. It's all in the tapes. . . . Oh, you don't know about the tapes? Well, you see, soon after your master took over the Presidency he decided to record the conversations of everyone he came in contact with—without their knowledge, except for H. R. Haldeman. You don't know Haldeman? He was Mr. Nixon's closest aide—he ran the White House with John Ehrlichman—they've both been indicted for the same crimes that finally caught up with your master.

"Anyway, the tapes were the only evidence that could convict Mr. Nixon, and he turned some over to the justice people, and he was ordered to turn over other tapes by the courts. I know what you're going to ask, 'Why didn't he burn the tapes?' Nobody knows the answer to that question, Checkers. Either he was stupid or he was so contemptuous of the laws of this country he didn't believe anyone would ever get to hear them. Once he was ordered to turn over the tapes that implicated him, his goose was cooked.

"But do you want to know the worst thing your master did? He lied to the American people. He lied to his friends, his lawyers, his own party, and everyone who believed in him.

"Why, Checkers, why? You knew him better than we did. Why would a man think the American people would keep him in office after he deceived them time and time again?

"Was it scorn for us that made him do it? Was it some insecurity in his character that kept him from playing by the rules? Or was it simply a case of a man who was a born loser even when he became President of the United States?

"Well, I've got to be going now. The country will survive, Checkers. We're much better than your master thinks we are. And we do have some consolation. If things hadn't worked out the way they did, Agnew might have become President and then we would have had to impeach him."

How Kissinger Got Married

The marriage of Secretary of State Henry Kissinger to the former Nancy Maginnes came as a surprise to everyone. Not even the Pentagon was let in on the secret, and members of the Senate Foreign Relations Committee are still mumbling that it was typical of Kissinger to do something like that on Saturday, when most Congressmen were out of town.

Although the State Department has remained mum on what led up to the marriage, I have been able to put pieces of the story together.

Kissinger came back from the Soviet Union on Thursday and immediately plunged into talks with Moshe Dayan in Washington. These talks were continued until lunch on Saturday.

At about noon Kissinger finished his conversation with Dayan, bade good-bye to him and then turned to his aide and asked, "What do I have on my schedule now?"

The aide said, "I don't see anything on your schedule, Mr. Secretary. You're free the entire afternoon."

Mr. Kissinger was incredulous. "What do you mean, I have nothing on my schedule? I always have *something* on my schedule. I think I'll go see the President."

"He's in Key Biscayne meeting with his lawyers." the aide said. "He can't see you until Sunday."

"All right then," Kissinger said, "I'll take a trip somewhere. I think I'll go to India. I haven't been there in sometime."

The aide replied nervously, "If you go to India this afternoon, you'll have to go to Pakistan as well, and you won't be able to get back in time for a reception at the Iranian Embassy on Monday."

"Well, is there any head of state visiting this country whom I can see?"

"King Hussein is in Palm Beach, but if you see him right after you saw Moshe Dayan, Sadat of Egypt might get angry."

Kissinger started pacing up and down the office.

"What about Africa? Couldn't I go to Africa this afternoon?"

"North or South Africa?"

"What difference does it make?" Kissinger asked. "Maybe I could work out a detente between the two of them."

"I wouldn't advise it, sir. If you go to Africa now, it will just stir up the Soviets and the Chinese."

"Chinese? There's an idea. Why don't I go see Chou En-lai? Get me Peking on the phone. . . . Hello, Chou. . . . This is Henry. I thought I'd come over for the afternoon, and we could have a bowl of rice together. . . . Oh, you've got tickets for the opera? . . . No, no that's all right. We'll do it some other day. . . . Yeah, sure, I'll give you some notice the next time."

Kissinger hung up the phone in despair. "Are there any movie premieres I could go to?" he asked his aide.

"You missed *The Great Gatsby* by three days," the aide said.

Just then Nancy Maginnes walked into the office.

"Hi, Henry, I was just driving by, and I stopped in to say hello. I won't keep you."

"No, no, sit down. I'm glad to see you. I don't have anything to do this afternoon."

"You must be kidding," Miss Maginnes said.

"I wish I was. My staff goofed up and left me without a trip, a negotiation or an appointment. I'm sick."

Miss Maginnes nodded sympathetically. "This is just a suggestion, Henry, but since you're free for the rest of the day, why don't we get married?"

Henry was shocked. "Married? It never occurred to me. I could probably get married this afternoon, couldn't I?"

"I'll check it out with protocol," the aide said, "but I'm sure they'd have no objection."

"Why not?" Kissinger asked Miss Maginnes. "It will be a fun way to kill the day before I go off to Damascus."

A Humdinger Explanation

It seems the mystery of the 18½-minute hum on one of the key Presidential tapes may never be resolved. Rose Mary Woods, President Nixon's lawyers and even Judge Sirica have no idea how it happened. Every possible theory has been advanced and rejected — except one.

The one explanation that no one has mentioned is that the President was humming by himself for the entire 18½ minutes.

I was put on to this theory by a former White House aide who says that one of President Nixon's biggest secrets is that he likes to hum when he's struggling with the major problems of the world.

"You mean the entire eighteen and a half minutes of hum on the tape could have been made by the President?" I asked.

"Easily. I've seen the President hum for hours at a time. It relaxes him and helps him tough it out. He hummed all during the Vietnam War, and I wouldn't be surprised if he's been humming ever since Watergate."

"But if the eighteen and a half minutes of humming was made by the President, why didn't he just say so and save us all from thinking the worst?"

"Because the President doesn't want anyone to know he hums. He'll do anything to keep people from finding out."

"But why?" I asked.

"He is afraid if the American people know he hums, they may think he's not cool. He doesn't want to go down in history as the first American President who was known as a nervous hummer."

"There's nothing wrong with humming. Lots of people do it."

"Yes, but the President doesn't hum very well. If you listen to the disputed tape, you'll realize his voice is a terrible monotone. Can you imagine what the media would do to him if they discovered the eighteen-and-a-half-minute hum on the tape was actually made by the President of the United States?"

"Then you think Rose Mary Woods was aware that the hum she heard was made by her boss?"

"I'm certain of it. She's been trying to break him of the humming habit for twenty-five years."

"What about the President's lawyers? Did they know?"

"I'm not certain of that. The President only hums around people he really trusts. When he goes out boating with Bebe Rebozo, he hums, and when he screens *Patton* with his family, he hums, and when he watches the Redskins, he hums."

"Wait a minute. On the tape there were two distinctive hums. One went for five minutes and was very loud, and the rest of the time the hum was much lower. How do you explain that?"

"The President was probably doing two different things. He may have hummed loudly when he was reading the Washington *Post,* and he could have hummed softly while he was working on his income taxes."

"Of course," I said, "that explains it. And to think Rose Mary Woods is taking the rap for the hum."

"That," said the White House aide, "is what secretaries are for."

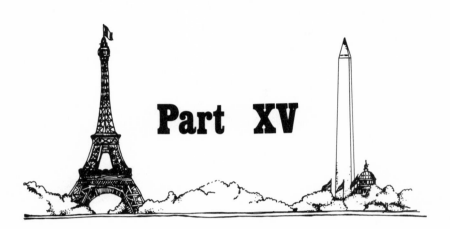

Part XV

Recycling Oil Money

PARIS—"There's your problem," said François as an Arab sheikh walked by the bar at the Hôtel George V.

We were talking about the economy in Europe, and François was trying to explain it to me.

"You mean there are too many Arab sheikhs?" I asked him.

"No, I mean there are not enough sheikhs—oil sheikhs to be specific. This shortage of Arab potentates is killing everyone."

"How's that?"

"It's called recycling. When you Americans once had money, you came by the millions to Europe and spent it here. When you ran out of money and the Japanese had it all, they came here to spend it. We always complained about tourists, but it was one of the best ways to keep the money in circulation.

"Now," said François sadly, "the Arabs have all the money, and there are not enough of them to spread it around."

"I thought there were a lot of Arabs in the world," I said.

"There are," replied François, "but they are not the right kind. Only a few of them have any of the oil money. The king of Saudi Arabia, for example, who must have made twenty-one billion dollars on oil this year, has about one hundred and thirty-two sons and nephews. That means each son or nephew would have to spend one hundred and sixty million dollars for the rest of us to get even."

"That would be tough to do," I admitted.

"Most of the oil sheikhs leave their wives at home, so you don't get any business at Dior, Balenciaga or Givenchy. They don't buy any art, and they're not known for their wine consumption. What can they spend their money on?"

"Postcards?"

"Exactly. Even if they ate at Maxim's twice a day, they wouldn't be able to use up all the money that's rolling in. The other oil sheikhdoms are no better. I would say at the maximum there are about one thousand Arab families who are responsible for recycling forty billion dollars a year. There is no way they can do it."

"What's the answer, François?"

"The oil kingdoms have to produce more Arabs. We have to start a population explosion program in Saudi Arabia, Abu Dhabi, Bahrain, and Kuwait so the royal families will give birth to more princes."

"Won't that take time?" I asked.

"Maybe, but if they start now, at least we'll have a change in the eighties when our oil bill will be somewhere around one hundred billion dollars."

"How do you persuade the Arab sheikhs to have more children?" I asked François.

"You give them free 'birth explosion' pills. You set up an Unplanned Parenthood Agency where you counsel them on the joys of having very large families. You persuade the sheikhs that the more mouths they have to feed, the easier it will be for them to get rid of their money."

"It sounds like a dream to me, François."

"Perhaps," he replied, "but if it works, I can see the day when there will be nothing but Arab princes walking down the Champs-Élysées. The Place de la Concorde will be filled with Cadillacs, the Folies Bergère will be jammed with burnooses, and there will be so many sheikhs in Paris that Frenchmen will scrawl in chalk on their walls, 'ARABIANS GO HOME!' "

The Arab sheikh came into the bar with three bodyguards. They ordered Coca-Colas.

François whispered to me, "You see what I mean? How can you recycle a twenty-one-billion-dollar oil bill when all they buy is four Coca-Colas?"

Mother of Exiles

The Statue of Liberty was gazing toward Europe when I tapped her on the shoulder. "Ma'am," I said, "if you look the other way, we have about one hundred and thirty thousand Vietnamese refugees coming in from Guam and the Philippines. I thought you might hold your torch high and light the way for them."

The statue seemed irritated. "We have too many people in this country now. What am I going to do with one hundred and thirty thousand Orientals?"

"The same thing you did with everybody else. Welcome them. They're tired, and they're poor, and they are yearning to breathe free."

"And what about jobs? Who is going to support them?" she said petulantly.

"You never worried about that before," I said. "Whoever came to this country eventually found jobs, and almost all of them made very good citizens. There is no reason to think the Vietnamese will be different. After all, you are the mother of exiles."

"Times have changed," she growled. "The American people aren't that thrilled about having a bunch of refugees dumped on them. Who is going to feed them? How many will go on welfare? How do we know their kids won't get in trouble in the streets? We have enough problems in this country without asking for more."

"But," I pleaded, "we're responsible for them being refugees. We screwed up a country like it's never been screwed up before. We supported their corrupt governments, loaded them down with weapons they couldn't use, defoliated their rice paddies, and wrecked their families.

"We left the country in a mess. The least we can do is take in whatever huddled masses escaped to our teeming shore."

"That's easy for you to say," the Statue of Liberty replied, "but we have to think of Americans first. They don't want any more foreigners in this country."

"But most of our fathers and grandfathers and great-grandfathers were foreigners. You've welcomed them all. Tell me the truth. Do you have anything against Orientals?"

"I don't personally. But you know how some people are. The Vietnamese have different habits, and they're from another culture. They just don't fit in. Besides, I'm supposed to welcome the homeless from Europe. That's why I'm looking in that direction."

"These people need refuge," I protested. "Their lives are in ruins. Remember when they flew in orphans from Vietnam and Cambodia? Nobody seemed to object to that."

"It's not the same thing," the statue said. "You can adopt orphans. But what can you do with refugees?"

"Help them find homes, jobs, make them citizens."

"It's out of the question. It isn't our fault they lost the war. Look, no one minds one or two Vietnamese in a community. But you're talking about thousands. They'll stick out like a sore thumb. The unions would never stand for it."

"Please don't turn your back on them," I begged. "If somebody just said, 'Welcome. We're glad you came,' most Americans would go along with it. The American people gripe a lot, but they'll do the right thing if somebody leads them. If you could shine your torch toward the Golden Gate Bridge, perhaps the people will be ashamed of the way they've behaved."

The Statue of Liberty turned slowly. There was a tear in her eye. "I've been here so long I almost forgot why I was holding this lamp. Where did you say I should shine my torch?"

"Over there. Hold it as high as you can and point it toward the West so every American can see it. That's it. Now repeat after me, 'Send these, the homeless, tempest-tossed to me, I lift my lamp beside the golden door.' "

Medical Advertising Is Almost Here

The Federal Trade Commission (FTC) has attacked the American Medical Association (AMA) for illegal price fixing. It also says doctors keep patients from getting medical information by forbidding AMA members to advertise.

The big question raised by this attack is what kind of advertising the public will be exposed to if the FTC wins its case.

My friend Beezlebub, who owns an advertising agency, has already been working on some campaigns and hopes to garner a lot of accounts as soon as medical advertising becomes legal. He gave me a preview of what he had worked up.

First he showed me a large full-page ad for a newspaper with a black headline on the top: SPECIAL GEORGE WASHINGTON BIRTHDAY SALE ON ALL MAJOR OPERATIONS.

Madman Dr. Kelly announces the greatest surgery bargain in history. The first 100 people who show up at the Wesley Heights Clinic on George Washington's Birthday will be given a complete operation, including anesthesia and postoperative care, for $2.

Yes, for only $2 you could be lucky enough to have any organ in your body removed at once-in-a-lifetime prices.

Other Bicentennial bargains Madman Dr. Kelly is giving away include a brain operation for $14.95, a kidney transplant for $29.50, and a complete blood transfusion for $3.95.

If you can find a doctor in town who will charge less, Madman Dr. Kelly will give you FREE, yes, we said FREE, a plastic surgery nose job. Don't forget for one day only the greatest surgical sale in history at Madman Dr. Kelly's. No phone orders, please.

"How do you like it?" Beezlebub asked me.

"It's a heck of an ad," I admitted.

"Come on in the screening room. I want to show you some commercials my TV people worked out." Beezlebub pushed a button, and John Cameron Swayze came on the screen.

He was standing on the top of a cliff. "Ladies and gentlemen, I am standing on the highest cliff overlooking Acapulco. With me are two gentlemen, both of whom have had pacemakers implanted in their hearts. One was implanted by Dr. Wallace Welby. The other by a heart surgeon who charges three times what a Welby implant costs. We're going to do a little experiment now. Are you ready, gentlemen?"

The men nod.

John Cameron Swayze pushes both men off the cliff, and they plunge 300 feet to the rocks below.

The commercial picks up Swayze at the bottom, standing over their bodies. A doctor with a stethoscope is listening to their hearts.

"Well, Doctor?"

"This man's pacemaker is still working. This other man's heart has stopped." Swayze pulls off a bandage on the body of the man whose pacemaker is still working. The camera zooms in on a tattoo which reads "Welby, M.D."

Swayze looks out at the audience. "This proves you don't need an expensive doctor to insert a pacemaker. Dr. Welby is cheap in price, but not in work. Call this toll-free number today. Dr. Welby's pacemakers start at thirty-nine fifty, including installation and a three-month guarantee."

"I like it," I told Beezlebub.

"Here's one which I call the average-woman-type commercial." He pushed a button.

A man with a microphone is standing in a large doctor's office. In the background are three women on couches.

He goes over to the ladies. "Now, ladies, we're going to have some fun today. We're going to blindfold you and have you analyzed by three psychiatrists. After they're finished, I want you to tell me which one you liked the best."

A sign flashes on the screen which says, AFTER 50 MINUTES.

"All right, ladies, which doctor did you prefer?"

The first lady, after her blindfold is taken off, says, "I liked number two. He had a nice soft voice."

"Number two," the second lady says. "He seemed to understand my problem."

The third lady says, "I don't know who he is, but I'm switching to number two."

The announcer says. "And now, let's see who number two is. It's Dr. Adolph Fremluck, America's favorite psychiatrist. Yes, folks, everyone is switching to Dr. Fremluck, not only for the quality of his work but for his low fees. If you are depressed, paranoid, schizoid, or just plain neurotic, Dr. Fremluck has a cure for you. He's open every night until ten, and if you take advantage of his special January blues rates, he will give you absolutely free a set of Walt Disney coffee mugs with Mickey and Minnie, Donald Duck, and all the other characters that made your childhood so miserable. Don't delay. If you're sick in the head, Fremluck wants to hear from you today.

Dinner in Paris

PARIS—The last time I was in Paris, six years ago, I wrote a column titled "Paris on $500 a Day." The thrust of the piece was that it was still possible to get by in the French capital on $500 if you passed up lunch. My French friends, as well as Americans living in France, thought the article was very funny. But they aren't laughing anymore.

When it comes to inflation, the United States is *Mary Poppins* and France is *Deep Throat*.

But if you don't worry about prices, you can still have a marvelous time in Paris. What you have to do is forget everything and just decide to live for the moment.

I did this the first night I arrived in town. My wife and I went to a small bistro that boasted two stars in the *Guide Michelin*.

When the waiter gave us the menu, I thought he made a mistake.

"I beg your pardon, monsieur," I said. "But I believe you have made an error. You gave me the Bank of France's financial report for the month of May."

"No, monsieur, that is the *carte pour* dinner."

My wife, who always gets nervous when she sees melon selling for more than $15 a portion, whispered to me, "Let's get out of here."

"Don't be silly. We don't get to Paris very often. Let's enjoy it." I studied the menu carefully. "Now we have our choice. We can have the white asparagus or send Joel to college in the fall."

She said, "You mean to say that white asparagus costs as much as Joel's tuition?"

"Yes," I replied, "but they're the large white ones with Hollandaise sauce. You can only get them in the spring."

"But," my wife, always the practical one, said, "Joel had his heart set on going to college."

"Look, Joel can go to school anytime. But how often do we come to France and have a chance to order white asparagus? I know if we explain it to him, he'll understand."

There were so many dishes to choose from after the first course that I couldn't make up my mind.

Finally, I said to my wife, "Remember that house we were going to buy in Martha's Vineyard?"

"The one overlooking the ocean?"

"That's the one," I said. "Let's have the lobster instead."

"You mean you'd rather have lobster than own a house on Martha's Vineyard?"

"But this lobster is cooked in a special cream sauce of the chef. It could be years before we have a lobster like this again. We have to think of our old age."

"I don't know," my wife said. "I had my heart set on that house."

"Well, I have my heart set on lobster, and since they're both the same price, I think our stomachs should come first."

The waiter handed me the wine card.

"There's a very nice Pouilly-Fuissé," I said.

"Can we afford it?" my wife asked.

"We can if we sell the car when we get back home."

"I need a car," she protested.

"All right," I said. "We'll order an inexpensive Sancerre and cancel the orthodontist's work on Connie's teeth."

My wife was becoming agitated. "If it's costing this much for dinner, how are we going to pay our hotel bill?"

"Will you stop worrying? What do you think the World Bank is for?"

Collect Call

"Hello, I have a collect call from Miss Joyce Robinson in Oshkosh, Wisconsin. Will you accept the charges?"

"Yes, operator, we will."

"Hi, Pops. How are you?"

"Fine. What are you doing in Oshkosh? I thought you were driving to Cape Cod to visit Aunt Rose."

"We were, but Cynthia wanted to stop off and visit a boy she knew from school who lives in Minneapolis."

"Who is Cynthia?"

"She's a girl I met in New Orleans."

"New Orleans? I didn't know you went to New Orleans."

"I wasn't planning to, but Tommy said there was a great concert of the Grateful Dead scheduled to play in the stadium. He got the day right, but the wrong month."

"Tommy?"

"He was hitchhiking on Ninety-five."

"You started out with Ellen Mulberry. Where is she?"

"She met some kids she knew in Fort Lauderdale, and they were driving to Mexico, so she decided to go with them."

"Do Mr. and Mrs. Mulberry know this?"

"I think Ellen called them after the accident."

"What accident?"

"The camper she was in had a blowout, and Ellen got banged up a little."

"So you're now traveling with Cynthia and Tommy."

"No. Tommy stayed in New Orleans, and Cynthia left yesterday. She said she couldn't wait until my car was fixed."

"What's wrong with your car?"

"The motor fell out. That's what I'm calling you about. The garageman said it will cost five hundred and fifty dollars to fix it up."

"That's a fortune!"

"You don't have to pay it if you don't want to. I can leave the car here. I met a guy who has a motorcycle, and he says he'll take me as far as Detroit."

"I'LL PAY IT!"

"How's Mom?"

"She's on the extension. I think she was fine until we got your call. Where are you staying until you get your car fixed?"

"I met some nice kids who have a religious commune near here, and they said I could stay with them if I promise to devote the rest of my life to God."

"That's nice."

"The only problem is I have to shave my head."

"Can't you stay at a motel?"

"I don't have any money left."

"What happened to the three hundred dollars I gave you?"

"Two hundred went for expenses, and one hundred of it went for the fine."

"What fine?"

"We were fined one hundred dollars for speeding in this little itty-bitty town in Arkansas."

"I told you not to drive fast."

"I wasn't driving. Fred was."

"Who the hell is Fred?"

"He's a vegetarian, and he says capitalism is finished in the West."

"That's worth one hundred dollars to hear. Are you going to Cape Cod to visit Aunt Rose or aren't you?"

"As soon as I get the car fixed, Pops. Send me the money care of Western Union. You don't want the man to fix the dented door at the same time?"

"Your car had no dented door."

"It does now. I have to go, Dad. Some kids I met are going to take me white-water canoeing. Good-bye. And, Pops—have a nice day."

The Most Unforgettable Swordsman I Ever Met

As a man who lives his sexual fantasies through his friends, I have made a lifelong study of the techniques of others in the pursuit of ultimate physical happiness.

The prize after all these years still goes to a friend I served with in the United States Marine Corps during World War Two. His name was Dooley and we were stationed together at the El Toro Air Base in Santa Ana, California.

Dooley was as unlikely a Marine or a swordsman as you could find in the Corps. He was 19 years old, suffered from an acne condition, was thin as a rail, walked with a slouch and his uniform made him look like a scarecrow.

We spent most of our liberty in Los Angeles, with side excursions to Newport Beach, Hollywood and Santa Monica. These trips in search of female companionship and liquid refreshment proved almost always productive for Dooley and almost always unproductive for me. Inevitably, Dooley wound up in the hay with a girl, while I usually found myself hitchhiking back to El Toro by myself at three o'clock in the morning, trying to figure out what the hell I had done wrong.

Except for admitting that he had scored, Dooley never talked too much about his successes; and after ten liberties, I was going out of my mind, trying to discover what Dooley had that I didn't. I will say right here, without bragging, that in those days, I looked like a Marine, talked like a Marine and, by all the laws of nature, it should have been Dooley rather than me who kept striking out.

One day I couldn't take it anymore and I said to Dooley while we were sitting on the flight line waiting for our planes to come back, "Goddamn it, Dooley, how do you do it?"

"How do you do what?" Dooley asked, rubbing grease all over his trousers.

"How do you make it with the broads?"

Dooley stared down at his dirty fingernails and said nothing.

"Come on, Dooley. I'm your buddy. Tell me your secret. Last night, we both walked into the bar together, we met two girls together, we both bought them drinks, I was twice as amusing as you were, and yet at the end of the evening, your girl took you home and my girl wouldn't even let me take her to her door. What the hell do you tell them?"

Dooley lay down outstretched on the concrete and shielded his eyes from the sun. "You really want to know?"

"You're damn right I want to know."

"OK," said Dooley, "I'll tell you, but only on the condition you never tell anyone my secret. Do you promise?"

"I promise! I promise!"

"I tell them I'm queer."

"What?"

"I tell them I'm queer. I tell them I can't make it with them sexually."

"How can you do that? You're a Marine."

"That's just the point. I tell them it's a secret. That I lied to get into the Marine Corps."

"I still don't get it. Why would you say a stupid thing like that?"

"Because almost every woman takes pity on a queer and decides it's her personal mission in life to make him go straight."

"Oh, my God!" I cried. "I don't believe it."

"It's true. I read it in a book once. Some guy thought he was queer and this older woman decided to prove to him that he wasn't, so she started taking her clothes off and, bam!"

"You couldn't get away with it," I protested. "You just couldn't."

"Well, I do."

"I don't believe you."

"OK," Dooley said, "I'll tell you what I'll do. One of these nights, when we go out, I'll take you along with me and you can watch me operate."

"I can't believe it, I can't believe it."

Three weeks later, Dooley and I were in a bar in Santa Monica and before the evening was out, we were sitting with two secretaries from Metro-Goldwyn-Mayer.

It turned out that one of them had an apartment a few blocks away and Dooley told the girls we had no more money to spend. His girl suggested we go up to the apartment, which I, of course, seconded.

As we were leaving the bar, Dooley whispered, "Now, watch me closely."

It was a nice one-bedroom apartment, with a large living room and two couches facing each other.

Dooley's girl brought out the ice and produced a bottle of Scotch. Then she turned on the record machine.

I tried to kiss my girl, but she pushed me away. "None of that stuff," she said. "We've only invited you up for a drink. Then you have to leave."

Dooley just sat on the couch, staring at his hands.

His girl said, after a while, "What's the matter?"

"I think I better tell you something, before we get to be good friends," he said, biting his lip. "You see, I like you a lot, but . . . but . . . " He put his head in his hands.

Dooley's girl sat down next to him. "What's wrong?"

He looked at her with large basset eyes. "I can't make it with a girl."

"Were you hurt in the War?" she asked.

"No, it's not that." Dooley gulped. "Christ, I wish it was. It's just that I've never been able to make it with a girl. Please, I better go."

His girl and my girl stared at Dooley. My girl said, "You mean you're . . . you're . . . "

"Yes," Dooley said. "You can say it. I'm queer." He hid his face in his hands.

Dooley's girl put her arm around his shoulder. "Have you ever tried?"

Dooley nodded his head. "Many times. It's just no good. Maybe it has something to do with my mother. She always dressed me in girls' clothes. I don't know why. Nobody can help me."

"You poor kid," my girl said.

"Maybe I could help you," Dooley's girl said.

Dooley tried to push her away. "It's no good. Believe me. Let me go home. I'm so ashamed."

Dooley's girl said. "Look at me. Just look at me. Do you find me pretty?"

"Yes, you're beautiful."

"Do you find me sexually attractive?"

"I don't know. Oh, why are you asking me all these questions?" Dooley cried, trying to turn away from her.

She held his face in her hands. "I can help you."

"Nobody can help me," Dooley said.

I didn't know whether to laugh or cry as I watched Dooley's Academy Award performance.

"Dooley," his girl said, "kiss me."

"I can't, I can't."

"Then I'll kiss you." She put her lips on his and held them there.

"How was that?" she asked.

"OK, I guess," Dooley said.

"All right," she said, "the next thing I want you to do is open your mouth when I kiss you."

"Why?" Dooley asked.

"Don't ask questions. Just do as I tell you."

Dooley opened his mouth and she kissed him, only this time, much longer.

I was getting pretty excited and I put my hand on my girl's thigh. She immediately brushed it off and said, "Watch your hands, Marine." I went back to watching Dooley.

Dooley's girl started unbottoning her blouse.

"Now," she said, "put your hands on my breast."

"No," Dooley said. "No."

"Do as I tell you," his girl whispered. Then she took his hand and put it on her breast and held it there.

"Does that feel nice?" she asked.

"Yes. It does."

"Now I'm going to release my hand and I want you to rub my breast gently. Do you understand?"

"You want me to rub your breast gently?"

"Yes, and kiss me at the same time."

I was going berserk on my couch and I made a grab for my girl, who whispered angrily, "Stop it. You'll spoil everything."

Dooley's girl had now unbuttoned her blouse and had removed her bra.

"Now," she said softly, "kiss my breast."

Dooley looked up at her. "Do I have to?"

"Yes, you do." She started shoving Dooley's head down to her breast.

Dooley tried to fight it, but soon he was kissing her breast.

"Now the other one."

"It's nice." Dooley said. "It's different with you. Why is it different with you?"

"You're not queer, Dooley," his girl said. "You're just afraid. Let's go into the bedroom now."

"No," cried Dooley. "I couldn't do that. Not the bedroom."

"I won't hurt you, Dooley. I promise." She lifted him off the couch. "It will be a beautiful experience."

Dooley let her lead him into the bedroom. "I hope you're right."

"I know I'm right," she said. "Believe in me."

They disappeared into the bedroom and shut the door.

My girl had tears in her eyes. "It's the most moving thing I ever saw."

"It sure as hell was," I said, trying to pin her against the couch.

"Get away from me, you animal," she said, shoving both elbows into my face.

"I'm not an animal. Why can't we do it, too?"

"Because," she said, getting up from the couch, "that's all you want from me."

I could hear moans coming from the bedroom.

"What's that got to do with it? They're doing it."

"Yes, but only because she's trying to make a man out of him. I would have done the same thing."

I put on my jacket and grabbed my hat.

"Aren't you going to wait for Dooley?" she asked.

"No," I said. "Let the queer son of a bitch find his own way home."

Twenty-five years have gone by since that excruciating evening, but it still remains vivid in my mind and I can't help thinking everytime I drive through Southern California that among those houses and apartments must be at least 200 middle-aged housewives, all of whom secretly believe that their ultimate sacrifice made a man out of Dooley.

* * *

Breaking the Tax Code

Deep in the bowels of the Internal Revenue Service building is a large steel door with a sign outside of it which says RESTRICTED AREA— AUTHORIZED PERSONNEL ONLY.

Two armed guards are stationed in front of it, and everyone who goes in and out is checked twice. This special bureau, called FITF, is in charge of devising federal income tax forms that no one can understand. A staff of cryptographers and code experts work day and night to devise new methods of foxing the taxpayer so he will be unable to fill out his 1040 form.

Last May an IRS agent in the Minneapolis office started to go over the 1974 return of a soybean farmer in Duluth when he sat up with a start. The form had been filled out by the farmer himself, and there were no mistakes.

He immediately picked up his phone and called the director of FITF.

"Sir," the agent said, "I think someone has broken our 1040 Code. I have a soybean farmer in Duluth who filled out his tax return without the aid of an accountant or a tax lawyer."

"Are you sure it just wasn't an accident?" the director said.

"Certain, sir. He was even able to fill out Part III 16 B which refers to Section D Lines 12(a) and 14(c) by combining the amounts shown on lines 5 and 13."

"Oh, my God," the director said. "Did he get Part V Question 40 by reducing his gain on line 18 to the extent of the loss, if any, on line 39, as referred to in Instruction K?"

"Perfectly, sir. It's as if he had our code book in front of him while he was filling out the form."

"I'll notify the commissioner and secretary of the treasury at once." The director hung up and picked up his red hot-line phone.

An hour later a group of grim-faced people were sitting in the office of the secretary of the treasury, who was pacing up and down. "How did it happen?" he shouted at the commissioner of internal revenue. "You promised me that no one would be able to make head or tail of the 1974 return."

The commissioner looked angrily at the director of FITF. "What happened, Mulligan?"

"I don't know," said Mulligan. "Maybe the soybean farmer is some kind of mathematical nut. We tried the 1974 form out on ten thousand people, including a thousand IRS agents, and not one of them understood it. It seemed foolproof."

The secretary of the treasury walked over to his window. "Do you know what this means? If a soybean farmer in Duluth has the key to our 1040 returns, that means other people will soon have it. We'll have millions of people filling out their own income tax forms. It could destroy every tax law and accounting office in the country."

The commissioner said, "It looks like we have no choice. We're going to have to change the 1040 form and make it so complicated that even H & R Block won't understand it. Can you do it, Mulligan?"

"Yes, sir," Mulligan replied. "But I'll need more people."

"Take anyone you want," the secretary of the treasury said. "This has highest priority. The very fabric of the American tax system is at stake. I want daily reports on your progress. I want that form to look like the greatest bunch of gobbledygook anyone has ever read."

The commissioner said, "We'll do it, sir. By the time the new returns are sent out there won't be five people in the country who will know how to fill it out."

"Not five people!" the secretary said. "I don't want anybody to understand it, including myself."

Mulligan replied, "Don't worry, Mr. Secretary. When my people get finished with it, the American taxpayer won't even be able to find the right line for his name and address."

The rest is history. As everyone who received his 1040 Tax Form for 1975 knows, FITF came up with a return that defied imagination. The secretary was so pleased he presented Mulligan with the U.S. Medal of Bureaucratic Balderdash with an Oak Leaf Cluster, the highest award the tax agency can bestow on an IRS employee in peacetime.

The Washington Triangle

By now everyone must know about the Bermuda Triangle, a vast body of water extending from Bermuda in the north to Southern Florida and then east to a point in the Bahamas past Puerto Rico.

Charles Berlitz, who has written a best-seller about it, claims 100 ships and planes have vanished in the area without a trace, and more than 1,000 lives have been lost since 1945.

There are many theories concerning the mystery. Some people believe that UFOs are responsible. Others feel the disasters may have been tied in with the lost colony of Atlantis. In any case, the Bermuda Triangle has caused quite a stir.

What has not been publicized is that there is a similar phenomenon right here in Washington, D.C. It is called the Washington Triangle, and it also has been a great source of mystery and unexplained disappearances.

The triangle area is located between the White House, the Capitol, and the Jefferson Memorial. Most of the accidents have taken place in the Tidal Basin, a rough, treacherous sea, five feet deep, which twists and turns as it empties into the Potomac River.

Jonathan Stone, who discovered the Washington Triangle, said, "The triangle is a frightening place. In a period of ten years we've lost thirty-four hundred trial balloons, two hundred congressional reforms, four hundred and fifty-three executive mandates, two hundred and thirty tax cuts, and one ship of state. They seem to have disappeared without a trace."

"But there must be some explanation," I said.

"The biggest disaster was the sinking of the SS *Watergate* with all hands aboard, including the President of the United States. A search of the area produced nothing but an empty lifeboat with the pathetic message 'I am not a crook' scrawled on the side."

"What do you think happened to the crew?" I asked Stone.

"They lost their moral compass. Something happens to people's sense of direction when they enter the triangle. The best political navigators forget which end is up and which end is down."

"What other disasters have taken place in the basin?"

"One day a Judge Carswell sailed out of the White House toward the Capitol to be confirmed as Supreme Court justice. Then a mysterious storm came up, and Carswell disappeared, never to be heard from again," Stone said.

"That's terrible," I said.

"Recently, President Ford sent up an energy message to the Hill and it sunk without a trace.

"At least a half dozen bills that Congress has sent down to the President to sign have drowned in the black, murky waters of the triangle. Budgets have been smashed on the rocks; campaign promises have vanished into thin air. Even a cargo of prayer breakfasts was lost without a trace or explanation."

"Do you suppose there is some supernatural power at work in the triangle that is responsible for so many disasters?" I asked.

"I'm sure of it," Stone said. "There is one theory that sophisticated beings from another planet live on the bottom of the basin and magnetically attract all the traffic between the White House and the Hill."

"I believe it," I said.

"Some say that there is a prehistoric monster in the water that eats nothing but budgets, presidential messages, government servants, and an occasional vice president of the United States."

"That could make sense, too," I agreed.

"There is also the possibility that the bottom of the Tidal Basin could be the lost colony of Atlantis," he said.

"You mean Fanne Foxe could be from another world?"

"There are many people, including respected scientists, who believe it."

They Need a Rest

The big question everyone in Washington is asking this week is: "Can congressmen chew gum and walk at the same time?" It's impossible to answer because all of them have gone on vacation for ten days.

The decision to take ten days off was not one of those spur-of-the-moment actions that the House of Representatives is noted for. It was carefully thought out and approved by the leadership.

I went up on the Hill Monday to find out what was going on while the congressmen were away.

The only one I could find, who wasn't on vacation, was a cleaning woman who had been asked to act as a liaison with the press.

After she finished mopping the floor in one of the congressmen's offices, she agreed to speak to me.

"Why would the House, after only being in session for one month, take a ten-day vacation?"

"They have to go home to make speeches in their districts telling their constituents what a mess this country is in because nobody in Washington is doing anything."

"Wouldn't it have been better if they stayed in Washington and tried to get us out of the mess?" I asked.

"Everyone needs a rest. You can't expect a legislator to work for thirty days and not get tired. When they come back from vacation, they'll be fresh and able to deal with the momentous problems of the country."

"I hate to say this, but there doesn't seem to be the sense of urgency around here that the times would require."

"That," she said, as she squeezed out her mop, "is because you don't understand how congressmen work. They have to know what the people are thinking. They can't pass laws if they don't have their ears to the ground."

"But all you have to do is pick up the newspapers and you'll know what people are thinking. They want jobs, a halt to inflation, and some sort of tax reform."

"You wouldn't get that in ten days even if they were all here," she retorted.

"But they could get started," I protested.

She emptied out her pail in the sink and filled it with fresh water.

"If the House thought they could have done something, they would have stayed here," she said. "But since the situation is hopeless, why sit in session and fret about it? Maybe they'll get some ideas while they're skiing."

"Haven't you heard from voters who have protested the House taking so much time off?"

"There has been a lot of mail," she said, "but I haven't been able to get to it yet because I still have to mop the hall."

"Are you going to answer the mail?"

"The congressmen said I could do anything I wanted as long as I didn't break any bric-a-brac on their desks. But I doubt if I'll get to the mail. I have to see Jerry Ford at four."

"You're going to see the President?"

"He called up and said he wanted to see Carl Albert and Tip O'Neill. I told him they weren't here. Then he said he would speak to any congressman. I had to tell him they were all on vacation. So he asked me to come over to discuss congressional problems with him. I said I would as soon as I got finished dusting Sam Rayburn's bust."

The phone in one of the congressmen's offices rang.

The cleaning lady picked it up. "Who is this? Senator Jackson? No, no one is here. This is Eliza in the Rayburn Building. No, I haven't gotten around to writing the energy legislation yet, I'll work on it tomorrow. For heaven's sakes, Scoop, I've only got two hands!"

The Great Leap Forward

The power struggle in Washington goes on unabated and foreign ambassadors stationed in Washington are sending long cables back to their countries trying to explain it.

Here is one of the cables sent by a representative of the People's Republic of China who is living in D.C.

"Momentous historical events are taking place here in Washington with the opening salvo of President Ford's Great Cultural Revolution. At first it was believed that Henry Kissinger was behind the cultural revolution to bring disgrace on Defense Minister James Schlesinger. But now Kissinger is in disgrace himself and has been demoted to only one inconsequential post as secretary of state. He has also been cited for contempt by the People's Congressional Subcommittee. Official American newspapers are predicting he will soon be sent to North Dakota to harvest grain at a state farm run by Agriculture Minister Earl Butz.

"Kissinger is now called a revisionist and counterrevolutionary by a majority of the People's Congress for advocating détente with the Soviet lackeys in the Kremlin.

"Defense Minister Schlesinger has been exiled to the Johns Hopkins School of International Affairs in the purge and has been replaced by Donald Rumsfeld, a young member of the Ford clique who has been involved in a power struggle with the Kissinger loyalists for over a year.

"Rumsfeld has denied he was the instigator of the palace revolt, but his picture with Ford has been plastered on posters all over the outside walls of the Pentagon.

"Another victim of the purge was William Colby, director of the People's Central Intelligence Committee. Colby's main crime was that he publicly confessed to the People's Congress about antigovernment activities committed by his cadres in the name of national security.

"He is being replaced by another Ford disciple, George Bush, formerly chairman of the People's Republican Party. He was sent to China when the party fell into disgrace after Nixon's fall from power after the August, 1974, revolution.

"The biggest shock was the demotion of President Ford's Vice President, Nelson Rockefeller, who still remains in his job, but only as a figurehead with no power.

"Rockefeller, with no dissent from Ford, was accused by conservative elements of the People's Republican Party of being a counterrevolutionary bourgeois radical revisionist arrogant dog. The conservative faction led by Ronald Reagan, a former governor of the province of California, threatened that unless Rockefeller and his ilk were brought to their knees, they would see that Ford was removed from the presidency at the next People's Republican Congress in Kansas City.

"To appease this faction, Ford made Rockefeller confess to the disastrous bond crop failure of New York and ordered all photographs of Rockefeller to be taken down from the country's post offices.

"The Reagan Guard still does not seem to be satisfied with the purge. There is now a power struggle going on in the People's Republican Party over the leadership, which may be fought out between the factions in the province of New Hampshire. Be advised when President Ford comes to the People's Republic of China next month, he will be constantly looking over his shoulder to see if Reagan is standing there.

"At the moment Ford is attacking the People's Congress and blaming it for the failure of his two-year plan. He is calling on the peasants and workers to throw out the People's Democratic Party in 1976.

"How are the masses reacting to all this? So far they have refused to support Ford mainly because every time the President tries to make a Great Leap Forward, he trips over somebody's wheelchair."

Lockheed Kickback 1100

Lockheed Aircraft has just developed a new supersonic Bribe that can fly two times the speed of sound. The Bribe, which took ten years to get off the drawing board, is called the Kickback 1100. Lockheed salespeople are claiming it is the most modern, versatile Bribe vehicle of its kind.

One of the people involved in the project told me in strictest confidence the Kickback 1100 can carry a payload of up to $10,000,000 to any corrupt official in the world.

"Northrup Corporation doesn't have anything to compare with it," he said proudly.

"How does it differ from the Bribe vehicles of the past?"

"Speed for one thing," he said. "We can now Bribe an Italian general in three and a half hours, whereas it took us seven hours to get the bag to him in the past."

"Boy, what will you space people think of next?" I said.

"The Kickback also has special navigational equipment which is so accurate it can land a million dollars on a Swiss bank vault with less than a ten-foot ceiling."

"You say it, but can you do it?"

"We did the other day. An African high government official asked us for one million dollars to okay a contract for several of our air buses. He gave us the name and the number of a Swiss bank account. The Kickback 1100 took off from Nassau and landed in Geneva in a safe at three o'clock the next morning. The African official was so pleased he ordered another Kickback for his brother."

My informant, who had too many drinks or he never would have talked so much, said, "The old defense Bribes were too noisy. Everyone heard about them. We told our engineers to completely redesign the Bribe so no one would recognize it. We wanted a model that would be smooth, fast, safe, and so quiet that nobody in Congress could complain about the sound. It also had no odor. The worst thing about a Bribe is that it eventually smells fishy."

"That must have been a tall order for the research and development people."

"We underestimated the cost of what it would take to develop a new Kickback by forty million dollars."

"How did you get the money to make up for the overrun?"

"We took several people from the Pentagon to our duck hunting club and explained the problem."

"That was good thinking. It's hard for a guy in a duck blind to say no to someone who has an overrun."

"Anyhow, we now have all the bugs out of the Kickback 1100, and we predict it will be the Bribe of the future. Everyone wants one. We have an order for three from a Japanese war criminal in Tokyo. He wants his painted gold. A South American president has asked for one decorated in German marks, and a member of a European royal family wants his covered with Dutch guilders."

"Some senators have complained about the dangers of the Kickback particularly as it's related to the ozone level. Are you certain the new Lockheed Bribe can stand an environmental study?" I asked.

"I'm certain of it. We tested our Bribes against those of France and England and many other foreign aviation companies. Not only were our Kickbacks larger and more comfortable, but we have a five-year guarantee behind them. You don't have to take my word for it. Ask any Arab prince in the Middle East."

The World Loves a Lobber

MONACO—I was invited to play in a pro-celebrity tennis tournament in Monaco. It was one of the events scheduled to celebrate the twenty-fifth anniversary of the reign of Prince Rainier. The reason I was invited is that Prince Rainier was trying to bring the lob back to Monte Carlo. Since this is a tennis stroke that I have become famous for, he insisted I be part of the tournament.

For those who do not play tennis, the lob is one of the most beautiful and difficult shots in tennis. The object is to hit the ball gently in the air over the head of the opponent and still keep it in the court. All the world loves a lobber, and wherever tennis is played, he is the most talked-about person on the court.

The lob shot was invented in 1893 by a Polish count named Leopold Lob. Leopold had studied to be a violinist, but when he bet his Stradivarius on black at the Monte Carlo casino one night and the ball dropped in the red slot of the roulette wheel, he had no choice but to give up music and become a tennis pro. He played tennis the way he played the violin, and pretty soon he was hitting the ball high in the air—the first time anyone had ever done it. In his honor, Prince Rainier's grandfather named the shot "the lob" or *le lob* as it is known in France.

By sheer coincidence, my grandfather had taken four lessons from Leopold Lob while vacationing one summer in Monaco and brought it back to his village in what was then the Austro-Hungarian Empire. When my grandfather wasn't being beaten up by Hungarian "Cossacks," he practiced the lob and taught it to my father.

My father brought it to the United States just before World War I. After I was born, he took me out to Coney Island every Sunday and made me practice it. (Since we were playing on the sandy beach, it was actually the only shot you could hit without the ball going dead.)

Prince Rainier had heard about my proficiency at the lob through Princess Grace, who still has relatives in Philadelphia.

He explained when I arrived why he was trying to bring the lob back to Monte Carlo.

For years Monaco had attracted the best-looking and richest lobbers in Europe. But in the fifties they started drifting away to other resorts such as St.-Tropez, the Italian Riviera, the Costa Brava in Spain, and Acapulco in Mexico.

Lobbers, you must understand, are not only great tennis players, but voracious gamblers as well as big spenders. One lobber will spend four times as much on tennis balls in one day as a backhander will spend in a week.

Lobbers also attract the most beautiful women. For some reason a woman just can't keep her hands off a man who hits a tennis ball up in the air.

Prince Rainier told me if he could bring back the lob to Monte Carlo, he was certain his principality would once again become the most important resort in the world.

The day I accepted the invitation to play in his pro-celebrity tournament, Prince Rainier built a new $10,000,000 casino. He didn't waste his money.

On the first morning of the tournament I drew Gardnar Mulloy as my partner. As soon as I got on the court and started to lob Dan Rowan and Dennis Ralston, the word went all the way down the Riviera: "Lobbing has come back to Monte Carlo."

By afternoon all the roads leading to Monaco were jammed with millionaire tennis players.

Every yacht in the Mediterranean within 3000 miles changed course and returned to the principality. Not since the early days of the century had Monaco seen anything like it.

Although Mulloy and I were eliminated on the first day, a grateful prince and princess presented me with the first issue of a new Monacan stamp. It was a two-franc airmail stamp with a beautiful etching of Count Leopold Lob hitting his first tennis ball high, high in the air.

Mother's Tennis

The explosion of tennis in the United States has produced all sorts of innovations in the game. One of the most exciting is called Mother's Tennis. It differs from regular tennis in that it requires not only four players, but also a number of children, several dogs, and an occasional irate husband.

The game is played on a regular court with two players on each side. But the thrill comes not from hitting the ball back and forth, but from the unexpected intervention of children and dogs onto the court during play.

I was introduced to Mother's Tennis at Martha's Vineyard last summer, and this is how it went.

One of the mothers was about to serve the ball when her seven-year-old child ran up to the fence and shouted, "Mommy, Johnny has climbed on the roof and he's crying because he can't get down."

"Well, tell him to stay up there until I finish the set," she said.

"He says he's afraid of falling."

"Tell him to hang onto the chimney."

A few minutes later during a heated volley a large black Labrador walked across the court. The rules of Mother's Tennis say play must be stopped when a dog comes on the court.

We all stopped while one of the mothers shouted at the dog, "Parkinson, go home."

Parkinson sat down next to the net and stared at all of us.

The mother-owner of the dog shouted to her daughter, "Polly, take Parkinson home."

"I can't," the daughter shouted back. "I have to take a sailing lesson."

The mother grabbed Parkinson by the collar and said to the rest of us, "I'll be right back."

Fifteen minutes later she returned, and play resumed.

For three minutes. Then another child appeared at the fence. "Mom, Dad wants to know where his bathing suit is."

"It's on the porch where he left it to dry."

"He says it isn't there now."

"Well, tell him to look in the laundry room."

"You better tell him. He's mad as heck. He had to make his own breakfast, and he cut his finger opening a grapefruit."

"I'll be home in a half hour."

We managed to get through one game when a lady appeared and shouted, "Sally, do you have a list of the sponsors for the wildlife benefit next week? I need it for the printer right away."

"The list is in my car. I'll get it." Sally went to her car while the rest of us kept swinging our rackets in the air to keep warm.

Game was about to resume when Lucy's three-year-old walked out on the court and sat on the baseline.

"Peter, please don't sit on the baseline," Lucy begged. "Go over there by the bench."

Peter just sat there, scratching himself.

Lucy was becoming angry. "Peter, if you don't get off the court, I'm going to give you a good spanking."

Peter pursed his lips and then started to cry.

Lucy made a dive for him, but he escaped and ran to the other side of the net.

He was finally grabbed by one of the other mothers and was dragged, howling and kicking, off the court. He didn't stop screaming for the rest of the morning.

During the set one husband showed up looking for his car keys, and two more dogs appeared on the court—one in heat.

It was a typical Mother's Tennis match, and no different from any I played all summer. The beauty of Mother's Tennis and where it differs from regular tennis is that no one keeps score. Who can remember?

* * *

Mail Day

POST OFFICE THREATENS TO CUT DOWN DELIVERIES TO THREE TIMES
A WEEK—headline in a recent newspaper.

It had to happen. In the year 1980 the postmaster general went on
television and announced to the country that because of a $600 billion
deficit and Congress' refusal to permit him to charge $5 for a first-class
stamp, the American people would receive their mail only *one* day a
year. This would be known as Mail Day and would be considered a national holiday. He regretted the decision but assured the American
people that they would still receive the best service of any postal system in the world, and he assured everyone that with only a few exceptions no one would be inconvenienced by it.

At first people were angered by the news, but pretty soon they accepted it as they have everything else the U.S. Postal Service has done
to them.

In a few years Mail Day became as popular as Christmas, and the excitement built up as the day came near.

Little children were told that if they were bad the Mailman (he was
pictured as a man in a blue uniform with a long white beard) wouldn't
bring them any Records of the Month. Department stores hired men to
play the role of Mailman, and men and women and children would sit
on his knee and tell them what they wanted for Mail Day.

People decorated their doors and windows with old birthday and get
well cards and put colored lights on their mailboxes.

The hit record played for weeks before Mail Day was Bing Crosby's
rendition of "I'm Dreaming of a Sears, Roebuck Catalogue." There was
a great spirit of goodwill associated with the holiday. Doormen and elevator operators and building superintendents became kinder and more
attentive. People greeted each other by saying, "Have a Merry Mail
Day." Charity organizations raised funds on the streets for poor people
who had no one to share their mail with.

Fraternal groups got together and walked through the streets singing Mail Carols. The churches and synagogues stayed open on Mail
Day Eve so people could pray for letters from their children.

When youngsters asked where the mailman lived, their parents told
them he lived at the North Pole and he spent the entire year canceling
stamps on letters and packages so he could leave them on Mail Day
morning for them. When they asked how he delivered the mail, they
were told he put it in bags and came down the chimney when everyone
was sleeping. But if there were a dog in the house, he would pass it by.
Everyone locked up their dogs on Mail Day Eve.

On the morning of Mail Day the entire family came downstairs and opened their bags of mail. Mothers got all the bills; fathers got all the newspapers and magazines that had piled up for the year. There were letters and postcards and birthday cards and Christmas cards for everyone. Grandmothers and grandfathers opened their Social Security checks. Children gleefully ripped open the junk mail with four-color catalogues and appeals from Indian reservations that didn't exist. There were also packages from stores and mail-order houses and tax returns and alumni fund appeals.

It took all day for people to open the mail. In the evening relatives came by to exchange canceled stamps and have Mail Day dinner with each other. Every TV network put on a televised football game, and Andy Williams had a special Mail Day TV program with his entire family.

For ten years Mail Day was the most exciting day of the year. But then in January, 1990, the postmaster general appeared on television and said that because of rising costs and a $2 trillion deficit the post office would be unable to deliver mail once a year as it had done in the past.

In the future, he said, mail would be delivered only one day during leap year. He felt that in this way the post office could operate with more efficiency and still provide the services that so many people depend on. But he warned that if Congress did not raise the price of a first-class stamp to $49 a letter, the post office would have to take more drastic measures, which included only delivering the mail once every bicentennial year.

How the Recession Happened

The recession hit so fast that nobody knows exactly how it happened. One day we were the land of milk and honey, and the next day we were the land of sour cream and food stamps.

This is one explanation.

Hofberger, the Chevy salesman in Tomcat, Virginia, a suburb of Washington, called up Littleton, of Littleton Menswear & Haberdashery, and said, "Good news, the new Impalas have just come in, and I've put one aside for you and your wife."

Littleton said, "I can't, Hofberger. My wife and I are getting a divorce."

Hofberger said, "That's too bad. Then take the car for yourself. I'll give you a hundred dollars extra on a trade-in because of the divorce."

"I'm sorry," Littleton said, "but I can't afford a new car this year. After I settle with my wife, I'll be lucky to buy a bicycle."

Hofberger hung up. His phone rang a few minutes later.

"This is Bedcheck, the painter," the voice on the other end said. "When do you want us to start painting your house?"

"I changed my mind," said Hofberger. "I'm not going to paint the house."

"But I ordered the paint," Bedcheck said. "Why did you change your mind?"

"Because Littleton is getting a divorce and he can't afford a new car."

That evening, when Bedcheck came home, his wife said, "The new color television set arrived from Gladstone's TV Shop."

"Take it back," Bedcheck told his wife.

"Why?" she demanded.

"Because Hofberger isn't going to have his house painted now that the Littletons are getting a divorce."

The next day Mrs. Bedcheck dragged the TV set in its carton back to Gladstone. "We don't want it."

Gladstone's face dropped. He immediately called his travel agent, Sandstorm. "You know that trip you had scheduled for me to the Virgin Islands?"

"Right, the tickets are all written up."

"Cancel it. I can't go. Bedcheck just sent back the color TV set because Hofberger didn't sell a car to Littleton because they're going to get a divorce and she wants all his money."

Sandstorm tore up the airline tickets and went over to see his banker, Gripsholm. "I can't pay back the loan this month because Gladstone isn't going to the Virgin Islands."

Gripsholm was furious. When Rudemaker came in to borrow money for a new kitchen he needed for his restaurant, Gripsholm turned him down cold. "How can I lend you money when Sandstorm hasn't repaid the money he borrowed?"

Rudemaker called up the contractor, Eagleton, and said he couldn't put in a new kitchen. Eagleton laid off eight men.

Meanwhile, General Motors announced it was giving a rebate on its new models. Hofberger called up Littleton immediately. "Good news," he said. "Even if you are getting a divorce, you can afford a new car."

"I'm not getting a divorce," Littleton said. "It was all a misunderstanding, and we've made up."

"That's great," Hofberger said. "Now you can buy the Impala."

"No way," said Littleton. "My business has been so lousy I don't know why I keep the doors open."

"I didn't know that," Hofberger said.

"Do you realize I haven't seen Bedcheck, Gladstone, Sandstorm, Gripsholm, Rudemaker, or Eagleton for more than a month? How can I stay in business if they don't patronize my store?"

No Frills on the Airlines

The "no frills" airline fare has gone into effect. National Airlines received permission to sell tickets on their planes for 35 percent less. Other airlines are expected to follow.

All the passenger would get on the plane would be a seat. He would have to bring his own food, his own drink, and provide his own Wash 'N Dry towelettes.

It's quite possible that the "no frills" part of the aircraft could be not only the most economical but the most fun as well.

I can see the scene.

Fifty people are seated in the back of the plane without so much as a stewardess in sight.

Each of them has a picnic basket or a box lunch on his lap.

As soon as the plane gets in the air, one of the passengers yells, "Does anybody want to trade a chicken salad with lettuce for a corned beef sandwich on rye?"

A man in the back says, "I'll give you a bacon, lettuce, and tomato for the chicken salad and throw in a hard-boiled egg."

His wife says, "I worked all morning to make the bacon, lettuce, and tomato sandwiches. How could you trade them for chicken salad?"

"I'll give you my corned beef sandwich," a man yells, "for the chicken salad plus three brownies, and I can keep my pickle."

"Done," says the man with the chicken salad.

A couple set up a hibachi stove in the aisle and started to barbecue spareribs.

"Hey," says a man sitting across from them. "Are you sure you're allowed to barbecue ribs on the plane?"

The lady who was putting the barbecue sauce on the ribs says, "There's nothing in the ticket that says you can't cook your own meals in the no frills section of the plane."

"Well, in that case," replies the man, taking a sword out of his briefcase, "I'm going to have some shashlik."

The odors of the cooking start to permeate the cabin. A lady preparing a cheese fondue on the seat next to her asks the lady in front if she can borrow a cup of oil.

The lady gives her the oil in exchange for some sugar which she needs for her pancake batter.

By this time the passengers in tourist and first class smell all the food. An angry first-class passenger who has wandered into the no frills cabin by mistake comes storming back and says to the stewardess, "How come they're eating shashlik back there and we're eating this glop which you call chicken?"

"It's quite simple. If you have a no frills ticket, you don't get the airline's food."

"If we have to eat your food, we're the ones who should get thirty-five percent off," the first-class passenger says.

By this time all the passengers in the no frills cabin have finished their meals.

"What do we do for entertainment?" someone asks.

"I've got some great home movies of a trip we took to Greece," a man says.

"Great, let's see them," a lady says. "Then my son will play the guitar for you."

"We could have some singing afterwards."

"I have a bingo game if anybody wants to play."

A barrel of beer that one of the passengers had brought on board is opened, and paper hats are passed out by a party-favor salesman.

Several of the first-class and tourist passengers try to get back in the no frills section, but they are stopped at the curtain by the stewardess, who tells them sternly, "Go back to your seats, or I won't give you any coffee, tea, or milk."

God Bless Little Old Ladies

What happened to all the little old ladies in tennis shoes? I am happy to report that they are alive and well, and most of them are on package tours in Europe.

Because traveling abroad has become so expensive, you do not see many Americans on the Continent anymore.

Occasionally a bearded kid with an American flag on the seat of his pants may walk by your café table, but it isn't like the old days when there wasn't a corner of Europe that didn't have a "U.S. Go Home" sign.

If it weren't for the little old ladies in tennis shoes, no one would be aware that the United States still existed, and it makes any red-blooded American's chest swell with pride when he sees a battalion of them marching down the Champs-Élysées, Piccadilly, or the Via Veneto to the tune of "Colonel Bogie's March."

Make no mistake about it, the little old ladies in tennis shoes still strike terror in the hearts of every tour director in Europe.

Most of the ladies are veterans of previous overseas tours— experienced in hand-to-hand combat at flea markets, versed in the skills of fierce haggling in souvenir shops, trained to assault churches and museums, and prepared for sneak attacks on any American Express branch in the country.

The cemeteries of Great Britain, France, Italy, the Benelux and Scandinavian countries are dotted with graves of tour guides who expired trying to keep up the pace set by these indomitable souls.

At airports all over Europe you see fresh young guides barely out of college, wearing their tour uniforms waiting nervously for their group to jump off the plane and encircle the city. Screaming, "We take no prisoners," the little old ladies, carrying their duty-free shopping bags from the previous airport, climb aboard their buses, determined not to miss one single thing included in the price of the tour.

No mountain is too high for them to climb; no fjord is too wide for them to cross. Heaven help the guide who forgets to stop for tea in Zermatt (included in the package) or leaves out a church in Montmartre. Let a waiter skip a salad course in Salzburg or a cheese plate in Brussels, and he'll get a karate chop he'll remember for the rest of his life.

In the last thirty years Europeans have seen their countries invaded by American, Japanese, and now Arab tourists. But none of them has ever shown the strength, the moral fiber, or the staying power of the little old ladies in tennis shoes.

Why do they do it? Why, when most Europeans have lost interest in tourists, when waiters and concierges and shopkeepers have become more surly, when most things are cheaper in the States, do the ladies keep traveling abroad?

The answer came from a little old lady sitting next to me at Fouquet's. "Someone has to carry on," she said simply.

"The young people can't do it because they don't have the money; the middle-aged people can't do it because they don't have the stamina. If it weren't for us little old ladies in tennis shoes, no one would remember what an American looked like. We've all taken a vow that as long as we can climb the steps of the Piazza di Espagna in Rome or wade on the beaches of Monte Carlo, we will see that the sun never sets on an

American tourist. Besides, I promised my grandson a sword from Toledo."

I almost broke into tears. Twenty years ago the American traveler ruled Europe from Gibraltar to Helsinki. Our traveler's checks were coveted from Dublin to Istanbul. There wasn't an arcade in Venice or a bazaar in Athens that didn't have a sign ENGLISH SPOKEN HERE. Those were the golden days for Americans, and we may never see them again.

So let's hear it for the little old ladies in tennis shoes. God bless them for showing the flag in the Old World. As long as they have the money and the time and the grandchildren, the spirit of American tourism will never die.

Guess Who Came to Dinner!

I was invited to a state dinner by the White House in honor of Prime Minister Bhutto of Pakistan. This was the first time I ever went to the White House officially. The Fords keep inviting strange people to their parties, and the only thing White House dinner watchers can figure out is that they're working from an old Nixon enemies folder, which they mistakenly believe was the previous President's social list.

There is always the danger when a newspaperman is asked to break bread with a President and his lovely wife that he can be compromised. How can he partake of the food and wine and still keep his objectivity? This is a problem most White House press people have to deal with. I am happy to say that the Bhutto dinner has not affected my attitude toward the administration one bit.

I still believe President Ford is the greatest leader this nation has ever known. His economic program is flawless, and his budget is probably the clearest document since the Declaration of Independence.

It is inconceivable that a free-spending Congress would set up roadblocks in the way of the administration's program. In dealing with the recession and inflation, the President has presented the most comprehensive plan ever worked out by brilliant economists, oil experts, and financial advisers. If this program were adopted, prices would go down, employment would go up, and America would once again enjoy the prosperity and good life that it so richly deserves.

The problem, as I see it, is that Congress refuses to bite the bullet. Instead of joining forces with our great President, they are voting inflationary programs that could break the back of Mr. Ford's efforts to hold down government spending.

By voting day after day to reject the needed legislation to turn this country around, the Democrats are playing politics with the economy of the country.

It is inconceivable to me that our lawmakers would make a partisan issue out of the magnificent effort by the President to solve our temporary woes.

I have always had an open mind on the energy problems the United States faces. But after President Ford explained it to me, while we were drinking coffee, I am now convinced that the only answer to this nation's self-sufficiency is a $3 tariff on imported oil, deregulation of prices for domestic gas reserves, and a postponement of environmental regulations in favor of getting coal and oil out of the ground.

I had the good fortune of talking to Secretary of State Henry Kissinger at the same dinner, and it's lucky I did, because I have now concluded it was a mistake to cut off aid to Turkey, refuse arms to South Vietnam and Cambodia, and investigate the CIA.

Our foreign policy has been severely wounded by the ambitions of certain Democratic senators who have their eye on the White House in 1976. Congress must leave the President and Kissinger alone if we are to achieve the goals of peace that all of us so desperately pray for. It was no accident that Secretary of Agriculture Earl Butz and I agreed over cognac and a cigar that his farm policies were the only ones that this country should follow. I couldn't believe that this fine man had been vilified by a scandal-mongering media that wouldn't know the truth if it was right in front of their eyes.

As I danced with Mrs. Ford after dinner, I decided I was glad I had accepted her invitation to eat at the White House. All my fears about being taken in by the administration were groundless. One meal cannot change a man's opinion of our President or his gracious First Lady. Not since Dolley Madison. . . .

Good Business for CIA

Many stories have come out about the CIA, but this is one that is still buried secretly in the archives. It has to do with an agent named Greensleeves. He was young, energetic, and imaginative. The CIA decided to set him up in a souvenir shop across the street from the palace of a South American dictator, where he could keep tabs on the comings and goings of government officials.

They gave him enough money to buy the shop and the souvenirs so the operation would be legitimate. This exchange of cables, after they were decoded, tells the story.

"CIA Headquarters, Langley: Business excellent. Have sold $16,000 worth of souvenirs thanks to Dictator Tacos three-day anniversary celebration in front of palace. Please tell our people in Taiwan I need more Tacos ashtrays, paperweights, and letter openers. If all right with you, am planning a sale on Dictator Tacos music boxes that play 'South of the Border.'—Greensleeves."

"Greensleeves, Paella, South America: Glad to hear you are doing well businesswise, but what the hell is going on at the palace? We hear Tacos may be overthrown by right-wing colonels. Please advise at once.—Frogmaster."

"CIA Headquarters, Langley: Sorry I have been too busy taking inventory to pay much attention to palace, but have good news. Discovered a factory outside Siesta that makes cuckoo clocks and hand-painted scarves. Have bought three gross at half-price. Expect sales figures in June up 20 percent over May. Had to pay off customs to get cigarette lighters into country, but will add bribe to price of item.—Greensleeves."

"Greensleeves, Paella, South America: Why no word from you on Tacos assassination attempt and his exile from country? Who is now in charge of Paella? Urgently need list of junta and whether it's pro-or anti-American.—Frogmaster."

"CIA Headquarters, Langley: Agency has nothing to fear from Tacos overthrow. I got wind of it two weeks ago and had Tacos Birthday Sale on Saturday, where I marked down all Dictator Tacos items 50 percent. The bronze busts moved especially well, as did Tacos pillowcases. We also unloaded 4,000 plates with portraits of Mrs. Tacos. Only item that didn't sell as well as expected was night-light of Tacos standing next to Virgin Mary. But I plan to remove Tacos and just sell them as Virgin Mary night-lights. Tell our Hong Kong people that I am sending them photograph of Colonel Chili which I would like them to have framed with sea shells. Also need 3,000 beer mugs commemorating the junta's revolution of July 5. By the way, tell our Hong Kong man to check packing. The ashtrays they sent came in all damaged. Am seeing insurance company tomorrow—Greensleeves."

"Greensleeves, Paella, South America: What information do you have concerning naval attack on Paella by neighboring country of Enchilada? Understand shelling destroyed half of downtown as well as Soviet, British, French, and Chinese embassies.—Frogmaster."

"CIA Headquarters, Langley: Your information correct. I heard about it ten days ago from Enchilada defector and moved all breakable items to the basement. Also boarded up windows. You'll be happy to know we had the only souvenir shop in Paella that opened for business the next day. Since the invasion started, I have added a toy line with tanks, soldiers, missiles, and fighter planes. Believe they will be big sellers. Took it on myself to give 10 percent discount to any Paella soldier or sailor in uniform. Have also ordered music boxes which say 'Mother' on the top in Spanish. Understand Mother items sell well in time of war."

"Greensleeves, Paella, South America: What has happened to U.S. ambassador? Is he being held hostage by revolutionary urban guerrillas as reported by AP, UPI, Reuters, and Agence France Presse?"

"CIA Headquarters, Langley: U.S. ambassador was kidnapped three days ago. One of my salespeople has a brother who told her about kidnapping plans last week. I immediately took steps to check his charge account. He owed us $89. On a ruse that we were collecting accounts receivable early this year, I managed to get his check before he was grabbed. We haven't lost a dime on him. Any chance of shipping Fidel Castro coffee mugs? They're expecting 15,000 male Cuban tourists, and it could be a big item this summer."

Gift Giving in Washington

In years past gift giving between the President of the United States and a head of state was a simple matter. One of the President's staff would call up Tiffany's or Steuben Glass or Neiman-Marcus and ask them to select something appropriate for a foreign dignitary.

But those days seem to be gone, and now when a head of state comes to the White House, he expects a lot more.

Just the other day the president of Lovlost-by-the-Sea paid a state visit to Washington, and this was what transpired.

President Yak of Lovlost-by-the-Sea gave his gift first. "President Ford, on behalf of the citizens of Lovlost-by-the-Sea I present you this beautiful silk tie woven by one of our most famous weavers and sewn by hand by six virgins from the Calico Mountain area of my beautiful country. And for your lovely wife I present this beer mug which was made especially to celebrate the occasion of the tenth anniversary of our independence."

"Thank you very much, Mr. President. On behalf of the people of the United States I would like to give you a brand-new steel foundry which we shall finance for you."

"That's lovely, Mr. President. I also would like to present to you a book of proverbs written by our most famous poet, Lo Tak, before he was put under house arrest for attacking my government."

"Thank you, President Yak. And although I cannot present it to you personally, I want you to have as a token of our friendship a squadron of F-4 fighter planes which will be delivered to your country in the next six months."

"That is very kind of you, President Ford, and it brings tears to my eyes. In exchange, please accept this coconut, which, as you will notice, has a face carved on it that bears a great resemblance to me."

"I am overwhelmed, President Yak. Would you consider it out of line if I gave you three hundred heat-seeking missiles to go with your fighter planes?"

"You've given us so much already, but I would not insult you by refusing your wonderful gesture. I hope you will not be offended to accept, in exchange, this straw basket, which was made by one of our greatest artisans before he was shot for treason after the last coup d'état."

"A real straw basket! I shall build a special case for it. And now I have a surprise for you. Henry tells me you have your heart set on a nuclear energy plant."

"I told Henry it was just a dream."

"Well, we're going to make your dream come true. Just present this certificate to any U.S. nuclear energy company, and they will honor it."

"President Ford, what can I say? Would you accept in exchange for it this elephant bracelet made by the widow of one of my former colonels in the army?"

"I've always wanted an elephant bracelet. Henry, is there anything else we can give President Yak?"

"You forgot the submarines, President Ford."

"Of course. President Yak, in honor of the long friendship between our two great countries we are presenting you with ten new submarines in any color you wish to choose."

"I shall tell my people that you are truly the greatest President the United States has ever had."

"There's just one more thing, President Yak. Why does your country always vote against the United States on every United Nations resolution?"

"Because, President Ford, we have no choice. We have to vote with our friends."

* * *

And Nobody Laughed

The last person to laugh in the United States was Robert Ketchum on Monday, August 3, 1978. There was no law passed to prevent people from laughing; they just quit voluntarily.

No one knows exactly when people gave up laughing in America. The Republicans claimed it was during the Johnson administration, and the Democrats said it happened during President Nixon's term in office. Putnam Toynbee, who in 1984 wrote *The Definitive History of the Seventies*, claims the first culture group to give up laughing was students.

"There's nothing to laugh about," they said to each other in despair. "Everything is rotten. The government, the establishment, the system and life itself. We're doomed to a plastic existence, and we'll be damned if we're going to laugh about it. If we show in any way we're happy, it will be a sign of weakness."

Toynbee points out that anything youth did in the United States was eventually picked up by the adult population, and when young people stopped laughing, older people started to emulate them.

Scowling became very fashionable in the with-it crowd. Articles began appearing in the chic magazines that laughter was out. Pretty soon the word had filtered to the hinterlands that anyone who laughed about anything was a fool or a knave.

Advertisers, sensitive to the mood of the consumer, canceled all comedy shows on television; the networks put out memos ordering all laughter bleeped from their programs, and newspapers dropped any stories or comic strips which might produce a chuckle for the reader.

Toynbee says in his book that it was difficult for a certain segment of society to give up laughing, but these people did it privately in their homes, where no one could see them.

A group of friends would get together, send the children off for the night with relatives, and then laugh for two or three hours among themselves.

There were certain key clubs where people could go to hear a comedian or see a funny motion picture from the past. But as the older generation started dying out, the clubs went bankrupt, as there were no young laughers to take their place.

Laughter in public buildings was forbidden and considered exceptionally bad taste. Anyone who laughed in a restaurant or theater was asked to leave.

If someone attempted to laugh on the street or in a park, he was met with stony stares or assaulted by angry passersby.

The government contributed to the antilaughter campaign by issuing pronouncements every day that things were worse than they were the day before.

To make sure that people wouldn't go back to their old ways, Washington raised taxes, passed outrageous laws, told of international threats, and gave out grim economic reports. Life indeed presented a dismal picture.

Toynbee claims the last person in the United States known to have laughed in public was Robert Ketchum, who lived in Salem, Massachusetts.

Ketchum was standing on a street corner when a friend of his, Adolph Green, walked by and slid on a banana peel. Before he realized what he was doing, Ketchum burst into laughter.

An angry crowd gathered and grabbed Ketchum and dragged him to the center of the square, where they tied him to a post, threw branches from trees at his feet, and burned him at the stake. All three networks covered the event, and the lesson was not lost on the populace. Toynbee feels it will be some time before anyone laughs in public in the United States again.

Advantage, God

LONDON, ENGLAND—Art Buchwald, the oldest professional tennis player in the history of the game, dropped dead today of a heart attack on the Centre Court at Wimbledon. He was 93 years old.

Mr. Buchwald was playing in the final match of the men's singles against Pancho Romero and was leading 6-1, 6-0, when, in the third set with the score 4-2, Romero hit a blazing drive down the middle of the court. Buchwald clutched his heart, blood drained from his face, but he managed to return the ball, much to the surprise of Romero, who hit it into the net.

He was rushed to Queen's Hospital in an ambulance but was dead on arrival. An attendant said Buchwald's last words were, "Tell Romero he was lucky this time, but I'll be waiting for him to play that final championship game in the sky."

Art Buchwald started late in the tennis business. The early years of his life were spent writing a newspaper column on politics and the human foibles of our society. Then, at 45, he started searching for new worlds to conquer. One day he picked up a tennis racket in a friend's house.

"What's this?" he asked.

The friend said, "It's a tennis racket."

"Show me how the game is played."

The friend took Buchwald out onto his tennis court and in an hour Buchwald managed to get the hang of it. In two hours he was beating his friend with what has since been described as "the fastest second serve in tennis."

The friend told Buchwald he was a natural and should join the professional ranks, but at first the columnist was reluctant to take the sport seriously. It's true he played at Forest Hills and Indianapolis the following year, winning both the men's grass and the clay championships, but it wasn't until 1975 that Buchwald started to play for money.

He gave up his column and his writing career to concentrate on tennis and never touched a typewriter key again.

In 1976 Buchwald toured Australia, where he was unscored upon in 47 matches. In 1980 he won $3,500,000 in prize money, not counting fees he earned for shaving-lotion testimonials.

Mr. Buchwald invented the backhand cocked serve, which is now used by every professional tennis player of any note. The serve puts a spin on the ball that causes it to go through the legs of the opponent.

He will also be remembered for his "choked forehand," where the ball is hit first as a lob but then drops dead in the forecourt.

A favorite with the ladies, the silverhaired Buchwald was followed everywhere he played by what was called Artie's Army.

He had to pay two bodyguards to escort him out of stadiums, because women would always try to rip the crocodiles off his tennis shirts.

Buchwald never believed in training and the night before a particularly rough match he could be found in a cabaret, dancing with three or four movie stars until five in the morning.

Once, when he was 75, he was criticized for setting a bad example for American youth. Buchwald replied: "I play better when I dance the night before." At least that's how it came out in the newspaper.

Although he was a terrific competitor and fought for every point, Buchwald never questioned a linesman's call. He always praised his opponents, no matter how badly he beat them, and sometimes shared his prize money with them when he felt they had played particularly well.

Besides winning every possible tennis championship in the world, Buchwald had been a member of the Tennis Hall of Fame for 40 years. An entire wing of the hall had to be built to house all his trophies.

Because of his tennis, Buchwald had friends among kings, presidents and emperors. He had been knighted for teaching King Charles's daughter the game.

He had also received the Order of Mao Tse-tung for introducing tennis to the People's Republic of China.

When President Christopher Kennedy was informed of Buchwald's untimely death, he ordered every tennis net in the United States to be lowered to half-mast.

The President said, "America has lost its greatest top-spinner. It will be impossible to find someone to replace him. But after a month of mourning, I have ordered the game to be played again. Art Buchwald would have wanted it that way."

You Kept Telling Me There Was No Better Place to Live

Dear Pop,

It's been four years since you passed away at the age of 79. On this Bicentennial holiday with all the hoopla and overkill, I am not taking the 200th Anniversary of the Country lightly, mainly because I know you wouldn't.

First I would like to thank you for leaving your home in Galicia, which you once explained was part of Poland, in 1910 when you were 17 years old. I know it wasn't an easy trip for you. You had to cross Europe all by yourself, and then you had to find a ship in Rotterdam that would take steerage passengers to New York City.

I've tried to imagine what it was like for a 17-year-old boy to arrive at Ellis Island without being able to speak a word of English. There were thousands like you and fortunately there were people who came before you to help you through the maze of paperwork and bewildering ways of New York City.

You wound up on the Lower East Side with so many of your fellow immigrants. They offered you a chance to go to night school, but you said you would learn English by reading every New York City newspaper every day. You kept reading them for 62 years and you seemed to know more about the country and the world than any of your children who had been "educated" in American schools.

I know you started out working in a raincoat factory 14 or 15 hours a day and when World War I came you worked even longer. They wouldn't let you serve in the army because you were considered an "enemy alien." Once I asked you if you missed being a soldier and you replied, "Yes, only because it would have gotten me out of making raincoats."

Then you went into the curtain and drapery business—the Aetna Curtain Co. The business consisted of you, a man named Sammy who helped you hang the drapes, and a seamstress. "Gimbel's we're not," you used to tell me, much to my chagrin.

But you did save enough money to bring your two sisters and a brother to America. And you did manage to get out of the Lower East Side.

"Making it in America, in those days," you once told me, "was moving to the Bronx."

You even got as far as Mt. Vernon, N.Y., when business was good, before the Depression. Then during the Depression it was back to the Bronx.

The thing I shall always remember is how you felt about the United States. You kept telling me there was no better place to live than America, and I could never appreciate this unless I was a Jew who had lived in Europe. Once when I was working in Paris I offered you a trip to Europe and you replied, "What do I want to go to Europe for? I've been there already."

You were like so many foreign-born Americans, Jewish, Russian, Italian, Irish, German, Scandinavian and Greeks, who considered this country the only land where your children would have a chance to become what they wanted to be.

You told me, "Everyone has dreams for their children, but here it's possible to make them come true."

Well, Pop, I just wanted you to know, as far as your children are concerned, you made the right decision when you left Poland. There are four of us, all first-generation Americans, and we will be celebrating the Fourth of July with many other first-generation Americans whose mothers and fathers arrived here in more or less the same way.

I don't know if all those great men in 1776 had you immigrants in mind when they signed the Declaration of Independence and formed a new country, but even if they didn't, they made it possible for you and millions like you to come to a free land.

So let the tall ships sail and the fireworks explode. We're probably overdoing it, but if you were here I'm sure you would say, "It's probably a good thing people remember what a great place this country is, even if it's going to cost the city a lot of money."